Winston Churchill
The Era and the Man

Virginia Cowles

First published in 1953 by Hamish Hamilton, Ltd.

This edition published in 2018 by Sharpe Books.

To the enduring inspiration of my mother
Florence Jaquith Cowles

Table of Contents

FOREWORD

IN THIS book I have attempted to tell of Mr. Churchill's early days, the influences brought to bear upon him as a young man, and to present, as objectively as possible, an account of his prodigious career. I have not tried to draw a veil over the less successful periods nor, I hope, have I withheld praise and admiration for his great contributions.

Mr. Churchill stands out as a titan among his fellow men. Consequently his mistakes and triumphs are often intermingled on a grandiose scale, and his personality seldom fails to draw a challenge. As a statesman he moved through four decades of tumultuous events before he reached the grand climax of his life. But in retrospect his political misfortunes seem providential, for without them he might not have been set apart, or 'spared', as Mr. Attlee once put it, to lead his country in the stirring days of 1940.

When I saw Mr. Churchill at the French Embassy in 1950 and told him I was planning to write his biography he growled good-naturedly: 'There's nothing much in *that* field left unploughed.' However, he did not take into consideration the unusual fertility of the ground and I hope the reader will not be disappointed in the harvest. I have been helped by the innumerable biographies and memoirs to which I have given acknowledgment, by the newspapers and magazines of the last fifty years, and by information gathered from people whose paths at one time or another have crossed those of Mr. Churchill.

A number of friends were kind enough to offer comment and criticism on the finished work. Although I do not pretend to reflect their views in the interpretation I have given, I would like to thank Mr. Leo Amery, Mr. Robert Boothby and Mr. William Deakin for reading the book in manuscript form.

VIRGINIA COWLES

Kingsbridge,
Steeple Claydon,
Buckingham.
January, 1953

Acknowledgements

MY THANKS are due to

Mr. Winston Churchill for permission to quote from many of his books and to the publishers concerned, namely Odhams Press Ltd. (*My Early Life*, *The Aftermath*, *The World Crisis*, *Thoughts and Adventures*, *Great Contemporaries* and *Lord Randolph Churchill*), George G. Harrap & Co., Ltd. (*Marlborough: his Life and Times*) and Cassell & Company Ltd. (*The Second World War*); also to Charles Scribner's Sons and Houghton Mifflin Company, who control Canadian publication rights in *The World Crisis* and *The Second World War* respectively.

The Author and Christophers for permission to quote from *Incidents and Reflections* by J. B. Atkins; the Executors of the late Admiral Sir Reginald Bacon and Hodder & Stoughton for permission to quote from *The Life of Lord Fisher* by Admiral Sir Reginald Bacon; Lord Beaverbrook for permission to quote from his *Politicians and the War* and from *War Memoirs of David Lloyd George*; Martin Seeker and Warburg Ltd. for permission to quote from *My Diaries* by Wilfrid Scawen Blunt; J. M. Dent and Sons, for permission to quote from three books by A. G. Gardiner, *Certain People of Importance*, *Pillars of Society* and *Prophets, Priests and Kings*; the Society of Authors as the literary representative of the Trustees of the A. E. Housman estate and Jonathan Cape Ltd., publishers of A. E. Housman's *Collected Poems*, for permission to include an extract from *A Shropshire Lad*; The Hogarth Press Ltd. for permission to quote from *The Economic Consequences of Mr. Churchill*, by J. M. Keynes; the Author and Ivor Nicholson & Watson Ltd. for permission to quote from *C. F. G. Masterman* by Lucy Masterman; Cassell & Company Ltd., for permission to quote from Lord Oxford and Asquith's *Memories and Reflections*, also to Little, Brown & Company who control Canadian rights; the Author and *The Sunday Times* for permission to quote from Sir John Rothenstein's article *Mr. Churchill: the Artist*; Gerald Duckworth & Co., Ltd., for permission to quote from *Anglo-American Memories* by George Smalley; the Executors of the late Frances, Countess of Warwick and Hutchinson & Co. (Publishers) Ltd. for permission to quote from *Life's Ebb and Flow* by Frances, Countess of Warwick; Longmans Green & Co., Ltd., for permission to quote from *Our Partnership*, by Beatrice Webb; William Heinemann, Ltd., for permission to quote from *Fighting in Flanders*, by E. Alexander

Powell; Victor Gollancz Ltd. for permission to quote from Lord Riddell's *Intimate Diary of the Peace Conference and After*, and Ivor Nicholson & Watson Ltd. for permission to quote from *Lord Riddell's War Diary*.

**Part One
The Present**

Chapter One — An Introduction

DURING THE Festival of Britain in the summer of 1951 Winston Churchill visited the Dome of Discovery and was taken up in a lift to a telescope where, he was told, he could view the outer spaces. He viewed them, and said: 'Take me down. I am more interested in what is happening on the earth.'

The earth has had the benefit of Mr. Churchill's attention for over half a century; and the fact that as a boy he heard Mr. Gladstone speak might be said to join his hand with another half a century. To-day at the age of seventy-eight with the authority of fifty years of Parliamentary experience behind him, with the mantle of Fame wrapped securely around his shoulders, and with an ardour for life as fierce and fresh as ever, he is serving for the second time as Britain's Prime Minister.

But his career is not only spectacular for its triumphs but for the long, intense struggle before he achieved his ambition as His Majesty's First Minister. Now that the colours of the canvas are nearly complete they offer a sharp and surprising contrast. His dazzling gifts were acknowledged from the very first, yet it took him forty years to reach his goal. He is one of the great orators of the day, yet he has lost more elections than any other politician. He is the leader of the Conservative Party, yet he has spent three-quarters of his life fighting Conservative Party leaders. He has been deeply distrusted by each political party in turn, yet in 1940 he was unanimously entrusted with the life of the nation.

Winston Churchill has had to fight for everything he has got. No man has aroused more heated opposition, or, for that matter, been more bitterly hated in his time. Recently Mrs. Churchill reminded a friend that in the days of the Lloyd George Budget and the House of Lords Reform, 'Winston was as ostracized as Oswald Mosley is now'. Three times his political career has lain in ruins and three times he has made an apparently impossible come-back.

His stormy passage has been the natural result of his own fierce partisanship. To Mr. Churchill the excitement of life has always lain in the clash of wills and the dangerous struggles which have fashioned the outline of history. He has never played for safety. Endowed with a highly emotional nature, he usually acts on impulse and intuition rather than on calculation or even logic. He is incapable of assessing a situation dispassionately, but once he has taken a stand he has never been at a loss to find closely reasoned arguments to support it. Thus on paper he appears to be a cool and highly rational being, while on the political stage he often seems rash and impetuous. This apparent contradiction has always perplexed his contemporaries, who regard him as the most incalculable figure in public life.

Yet there is one constant note in his character which is the very essence of his nature and of his genius as well. That is his Romanticism. It may well be that in the years to come historians will describe him as the last great Romantic that England produced. Mr. Churchill is incapable of seeing life in terms of monotones. Whatever subject his mind touches is at once transformed into shimmering lights and colours.

Just as when he paints he has little use for the dull browns and greys, as a politician and a writer he feels compelled to reach out for the vivid hues. He does not see life in any other way, for every subject his mind touches is at once transformed into a brilliant drama. His world is a world of good and bad, of righteous causes and shining swords, and of dark and evil foes. There is always a hero and a villain, and the fact that Mr. Churchill never fails to cast himself in the leading role not only annoys his opponents but often irritates his colleagues as well.

Although Churchill's Romanticism undoubtedly is the natural consequence of a brilliant fancy and a highly emotional nature, it was bred in him as well. Blenheim Palace, where he was born, kindled in his mind the splendour of military exploits, and his father's sensational career opened his eyes to the fame that awaits the orator. Of the two careers, soldiering attracted him the more. Surprisingly enough, until he was nearly forty he dreamed of glory on the battlefield. That is why in the 1914 war he begged to resign his office as First Lord of the Admiralty to take charge of Antwerp; that is also why, when he joined a regiment in France a year later, he was bitterly disappointed not to be allowed an important field command. Throughout his long Parliamentary career he has never lost his interest in the science of battle. Of over thirty published volumes to his credit, twenty-five deal with some aspect of war. And the two books he would like to have written, had time allowed, are the life of Napoleon and the life of Julius Caesar.

Although Mr. Churchill left the army at the age of twenty-four, first to earn a living, and second, because in those peaceful days it seemed unlikely that Britain would ever again become embroiled in a world-wide conflict, he brought the smoke of the battlefield with him to Parliament. From the very first he was a natural storm centre. He never failed to take a stand and he usually took it in the most provocative way possible. Consequently the House of Commons always crowded to hear what he had to say. This was a triumph, for as a young man he was not an accomplished orator. Although he could write a compelling speech, his delivery was poor and the cut and thrust of debate did not come easily to him. Indeed, Arthur Balfour once taunted him with the remark that 'the Right Honourable Gentleman's artillery is very powerful but not very mobile'.

Churchill was determined to master the art of debate and spent long hours practising his speeches out loud, pausing for interruptions, and thinking up appropriate and acrimonious retorts. Gradually, by sheer effort, he developed a facility for impromptu intervention, and to-day he has few equals. His opponents are forced to recognize him as one of the greatest Parliamentarians England has ever produced.

When he comes into the Chamber you feel a stir in the galleries as the whole atmosphere electrifies. He sits on the front Government bench with his shoulders hunched, his bulldog head thrust forward, straining to catch every word. There is not a trick of the trade which he does not know. Quick to strike and quick to defend, few opponents score off him. Often, when he rises to speak, he begins in a deliberately low voice to command attention. Once when he was Leader of the Opposition there were cries from the Labour benches: 'Speak up! Don't be afraid.' He paused and surveyed them critically. The House grew still in anticipation. Then in a whisper which could be heard from one end of the Chamber to the other, he said: 'I find I speak quite loud enough to silence any of *you* when I like.'

No one has a deeper respect for the power of the House of Commons than Churchill. He observes parliamentary procedure with care, but this does not prevent him from employing his talent for abuse and ridicule to the fullest and he often whips the Chamber into such an uproar with insults and accusations hurled back and forth that the Speaker rises to maintain order. Following one of these hubbubs in 1947, several letters appeared in the *Daily Telegraph* deploring the fact that Churchill was not accorded the deference of the Elder Statesman. Little did the writers understand the man's temperament for if the day ever comes when he fails to draw the fire of the other side, he will consider his usefulness in Parliament at an end. In fact, his provocations are often such carefully planned traps that Labour M.P.s are sometimes instructed by the Whips not to interrupt him during a debate so that he will not have the opportunity of getting the better of them.

The secret of Mr. Churchill's parliamentary mastery lies in his ability to change the mood of the House. Although he can provoke an angry storm he can also turn the storm into roars of laughter by a sudden shaft of wit. His humour is not the cold, polished variety; it smacks much more of the Music Hall with comic, impish, even schoolboy jokes which few people can resist. In 1939 when he was serving as First Lord of the Admiralty he told me with relish how a destroyer had dropped a depth charge, but instead of finding a submarine, bits of an old wreckage had come to the surface. 'And would you believe it,' he added with a grin, 'there was a door bobbing around with my initials on it! I wanted to recount this important occurrence in a speech, but Mr. Chamberlain cut it out.' He added with a twinkle, 'He thinks my taste is questionable.' On another occasion, near the end of the war, when he was reminiscing about his career and the fact that he had changed his Party twice, I remember him startling his luncheon guests by proclaiming solemnly: 'Any one can rat but it takes a certain amount of ingenuity to re-rat.'

In the House of Commons his humour often lies in the emphasis and hesitation of his voice. Sometimes he treats the assembly to an act which borders on pantomime. A few years ago when a Labour Minister rose to speak Mr. Churchill suddenly began feeling in his pockets with an air of consternation, then looking down towards his feet. The eyes of the members left the speaker and began to follow his puzzling movements, and soon even the people in the Galleries were craning in his direction. Suddenly with an elaborate start he apologized to the Minister: 'I was just looking for my jujube,' he explained innocently.

An example of his ability to turn an awkward situation into a humorous one was illustrated recently over the controversy about American and British naval commands. When Churchill was Leader of the Opposition he had attacked the Labour Government hotly for having consented to an American Admiral as Commander of the Atlantic, insisting that the British should have the Atlantic and the Americans the Mediterranean. When, however, he lost the arguments about the Atlantic he dismissed the reasons he had advanced about the advantages of an American in the Mediterranean and insisted that the Mediterranean must remain under British control. The Socialists could not resist baiting him about his change of mind. In order to force him into a corner, one of them asked him to state categorically whether or not his views were the same now as they had been twelve months previously. 'My views,' he began ... 'Change,' interjected a Socialist.

'My views,' he continued placidly, 'are subject to a harmonious process which keeps them in relation to the current movements of events.'[1] Even the Labour benches could not refrain from laughter.

*

Time has mellowed Mr. Churchill and greatness has softened the antagonism of his opponents. As a young man he was far from popular. It was part of his Romanticism that from his earliest days he believed he had been put upon earth to fulfil some great purpose. This presentiment led him into many disastrous blunders, for he was not merely ambitious as other men are, but openly and impatiently in search of Fame. As a result he gave the impression of seizing issues indiscriminately in order to project himself into the limelight. No man in public life seemed to have a greater facility for veering from the role of statesman to that of politician. Indeed, as recently as 1945 Churchill gave a striking example of this dual capacity, by opening the election campaign with the sensational warning that Socialism would mean 'a Nazi state' and 'a Gestapo'. People were shocked because they remembered the many tributes he had paid to Attlee, Morrison, Bevin and other Socialist leaders when they were serving in his wartime coalition Government only a few weeks before; to turn on them so wildly to cadge votes was considered 'un-English'. One could not help recalling the lines H. G. Wells once wrote: 'There are times when the evil spirit comes upon him and I think of him as a very intractable, a very mischievous, dangerous little boy, a knee-worthy little boy. Only thinking of him in that way can I go on liking him.'

Churchill's egoism and impetuosity filled the public with a deep distrust which proved a fatal stumbling block to him for nearly four decades. People became convinced that he was less interested in a cause for its merits, than as a vehicle for his own ambitions; and the fact that he changed his party twice did not help to dispel the impression. His opponents branded him as a cynic and an opportunist, while his colleagues, disconcerted by the fact that he found it difficult to serve as a member of a team but instinctively reached out for the reins, openly referred to him as 'a trouble-maker'.

Mr. Churchill never got accustomed to his unpopularity. He was genuinely hurt and astonished by the animosity he aroused, for he was so absorbed by his projects and plans that he gave very little thought to the complexities of human nature. Ideas, not people, interested him,

---

[1] *Hansard*: 5 May, 1952.

and as a result the reactions of his fellow beings invariably burst upon him as a complete surprise. Sometimes moody and preoccupied, at other times tactless and aggressive, he frequently wounded sensibilities without even knowing that he had done so. Once he cried out mournfully: 'I have never joined an intrigue. Everything that I have got I have fought for. And yet I have been more hated than anybody!'[2]

These protests came from the heart, for Churchill himself is remarkably free from malice. His lack of interest in the human element eliminates all pettiness from his nature, and his sudden, unexpected, emotional surges of generosity have disarmed more than one opponent. Once when Ernest Bevin was Foreign Minister he paid Churchill a heart-felt tribute in the House, and the latter was so moved he could not keep back the tears. On more than one occasion during the 1945-51 Parliament, when Mr. Attlee was Prime Minister, Churchill entered the smoking-room, sometimes after a particularly acrimonious debate, saw 'Clem' sitting at a table, promptly joined him and congratulated him on his speech. Members also remember how in 1951, when his most formidable critic, Mr. Aneurin Bevan, opened the Defence Debate, he sat attentively in his place admiring the brilliance of the speech. Then Mr. Bevan began to liken some of his methods to those of the Nazis. Churchill put up his hand in protest. 'I had nothing to do with the Nazis,' he beamed. 'Do not spoil a good speech now.'[3] Recently when Churchill visited his old school, Harrow, the boys asked him who he thought was the greatest man who had ever lived. 'Julius Caesar,' he replied, 'because he was the most magnanimous of all the conquerors.'

*

I first met Mr. Churchill in the beginning of 1938, when his political career was at one of its lowest ebbs. He was not a member of the Government for although his colleagues recognized his ability they were deeply suspicious of his 'unreliability' and his 'exhibitionism'. 'The trouble with Winston,' people said, 'is that you never know what he will do next.' But despite his exclusion from power, he was still the most colourful and controversial figure in English political life. I had sat in the gallery of the House of Commons and watched the Chamber

---

[2] *My Diaries*: Wilfrid Scawen Blunt.

[3] *Hansard*: 15 February, 1951.

crowd to hear him speak. In the distance he looked extraordinarily old-fashioned in his black coat, his winged collar and bow-tie, and even his rolling prose suggested a more leisurely and cultivated century. But what he had to say was not of the past; when he leaned forward to warn his colleagues of the dangers of Nazi Germany he became the incarnation of a pugnacious and perennial John Bull. You felt the imagination of the House stir with the brilliance of his words, but unfortunately the magic ended with his eloquence. When you went into the tea-room half an hour later you heard people chattering about what he had said with an alarming light-heartedness.

Churchill spent most of his time at his country house, Chartwell in Kent, and one Sunday his son took me there for lunch. I remember being surprised by his round pink face. I had not expected such a formidable man to have such a cherubic appearance. Later I heard that a woman had once told him that her baby looked like him, to which he replied firmly: 'All babies look like me.' I was also surprised by the fact that even in private conversation his phrases were as rounded and polished as when he is speaking in the House. He delighted in the use of such Victorian expressions as 'I rejoice', 'I am greatly distressed' and 'I venture to say', which were emphasized by the impediment in his speech that prevented him from pronouncing distinctly the letter 's'.

During lunch the conversation centred on world affairs and Mr. Churchill talked with the brilliance I had expected but I later learned that I was lucky, for often he is absorbed with his own thoughts and makes no attempt at conversation. Small talk does not interest him; it is a question of silence or a monologue, and nothing in between. On this day, however, he expressed his fear that England would not only refuse to show her hand until it was too late to avoid war, but too late to win. 'Mr. Chamberlain can't seem to understand that we live in a very wicked world,' he said. 'English people want to be left alone, and I daresay a great many other people want to be left alone too. But the world is like a tired old horse plodding down a long road. Every time it strays off and tries to graze peacefully in some nice green pasture, along comes a new master to flog it a bit further along.'

After lunch I was taken upstairs to see his large, high-ceilinged, oak-beamed study. He showed me several stacks of manuscript of the history of the English-speaking people which he was then writing. 'I doubt if I shall finish it before the war comes,' he said morosely, 'and if I do, the part the English-speaking people will play will be so decisive I will have to add several more volumes.' He paused. 'And if it is not decisive no more histories will be written for many years.'

One had an impression of restless, pounding energy, and a prodigious capacity for work. In the course of the afternoon I was shown the goldfish pond (fish are one of Churchill's hobbies), the swimming pool and the cottages, all of which he had built with his own hands. I was also shown another cottage that he had turned into a studio and which was filled with pictures he had painted. In 1951 Sir John Rothenstein, the Director of the Tate Gallery, and one of the foremost art critics in England, paid him the compliment of saying: 'Had the fairies stuck a paint brush into his hands, instead of a pen into one and a sword into the other, had he learnt while still a boy to draw and to paint, and had he dedicated an entire laborious lifetime to art, Mr. Churchill would have been able to express himself, instead of one small facet. He would have painted big pictures.' Churchill, however, regarded painting as a recreation, not as hard work. In 1949 he commented to Rothenstein, 'If it weren't for painting I couldn't live; I couldn't bear the strain of things.'[4]

*

Although Mr. Churchill has a reputation for enjoying luxury, few men have devoted their lives more completely to intellectual pursuits. He has never moved in social circles; idle conversation or aristocratic companionship has never had an appeal for him. Throughout his life his closest friends have all been men from humble backgrounds who have made their own way to the top; Lloyd George, 'F. E.' Smith, 'Prof' Lindemann and Brendan Bracken. It was Churchill who recommended the last two, now Lord Cherwell and Lord Bracken, for peerages.

Churchill often attends official functions, but he rarely can be persuaded to spend a week-end away from home. He is devoted to his wife, and idolized by his children, and is very much the master of the household. The one thing he insists upon is comfort, and his ideas on this subject are based, rigidly, on Victorian standards. Delicious food and well-trained servants are regarded as absolutely essential. And if he can help it, he never travels without a valet. Before the war, he once arrived at Maxine Elliott's villa in the South of France by himself, and Vincent Sheean heard tell him his hostess with a broad grin, 'My dear

---

[4] *Mr. Churchill: The Artist*: Sir John Rothenstein (*Sunday Times*, 7 January, 1951).

Maxine, you have no idea how easy it is to travel without a servant. I came here all the way from London alone and it was quite simple.' 'Winston, how brave of you,' replied Miss Elliott.[5]

Any deviation from comfort, arranged in the name of pleasure, fills Churchill with gloom. For example, Lady Megan Lloyd George tells the story of a time many years ago when her father and he went on a trip to North Africa. A prominent prince of the desert gave a large dinner in their honour. The feast was served in the open and the guests sat in a circle on the ground around a huge cauldron of steaming food. There were no forks or knives and everybody was expected to help himself from the common bowl and to eat with his fingers. Lloyd George enjoyed anything out of the ordinary and at once flung himself into the spirit of the occasion. But Churchill sat silent and glowering, refusing to make a move of any kind. Some of the guests eyed him nervously for fear their host would take offence at his sullen mood. Suddenly he rolled up his sleeves and with a fierce defiance plunged his arm into the bowl growling: 'Come on, Megan, to hell with civilization!'

Mr. Churchill occasionally plays a game of Canasta, and has a weakness for romantic or humorous films. During the war he saw *Lady Hamilton* eight times and rewarded the producer, Alexander Korda, with a knighthood. The news of Rudolph Hess's arrival in Britain is said to have been delivered to him while he was watching the Marx Brothers. Another one of his amusements is singing old and familiar songs. During the last twelve years he has never missed an annual evening visit to Harrow during which all the old school songs are sung. However, he is like a child about music, and a change of tune can turn him instantly from one mood to another. In the war his son-in-law Vic Oliver was playing 'The Blue Danube' on the piano at Chequers, when Churchill came through the door and slowly began to waltz. Suddenly Oliver jokingly struck the sombre chords of Chopin's Funeral March. The Prime Minister broke off angrily, and left the room.

Churchill's recreations are simple enough, for the answer is that he has derived his real pleasures in life from a great creative output, whether it is building houses, writing books, painting pictures, or making speeches. Once he remarked to me with a twinkle: 'With all the fascinating things there are to do in the world, some people

---

[5] *Between the Thunder and the Sun*: Vincent Sheean.

actually while away their time playing Patience. Just fancy!' Few people will accuse him of such a weakness.

*

It is a great tribute to Democracy that when war came Mr. Churchill was unanimously accepted as leader of the nation. The antagonisms and the quarrels that he had had with all three political parties, some of them stretching over nearly four decades, were put aside at once. Politicians and public alike recognized that by temperament, application and genius he was the one man superbly fitted to command the battle. Never in history have the people of Britain been so solidly behind a Prime Minister.

Mr. Churchill did not fail them. At last the canvas was high and broad enough to work on; at last his brilliant colours were needed to depict the terrible and majestic glow on the horizon. He thrilled the western world to its mission as no other man could have done. The very fact that he saw life in terms of broad events rather than through the individual, which hitherto had been his greatest weakness, now became his greatest strength. When he spoke of Man, he was thinking of Mankind; and the future of Mankind hung in the balance.

**Part Two
The Making of a Man**

Chapter Two — His Background

BLENHEIM PALACE is one of the great houses of England. It was built nearly two hundred and fifty years ago with money voted by Parliament as a princely home for John Churchill, the first Duke of Marlborough, whose military genius saved Europe from the domination of Louis XIV.

From that time to this the palace has been occupied by the dukes of Marlborough and in 1950 its present owner announced that on certain days of the week the Great Hall and the West Wing would be open to the public. Since then thousands of sightseers have strolled across the rolling green parklands and wandered through the house inspecting the priceless tapestries and murals, the wonderful carved ceilings, the gold and silver work, the china and furniture wrought in the days of Queen Anne. Many of these tourists write their impressions in a 'Suggestions Book' in the chapel, and it is amusing to notice that whereas the English visitors usually comment on the beauty of the treasures, many of the Americans remark on what a privilege it has been to see 'the home of Mr. Winston Churchill'.

Blenheim, of course, has never been Mr. Chur chill's 'home'. His father, Lord Randolph Churchill, was the third son of the seventh Duke of Marlborough, and lived in the palace from the age of eight until he married. The estate eventually passed to his eldest brother, and then in turn to his nephew, and is now in the possession of Winston Churchill's second cousin, the tenth Duke. Strictly speaking Winston arrived in the world as the poor relation of a great ducal family. Nevertheless from the very first he asserted himself and with a fine disregard for propriety managed to be born at Blenheim.

The circumstances of his birth were unusual. His mother, a beautiful, vivacious young bride, was seven months with child. She loved gaiety and against the advice of her doctors insisted on attending the St. Andrew's Ball, held at Blenheim on the night of 30 November. In the middle of the evening she was rushed from the ballroom to the cloakroom where, amid a setting of silk hats, velvet capes and feather boas, she gave birth to Winston.[6]

---

[6] This story was told to me by Sir Shane Leslie, who heard it from his mother, Lady Leslie, Lady Randolph Churchill's sister.

This fact has caused the owner of Blenheim a certain amount of embarrassment. For although Winston's birthplace was once the bedroom of the first Duke's chaplain, Dean Jones, it is more suitable as a cloakroom than a boudoir. It is on the ground floor, small and plain, overlooking a sunless well. It has been fitted with a modest bed and a few pieces of furniture, and when the tourists file through one always sees looks of surprise, and hears whispered comments on the disappointing lack of regality. The present Duke has criticized Winston's lack of showmanship in failing to arrive in the Yellow Room or some other suite which could be shown off to advantage.

Winston's birth was announced by *The Times* in a single line: 'On the 30th November at Blenheim Palace, the Lady Randolph Churchill, prematurely, of a son.' Nevertheless the event caused excitement among members of the Churchill family who interpreted the circumstances as an omen that one day he would succeed to the Marlborough title. Although this prediction did not come true, the accident of his birth had a profound effect on his character and outlook. It aroused in him a passionate interest in Blenheim and its history, and a veneration for tradition and continuity which developed into a fierce family pride. The two heroes of his youth, about whom he later wrote biographies, were men whose blood flowed in his own veins; the first Duke of Marlborough, and that brilliant, erratic Victorian statesman, his own father. The fact that both these men had lived at Blenheim where he had so unexpectedly intruded did not make him dream of inheriting the Marlborough riches, but of being the true heir to the genius in the Churchill line. As a Churchill he felt he had a special obligation and a special mission.

*

The first Churchill about whom anything much is known was the son of a lawyer and the grandson of a blacksmith. He was born in 1620 and grew up in the county of Dorset; like his descendant of to-day he was a soldier, a writer, and a member of Parliament, and his name was Winston. He was a passionate supporter of Charles the First and in the Civil War took part in the fighting at Lansdowne House and Roundway Down, where he was wounded. When the Parliamentarians triumphed he was a ruined man and spent thirteen years bringing up a large family under the poverty-stricken roof of his mother-in-law, Lady Drake, a sister of the Duke of Buckingham. Nevertheless he occupied himself in doggedly writing a long and laborious book entitled *Divi Britannici* in which he traced from 'the year of the world 2855' downward the Divine Right of Kings, insisting that the monarch should have the power to levy taxes without consulting Parliament, an idea which, even in those days, caused some astonishment. When the Restoration came and Charles II ascended the throne Winston's fortunes took a turn for the better. He was awarded a knighthood and allowed to place one of his daughters at Court. Whether he considered this due recompense is not known, for he had despairingly emblazoned on his coat-of-arms the motto, 'Faithful but Unfortunate'.

Lord Macaulay refers to Sir Winston in his *History of England* as 'a poor Cavalier Baronet who haunted Whitehall and made himself ridiculous by publishing a dull and affected folio, long forgotten, in praise of monarchy and monarchs'. Nevertheless, Sir Winston produced three remarkable children. One was Arabella, who became the mistress of James the Second and bore him a son, the Duke of Berwick, who was one of the great generals of Louis XIV;[7] another was a George Churchill who rose to be an admiral in the British Navy; the third was John Churchill, the first Duke of Marlborough, who proved himself one of the greatest soldiers of all time.

It is not surprising that the Winston of to-day should have been thrilled by the story of the Duke, for there is no more fabulous character in English history. In 1688 England embarked on a war which soon involved all the civilized countries of the world and lasted, with one brief period of peace, for a quarter of a century. This war was not only fought to defend the Protestant faith but to prevent Louis XIV from bringing all Europe under his control, thus destroying the independence of England. It was as perilous a struggle as the war against Hitler, and for ten campaigns stretching over the years John Churchill led the armies of Europe. 'He never fought a battle which he did not win nor besieged a fortress which he did not take ... Nothing like this can be seen in military annals,' writes the present Winston Churchill. 'Until the advent of Napoleon no commander wielded such widespread power in Europe. Upon his person centred the union of nearly twenty confederate states. He held the Grand Alliance together no less by his diplomacy than by his victories. He rode into action with the combinations of three-quarters of Europe in his hand. His comprehension of the war extended to all theatres, and his authority

---

[7] In 1939 the present Duke of Berwick and Alba, a lineal descendant of the victor of Almanza, was appointed Spanish Ambassador to Britain. He held the post throughout Mr. Churchill's premiership until 1945.

alone secured design and concerted action … He was for six years not only the Commander-in-Chief of the Allies, but, though a subject, virtually Master of England.'[8]

Marlborough has been described by his contemporaries as 'cold and proud' and 'the handsomest man in Europe'. His powerful position invited bitter attack, and for years the Tories blackened his name while the Whigs only defended him with indifference. He was accused of avarice, immorality, corruption and even treachery; and long after he died scurrilous stories were repeated by famous writers which for many years prevented his countrymen from according him his just due. Twice he was dismissed from his offices, once by King William who believed that he was intriguing against him, and once by Queen Anne who listened to tales of corruption, but both times he was later reinstated. Through all his vicissitudes he had the support of his beautiful, dynamic wife, Sarah. The passionate feelings of these two through nearly fifty years of married life constitute one of the great love stories of history. When Sarah was widowed at the age of sixty-two, the wealthy Duke of Somerset proposed to her, and she made her famous reply: 'If I were young and handsome as I was, instead of old and faded as I am, and you could lay the empire at my feet, you should never share the heart and hand that once belonged to John, Duke of Marlborough.'

After Marlborough's victory at Blenheim in 1704 Queen Anne made him a gift of fifteen hundred acres at Woodstock, a few miles from the city of Oxford, and Parliament approved the sum of £24,000 for the building of a house. It was arranged that the quit-rent of the palace would be 'one standard, or colours,' with flower-de-luces painted thereupon', presented at Windsor Castle every August on the anniversary of the Battle of Blenheim. This custom is still observed to-day, and when the present Winston Churchill wrote his brilliant life of Marlborough he paid his forbear an added tribute by carefully dating the foreword of each volume August the 13th.

When Marlborough died he left no son and the title passed through his daughter to his grandson whose family name was Spencer. In 1817 the Marlboroughs received permission to add Churchill to their name, and since that time members of the family have styled themselves Spencer-Churchill.

---

[8] *Marlborough: his Life and Times*: Winston S. Churchill.

For a century and a half the dukes of Marlborough and their Churchill kin led surprisingly uneventful lives. They passed their days as undistinguished members of the landed gentry occupying themselves with the traditional duties of the aristocracy. Not until 1874 did the pulse of Blenheim quicken with excitement, as once more it felt adventure in the air. That was the year that Lord Randolph Churchill, a younger son of the seventh Duke of Marlborough, stood as a candidate for Woodstock and was elected to Parliament; that was also the year that he brought his American bride to Blenheim. 'As we passed through the entrance archway and the lovely scenery burst upon me,' she wrote, 'Randolph said with pardonable pride, "This is the finest view in England". Looking at the lake, the bridge, the miles of magnificent park studded with old oaks … and the huge stately palace, I confess I felt awed. But my American pride forbade the admission.'[9]

And 1874 was also the year that the Randolph Churchills' son and heir, Winston Leonard Spencer Churchill, was born.

*

Winston grew up in the bright glow of his father's fame. If the Duke of Marlborough was his idol, Lord Randolph was his inspiration. Lord Randolph was one of the most spectacular men of the day, and it is small wonder that he excited his son's imagination for he astonished many other people as well. His career flashed across the late Victorian sky like a meteor while he advanced, by means of a brilliant and savage tongue, from the political back benches of the Commons to Leader of the House and Chancellor of the Exchequer. He was the outrageous idol of the hustings, the *enfant terrible* of British politics. He revitalized a defeated and dispirited Tory Party and led it to victory. He reached the pinnacle of success when he was only thirty-six; then in a moment of arrogance and folly flung away his position never to retrieve it again.

Lord Randolph entered politics and his son entered the world as the curtain was rising on the last twenty-five years of Queen Victoria's reign. During the first sixty years of that century Britain turned from her victory over Napoleon to develop the talents which soon transformed her from a landed society into the greatest manufacturing country in the world. She had no rivals, and as well as supplying the needs of Europe, extended her commerce to her great growing Empire

---

[9] *Reminiscences of Lady Randolph Churchill.*

across the seas. In 1868 she was proud and prosperous. The aristocracy and the newly rich manufacturers lived in affluence and style; and although they were divided by birth and breeding the public schools provided the necessary link by educating the children of both to be gentlemen of a single, approved pattern. These children were brought up to take their places in the powerful and exclusive oligarchy by which Britain was governed.

This oligarchy was based on wealth and position. Only men of property had the right to vote and only men of property were chosen as Parliamentary candidates. As a class they considered it their natural prerogative to rule, and proudly displayed to the world the strong, rich nation that had emerged under their guidance. But beneath this impressive show of prosperity there was also poverty, bitterness and unemployment. The lot of the working man was hard. He lived in crowded slums, labouring long hours for low wages, with the fear of the workhouse always in his mind. Without the right to vote his struggle for improvement was limited, but the fact that the Trade Unions were slowly gathering strength revealed his sombre determination.

The restlessness of the masses did not escape the notice of William Ewart Gladstone, who was Prime Minister from 1868 to 1874. He devoted his first administration almost entirely to attacking the privileges of the ruling class. He ended the patronage system by which the Civil Service was run and opened it to competitive examination; he stopped the buying and selling of commissions in the Army and opened it to talent; he extended primary school education throughout the country; and he extended further the vote to the middle classes.

Although he did not destroy the oligarchy but merely broadened its basis, such people as the Duke and Duchess of Marlborough considered Mr. Gladstone a dangerous Radical. When young Lord Randolph left Oxford they begged him to hold himself in readiness for the next election when he could stand for the family seat of Woodstock and prevent it from falling into the hands of the hated enemy.

As a boy Lord Randolph had none of the harsh insolence which characterized his career in the House of Commons. He grew up at Blenheim with his elder brother, Blandford, under the care of a doting father and mother. His parents followed the normal practice of the aristocracy in sending him to Eton and Oxford where he appears to have been an able though not a brilliant pupil. At Eton one of his masters, Mr. Brinsley Richards, described him as 'a rough and tumble urchin'. 'Churchill,' he wrote, 'was an easy lower boy to catch whenever anything had to be done, for his whereabouts could be ascertained by his incessant peals of laughter.'[10]

After graduating from Oxford Lord Randolph obediently idled away the next three years waiting for a General Election. He was not at all politically inclined but Woodstock had been represented by a member of the family for 'years and years' and he felt it his duty to maintain tradition. He travelled abroad for a year then returned to enjoy himself as a gay spark in the fashionable and exclusive circles of London society. At this period he is described by his biographers as 'cheerful and impulsive', which seems to be borne out by the fact that he went to Cowes in August 1873, met a beautiful, dark-haired, nineteen-year-old American girl, Jeanette Jerome, and forty-eight hours later proposed and was accepted. He sent her picture to his father with a long letter of explanation, in which he said: 'I do not think that if I were to write pages I could give you any idea of the strength of my feelings and affection and love for her; all I can say is that I love her better than life itself, and that my one hope and dream is that matters may be so arranged that soon I may be united to her by ties that nothing but death itself could have the power to sever.'

He then went on to say: 'Mr. Jerome is a gentleman who is obliged to live in New York to look after his business. I do not know what it is.'[11]

Mr. Jerome was a New York business man who had made and lost several fortunes. During the Civil War he owned and edited the *New York Times*. He was a passionate supporter of the Northern cause, to which he subscribed large sums. When the New York war party became discredited in 1862, furious mobs attacked the Times office. But Mr. Jerome had fortified his position with rifles and cannon and beat off the raid after some bloodshed. In his calmer moments he managed to found the first two great American race-courses, Jerome Park and Coney Island Jockey Club. He had two daughters besides Jeanette, both of whom married British subjects. One became the mother of Shane Leslie, the distinguished Irish writer, and the other of Clare Sheridan, the equally distinguished sculptress.

The Duke of Marlborough was alarmed by his son's precipitous action and although Lord Randolph assured him that Jeanette was

---

[10] *Seven Years at Eton*: Brinsley Richards.

[11] *Lord Randolph Churchill*: Winston S. Churchill.

beautiful, accomplished and rich, and that she moved with the most exclusive society in France, where she lived with her mother, the Duke was not enthusiastic about his son marrying an American. He insisted that the young couple must wait until time proved the worth of their affection. At the first sign of reluctance on the Duke's part Mrs. Jerome indignantly took her daughter to Paris and refused to let her see Lord Randolph except at infrequent intervals. A period of frantic letter writing followed, then suddenly Parliament was dissolved and Lord Randolph was faced with an election.

In those days only 1071 people in the Churchill family borough were eligible to vote. Disraeli's Act of 1867 had extended the franchise to the lower middle class but the agricultural labourers who made up the bulk of the population of Woodstock were not included. To-day, when the constituency of a Member averages fifty thousand voters, Victorian elections seem leisurely affairs. But evidently Lord Randolph did not think so, for he wrote to Jeanette: 'My head is in a whirl of voters, committee meetings and goodness knows what. I am glad it is drawing to an end, as I could not stand it very long; I cannot eat or sleep.'[12]

The suspense soon ended with victory for Lord Randolph, and victory for the whole Tory Party. Disraeli displaced Mr. Gladstone as Prime Minister. But Lord Randolph was more concerned with his personal triumph. He wrote Jeanette elatedly: 'There was such a burst of cheers they must have made the old dukes in the vault jump … There is nothing more to do but pay the bill which I have left to my father.'[13]

Shortly after this the Duke of Marlborough and Mr. Jerome amicably agreed to let the young couple marry. Lord Randolph brought his bride to England where she soon established herself as one of the most fascinating and popular figures in Society.

*

Lord and Lady Randolph lived in London for two years where they entertained Mr. Disraeli, the Prince of Wales, and many other illustrious figures of the day. Lord Randolph dutifully made his maiden speech but he was more interested in the pleasures of life than in Parliament. He attended the House only spasmodically, spending

---

[12] Ibid.

[13] *Lord Randolph Churchill*: Winston S. Churchill.

his time at balls, dinners and week-end parties. Then suddenly an event took place which altered the whole course of his life. In his biography of his father Winston Churchill states: 'Engaging in his brother's quarrels with fierce and reckless partisanship, Lord Randolph incurred the deep displeasure of a great personage. The fashionable world no longer smiled. Powerful enemies were anxious to humiliate him. His own sensitiveness and pride magnified every coolness into an affront. London became odious. The breach was not repaired for more than eight years and in the interval a nature originally genial and gay contracted a stern and bitter quality, a harsh contempt for what is called "Society", and an abiding antagonism to rank and authority.'[14]

This discreet statement by Mr. Winston Churchill was amplified some years later by Lord Randolph's nephew, Shane Leslie, who explained that the 'great personage' with whom Lord Randolph's brother, Lord Blandford, quarrelled was the Prince of Wales, later Edward VII. The quarrel was over a woman. Lord Blandford had succeeded the Prince in a certain lady's affections, whereupon the Prince, through pique, encouraged the lady's husband to sue for divorce and name Lord Blandford. Lord Randolph was outraged by this behaviour and audaciously intimated that 'any divorce case would bring to light some friendly letters which had escaped the Prince's pen and memory'.[15]

But how did Lord Randolph come into possession of the lady's letters? To threaten the Prince was bad enough; to brandish a lady's love letters was quite unthinkable. These were the points around which the scandal raged. The Prince declared that he would not enter any house which received Lord Randolph, and as a result all the doors of Society were firmly shut. The ban was severe and complete; and feeling ran so high that the Duke of Marlborough consented to accept the position of Viceroy in Ireland so that he could take his son with him as secretary.

*

The Randolph Churchills did not return to England for nearly three years. Soon afterwards Disraeli's Government came to an end and Gladstone was again in power. The Grand Old Man's second

---

[14] Ibid.

[15] *These Men are Different*: Shane Leslie.

administration lasted from 1880 to 1885. Its most important legislation was the Third Reform Bill giving the vote to the agricultural labourer and the miner. Otherwise it was concerned mainly with serious problems in Ireland, Egypt and Africa.

The Tory members took their places on the Opposition benches in a discouraged and uncertain frame of mind. They had been out of power for twenty-two years except for one short interval until Disraeli brought them back in 1874; was this the beginning of another long period in the wilderness? It seemed as though Mr. Gladstone exercised a magic spell which no one could break.

This was the stage on which Lord Randolph made his entrance. The five years he had spent in Ireland had whetted his appetite for politics and he was ready for a fight. 'The duty of an Opposition is to oppose,' he announced, and lost no time in doing it. He was no longer the amiable young man of London society. Many people still refused to receive him in their houses, but now he did not seem to mind. He had developed a hard, cold armour and his tongue had become a formidable weapon.

He at once plunged into the attack. Yet he did not only cross swords with the great Gladstone but turned on his own leaders as well, ridiculing them for their vacillation and defeatism. With three followers he sat below the gangway in the House of Commons, and carried on his own blistering opposition to the powerful Liberals, regardless of what his party leaders had to say. This small group became known as 'The Fourth Party'.

Lord Randolph's house gradually became a meeting place for all shades of politicians. 'Many were the plots and plans,' Lady Randolph wrote, 'which were hatched in my presence by the Fourth Party, who, notwithstanding the seriousness of their own endeavours, found time to laugh heartily and often at their own frustrated efforts.' She went on to add: 'Sometimes to hear … Randolph discussing the situation the uninitiated might have thought the subject was a game of chess.'[16] There is no doubt that Lord Randolph and his followers enjoyed themselves. They referred to their respectable, die-hard leaders as the 'Old Gang', and derisively nicknamed the weaker members 'The Goats'.

Under these circumstances it is small wonder that Lord Randolph was not popular. While he made his strenuous and unorthodox efforts

---

[16] *Reminiscences of Lady Randolph Churchill.*

to infuse a new spirit into the Tory Party and bring it back to power, the Tories stood by ready to benefit by his success, yet smarting with resentment. 'To them,' Winston Churchill wrote, 'he seemed an intruder, an upstart, a mutineer who flouted venerable leaders and mocked at constituted authority with a mixture of aristocratic insolence and dramatic brutality.'[17]

Not only this but he seemed a cad. His tactics were not the tactics of an English 'gentleman'. On one occasion he wrote a scorching letter to *The Times* criticizing Sir Stafford Northcote's 'pusillanimous' leadership in the House of Commons. His friends begged him not to send the letter, warning him against public disloyalty to his own leader, and reminding him that Sir Stafford had just recovered from an illness and enjoyed the sympathy and affection of many people. Lord Randolph persisted and when he entered the House the next day scarcely a soul would speak to him; and when Sir Stafford rose to ask a question he was greeted by a tremendous ovation. On another occasion Lord Granville, the Foreign Secretary, criticized Lord Randolph in the House of Lords, and the latter again wrote *The Times*; he accused Granville of 'the petty malice of a Whig'; 'of his usual shamelessness'; 'of sneaking down to the House of Lords to make without notice a variety of deliberate misrepresentations, deliberate misquotations and false assertions which were quite in accordance with the little that was known about the public career of Earl Granville, Knight of the Garter, and, to the misfortune of his country, Her Majesty's principal Secretary of State for Foreign Affairs'. *The Times* printed the letter but devoted a column and a half to dissociating itself from the insults and bad taste of the author.

Lord Randolph, however, continued along his sensational path with cold indifference. It must be borne in mind that a majority of the Members of Parliament were the same men who ruled the fashionable world which had turned its back on him. He was paying them back, and showing that he scorned their good will. Gradually he developed a creed for his small party, borrowed from Disraeli's political philosophy, which became known as 'Tory Democracy'. Upon examination there was nothing particularly new in this faith. 'Tory Democracy,' Lord Randolph once explained blandly, 'is a Democracy that votes for the Tory Party.' His tactics were to appeal to the patriotic sentiments of the English working man and to convince him that no

---

[17] *Lord Randolph Churchill*: Winston S. Churchill.

one could defend Queen and Country better than the Tories. This was accompanied by a slashing indictment of Mr. Gladstone's handling of Foreign Affairs. But when it came to the acid test, Tory Democracy faltered. Mr. Gladstone presented his Bill to extend the vote to the agricultural labourer and Lord Randolph opposed it. 'As the representative of a small agricultural borough he could not, as he himself said afterwards, be expected to look on a measure for the extinction of Woodstock "with a very longing eye",' his son explains somewhat naïvely.[18] As things turned out the extension of the vote did not mean 'the extinction of Woodstock' for Lord Randolph won his next election; and it remains a curious blot on the career of the Tory Democrat who toured the country crying: 'Trust the People'.

Nevertheless it did not seem to affect Lord Randolph's popularity with the masses. His meetings were packed and he went from strength to strength. He was greeted by cries of 'Yahoo Randy!' and 'Give it to 'em hot!' He complied with relish. During this period his range of invective was inexhaustible. He called Chamberlain a 'pinchbeck Robespierre' and Gladstone a 'purblind and sanctimonious Pharisee' and 'an evil and moonstruck monster'. He accused the Government of 'treachery and incapacity', of 'imbecility', of 'sinking below the level of slaves'; and he declared that 'general destruction and all around plunder are alike their pleasure, their duty and their pride.'

By 1884 Lord Randolph was a national figure. A slim man with bulging eyes and a huge moustache, he became the delight of the cartoonists. Although he was of medium height it pleased the artists to picture him as a diminutive figure; sometimes as Jack the Giant Killer; sometimes as a wasp, a pug dog, a monkey or a clown. This publicity served him well and helped to swell the already large, excited crowds. His wife flung herself into the political fray, and even fought an election for him. On this occasion Lady Randolph and her sister-in-law toured Woodstock in a smart tandem with the horses wearing brown and pink ribbons, Lord Randolph's racing colours. Soon the music halls were singing:

Bless my soul! that Yankee lady
Whether day was bright or shady
Dashed about the district like an oriflamme of war;
When the voters saw her bonnet
With the bright pink roses on it,

---

[18] *Lord Randolph Churchill*: Winston S. Churchill.

They followed her as the soldiers did the Helmet of Navarre.

As Lord Randolph's popularity in the country grew, the Liberals attacked him with increasing vehemence. A pamphlet entitled *The Woodstock Bantam* was published by a Mr. Foote, who wrote angrily: 'Incessant abuse of Mr. Gladstone has been the principal means of Lord Randolph Churchill's advancement. The Tories hate the great Liberal chief who is at once its Nestor and its Agamemnon; and they are ready to applaud any young jackanapes who will pull him by the beard. Finding how cheap and easy it was to bait Mr. Gladstone and what golden honours the performance won among the Conservatives, his lordship flew at the Premier night after night like an impudent bantam. Out of doors he was still more insolent. There is scarcely an epithet in the vocabulary of vituperation which he has not flung at Mr. Gladstone from Tory platforms ... At a recent Woodstock election his lordship circulated a printed certificate of his good manners from no less a person than Mr. Gladstone himself. It was a sign of that great man's magnanimity but it was also a sign of Lord Randolph Churchill's consummate meanness. After blackguarding the Liberal chief for years no one but a miserable sneak would have condescended to have availed himself of an exculpation from the object of his malicious insults.'

*

In 1885 Mr. Gladstone resigned and the Tories formed a Government. Lord Randolph was made Secretary of State for India. A few months later Mr. Gladstone again formed a Government; then in the summer of 1886 a General Election took place.

This election was fought on the stormy issue of Home Rule for Ireland and was one of the most bitter contests that have ever taken place in English parliamentary life. Home Rule was the great dream of Mr. Gladstone's old age; but it split the Liberal Party in two. The dissentients lined up with the Tories and together the 'Unionists', as they were called, scored a sweeping victory.

Historians do not go so far as to declare that without Lord Randolph the Tory battle would have been lost, yet no one denies that by his force and personality he played a major part. Lord Salisbury, the Tory Prime Minister, rewarded him by appointing him Leader of the House of Commons and Chancellor of the Exchequer. He was at the top.

He did not hold his position long. In December 1886, less than six months later, he suddenly resigned. He informed the Prime Minister that unless the Army and Navy cut the amount of money they were spending he would not be able to construct the Budget as he wished.

The Navy acquiesced but the War Minister stood firm. Lord Randolph had forced his colleague to do as he wished twice before by threatening resignation; why not a third time, particularly when, as Leader of the House of Commons and the greatest platform orator of the day, his influence was at its zenith?

But this time the move failed. Lord Salisbury accepted his resignation. The news caused a sensation not only in England but throughout Europe. The public were astonished and all sorts of rumours began to spread as people insisted there must be a more important reason than the one given in the press. The Tory Party was openly alarmed. Could Lord Salisbury's administration continue, deprived of the support of its most glittering figure?

As it became known that Lord Randolph's resignation was not based on a great principle, but on a minor disagreement, opinion quickly hardened. *The Times* rebuked him indignantly, declaring that Conservative circles regarded him as highly 'unpatriotic'; and the following day printed an excerpt from the Vienna *Tageblatt* which almost equalled Lord Randolph's own invective: 'He is one of those men who will always play second fiddle and play out of tune. The Continental Cabinets which were astonished and perplexed by his sudden rise, must rejoice that Lord Salisbury has not allowed himself to be dictated to by a mere jackanapes. Lord Salisbury's resignation would have been a very serious thing for Europe; Lord Randolph's resignation means simply this — that a noisy personage, who was never fitted to be a Cabinet Minister, has reassumed his proper part as a political brawler.'[19]

Lord Salisbury's Government staggered, then quickly righted itself. Practically no voices were lifted in Lord Randolph's defence and no one mourned his going. Punch printed a cartoon of a clown walking out of the circus ring, saying: 'I shan't play any more.' Underneath was the caption: 'The Great Little Random', and the following verse:

Pet of the Public and pride of the Ring
Master of excellent fooling
Beating in patter and tumble and fling
Fellows with ten times his schooling
Great Little Random the company led
Was it a wonder he went off his head?

---

[19] *The Times*: 25 December, 1886.

Lord Randolph remained in Parliament but returned to the back benches where, only six years before, he had begun his career. In January 1895, at the age of forty-five, after a protracted and lingering illness which resulted in paralysis of the brain, he died. His son, Winston, was just twenty.

Chapter Three — His Schooldays

WINSTON'S EARLIEST memories are of Dublin. He was not quite two years old when his father quarrelled with the Prince of Wales and his grandfather accepted the position of Viceroy of Ireland in order to remove the impulsive Randolph from the wrath of London Society. The latter received an official appointment as the Duke's Private Secretary and installed himself and his family in the Little Lodge, a house in the park of the Viceregal Mansion. One of Winston's first recollections is the forbidding figure of his grandfather unveiling a statue to Lord Gough with the thrilling words 'and with a withering volley he shattered the enemy lines'.

Although Winston left Ireland before he was five, Dublin made a vivid impression on his mind. He remembers the red-coated soldiers, the emerald grass, the mist and the rain, and the excited and sometimes whispered talk about 'the wicked Fenians' who were trying to terrorize the British administration. Once when he was riding a donkey led by his nurse, Mrs. Everest, a group of soldiers appeared in the distance. There was a moment of panic as the nurse mistook them for Fenians; the donkey kicked and threw Winston to the ground, which resulted in a slight concussion of the brain. On another occasion arrangements were made to take a group of children to the pantomime. When Winston and Mrs. Everest reached the Castle where they were to meet the others, people with long faces came out and said that the theatre had been burned down. All that was left of the manager, they added lugubriously, were the keys that were in his pocket. Winston asked eagerly to see the keys, but this request, he wrote years later, 'does not seem to have been well received.'

The early pictures of Winston show a pug-nosed, determined little boy with a mass of untidy curls framed by the round sailor hat so dear to the hearts of the Victorians. He was red-headed, freckle-faced and obstreperous and from the moment he learned to talk, he talked incessantly. The recipient of his confidences was Mrs. Everest, a large, fat, homely woman who loved her small charge and who was rewarded by an unswerving devotion which lasted until her death.

He did not see much of his parents. His father was engrossed in Irish politics and his mother caught up in a busy social life. Neither considered children a vocation, and, in the way of most aristocratic families at that time, regarded the nursery, like the kitchen, as necessary adjuncts to the well-run household, but ones which should be hidden. Winston admired his mother from a distance like a beautiful, far-away evening star. She obviously had dazzling qualities for Viscount D'Abernon wrote of her at this time: 'I have the clearest recollection of seeing her for the first time. It was at the Viceregal Lodge at Dublin. She stood at one side to the left of the entrance. The Viceroy was on a dais at the farther end of the room surrounded by a brilliant staff, but eyes were not turned on him or his consort, but on a dark, lithe figure, standing somewhat apart and appearing to be of another texture to those around her, radiant, translucent, intense. A diamond star in her hair, her favourite ornament — its lustre dimmed by the flashing glory of her eyes. More of the panther than of the woman in her look, but with a cultivated intelligence unknown to the jungle. Her courage not less great than that of her husband — fit mother for descendants of the great Duke. With all these attributes of brilliancy such kindliness and high spirits that she was universally popular. Her desire to please, her delight in life, and the genuine wish that all should share her joyous faith in it, made her the centre of a devoted circle.'[20]

Winston was supremely happy until he was seven years old. His parents moved back to London after their three years in Ireland and he was given a large nursery equipped with all the things that a small boy likes best. He had a thousand tin soldiers, a magic lantern, and a real steam engine. Furthermore, when he was six his mother presented him with a brother, John, whom he regarded as a curious and amusing new possession.

The following year adversity set in. His mother announced that the time had come for him to go to boarding school. She had selected an expensive, modern school near Ascot which specialized in preparing boys for Eton. Winston dreaded the idea of leaving his untrammelled existence with Mrs. Everest and, as things turned out, his worst forebodings were fulfilled; he spent two years at St. James's School and hated every minute of it.

His departure had an almost Dickensian flavour. He was only seven and until then had led a happy and sheltered life. He remembers the ride in the hansom cab with his mother, his growing apprehension, and finally the awful moment when good-byes had been said and he was left alone with a stern, unbending master. The latter led him to an empty classroom and told him to sit down and learn the First

---

[20] *An Ambassador of Peace*: Viscount D'Abernon.

Declension of the Latin word for table, *mensa*. One can imagine the child's sinking heart as he looked at the strange, incomprehensible words. He did as he was bid and memorized them, but when the master returned, inquired boldly:

'And what does O table mean?'

'*Mensa*, O table, is the vocative case … You use it in speaking to a table.'

'But I never do,' insisted young Winston.

'If you are impertinent, you will be punished, and punished, let me tell you, very severely,' said the master angrily.[21]

This was the beginning of a bad two years. Discipline at St. James's was rigidly strict and, according to Winston, the headmaster was cruel and perverted. He delighted in assembling the little boys in the library, singling out the culprits one by one and taking them into the next room where he beat them until they bled. The other boys were forced to sit silent and listen to the screams of their schoolmates. Winston rebelled. He was beaten often and freely and with a violence which, he declares, not even a reformatory would tolerate to-day. Nevertheless he refused to surrender; he refused to write the Latin verses which he declared he could not understand, he refused to curry favour, he refused to repent. Once he even kicked the headmaster's straw hat to pieces which made him the hero of the school.

Winston nursed such a grievance against this man that for years afterwards he brooded on revenge. He planned to return one day, denounce the master before all his pupils, then subject him to the same punishment he had inflicted on his helpless charges. At the age of nineteen he actually drove to Ascot, but when he reached his destination he found that the school had been abandoned long before and the hated headmaster had disappeared.

Although Winston's lion-hearted resistance soon became a legend at St. James's his health suffered badly and after two years his family doctor advised Lady Randolph to remove him to Brighton where he would gain the benefit of sea air and more freedom. Here his fortunes improved. He was put under the care of two kind and elderly ladies who encouraged him to study the things he liked such as English, history, French and poetry. He was also allowed to ride and swim and to read Rider Haggard's thrilling books *King Solomon's Mines* and *Allan Quatermain*. Other activities included a school paper called *The*

---

[21] *My Early Life*: Winston S. Churchill.

Critic in which he lost interest after the first number, and a production of *Aladdin* which was so ambitious it never saw the light. He was happy once again, but in all fairness to the masters of St. James's it must be said that his new freedom did not bring about any magic change in him so far as obedience was concerned. He had such bounding vitality he could not, it seemed, keep out of mischief. His dancing mistress, Miss Vera Moore, described him as 'a small, red-headed pupil, the naughtiest boy in the class; I used to think he was the naughtiest small boy in the world'. There seemed to be no field in which Winston's peculiar brand of cheekiness did not flourish. Once one of the teachers asked the children to call out the number of good conduct marks they had lost. 'Nine,' cried Winston. 'But you couldn't have lost nine,' the teacher protested. 'Nein,' repeated Churchill triumphantly. 'I am talking German.'

Even Winston's relatives found him a handful. He usually spent his holidays visiting one of his many aunts and uncles, and the occasions rarely passed without some dramatic incident taking place. Sometimes he went to Bournemouth to stay with his father's sister, Lady Wimborne, and sometimes to Blenheim to stay with his father's brother, now the eighth Duke of Marlborough. Winston loved Blenheim, for every corner of the resounding halls and majestic rooms breathed the splendour of the great defender who had saved England from the rule of a tyrant. The little boy was dazzled by the uniforms and armour, by the wonderful trophies, and by the battle scenes that decorated the walls; but best of all he loved the toy soldiers that brought to life the armies which his famous ancestor had commanded. He modelled his own collection on this impressive array and often refought the Battle of Blenheim with himself as the heroic leader. He resolved that his life too would be filled with excitement and glory.

When Lady Randolph was abroad, as she frequently was, her elder sister, Lady Leslie, took Winston under her wing as part of her own family. When he was twelve years old she wrote the following letter to the celebrated author, Mr. Rider Haggard: 'The little boy Winston came here yesterday morning, beseeching me to take him to see you before he returns to school at the end of the month. I don't wish to bore so busy a man as yourself, but will you, when you have time, please tell me, shall I bring him on Wednesday next, when Mrs. Haggard said she would be at home? Or do you prefer settling to come here some afternoon when I could have the boy to meet you? He really is a very interesting being, though temporarily *uppish* from the restraining parental hand being in Russia.' Shortly after the meeting

Winston wrote to Mr. Haggard: 'Thank you so much for sending me *Allan Quatermain*; it was so good of you. I like *A.Q.* better than *King Solomon's Mines*; it is more amusing. I hope you will write a good many more books.'

When Winston was not at Bournemouth or Blenheim or with Lady Leslie, in her house near Dublin, he sometimes stayed with his mother's younger sister, Mrs. Frewen, in London. And other times the Leslie and Frewen children came to visit him at various houses which the Randolph Churchills rented for the summer. The three Jerome sisters had produced between them six boys and one girl, so there was no shortage of playmates. A picture taken in 1889 shows Lady Randolph with her two sons, Winston age fourteen and Jack age eight; Mrs. Frewen with Oswald, one, Hugh, six, and Clare, four; and Lady Leslie with Shane, four, and Norman, three.

Winston was the undisputed leader of the group, being six years older than any of the other children, and his leadership was of a stirring and wilful character. His cousin, Shane Leslie, remembers the agitated consultations between nannies and nursery maids as to how to handle the headstrong boy. He was the true *enfant terrible*. Once when he was defying his nurse he searched his brain for something 'wicked' with which he could threaten her; finally remembering her low church principles he declared boldly that if she would not let him have his way he would 'go and worship idols'.

The cousins regarded Winston with fascination and awe. 'We thought he was wonderful,' Shane Leslie explains, 'because he was always leading us to danger.' Sometimes the danger rested in hazardous bird's-nesting expeditions, sometimes in fights with the village children, sometimes in full-scale battles over carefully built fortresses. Once he persuaded Mrs. Everest to organize an expedition to the Tower of London so that he could give the younger children a detailed lecture on the tortures.

His cousin, Clare Frewen, who later as Clare Sheridan became widely known as a sculptress and a writer, describes in her memoirs the impression he made on her:

'Winston was a large school boy when I was still in the nursery. He had a disconcerting way of looking at me critically and saying nothing. He filled me with awe. His playroom contained from one end to the other a plank table on trestles, upon which were thousands of lead soldiers arranged for battle. He organized wars. The lead battalions were manoeuvred into action, peas and pebbles committed great casualties, forts were stormed, cavalry charged, bridges were destroyed — real water tanks engulfed the advancing foe. Altogether it was a most impressive show, and played with an interest that was no ordinary child game.

'One summer the Churchills rented a small house in the country for the holidays. It was called Banstead. Winston and Jack, his brother, built a log house with the help of the gardener's children and dug a ditch around it which they contrived to fill with water, and made a drawbridge that really could pull up and down. Here again war proceeded. The fort was stormed. I was hurriedly removed from the scene of action as mud and stones began to fly with effect. But the incident impressed me and Winston became a very important person in my estimation.'[22]

During the first three years that Winston was at school in Brighton, Lord Randolph was moving rapidly towards the glittering height of his career. Even though Winston was only nine he realized with immense pride that his father was a great national figure. The newspapers were full of his utterances, and the magazines ran dozens of cartoons. He noticed proudly that strangers even took off their hats when Lord Randolph passed and he heard grown-ups speaking of him as 'Gladstone's great adversary'. He pored over the daily papers and read every word of his father's speeches. He bought a scrap-book and pasted in the cartoons. He listened to whatever snatches of political talk he could hear, and acquainted himself with knowledge of all the great personalities of the day. And, of course, he lined up firmly on his father's side.

Anyone who was not interested in politics, he decided, must be very stupid indeed. Once when he visited the Marylebone swimming baths in London he asked the attendant if he were a Liberal or a Conservative. 'Oh, I don't bother myself about politics,' replied the man. 'What,' gasped Churchill in indignation, 'you pay rates and taxes and you don't bother yourself about politics? You ought to want to stand on a box in Hyde Park and tell people things.' On another occasion Winston refused to play with a certain friend any more, and when the friend's father inquired why, the boy answered: 'Winston says you're one of those damned Radicals and he's not coming over here again.'

Lord Randolph was apparently unaware that he had such a staunch supporter in his elder son. He was completely centred in his own

---

[22] *Nuda Veritas*: Clare Sheridan.

affairs and spared little time for his children. They were almost like strangers to him and yet when Winston was thirteen his father introduced him to Bram Stoker, the author of *Dracula*, saying: 'He's not much yet, but he's a good 'un.' Winston was enormously pleased by this tribute but during the next few years was doomed to fall considerably in his father's estimation.

The trouble, once again, was school; and this time it was Harrow. From the very first he was a failure. Most members of the Churchill family went to Eton, but since Winston had suffered from pneumonia twice his mother decided to send him to Harrow which, since it stands on a hill, was supposed to be healthier for a boy with a weak chest. The Latin entrance examination paper which Winston handed in, however, contained nothing more than a figure one in brackets, two smudges and a blot. However, Dr. Welldon, the Headmaster, took the unusual step of examining his other papers himself, and being convinced that it was impossible for Lord Randolph's son to be totally devoid of intelligence, persuaded himself that they showed traces of originality. On the strength of his intervention Winston was admitted.

Things went from bad to worse. Winston passed into Harrow the lowest boy in the lowest form, and he never moved out of the Lower School the whole five years he was there. Roll call was taken on the steps outside the Old School and the boys used to file past according to their scholastic record. Although in 1888 Lord Randolph was out of office he was still a world figure and sometimes visitors gathered to catch a glimpse of the brilliant man's son. Winston often heard them exclaim in amazement: 'Why, he's the last of all!' Many years later he proclaimed firmly: 'I'm all for the Public Schools but I do not want to go there again.'

The masters struggled with Churchill in bewilderment and indignation. He was self-confident and assertive; he could talk the hind leg off a donkey; why could he not learn the rudiments of Latin and Mathematics? Churchill insists that where 'my reason, imagination or interest was not engaged I could not or would not learn'.[23] There is no doubt that stubbornness played a considerable part for when his twelve years of school came to an end he declared with some pride that no one had ever succeeded in making him write a Latin verse or learn any Greek except the alphabet.

---

[23] *My Early Life*: Winston S. Churchill.

As a result he remained perpetually at the bottom of the class; and as a further result he was thoroughly grounded in English. If he was too stupid to learn Latin he could at least learn English. He was drilled over and over again in parsing and syntax. 'Thus,' he writes, 'I got into my bones the essential structure of the ordinary British sentence — which is a noble thing. And when in after years my schoolfellows who had won prizes and distinction for writing such beautiful Latin poetry and pithy Greek epigrams had to come down again to common English, to earn their living or make their way, I did not feel myself at any disadvantage.'[24]

Churchill loved to experiment with the use of words and was passionately fond of declaiming. He astonished the Headmaster, Dr. Welldon, by reciting twelve hundred lines of Macaulay's *Lays of Ancient Rome* without making a single mistake, for which he won a school prize. 'I do not believe I have ever seen in a boy of fourteen such a veneration of the English language,' Welldon once declared. Other testimony comes from Mr. Moore, who ran the Harrow Bookshop. 'Mr. Churchill ... in his schooldays already showed evidences of his unusual command of words. He would argue in the shop on any subject, and, as a result of this, he was, I am afraid, often left in sole possession of the floor.'[25]

Churchill was no better at sport than he was at Latin or Greek. He hated cricket and football and the only distinction he won was the Public Schools Fencing Competition. He was not a popular boy. Instead of being subdued by his failures he grew more self-assertive than ever. Once he crept up behind a small boy standing on the edge of the swimming pool and pushed him in. As the dripping and indignant figure climbed out, some of the boys who had watched the incident chanted with delight, 'You're in for it,' for the victim was none other than Leo Amery, a Sixth Form boy, who was not only Head of his House but a champion at gym. When Winston realized the full implications of his act he went up and apologized. 'I mistook you for a Fourth Form boy,' he explained, 'you are so small.' Then, sensing that this had not improved matters, added quickly: 'My father too is small and he also is a great man.' Leo Amery, who in later years sat

---

[24] Ibid.

[25] *Winston Churchill and Harrow*: Ed. by E. D. W. Chaplin.

in many of the same Cabinets with Churchill, burst into laughter and warned the miscreant to be more careful in the future.

Amery got his own back on Winston a short time later when the latter wrote several letters to the school magazine criticizing the gym. Amery was one of the schoolboy editors, and when Churchill's second contribution was sent in, containing an even more spirited attack than the first, he wielded the blue pencil firmly. With tears in his eyes Winston remonstrated that Amery was deleting his best paragraphs, but the latter was adamant and the letter was published with the following footnote: 'We have omitted a portion of our correspondent's letter, which seemed to us to exceed the limits of fair criticism. — Eds. *Harrovian.*'

Churchill's letters were published under the pen-name, Junius Junior, and even with the excisions Welldon felt that he was going too far. He summoned him and said that he had noticed certain articles of a subversive character critical of the constituted authorities of the school; that as the articles were anonymous he would not dream of asking who wrote them, but that if any more of the same sort appeared it might be his painful duty to swish Winston.

Churchill, however, was not intimidated by a dressing-down. Mr. Tomlin, who was the Head of School in Winston's second year, wrote that when Welldon once had Winston 'on the carpet' and said, 'Churchill, I have very grave reason to be displeased with you,' the boy retorted brightly, 'And I, sir, have very grave reason to be displeased with you.'[26] Despite Winston's sauce, Welldon confided to a friend that he was one of his favourite pupils.

Churchill's literary efforts did not extend much further than his attacks on the gym, save for a long poem on an epidemic of influenza. One of the verses went:

And now Europe groans aloud
And 'neath the heavy thunder-cloud
Hushed is both song and dance;
The germs of illness wend their way
To westward each succeeding day
And enter merry France.[27]

---

[26] *Winston Churchill and Harrow*: Ed. by E. D. W. Chaplin.

[27] Ibid.

Churchill did not worry about his unpopularity with his schoolmates, for he was not a boy who feared to be alone; he could always find something amusing to do with his leisure. When he was fifteen he made an experiment which fortunately escaped the notice of the masters. In the town of Harrow there stood an old deserted house with a large garden. As the building fell into decay it became known as 'The Haunted House'. There was an old well in the garden and people claimed that a passage at the bottom led to the Parish Church. Winston thought it would be fun to find out whether this was true and hit upon the happy idea of blowing it up. With some gunpowder, a stone ginger-beer bottle and a homemade fuse he assembled an elementary but effective bomb, and placed it at the bottom of the well. Nothing happened and he leaned over the wall. At that moment the bomb exploded. Winston was not hurt but his face was blackened and his hair and eyebrows singed. The neighbours hurried to their windows and Mr. Harry Woodbridge, who still lives in Harrow, declares that his aunt ran out to help the boy. She brought him into the kitchen and bathed his face. When he left he thanked her and said: 'I expect this will get me the bag.' But the masters did not hear of the incident and his fears were not realized.

Winston's indifference to his schoolmates probably revealed itself most nobly in his attitude to the devoted Mrs. Everest. English Public Schools are cruelly critical of the outward display of affection, and for this reason boys have even been known to beg their parents to keep away. Winston not only invited Mrs. Everest to visit him but when she arrived, enormously fat and smiling, kissed her in front of all the boys and walked down the street with her arm in arm. Jack Seely, an old Harrovian who afterwards became one of Churchill's Cabinet colleagues, and won the D.S.O. in the First War, witnessed the incident and described it as one of the 'bravest acts' he had ever seen.

*

Lord Randolph was startled and worried by his son's scholastic failures. He felt that the boy must be backward and for the first time began to concern himself about his future. Occasionally he visited him at Harrow and followed the approved pattern of parental behaviour by taking him and his school friend, Jack Milbanke, to luncheon at the King's Head Hotel. Winston sat awkward and silent, listening to Milbanke conversing so easily with his brilliant father and wishing with all his heart that he could do the same. But Lord Randolph intimidated his son. He was remote and impersonal and even then made no effort to gain his confidence. The son was filled with admiration for his father, yet in his presence was *gauche* and self-conscious.

One day when Winston was fourteen and home on holiday Lord Randolph went up to the nursery. He found the boy playing with his soldiers which were then over fifteen hundred strong. He studied them as they stood arrayed in line of battle and asked him if he would like to be a soldier. Winston was delighted to think that his father had discovered in him the seeds of military genius and did not realize for many years that Lord Randolph had decided that soldiering was the only career for a boy of limited intelligence.

Winston was immensely pleased at the prospect of a military life. He took a special course at Harrow to prepare him for his Sandhurst examination, but even here he did not succeed. Twice he took the examination and twice he failed. In exasperation his father removed him from Harrow and sent him to a crammer. He took the examination for the third time and passed, but so low that he was not qualified to enter any regiment but the cavalry. The cavalry accepted a lower standard since its primary requisite was for young men of independent means who could and would pay for their own horses.

When Lord Randolph heard of his son's latest failure he was very angry and wrote him a terse letter warning him that if he did not pull himself together he would be a 'social wastrel'. Lord Randolph had set his heart on Winston's joining the 60th Rifles, and now he had the humiliating duty of writing to the Colonel of the Regiment and explaining that his son was too stupid to qualify.

Despite his father's indignation Winston was thrilled at the thought of becoming a cavalry officer. Riding was more fun than walking. He entered Sandhurst with a light heart.

*

Just before Winston passed his final examination for Sandhurst he had a serious accident. He went to visit his aunt, Lady Wimborne, at Bournemouth. He was being chased by his cousin and his brother and suddenly found himself cornered on a bridge, under winch lay a ravine covered with pine trees. He rashly decided to avoid capture by jumping into the ravine, hoping that the trees would break his fall and deposit him on the earth unhurt. His plan misfired and he fell twenty-nine feet on to hard ground. The two boys ran into the house and fetched Lady Randolph, saying: 'Winston jumped over the bridge and he won't speak to us.' For three days he was unconscious. His father hurried from Ireland and all the most eminent specialists of the day were summoned. He had a ruptured kidney which called for an immediate operation. The news went round the Carlton Club that Lord Randolph's son had met with a serious accident playing 'Follow my Leader', to which the wits replied: 'Lord Randolph will never come to grief that way.'

Winston was laid up for nearly the whole of the year 1893. But his convalescence, far from proving dull, opened up for him the exciting world of politics that he had hitherto only read about. His parents took him to London where they were living with his grandmother, the dowager Duchess of Marlborough, at 50 Grosvenor Square. Lord Randolph was a sick man; he was shrunken and pale and had grown an enormous, shaggy beard that seemed to accentuate his illness. Yet he still dreamed of retrieving his position. He felt he had been badly used and Winston had heard him refer bitterly to the Tories as 'a Government and a party which for five years have boycotted and slandered me.'[28] He had therefore gained a certain amount of satisfaction when, a few months previously, Gladstone had beaten the Tories at the polls and ascended the throne once again.

Lord Randolph's sister was married to Lord Tweedmouth, Gladstone's chief whip, so the Churchills found themselves in the Liberals' inner circle. Every day there were people for lunch and dinner and here the eighteen-year-old Winston met for the first time many of the great figures whom he was destined to know as colleagues in the days to come. He met Mr. Chamberlain, Mr. Balfour, Mr. Edward Carson, Mr. Asquith, Mr. John Morley, Lord Rosebery and many others. He often attended the House of Commons, and heard Gladstone wind up the Third Reading of the Home Rule Bill. One evening when Edward Carson came to dinner and discovered that Winston had spent the afternoon in the gallery, he said: 'What did you think of my speech?' Winston replied solemnly: 'I concluded from it, sir, that the ship of State is struggling in heavy seas.'

What fascinated Winston most about the House of Commons was that although the battle across the floor was sharp and fierce, when opponents met outside the Chamber they were friendly and courteous. On one occasion he heard his father and Sir William Harcourt exchanging very acrimonious charges. Sir William seemed to him unnecessarily angry and extremely unfair. He was therefore astonished when the latter came up to him in the gallery, shook his hand and smiled and asked him what he thought of the speech. The

---

[28] *Lord Randolph Churchill*: Winston S. Churchill.

lack of rancour impressed Winston. It was the truly sporting way to fight, he decided, as chivalrous as the knights of old; and it is worth noticing that he has always modelled his own conduct on these Victorian examples.

As the days passed he tried eagerly to draw closer to his strange father. A short time before his accident he had caught one fleeting glimpse of the inner man, which encouraged him and filled him with hope. He had let off a gun at a rabbit which happened to appear on the lawn just below Lord Randolph's window. The latter spoke to his son angrily, then suddenly melted. He talked gently about school and the Army, and the difficulties and rewards of life in general. At the end he said: 'Remember things do not always go right with me. My every action is misjudged and every word distorted ... So make some allowances.'[29]

The fact that Lord Randolph had unbent for these few minutes filled Winston with hope. Perhaps one day, when he had made his name and fortune, he would enter the House at his father's side and they would fight their way together. But this talk was the only intimate conversation he was ever to have with Lord Randolph.

*

Winston loved Sandhurst. For the first time he enjoyed studying for now the lessons consisted of Tactics, Fortification, Topography and Military Law. He learned how to blow up masonry bridges, constructed breastworks, made road reconnaissances, and contoured maps. The wars he particularly studied as 'the latest and best specimens' were the American Civil War, the Russo-Turkish War, and the Franco-German War.

Horses were his greatest pleasure. Besides the instruction he received at Sandhurst his father arranged for him to take an additional course in the vacations with the Royal Horse Guards. He spent all his money on hiring horses and much of his time in organizing point-to-points and steeplechases.

But he still retained a lively interest in politics, and during his last term made his first public speech. The circumstances were unusual and comic. In the summer of 1894 a certain Mrs. Ormiston Chant launched a Purity Campaign which received much publicity. The chief object of her attention was the promenade of the Empire Theatre, a large space behind the dress circle which was a lounge containing

---

[29] *Lord Randolph Churchill*: Winston S. Churchill.

several bars and usually filled with men and professional ladies. Since it was a favourite place of many of the Sandhurst cadets many of them were naturally indignant at Mrs. Chant's allegations of insobriety and immorality. The *Daily Telegraph* ran an article against the lady entitled: 'Prudes on the Prowl', and the battle was on.

Winston followed the controversy with immense interest, and one day read in the paper that a certain gentleman was proposing to form a League of Citizens under the name 'The Entertainments Protection League' and was calling on all interested people to come forward and help form committees.

He responded at once, and wrote to the founder saying that he would travel to London for the first meeting. He then sat down and composed a speech, dealing with the rights of the individual, which he learned by heart. On the appointed day he travelled to London with the good wishes of his colleagues. He was surprised to find the hotel small and dingy. But he was even more surprised to find only one person there, the founder. The latter admitted sadly that save for Cadet Churchill there had been no response. Winston swallowed his disappointment and returned to Sandhurst, pawning his gold watch on the way to pay for his dinner.

This was not the end of the story. Winston and his friends attended the promenade and were disturbed to see that screens had been put around the bars to divide them from the public. A young man tapped one of the screens with his cane; another pushed it, a third kicked. Suddenly two hundred people were rushing at the screens, Winston conspicuous among them. At the height of the excitement Churchill leapt on to a chair and delivered his speech, but it was no longer the cold, reasoned, constitutional effort. It was a heated, rousing speech shouted above the tumult. Although this maiden oration fortunately escaped the notice of the press, Richard Harding Davis, an American author who met Churchill in London, was given a version of the speech by Winston's fellow officers, and preserved a portion of it for posterity. 'Where does the Englishman in London always find a welcome?' cried Churchill. 'Where does he first go when, battle-scarred and travel-worn, he reaches home? Who is always there to greet him with a smile and join him with a drink? Who is ever faithful, ever true? The ladies of the Empire promenade!'[30]

---

[30] *Real Soldiers of Fortune*: Richard Harding Davis.

Luckily, this incident was not brought to the attention of Winston's commanding officer.

*

In January 1895, two months before Winston received the Queen's Commission, Lord Randolph Churchill died. It was a severe blow to his son, for although the disappointed statesman had been increasingly ill in the past few years the family clung doggedly to the hope that he would recover both his health and his political position. Winston was eagerly awaiting the day when his father would accept him as an equal. During the boy's two years at Sandhurst Lord Randolph had occasionally taken him to dinners and week-end parties and he was confident that they were moving toward a closer understanding. But Lord Randolph never really dropped his mask. 'If ever I began to show the slightest idea of comradeship, he was immediately offended;' Winston wrote many years later, 'and when once I suggested that I might help his private secretary to write some letters, he froze me into stone.'[31]

Lord Randolph knew his son so little that it never crossed his mind that Winston even toyed with the idea of entering politics. Certainly it never entered his head as a feasible proposition. Politics were expensive in those days and Members of Parliament were unpaid. Besides, he could not pretend his boy was clever. Some months previously he had even written a friend in South Africa asking if there were any prospects in the Colonies for he did not feel his son was likely to make his way in England.

Winston was just twenty when Lord Randolph died and he at once assumed his role as head of the family. Relatives remember him at the funeral, self-possessed and capable. They remember the hundreds of telegrams that poured in and the picture of Winston reading each one and impaling it dramatically on a spike. The young man's future was now a large question mark, for Lord Randolph had left his two sons no money. His estate just settled his debts, and there was nothing over. In Victorian days this was a severe handicap for a member of the ruling class, for without money the road to politics was completely barred. It was even necessary, of course, to have money as a cavalry officer. Lady Randolph gave Winston an allowance of £500 a year. He accepted it gratefully with a determination to make himself financially independent as quickly as possible.

---

[31] *My Early Life*: Winston S. Churchill.

Six months after his father's death Winston received another blow, which was an even greater emotional loss. Mrs. Everest died. Throughout the years the deep bond between her and Winston had remained as strong as ever. 'She was,' he wrote, 'my dearest and most intimate friend during the whole twenty years I had lived.'[32] When she had retired from the Churchills' service some years before, Lord Randolph had paid tribute to her devoted care by making a special trip in a hansom cab to lunch with Lord Rothschild in order to invest her savings.

Mrs. Everest lived in North London, and when Winston heard she was ill he hastened to her bedside. He had to return to Aldershot for an early morning parade, then hurried back to her again. He sat with her for many hours, and was with her when she died. He attended her funeral and when she was lowered into her grave he wept as he had never wept for his own father. Several years later, in India, he came across the passage Gibbon had written about his nurse: 'If there be any, as I trust there are some, who rejoice that I live, to that dear and excellent woman their gratitude is due.' This, he declared, would be Mrs. Everest's epitaph: and to-day her picture still hangs in his study at Chartwell.

---

[32] Ibid.

Chapter Four — Cuba, India and Egypt

TWO MONTHS after Lord Randolph's death, Winston was gazetted to the 4th Queen's Own Hussars. Although he was not a handsome boy, his appearance was striking. He was of medium height, strong and wiry, with a head that seemed too large for his body. He had a pug nose, large protruding blue eyes, a pink and white skin a girl might have envied, and a shock of red-gold hair that matched the braid on his uniform. An impediment in his speech prevented him from pronouncing the letter 's' clearly and gave him a slight lisp. Yet he was anything but effeminate. His blue eyes were impudent and challenging and his round face had the pugnacious look of the street urchin.

His birth and breeding automatically opened the doors to the powerful oligarchic society which ruled Britain. This society consisted of a few hundred great families who throughout the years had become widely interrelated by marriage. 'Everywhere one met friends and kinsfolk,' wrote Winston. 'The leading figures of Society were in many cases the leading statesmen in Parliament, and also the leading sportsmen on the Turf. Lord Salisbury was accustomed scrupulously to avoid calling a Cabinet when there was racing at Newmarket, and the House of Commons made a practice of adjourning for the Derby. In those days the glittering parties at Lansdowne House, Devonshire House and Stafford House comprised all the elements which made a gay and splendid social circle in close relation to the business of Parliament, the hierarchies of the Army and Navy, and the policy of the State.'[33]

Winston found this new world greatly to his liking. Not only was he free from the constraining atmosphere of the classroom but he was delighted to find himself moving on terms of social equality with the most distinguished men of the day. Furthermore, he had discovered in his mother a new and kindred spirit. Up till then Lady Randolph had paid little attention to her son, but now that Winston had reached an age where he could fit into her life she began to take an amused and genuine interest in him. She introduced him to whoever he wished to meet and made every effort to smooth his path. She did not attempt to

---

[33] *My Early Life*: Winston S. Churchill.

exert a maternal influence, and gradually a deep and affectionate brother-sister relationship developed which lasted until her death.

Winston, however, was not a universal favourite. He moved bombastically and assertively through the sedate circles of Victorian society. He was blunt and opinionated and indifferent to the social graces. His prolonged failure at school had increased, not diminished his aggressiveness, for he was so eager to impress people with his unrecognized ability that he seized every opportunity to force his ideas upon them. Small talk bored him and he made no attempt to conceal his impatience with stupidity. He did not hesitate to engulf his elders in a tide of rhetoric against which they often struggled helplessly; and as a result he soon won the reputation of being egotistical, rude and bumptious.

The young men of the 4th Hussars regarded him with good-natured amusement. The majority were rich, charming and intellectually lazy. Most of them had chosen a military career because it interfered less than anything else with hunting and shooting and the pleasures of the London season. In those days cavalry officers were paid only fourteen shillings a day, and were obliged to dig into their own pockets to support themselves and a string of horses as well. But their meagre salaries were balanced by certain advantages. They had five months' leave a year, and even when they were on duty their hours were neither arduous nor long. Although Winston's mother made him an allowance of £500 a year which in those days had considerable purchasing power, his brother officers lived at such a high standard he regarded himself as 'a poor man'.

However, Lieut. Churchill had not joined the army in order to embark on a social career. It was not for nothing that the Duke of Marlborough was his hero, or that he had arrayed his tin soldiers in line of battle and dreamt of heroic deeds suitably rewarded by Fame. He was determined to make a name for himself, but it was a depressing truth that there could be no sensational military exploits if there were no wars. He looked at the world of 1895 with dismay. If only he had been born at the end of the last century with twenty years of Napoleonic battles stretching out before him. The last war Britain had fought was in the Crimea in 1854, and still there was scarcely a cloud on the horizon.

The only place any fighting was going on was in Cuba and one could scarcely call a minor rebellion a war. However, he was soon to have a few months' leave and a rebellion was better than nothing. He persuaded Reginald Barnes, a fellow subaltern, to undertake the journey with him and secured a few letters of introduction to the Spanish authorities in Havana by writing to his father's old friend, Sir Henry Drummond-Wolff who was at that time British Ambassador in Madrid. Then he remembered that his father had once written several articles for the *Daily Graphic*. In those days there were no regulations which forbade Army officers to write for the press, and many newspapers commissioned serving officers to act as correspondents. Winston saw the editor of the *Graphic* and succeeded in securing a commission for a series of dispatches at £5 apiece.

The two young Hussars set out for Cuba early in November. Their adventures proved to be more comical than dangerous and more jovial than instructive; nevertheless the trip was an important turning point in Winston's life for it launched him on the career of a war correspondent which was to make him a national figure before five years had passed.

The Spanish authorities welcomed the two subalterns with surprising cordiality. They were attempting to suppress a Cuban thrust for independence, and they insisted on interpreting the visit of the Englishmen as an official gesture of friendship from a great and interested power. Every courtesy was shown them and every facility placed at their disposal. Arrangements were soon made to send them to join a Spanish column of four thousand men that was marching through a jungle in which many enemy patrols were operating.

It took the two Hussars several days to reach General Valdez's column. They travelled first by train, then by boat and finally caught up with him in the town of Sancti Spiritus. The General greeted them warmly, provided them with horses and explained to them that he was making a fortnight's march through the insurgent districts. The long column set off in the morning first moving through tangled jungles, then open spaces, then more jungles. The enemy was well hidden, but on the morning of 30 November, Winston's twenty-first birthday, a few bullets whistled over his head while he was camped near the roadside eating a chicken for his breakfast. This was his baptism of fire. The next evening another volley rang out while he and a group of officers were dressing after a swim, causing them a certain amount of inconvenience and a good many jokes. And later that night several more bullets lodged themselves in the thatch of the hut in which he was sleeping.

On the third day the Spanish column attacked. Churchill and Barnes were mounted and advanced with the General and his staff about fifty yards behind the Spanish infantry. They watched the puffs of enemy smoke in the distance and sat with dignity while bullets whistled around them. Soon the rebel fire died away and the Spanish soldiers occupied the insurgent positions. It was impossible to pursue the enemy because of the density of the jungle, and the battle was over. The next day the Englishmen left for England.

Winston sent several dispatches home. One opened with the jovial declaration that first sentences, whether of a proposal of marriage or a newspaper article, were always difficult. The other explained the handicaps under which journalists operated. 'While the Spanish authorities are masters of the art of suppressing the truth,' he wrote, 'the Cubans are adepts at inventing falsehoods.'

Churchill and Barnes felt that they had had their money's worth. Besides all the fun, they had learned to appreciate Havana cigars, rum cocktails, and the merits of the Spanish siesta. When the first World War came, Winston adopted the habit of the afternoon siesta and has continued it ever since. But more important still, the young men now considered themselves authorities on war. None of their fellow subalterns had been to a war and although their own experience was limited to three days they could boast triumphantly of 'having seen fighting in Cuba'.

They reached England to learn that the 4th Hussars were soon to sail for India.

*

The necessary regimental preparations took nearly nine months and it was not until the autumn of 1896, a year and a half after Winston had first received his commission, that the Hussars finally set forth. When the ship anchored in Bombay Harbour he was so anxious to get ashore that he embarked in a small boat. Upon reaching the quay he grabbed at an iron ring to pull himself up and dislocated his shoulder, which was to prove a handicap in later life.

The regiment was stationed at Bangalore. Winston moved into a pink and white bungalow covered with roses which he shared with three other officers. The young men pooled their money, organized their servants and settled down happily to enjoy themselves. They spent the mornings drilling, parading and attending to their regimental duties, and the afternoons in sleeping. But at five o'clock the real business of the day began. In the cool of the evening they had strenuous and thrilling polo matches, for polo was the pivot around which the life of all cavalry officers in India centred. Although Winston had to ride with his shoulder strapped he often played ten or twelve chukkas. His life was entirely carefree except for occasional money worries. Polo ponies were expensive, and the mess operated on a lordly scale. Every now and then he was forced to visit the native moneylenders where he borrowed money at the rate of twenty-four per cent interest a year. But in the end all these matters seem to have adjusted themselves.

Winston enjoyed his new existence to the full. Nevertheless he found himself beginning to think of more serious things, and for the first time he became painfully aware of the fact that he was badly educated. Years later he likened his education to a Swiss cheese — 'smooth on the surface but too many holes in it.' He wrote to his mother and asked her to send him some books. Gradually he developed the habit of reading for three or four hours each day. He read Plato's *Republic*, Aristotle on Politics, Schopenhauer on Pessimism, Malthus on Population, Darwin's *Origin of Species*. But the books that interested him most, first for their wonderful English and second for their thrilling subject matter, were Gibbon's *Decline and Fall of the Roman Empire* and Macaulay's *History of England*. He read and re-read these two authors, revelling in their wonderful, rolling phrases and memorizing long passages by heart. He tried to pattern his own writing on their style and subconsciously even began to phrase his thoughts in their polished language.

Although Winston admitted the deficiencies of his education he was careful not to allow anyone else to draw attention to them. He was as cheeky as ever. He could not refrain from criticism and advice, and was seldom able to flavour either with tact. An old Field-Marshal, who was serving as a captain in India at the time, told me of an occasion when Winston and several of his fellow officers were invited to dinner at the Viceroy's Palace. Pomp and ceremony blazed at such functions, and rules of procedure were observed with meticulous care. The young Army officers were kept at one end of the reception room, while the great ones of India, the governors and princes, or 'heaven-borns', as they were called, talked politics at the other end. Winston listened impatiently to the banal conversation of his contemporaries, then strode down the length of the room, pushed his way into the celebrated circle and began to give them advice on how to run the country. 'That sort of thing,' said the Field-Marshal, 'did not contribute to his popularity.'

And yet if Winston could be annoying he could also be disarming. He was aware of the unfavourable impression he created and was usually indifferent to it, but his indifference was never cold for he was incapable of holding any malice. He had the rare quality of never resenting the resentment of those to whom he had been rude, and often took his enemies unawares by offering a sudden warm apology. Once sufficient time had elapsed to give him perspective, he had the gift of surveying himself with humour and detachment. In *My Early Life* he produces a literary bonne bouche. in describing an occasion, shortly after his arrival in India, when he was in one of his most aggressive moods. The Governor of Bombay, Lord Sandhurst, entertained Winston and a brother officer at dinner. 'We … enjoyed a banquet of glitter, pomp, and iced champagne,' he wrote. 'His Excellency, after the health of the Queen-Empress had been drunk and dinner was over, was good enough to ask my opinion on several matters, and considering the magnificent character of his hospitality I thought it would be unbecoming in me not to reply fully. I have forgotten the particular points of British and Indian affairs upon which he sought my counsel; all I can remember is that I responded generously. There were indeed moments when he seemed willing to impart his own views; but I thought it would be ungracious to put him to so much trouble; and he very readily subsided.'

Although Winston enjoyed the Army life in Bangalore, and particularly the thrilling polo matches, he began to grow restless. The more he read and the more he talked, the more certain he became that he was intended for great things. A sharp driving ambition was growing within him that seemed to be increasing each day; and at the age of twenty-two he felt there was no time to lose. He must establish a name for himself as quickly as possible. But how could he show the world the stuff he was made of if his regiment remained in idleness? What chance was there for him to win his spurs in peaceful Bangalore?

He was in this impatient mood in the summer of 1897 when he was in England on leave. One morning he picked up a newspaper and read that fighting had broken out on the Northwest Frontier and General Sir Bindon Blood was in charge. Sir Bindon was a descendant of a notorious character named Colonel Blood who had tried to steal the Crown Jewels from the Tower of London in the reign of Charles II. Winston had made friends with the General at a social function in England the year before, and the latter agreed that if any trouble broke out on the frontier he would let the young subaltern join him. Churchill promptly sent him a telegram reminding him of his promise, and the reply came back that although there were no vacancies on his staff if Winston could get a job as a war correspondent he would be pleased to have him with him.

Winston left for India in a high state of excitement. He persuaded the editor of an Indian paper, the *Allahabad Pioneer*, to employ him, and even more important, persuaded the Colonel of the Queen's Hussars to grant him leave from his regiment. He then travelled two thousand miles across India to the frontier.

The command Winston joined was known as the Malakand Field Force. Its task was to suppress an uprising among the fierce Pathan tribesmen on the frontier, against a grandiose background of high rugged mountains, small mud villages and broad arid plains. Winston was allowed to attach himself to a brigade of cavalry and infantry which had been given orders to march through the Mamund Valley. The column started forth in war-like formation preceded by a squadron of Bengal Lancers, then broke up into small sections. Before the day was out Winston's group came into contact with a band of fierce Pathan savages. The Adjutant of his regiment was wounded a few yards from Winston, who saw a tribesman rush at the stricken officer and kill him with a slash of his sword. Then the savage picked up a stone, hurled it at Winston and waited for him, brandishing his sword. Churchill pulled out his revolver and fired several shots, then realizing he was alone and surrounded by the enemy he ran as fast as he could and took cover behind a knoll where he found a handful of his own soldiers. The fighting lasted several hours. Winston and his men carried two wounded officers and six wounded Sikhs back to safety.

For the next fortnight part of the Field Force carried out a punitive expedition through the valley which provided Winston with more fighting and more copy. When the operation finally came to an end Sir Bindon Blood stated in dispatches that the officer commanding the forces had 'praised the courage and resolution of Lieut. W. L. S. Churchill, 4th Hussars, the correspondent of the *Pioneer* newspaper, who had made himself useful at a critical moment.'

After this thrilling adventure Winston had no wish to return to the routine life of Bangalore. His mother had been busy on his behalf in London and had landed him a job as correspondent to the *Daily Telegraph*. He tried energetically to secure a permanent appointment to the Malakand Field Force, but suddenly operations came to an end and the command was disbanded. This was disappointing but at the same time news came that another force was being organized to carry out a punitive expedition in Tirah, another trouble spot on the Northwest Frontier. Winston began to pull strings, but by this time influential generals and colonels had formed a strong prejudice against the bumptious young officer. He could not resist offering them advice and lecturing them on strategy and he even had the effrontery to criticize them in his articles. Who did the young whippersnapper think he was, anyway? They would show him, and as a result Winston found his path firmly blocked. Sorrowfully he was forced to return to the uneventful life of Bangalore where his brother officers made it plain that they thought it high time he attended to his regimental duties.

But Winston did not abandon his efforts. He still cast wistful eyes towards Tirah, and with his mother's help in London he exerted all the pressure he could to advance his aims. He wrote letters, sent telegrams, inveigled and implored. Finally a letter arrived from an old friend, Colonel Ian Hamilton, informing him that a certain Captain Haldane was A.D.C. to Sir William Lockhart, the Commander-in-Chief of the expedition, and advising him that if he could impress himself sufficiently on Haldane the latter had sufficient influence to get him an appointment on the General's staff. Once again Winston obtained leave from his Colonel and once again he travelled across India. He was received by Captain Haldane who listened to his story and said he would have to discuss the matter with his chief. Ten minutes later he reappeared and to Winston's great joy announced that he could give him an appointment as an extra orderly officer on the Commander's staff.

This was such a stroke of good fortune that Winston strained every nerve to continue his good behaviour. For once he was neither bumptious nor cheeky. 'I behaved and was treated,' he wrote, 'as befitted my youthful station. I sat silent at meals or only rarely asked a tactful question.'

Captain Haldane obviously had no idea what an effort this cost Lieut. Churchill, for years later when he was an old, distinguished and retired general he wrote in his memoirs that although Churchill 'was widely regarded in the Army as super-precocious, indeed by some as insufferably bumptious' that 'neither of these epithets was applicable.' 'On the contrary,' he continued, 'my distinct recollection of him at this time was that he was modest and paid attention to what was said, not attempting to monopolize the conversation or thrust his opinions — and clear-cut opinions they were on many subjects — on his listeners. He enjoyed giving vent to his views on matters military and otherwise, but there was nothing that could be called aggressive or self-assertive which could have aroused antagonism among the most sensitive of those with whom he was talking.'[34]

It all went to prove that Lieut. Churchill knew how to conduct himself when his interests were at stake. However, his well-laid plans and his justifiable hopes were to come to nothing. Peace suddenly broke out and the expedition was abandoned. Once more Churchill returned forlornly to Bangalore.

*

While Winston was in Bangalore trying to attach himself to the Tirah expedition he was not idle. His dispatches on the fighting at the frontier had been colourful and amusing and he suddenly decided to write a book entitled *The Malakand Field Force*. He worked furiously and at the end of two months had produced a lively and detailed account of the campaign. The book soon found a publisher and when it came out a few months later the critics were friendly and the public enthusiastic. The Prime Minister, Lord Salisbury, read it, and the Prince of Wales wrote the author a letter of congratulation. Everyone was delighted except the Army. The generals noticed with annoyance and anger that 2nd Lieut. Churchill had been very free with his censure. He criticized the 'short service' system of recruitment; the fact that soldiers were not equipped with chocolate or sausages on their marches; that retiring companies were not covered by continuous fire; that civil officers were encouraged to collect military information from the enemy. And then ended undaunted: 'There will not be wanting those who will remind me that in this matter my opinion finds no support in age or experience. To such I shall reply that if what is written is false or foolish, neither age nor experience should fortify it; and if it is true, it needs no such support.'

Winston was so encouraged by the success of his book, that he promptly sat down to write another. This time he decided to try his hand at a novel. While his brother officers were taking siestas on the hot Indian afternoons, he worked. His theme was a revolt in Ruritania with a hero who overthrew the Government and was then threatened with a socialist revolution. The climax centred in an iron-clad fleet firing on the capital to quell the murderous radicals. The story was called *Savrola* and although it was not hailed as a masterpiece it was serialized in *Macmillan's Magazine* and earned the author £700. Winston was quick to see its literary defects and decided never again

---

[34] *A Soldier's Saga*: General Sir Aylmer Haldane.

to attempt fiction. 'I have consistently urged my friends to abstain from reading it,' he wrote in later years.

*

Winston felt in his bones that he was meant for the battlefield. But he was not content to lead a minor campaign. He wanted a career along the lines of Marlborough or Napoleon, but in 1898 people were saying emphatically that major wars were a thing of the past.

Reluctantly he came to the conclusion that if Fame was to be his quarry he must change his course. The more he studied his father's life the more it stirred him. The House of Commons offered excitement, and the prizes were great. Besides, there was no bar to youth and he was in a hurry. Lord Randolph had reached the Cabinet at the age of thirty-six, and perhaps he would do the same. He made up his mind to enter Parliament as soon as possible. He knew that he would be unable to secure a Conservative seat without money and a reputation, but he was confident that he could win both by his pen, if only Britain's 'little wars' would provide him with sufficiently exciting material to catch the public eye.

He was delighted to learn therefore, in the spring of 1898, that Sir Herbert Kitchener, the Commander-in-Chief of the Anglo-Egyptian Army, was planning a large-scale offensive to liberate the Sudan from the tyrannical rule of the Dervishes. This would be a thrilling campaign and he was determined to be in it. Once again he started pulling strings, but the hostility towards him in military circles had been growing and now extended to the powerful Kitchener himself. Although Winston obtained permission from the War Office to join the Egyptian forces, and leave from his regiment, and even wangled a commission with the 21st Lancers, Kitchener flatly refused to have him. Lady Randolph, who knew the General personally, wrote him a letter but the 'no' still remained firm.

Then one day Lord Salisbury, the Prime Minister, wrote Winston telling him how much he had enjoyed his book *The Malakand Field Force* and invited him to come and see him. The latter accepted with alacrity, and spent half an hour with the Prime Minister discussing military operations in India. When he left the aged statesman told him to let him know if he could ever be of any help to him. Winston took him at his word and asked him to intervene with Kitchener. But even Salisbury failed. Kitchener still said no.

Winston, however, never abandoned hope, and finally got his way through the rivalry which existed between Kitchener and the War Office. Sir Evelyn Wood, the Adjutant-General, felt that Kitchener was being too autocratic in picking and choosing officers despite the recommendations of the War Office. The case of young Churchill gave him an opportunity to assert himself. He declared that Kitchener was Commander of the Egyptian Army but not of the British Army; that the 21st Lancers were part of the Expeditionary Force and not under his control until they arrived in Egypt; and sent Winston a note informing him that he was attached to the Lancers, and ordering him to report at once to Regimental Headquarters in Cairo. 'It is understood,' said the communication, 'that you will proceed at your own expense and that in the event of your being killed or wounded in the impending operations or for any other reason, no charge of any kind will fall on British Army Funds.' With this our hero set off for the wars. Before leaving he signed up with the *Morning Post* to write articles at £15 each.

He arrived in Cairo on 1 August. He learned that two squadrons of the 21st Lancers had already started up the Nile and the other two were scheduled to leave in the morning. A troop in one of the leading squadrons had been reserved for him but because of the uncertainty of his arrival it had been given to Lieut. Grenfell. This was part of Winston's luck for Grenfell and his troop were destined to be cut to pieces in the battle to come.

The regiment travelled fourteen hundred miles into the heart of Africa. It took them nearly three weeks to reach the front, an outpost about twenty miles from the great city of Omdurman. They journeyed by train and steamer, then marched two hundred miles through blistering heat in full battle array. The tension and excitement mounted as they drew nearer their destination and heard the first reports of horsemen in white with shining, curved swords.

A few hours after the Lancers had reached their final camp Winston had his first sight of the enemy. He rode up to ail advance outpost where, with several other officers, he looked through field glasses and saw a long dark smudge on the horizon which was the massed Dervish Army sixty thousand strong. The shadow was beginning to move and Winston was ordered to ride post haste to Kitchener and give him the latest report. He was exhilarated at the thought of the coming action but filled with apprehension at having to face the Commander who had flatly refused to have him in Egypt. He cantered back seven miles, paused on a hill to watch the British Army advancing in splendid formation with their standards flying, and Kitchener himself leading the procession, then rode forward and delivered his message.

Kitchener asked a few questions, and then dismissed his informant; he did not know who he was.

That night all was quiet. The Dervish Army had not attacked after all. Several British gun-boats were anchored on the Nile not far from Winston's camp, and some of the naval officers chaffed with the soldiers about the coming battle. A young man named Beatty flung a bottle of champagne ashore which Winston picked up.

At dawn the great battle began. Kitchener's Army consisted of only twenty thousand men, but it was an uneven struggle. Some of the Dervishes had antiquated guns but most of them attacked with lances and swords and were mown down by the artillery and rifle fire of the British. At the end of an hour the ground was strewn with over twenty thousand Dervishes, dead and wounded. Winston watched the great clash from an observation post only four hundred yards away. The enemy swept across the sands like a great incoming tide cheering fanatically for God, his prophet, and the Khalifa. 'We were so close, as we sat spellbound on our horses,' he wrote, 'that we almost shared their perils. I saw the full blast of Death strike this human wall. Down went their standards by dozens and their men by hundreds. Wide gaps and shapeless heaps appeared in their array. One saw them jumping and tumbling under the shrapnel bursts; but none turned back.'[35]

The Lancers played no part in the initial assault but as soon as the main body of the Dervish Army was broken and retreating they had orders to reconnoitre and find out what enemy forces stood between Kitchener and Omdurman. The three hundred men of the 21st Lancers had little idea when they mounted their horses that they were going to provide the most dramatic chapter of the day's fighting.

They were riding forward when suddenly two thousand Dervishes who had been concealed in a water course rode up from the ground like magic. The Colonel intended to wheel around to their flank but the Dervishes opened fire and he had no choice but to charge them. 'The trumpet sounded "Right wheel into line", and all the sixteen troops swung around towards the blue-black riflemen,' wrote Winston. 'Almost immediately the regiment broke into a gallop, and the 21st Lancers were committed to the charge ... In one respect a cavalry charge is very like ordinary life. So long as you are all right, firmly in your saddle, your horse in hand, and well armed, lots of enemies will give you a wide berth. But as soon as you have lost a

---

[35] *My Early Life*: Winston S. Churchill.

stirrup, have a rein cut, have dropped your weapon, are wounded, or your horse is wounded, then is the moment when from all quarters enemies rush upon you. Such was the fate of not a few of my comrades in the troop immediately on my left.'[36] The charge took only two minutes. The Lancers lost twenty dead and fifty wounded, but the enemy was in full flight.

The story caused widespread interest in England, for even in 1898 the cavalry charge was almost a thing of the past. Revolvers, rifles and artillery were giving war a new technique, and the action in which Winston took part was almost the last of its kind in British history. But the newspapers of the nineteenth century were so staid and dull the *Morning Post* did not think to exploit its good fortune in having a well-known journalist as an eye-witness. It ran Winston's account without even bothering to sign his name, and however much their 'special correspondent' wrote, printed only one short paragraph on the day's fighting in the middle of a column of closely printed type. Very few people would guess that this is what came from Mr. Churchill's pen at the end of one of the most exciting days of his life:

Camp at Omdurman.
2 Sept.

THE GENERAL ENGAGEMENT

The Dervishes attacked our Zareba at Kerreri shortly before seven in the morning.

The battle lasted five hours, the enemy charging repeatedly.

The gunboats, artillery and Maxims did deadly execution at long range.

The enemy eventually wavered and fell back. Whereupon British Brigades, with the cavalry, advanced towards Omdurman.

A great mass of the enemy, accompanied by horsemen, suddenly charged the First and Second Brigades from the right flank.

Both sides showed great gallantry.

The Dervishes were completely destroyed, though our losses were not severe.

The Lancers suffered the greatest proportion of casualties.

Omdurman was taken at sundown.

The Khalifa has not yet been captured but troops are pursuing him.

Charles Neufeld, a European who has been a prisoner with the Dervishes for many years, has been released.

---

[36] *My Early Life*: Winston Churchill.

Besides Winston, only three survivors of the cavalry charge are alive to-day. One of them, Mr. Norris, a private soldier who now lives in retirement in Dublin, wrote me a letter about the part Churchill played. In contrast to the antagonism Winston aroused among his senior officers this touching tribute is interesting for the warm regard which the ordinary man felt for him. 'Mr. Churchill,' he says, 'was in command of my troop and I must say that he was a daring and a resourceful soldier. I was only nineteen years of age then and Mr. Churchill must have been about twenty-four years of age. The morning of the battle my regiment was told to scout out and turn their flank and during this manoeuvre I saw him dismount and firing his revolver at the Dervishes. When he was spotted by my colonel whose name was Martin he was told to mount his horse and join his troop, and no sooner had he joined when the regiment wheeled into line for the charge. We had a drop of six feet or more and the ditch was about twenty feet wide. They were lying in wait for us. I saw Mr. Churchill firing away for all he was worth. The troop went into the charge twenty-five strong but only twelve of us were left, some were killed and others wounded.

'After the battle that night when I was picketing my horse, down my foot came in contact with a bundle of rags and on picking it up I found it was a Dervish baby. Just then Mr. Churchill came down the line asking if anybody knew of any man who had done a great deed. When he came to me I handed the baby to him and like a gentleman he took it to the Sudanese lines as they had their wives with them and that was the last time I saw him. I would like to see him again before I leave this world. I am going on for seventy-three years of age.'

*

Three weeks after the charge Winston was on his way back to London and he now took a momentous step. He decided the time had come to leave the Army and strike out on his own. The *Morning Post* was impressed by his enterprise and he was certain they would give him a permanent job. But first he decided to write a book on the Egyptian campaign. With characteristic zeal he proceeded at once, working half the night on the ship that was taking him home. On the voyage he struck up a friendship with a newspaper correspondent, G. W. Steevens of the *Daily Mail*. The latter was immensely struck by the young man's energy and brilliance and wrote an article about him describing him as 'the youngest man in Europe'. He went on to predict: 'There will hardly be room for him in Parliament at thirty or in England at forty'.

60

Other people were not so complimentary, particularly the military hierarchy. They called him a 'young whippersnapper', a 'medal snatcher' and a 'self-advertiser'. Although he had held a commission in the 4th Hussars for four years they pointed out that he had spent less than six months on routine duty. This was true but what they failed to appreciate was his extraordinary capacity for hard work both physical and mental. While his brother officers spent their evenings talking and drinking in the mess, he was working. Although he was not yet twenty-five he had produced three books. Winston's outlook on these matters was distinctly Victorian. His philosophy was expressed by the hero of his novel *Savrola*. "'Would you rise in the world?" said Savrola. "You must work while others amuse themselves. Are you desirous of a reputation for courage? You must risk your life. Would you be strong morally or physically? You must resist temptation. All this is paying in advance."'

Although Winston was unpopular with generals another proof of the loyalty of his subordinates comes from an old man of eighty-two who served in Mr. Churchill's regiment in India as a sergeant-major. His name is Mr. Hallaway and he now lives on splendid memories in a little house in Wimbledon. I called on him there and found a charming person with bright blue eyes and a handsome snow-white moustache. He seemed pleased to talk of the old days and showed me pictures of the young gentlemen of the 4th Hussars in their wonderful uniforms with astrakhan collars and cuffs. ('They cost £150 apiece, madam.') 'Mr. Churchill was a real live one,' he beamed. 'Not at all stuffy like some of the other officers, if you know what I mean. Easy going, and always ready for a joke. He hated to see chaps punished. The officers used to inspect the stables every day and we never knew when they were coming. But Mr. Churchill would whisper to me "Eleven-thirty, sergeant-major". But perhaps you had better not mention that,' he broke off anxiously, 'he ought not to have done it. But the great thing about him was the way he worked. He was busier than half the others put together. I never saw him without pencils sticking out all over him. And once when I went to his bungalow I could scarcely get in what with books and papers and foolscap all over the place. Oh, he was a live one. He told me he was leaving the Army to earn some money. We always had one thing in common. Both of us was always broke …'

Winston returned to India, said good-bye to his regiment, and took part in a polo tournament which he won. Then he went to Egypt and discussed and checked his manuscript. The book was called *The River*

War and was published in two volumes. It aroused a good deal of interest but did little to appease military circles for the author did not hesitate to criticize Kitchener. He condemned him hotly for ordering the desecration of the Mahdi's Tomb. He told how the Mahdi's corpse was dug up and cut to pieces and commented acidly: 'Such was the chivalry of the conquerors!'

*

In June 1899, three months after he had resigned from the Army, he was invited to fight a by-election as Conservative candidate for Oldham, a great Lancashire working-class constituency. Purely political issues were far less absorbing in those days and Winston's opening speech was on the issue of high church versus low. He began with a diatribe on the 'lawlessness and disorder in the Church of England' caused by the introduction of 'ritualistic practice'. This was an opinion he had acquired from both his nurse and his masterful aunt, Lady Wimborne, and he fought their cause with fervour. He was sure, he told his audience, that this subject was uppermost in its mind.

He also fought on the well known Tory platform of 'unity of the Empire', the 'benefits of the existing system of society' and the 'virtues of Conservative rule'. However, as the election progressed it became apparent that the opposition was gaining ground by the unpopularity of a Tithes Bill which at that moment was being passed through the House of Commons. The Bill had been introduced to help the Church of England's poor clergy, but it was arousing widespread antagonism among Nonconformists, a large number of whom lived in Lancashire. Winston's Conservative supporters did not like the Bill, and in the middle of the campaign he suddenly threw it overboard, promising not to vote for it if he were returned to Parliament.

This spectacular move caused an uproar. In the House of Commons Liberals were able to jeer at the Government with the taunt that even their Conservative candidate did not dare face the electors on the issue; and Mr. Balfour, the Leader of the House, remarked acidly: 'I thought he was a young man of promise, but it appears he is a young man of promises.'

Winston was beaten at the poll. He returned to London to find himself the subject of general abuse, for even the newspapers were running leaders saying that in the future the Conservatives must not send raw young candidates to fight working-class areas.

Sadder, wiser, but still undaunted he turned his attention back to his book.

Chapter Five — Fame

THE WHEEL of Fortune holds many surprises. Six months after his defeat at Oldham, Churchill's name was ringing throughout England. He was a national hero.

The scene of his triumph was the South African War, a war which was denounced by many Radicals as 'shameful' and became the subject of bitter debates in Parliament. The war was brought about by the demands of the Tory Imperialists of the day led by Joseph Chamberlain. Gold and diamond mines had been discovered near Johannesburg which, in the past ten years, had attracted a rush of British pioneers and business men. These newcomers were bitterly resented by the Dutch or 'Boer' farmers who had settled in South Africa a century and a half before, and who had established two independent republics, the Orange Free State and the Transvaal. The Dutch were determined not to allow the British settlers to gain political control of their affairs, while the British Government, toying with the idea of building a railway from Cairo to the Cape, became increasingly attracted by the possibility of 'uniting' the length of South Africa under British rule. This was the fundamental issue underlying the events of 1899. Chamberlain demanded that British subjects residing in the Transvaal should be granted full rights of citizenship after five years of residence. As the crisis developed, the Boer President, Mr. Kruger, finally agreed to the proposals, but his concession only drew further demands from the British, and he finally dug in his toes. He sent an ultimatum to London and a few days later war had begun.

In those days Winston was not so much concerned with the rights and wrongs of an issue as with getting himself to the front. This time he had no difficulty, for his book *The River War* had been hailed by the critics as a brilliant military history. Shortly after the Boer ultimatum was published the *Morning Post* asked him to travel to South Africa as their special correspondent. They would pay all his expenses, and a salary of £250 per month which, at that time, was an unheard-of figure.

Delighted by his stroke of good fortune he sailed in the *Dunottar Castle* on 11 October. The ship contained many distinguished passengers including General Sir Redvers Buller, the Commander-in-Chief of the British Army, and his entire Headquarters Staff. Winston would have liked to have made the acquaintance of the General, but the latter had no time for 'journalists', so Churchill was forced to content himself with lesser fry. His great fear, as the ship moved slowly through the waters, was that the show would be over before he arrived. The Army believed that a war against untrained Boer farmers could not possibly last more than three months, but in fact it dragged on nearly three years, and cost the Treasury £200,000,000.

On the voyage Winston made friends with a young man, Mr. J. B. Atkins, who was correspondent of the *Manchester Guardian*. Atkins is now an old man of over eighty, a charming and soft-spoken person whose eyes gleam with humour and pride when he talks of his trip with Churchill. He was immensely struck by the latter's dynamic personality, and it is obvious that Winston found Atkins a sympathetic character, for he at once poured out his heart to him. Many years later Atkins recorded some of their conversation in his memoirs,[37] producing the most sensitive and amusing pen portrait of Winston at this period that has ever been published. 'I had not been many hours on board before I became aware of a most unusual young man,' he wrote. 'He was slim, slightly reddish-haired, pale, lively, frequently plunging along the deck with neck out-thrust, as Browning fancied Napoleon; sometimes sitting in meditation folding and unfolding his hands, not nervously but as though he were helping himself to untie mental knots. Soon we conversed. He told me that he was Winston Churchill, that he was correspondent for the *Morning Post*, that he had already seen fighting in Cuba in 1895, with the Malakand Field Force, with Lockhart's Tirah Force, and in Egypt where he had been in the charge at Omdurman. He coveted a political career above all.

'It was obvious that he was in love with words. He would hesitate sometimes before he chose one or would change one for a better. He might, so far, have been just a young writer or speaker very conscious of himself and his art. But when the prospects of a career like that of his father, Lord Randolph, excited him, then such a gleam shot from him that he was almost transfigured. I had not before encountered this sort of ambition, unabashed, frankly egotistical, communicating its excitement, and extorting sympathy ... He stood alone and confident, and his natural power to be himself had yielded to no man. It was not that he was without the faculty of self-criticism. He could laugh at his dreams of glory, and he had an impish fun: that was what it was in those days rather than an impish wit. It was as though a light was switched on inside him which suddenly shone out through his eyes; he

---

[37] *Incidents and Reflections*: J. B. Atkins.

compressed his lips; he contracted himself slightly as though gathering himself together to spring; the whole illuminated face grinned. I never heard him bring out a jocular or mischievous remark without these symptoms of his own preliminary relish.'

Atkins and Churchill agreed to knit their fortunes together. They decided to travel to Durban, a four-day journey by rail and steamer, then to try and get through to Ladysmith where they believed the heaviest fighting would take place, and where Winston's friend General Ian Hamilton had promised to give him 'a good show'. However, when they reached the town of Estcourt they found that Ladysmith had been cut off, and that troops were being hurriedly concentrated to protect the southern part of Natal from an impending attack.

Churchill and Atkins pitched their tent in the railway yard at Estcourt and talked far into the night. Winston showed his friend articles which had been published in the *Morning Post*, and two still in manuscript, and invited his criticism. 'He was gratified,' wrote Atkins, 'by the wide interest which his work had already aroused. When I read his articles, he said, "Now what do you think of them? Is the interest due to any merit in me, or is it because I am Randolph's son?" "Do you want a candid answer?" "Naturally. Any other would be useless." "Well," said Atkins, "I notice in your articles a sweep and a range of thought, particularly in your philosophical vision of a true Imperialism, which I should not find in articles of other correspondents. But, then, would your articles have excited so much interest if I had written them? I think not."

'"A fair verdict. But how long will my father's memory help me?"

'"Curiosity is very keen for a time, but only a short time. I should think it will help you for two or three years, but after that everything will depend on you. But I honestly don't think you will have to rely on your father."

'Winston told me,' continued Atkins, 'that the *Morning Post* had been very kind to him in his political campaigning so far. It had given a good deal of praise to his speeches, and had even allowed him to visit the office to revise proofs. On one occasion the Editor was surprised at the modesty of youth when Winston struck out "Cheers" at the end of a speech, but was still more surprised when he substituted "Loud and prolonged applause". "The worst of it is," went on Winston, "that I am not a good life. My father died too young. I must try to accomplish whatever I can by the time I am forty."

'He often turned our conversation to style, grammar and construction. He admired the rhythm and resonance of Gibbon. It had been said that he had taken Gibbon for his master. Did I find anything Gibbonian in him? But, after all, style was a matter of taste; what was more important to him immediately was correctness in construction and grammar. What, for instance, was a split infinitive and why was it wrong? And what was an unrelated, or misrelated, participle, which was said to be a frequent source of ambiguity and which I had happened to mention? He considered my explanations, such as they were, and sternly rejected my caveat that as great writers often carry a load of mistakes it is pedantic and priggish to let such things count for too much in a reckoning of genius. "It is better," he pronounced, "to be correct." I agreed to his maxim so far as it affected us. Ruskin could afford to invent his own grammar, but we could not. "Very well," he concluded. "I am never going to write, 'the plan is to frontally attack the position'."'[38]

Winston had not been in Estcourt more than a few hours before he found old friends. First he ran into Leo Amery, the Harrow schoolboy whom he had pushed into the bathing pool, and who was now a war correspondent for *The Times*. That same evening as he was walking down the street he met Captain Haldane, the young officer who had been in India and helped him to secure an appointment on Sir William Lockhart's staff for the Tirah expedition. Haldane had been wounded and had been given the temporary command of a company of the Dublin Fusiliers.

The position of the small force in Estcourt was precarious. No one knew from day to day whether a few thousand Boers might not sweep into the town. Each morning cavalry reconnaissances were sent out to find out if any sudden attack was likely. Then the General in command of the town decided to aid the cavalry by sending an armoured train along the sixteen miles of railway which was still intact. The armoured train was regarded by ordinary soldiers as a huge joke. It rumbled along at a slow pace and was nothing more than an engine with a few ordinary iron railway trucks covered with steel plates through which rifle slits had been cut. Everyone except the General seemed to know that if the Boers wanted to capture the train all they had to do was to blow up a bridge or culvert, and it lay at their mercy.

---

[38] *Incidents and Reflections*: J. B. Atkins.

Captain Haldane was put in charge of the operation, and asked Winston if he would like to accompany him. The latter enthusiastically said yes, and hurried off to extend the invitation to Atkins. But Atkins declined. He thought it was a crazy idea, explaining that his instructions were to follow the war on the British side, not to rush off and let himself get taken prisoner, and miss the rest of the war. 'That is perfectly true,' said Winston, 'I can see no fault in your reasoning. But I have a feeling, a sort of intuition, that if I go something will come of it. It's illogical, I know.'

Winston's instincts were right, for the journey on the armoured train was the beginning of a journey to fame. The train travelled along the line fourteen miles to Chieveley. Then two Boer guns opened fire. A few minutes later there was a crash and an explosion as the driver ran into a shell that had been placed on the track. Several trucks were derailed, and the engine trapped. Captain Haldane asked Winston to see what damage had been done to the line while he and his Dublin Fusiliers fired the small naval gun they had in the rear truck. Winston quickly surveyed the situation and decided that it might be possible to free the engine. With bullets rattling against the steel plates and shrapnel bursting overhead he called for volunteers, and was heard to say: 'Keep cool, men.'

The engine driver was grazed on the head, and he reassured him by announcing confidently: 'No man is hit twice in the same day.'

At last the engine was free. Since it was impossible to re-attach the trucks Captain Haldane decided that the engine should carry all the wounded, who were now numerous, and that the rest of the men should march home on foot, sheltering behind the vehicle which would travel very slowly. Winston climbed into the engine cab. Shells were still bursting overhead, and the driver could not seem to keep the pace slow enough. Gradually the infantry were being left behind. Winston forced the engine driver to stop, but by this time there was a gap of three hundred yards. He jumped out and ran back to find Captain Haldane. Suddenly he saw two figures in plain clothes on the line and realized they were Boers. He ran back towards the engine, with the men firing after him. He scrambled up the bank trying to make a dash for the river, but now he was confronted by a horseman galloping furiously towards him with a rifle in his hand. The rider pulled up and took aim. Winston reached for his pistol but it was not there. He had taken it off when he was trying to free the engine. The Boer looked along the sights of his gun. There was nothing for Winston to do but surrender. His captor led him back to the other

British soldiers where he found Captain Haldane. Together they were taken to Colenso Station, and then on a three-day journey to Pretoria where they were imprisoned in the State Model Schools. Captain Haldane describes in his memoirs their feelings as they trudged across the veldt together and relates how Winston thanked him for allotting him the 'star turn' of freeing the engine. He told Haldane he was certain it would be given much prominence in the English papers; and although he would lose his job as a war correspondent the incident undoubtedly would help him to reach the House of Commons. This strange conversation in such depressing circumstances gives the reader an indication of Winston's determination to succeed in life; it also shows how accurately he gauged the situation, for his fellow journalists received glowing accounts of his action which they sent home and which made front page news — the *Daily Telegraph* printed Reuter's dispatch which said: 'Mr. Winston Churchill's bravery and coolness is described as magnificent, and encouraged by him, all worked like heroes to clear the line and enable the engine and tender to get away.'[39]

Winston was a prisoner but he was also well on the way to being a national figure.

*

Sixty British officers were imprisoned in the State Model Schools which stood in the middle of a quadrangle bounded on two sides by a corrugated iron fence about ten feet high, and on the other two by an iron grille. Winston had no intention of remaining a captive for long. First he argued with the Boer authorities that he should be released because he was a civilian press correspondent. But the Boers had no intention of letting him go, for by this time they knew who he was. 'It's not every day,' one of them said, 'that we catch the son of a lord.' Besides, they had the law on their side. He had forfeited his non-combatant status by the part he had taken in the train fight.

The moment Winston realized that their decision was final his thoughts turned to escape. He hated the feeling of being confined, and found it impossible to play cards with his fellow prisoners or enjoy any lighter moments. Meanwhile Captain Haldane was working out a plan of escape with a sergeant named Brockie who spoke Tael[40]

---

[39] 17 November, 1899.

[40] Debased Dutch which was the local idiom.

fluently. Winston asked Haldane if he could join them but the latter was apprehensive at increasing their numbers. Besides, he felt that Churchill was already attracting too much attention to himself by engaging in animated discussions as to who was to blame for the war. Added to this, he was temperamental and unaccountable. For example, if any of the younger men indulged in whistling Winston made no effort to conceal his extreme exasperation.

In his memoirs, *A Soldier's Saga*, Haldane relates how Churchill continued to urge him to include him in his plan of escape. As bait, Winston emphasized that if they were successful, he would see that Haldane's name was emblazoned triumphantly across the press. The Captain declared that this did not interest him, for he felt it was his duty to escape. What worried him was the fear that the talkative soldier-journalist might compromise their chances of success. He discussed the matter with Brockie, who shared his apprehension and was strongly opposed to Churchill's inclusion.

Nevertheless Haldane felt responsible for having invited Winston to join the armoured train, and in the end gave in. He made no secret of Brockie's views and said that under the circumstances he could not extend a cordial invitation, but that if Winston, knowing of their mixed feelings, still wanted to join them, he could do so. Churchill at once replied that he would come, but said he did not think it would be fair to blame him if they were recaptured due to his presence. Haldane agreed, but made it clear that he expected Winston to 'conform to orders'.

The plan, as outlined by Haldane, was as follows. Since it would be difficult for all three men to climb out of the latrine at the same time, Brockie was to follow as soon as it was known that Haldane and Churchill had succeeded. Haldane had noticed that Churchill did not take much exercise and stood aloof while the other prisoners played fives and rounders and tried to keep themselves fit by skipping. Besides this, he had a weak shoulder. Haldane therefore was worried for fear he might not be agile enough to reach the roof of the latrine, which was about seven feet high, without a 'leg up'. In his effort to mount the top he might kick the metal side of the structure and attract the attention of the sentry. Haldane states bluntly in his book that his major anxiety about the success of the operation arose from Winston's 'accession to the party'. With only Brockie, he continues, there was nothing to fear; but with the impulsive and loquacious Churchill, he was gravely doubtful. Nevertheless the die was cast and he had to go on with it.

The three men decided to leave on 11 December. About ten minutes before the dinner hour, at six-fifty, Churchill and Haldane strolled over to the latrine in the company of several officers. These prisoners would return one by one in the hope that the sentry might think that all had left. If the guard behaved as he usually did he might move along a line of trees to talk to another sentry, which would give the three men their chance to scale the wall. On this night, however, the sentry did not budge and after waiting fifteen or twenty minutes Churchill and Haldane whispered to each other that they must abandon their efforts and try another time.

The next day continued to be one of anxiety. Haldane was alarmed by Winston's excited condition and the fact that he was striding up and down the yard with his head lowered and his hands clasped behind his back. He feared that the other prisoners would realize that something was up. Churchill said to Haldane, 'We must go to-night.' The Captain replied that if the chances were favourable they would certainly undertake it again that evening, but he must remember that there were three of them.

Winston relates the story of his escape in *My Early Life*. The next evening, shortly after Haldane and Brockie had made another unsuccessful attempt, he strolled out and secreted himself in the lavatory. He had not been there long before the sentry turned his back and the great moment had arrived. He drew himself up, and jumped over the wall. He was in a garden and people were moving about. He hid himself in the shrubs and waited there for over half an hour, then he heard a British voice from within the camp say: 'All up.' Winston coughed and the voice continued in a low tone: 'The sentry suspects. It's all up. Can you get back?'

No sensible person could really have expected Winston meekly to climb back into captivity. He had £75 in his pocket, four slabs of chocolate and a few biscuits, and although he was without a compass he decided to have a run for his money. Haldane declares in his *Saga* that he was 'bitterly disappointed to find that Winston had gone', and adds, 'I resist the temptation of stating what Brockie said on the subject.'

Friends who heard the story from both men saw that a genuine misunderstanding had arisen. Winston believed he was acting within his rights and Haldane felt he should have waited. Neither one has dealt with the disagreement in his memoirs. Churchill ignores it and Haldane alludes enigmatically to the proverb 'There is many a slip', and declares that things did not go 'according to plan'. He then goes on to say that at this point it is best 'to draw a veil over subsequent events', although by doing so he does not want his readers to suppose that he supports many of the versions of the story which appeared in print, often under the name of distinguished writers.

Those close to Haldane assert that he never forgave Winston. And as a result of his resentment Churchill was often accused on public platforms of having left his comrades in the lurch, which he always hotly denied. George Smalley, an American journalist who knew Churchill personally, and heard statements on both sides, including a full account from Winston, wrote: 'I think his conduct open to no reproach or even criticism.'[41]

Nevertheless aspersions continued to be made, and out of this story sprang another, that Churchill had broken his parole. No parole system existed and all prisoners were under armed guard. Many years later he sued *Blackwood's Magazine* for libel, and on other occasions issued writs which drew forth apologies.

*

Winston's lucky escapes in India and Egypt had made him superstitious. He was increasingly certain that he was destined for great events. Certainly there was an astonishing element of luck in his flight from the Boers. After waiting in the garden for nearly an hour he began to walk. He found the railway line, headed along it for some time, then managed to climb on a goods train. Before dawn he jumped off and making for the hills hid in a grove of trees near a ravine. That night he walked back to the tracks with the idea of taking another train. But he saw lights in the far distance, which he thought were Kaffir fires, and some strange instinct bade him approach them. He walked for many hours and as he drew nearer he suddenly realized that he was nearing a coal mine.

He had heard that there were a number of English residents in the mining district of Witbank and Middelburg and with trepidation decided to chance his luck. He knocked on a door and a tall man with a pale face and a moustache let him in. Winston said he was a burgher but the man eyed him with suspicion. Then he decided to make a clean breast of it. When he gave his name his host's face relaxed. 'Thank God you have come here,' the man said. 'It is the only house for twenty miles where you would not have been handed over.' The man was Mr. John Howard, the British mine manager, and living in the

---

[41] *Anglo-American Memories*: George Smalley.

house with him was a plump man named Mr. Dewsnap, of Oldham of all places. Howard decided that Winston must hide in the coal pit and Dewsnap led him there, shook his hand and whispered, 'They'll all vote for you next time.'

He remained under Howard's wing for three days. By then arrangements had been made for him to board a goods train heading for Portuguese East Africa. The plan worked easily, and Winston lay in one of the wagons covered by bales of wool. Three days later the train reached Lourenço Marques, and he jumped off a free man. He made his way to the British Consulate where he was given a hot bath, new clothes and a square meal. He learned that newspapers all over Europe had been speculating on his fortunes and that the Boers had advertised his escape widely, offering £25 for his capture dead or alive. The English press took a pessimistic view of his chances. One of them remarked laconically: 'With reference to the escape from Pretoria of Mr. Winston Churchill, fears are expressed that he may be captured again before long and if so will probably be shot.'

*

The war in South Africa had been going badly. Britain was smarting under a series of military rebuffs, and the news that Winston had reached safety was just the tonic that was needed. The public went wild with joy: overnight he became a symbol of British invincibility. The same day that he had arrived in Lourenço Marques he caught a steamer back to Durban. He arrived to find the town decorated with flags, bands playing, and cheering crowds in a state of excitement.

An interesting footnote to the whole episode is the fact that Captain Haldane and Sergeant Brockie also succeeded in escaping. After Winston's absence had been discovered they were unable to pursue the original plan of scaling the wall, but worked out another scheme; they had learned that all prisoners were to be transferred from Pretoria to another camp. A week before the change took place they hid under the floor of the barracks. While the Boers were searching for them they sat tight; but when the pursuit was finally abandoned and the move took place and the camp was deserted, they struck out for safety. However, by the time they reached the freedom of Portuguese territory, the gilt was off the gingerbread and compared with Winston's reception they were hardly noticed.

Sir Redvers Buller sent for Churchill and asked was there anything he could do for him. The young man replied that he would like a commission in the Army. This was difficult to arrange since a new regulation had been introduced, largely because of Winston's activities, forbidding serving officers to work for the press. Buller got round this order by granting him a commission unpaid.

Winston at once sent a dispatch to the *Morning Post* giving the War Office and the generals some clear, practical advice. 'We must face the facts,' he wrote. 'The individual Boer, mounted in suitable country, is worth from three to five regular soldiers. The power of modern rifles is so tremendous that frontal attacks must often be repulsed. The extraordinary mobility of the enemy protects his flanks. The only way of treating the problem is either to get men equal in character and intelligence as riflemen, or failing the individual, huge masses of troops ... It would be much cheaper in the end to send more than necessary. There is plenty of work here for a quarter of a million men, and South Africa is well worth the cost in blood and money. More irregular corps are wanted. Are the gentlemen of England all fox-hunting? ...'

The gentlemen of England did not take too kindly to this sarcasm. A group of colonels and generals in one of the London clubs sent a telegram: 'Best friends here hope you will not continue making further ass of yourself.' And the *Morning Leader* wrote acidly: 'We have received no confirmation of the statement that Lord Lansdowne has, pending the arrival of Lord Roberts, appointed Mr. Winston Churchill to command the troops in South Africa, with General Sir Redvers Buller, V.C., as his Chief of Staff.'

For the next few months Winston served in the South African Light Horse which he nicknamed the Cockyollybirds because of the plumes which they wore in their slouch hats. It was a thrilling life, riding half the day and talking over a camp fire at night. He took part in the fighting at Spion Kop and in the relief of Ladysmith. His brother Jack, now a lieutenant, joined him in this adventure but was wounded on the first day and put out of action. Lady Randolph Churchill arrived in Durban on a hospital ship which had been equipped with funds raised by a committee of American ladies married to Englishmen, and the three members of the family celebrated a reunion.

By the summer the British had captured Johannesburg and Pretoria. It looked as though the war would soon come to a close. The Conservative Government decided to take advantage of the public exuberance. In September the 'khaki election' was held and Winston hurried back to Oldham to try his luck.

*

Oldham gave Winston a spectacular welcome. The town was decorated, crowds lined the streets and the band struck up: 'See the

Conquering Hero Comes.' That night he addressed a large meeting in the assembly hall, and told them for the first time the full details of Iris escape. When he mentioned the name of Mr. Dewsnap, the Oldham man who had hidden him in the coal mine, the audience shouted: 'His wife's in the gallery,' and there were tremendous cheers. A girl in the front row expressed the sentiments of his supporters by wearing a sash with the words embroidered on it: 'God Bless Churchill, England's Noblest Hero.'

He fought his election campaign in a blaze of national publicity. Many London papers sent reporters to give it full coverage. Dozens of descriptive articles appeared about him. Julian Ralph of the *Daily Mail* wrote: 'Young Churchill is a genius. The species is not so broad or so over familiar that one can carelessly classify a man as such. In this case there is no doubt.' He then went on to describe his personality. 'He finds it easier to vault out of a landau than to open the door when he is getting out to address his electors and win their unqualified admiration if he can. He will take a bath thirteen minutes before dinner-time, will not hesitate to advise or admonish the Government in a newspaper letter, and will calmly differ from a bishop on a point of ecclesiastical law. But, mark you, he is usually diplomatic and considerate in speech and tone; he is boyishly handsome, has a winning smile, and is electric in brilliance and dash. That is why people rushed after him in crowds in Oldham, to see and hear him and to wring his hand. They called him "Young Randy" and shouted God's blessing after him.'[42]

The election was fought largely on the issue of the Boer War. The radical Liberals were bitterly opposed to the conflict; they thought it was wicked and unnecessary, and had been deliberately engineered by Joseph Chamberlain as a commercial venture. Winston was bound to defend the Government and as a result the Radicals made him the target for a malicious and outrageous whispering campaign. They suggested that he had left the Army in disgrace; that he had gone to South Africa as a correspondent rather than a soldier because he was a coward; that he would have been cashiered from the Army had he not resigned; and many other cruel slanders. On 27 September the *Daily Mail* reporter wrote: 'In nothing does Winston Churchill show his youth more than in the way he allows slanders to affect him … They deeply wound him and he allows men to see it. When some

---

[42] 2 October, 1900.

indiscreet supporter brings these stories to him, his eyes flash fire, he clutches his hands angrily, and he hurries out to find opportunity of somewhere and somehow bringing his traducers to book.'

The campaign grew in violence as the climax neared. Chamberlain had uttered the slogan: 'Every seat lost to the Government is as a seat gained to the Boers', which had increased the temperature still further. He came to Oldham to speak for Winston and the two men drove together to the meeting in an open landau. The hall was jammed with supporters and the entrance and streets were crowded with booing opponents. Both men loved the 'roar of the multitude' and Chamberlain's speech was an outstanding success. Polling day came and when the count was finally announced Winston had won by two hundred and thirty votes.

In those days constituencies polled over the space of six weeks. Churchill's result was one of the first. He walked to the Conservative Club to find a telegram of congratulation from the Prime Minister, Lord Salisbury, and a few hours later invitations were pouring in from all over the country asking him to address meetings. He spoke in Manchester for Arthur Balfour, the Leader of the House, and when he walked on to the platform the whole Hall rose and cheered him. After this he seldom addressed audiences of less than five or six thousand. 'Was it wonderful that I should have thought I had arrived?' he wrote in *My Early Life*. 'But luckily life is not so easy as all that: otherwise we should get to the end too quickly.'

Winston was now a Member of Parliament, which in those days was a thrilling but expensive occupation. He took stock of his financial position. His book *The River War* had sold well; besides he had written two small books on his South African experiences which, together with his salary from the *Morning Post*, gave him a net sum of £4,000. He felt that he must increase his capital by a lecture tour before taking his seat. First, he toured England speaking every night for five weeks at a fee of £100 to £300 a lecture. He banked £4,500. Then he travelled to the United States and for two months carried out a similar programme in America and Canada. In New York his meeting opened under the auspices of Mark Twain. His manager advertised him enthusiastically as 'the hero of five wars, the author of six books, and the future Prime Minister of Great Britain'. Altogether the New World provided another £10,000.

Just twenty-six years old he returned to London eagerly and joyously to take his seat in the House of Commons.

**Part Three
Parliament**

Chapter Six — Backbencher: Conservative

THE YEAR 1901 opened with the death of Queen Victoria after a reign of nearly sixty-four years. Five kings and forty members of the royal families of Europe followed her funeral cortège on its long and solemn procession through the streets of London. A month later King Edward VII opened his first session of his first Parliament: and in this Parliament Winston Churchill made his début.

Churchill sat in the House of Commons as a 'back-bencher' for five years. Those five years now appear in history as a bridge between the peace and power of the Victorian age and the violence of the new century, trailing in its wake global wars, turbulent reforms, and the steady decline of British world supremacy.

However, few Members of the Parliament of 1901 were aware that an era had ended. During Queen Victoria's lifetime Britain had risen from a largely agricultural country to the greatest industrial nation and the greatest empire in the world. At home she trod the path of slow, steady reform with the comfortable knowledge of a well-ordered and secure existence. A strong, unrivalled Navy not only protected her home shores but her far-flung trade routes, enabling her to remain aloof from all continental quarrels and to use her wealth for the benefit of mankind. She had not taken part in a conflict in western Europe since the defeat of Napoleon eighty-six years before. Her policy was Splendid Isolation.

Many of the Parliamentarians of 1901 saw no reason to doubt the Victorian creed. At home this faith was based on the firm conviction that Britain's astonishing success was due to the rule of an educated and enlightened oligarchy. At the same time Britain was a democracy; indeed, the harnessing together of these two political conceptions might be described as the most ingenious achievement of the Victorian age. Foreigners were openly puzzled by the strange paradox of a democracy governed by an oligarchy, and it is only fair to add that even the English were surprised that it worked. When it became apparent in the last forty years of Victoria's reign that the democratic idea was gathering strength, and that pressure was increasing for an extension of the franchise, the English upper classes became alarmed. The great constitutional writer, Walter Bagehot, stated firmly: 'Sensible men of substantial means are what we wish to be ruled by …' He went on to warn 'that a political combination of the lower classes … is an evil of the first magnitude; that their supremacy in the state they now are, means the supremacy of ignorance over instruction and of numbers over knowledge. So long as they are not taught to act together there is a chance of this being averted, and it can only be averted by the greater wisdom and foresight in the higher classes.'[43]

Under Disraeli and Gladstone the vote was widely extended. Those who voiced apprehension forgot that the British public had been taught to respect its betters; and when the newly-enfranchised, class-conscious mass went to the polls in 1885, and again in 1886, it elected a Conservative Government known to regard innovations of almost every kind with an unfriendly eye. The 'higher classes' drew a breath of relief and settled down to a long period of quiet consolidation. In 1901 a Conservative Government led by the same Conservative Prime Minister, Lord Salisbury, was still in power.

*

The House of Commons that Winston Churchill entered was an exclusive and wealthy body. Members of Parliament received no payment for their services and were expected to contribute substantial sums of money to their constituencies as well. Thus only men of means, or men with outside backing, could hope to be adopted as candidates.

Liberals and Conservatives were cut from the same expensive cloth. Conservatives could claim more supporters among the landowning gentry, whose younger sons found occupations 'fit for gentlemen' in the Army, Navy and diplomatic services, and who were now stretching a point by infiltrating into the financial precincts of the City. The Liberals could claim more supporters among the enterprising, self-made industrialists upon whom Britain's prosperity depended. Nevertheless, each party had a smattering of both.

Temperamentally, however, there was a clear division between the two factions. The Conservatives believed themselves to be the rightful guardians of Church and State, of continuity and tradition. They disliked change and usually made concessions only when it was impossible to withhold them. The Liberals, on the other hand, regarded themselves as the champions of individual liberty. They welcomed change so long as it promised to enlarge the opportunities for personal freedom. And because they were open to new ideas, they attracted a wing of Radicals who were determined to break down the

---

[43] *The English Constitution*: Walter Bagehot.

privileged oligarchic rule at Westminster, to reform the House of Lords, and establish the principle of *la carrière ouverte aux talents*.

However, these Radicals were not Leftists in the sense conveyed by that word to-day. All Liberal supporters were passionate believers in a *laissez-faire* economic system, and went even further than the Conservatives in their opposition to State interference. Both parties agreed that the Government's operational sphere should be extremely limited. The Government was expected to produce law and order at home, to protect British nationals abroad, and to conduct the country's foreign affairs to skilful advantage. It was also expected to leave the country's industrial life severely alone. Business matters were for business men and not for politicians.

In 1902 Charles Booth, a wealthy ship-owner, published a laborious statistical work entitled *The Life and Labour of London* which had taken him sixteen years to complete. Although London was regarded as 'the richest city in the world' he revealed that thirty per cent of the population were suffering from under-nourishment. But despite this astonishing revelation, poverty and unemployment continued to be regarded as subjects for private charity, and not for Government action. The Victorians accepted Malthus' theory that the population would always outstrip the means of sustenance, and therefore looked upon the poor as a permanent and unavoidable fixture brought about by God's Will rather than man's ineptitude. On Sundays church congregations solemnly sang:

The rich man in his castle
The poor man at his gate
God made them high and lowly
And order'd their estate.

And yet beneath the calm Victorian surface the threads of the pattern for the new century, which Elie Halévy, the eminent French historian, describes as 'hastening towards social democracy and towards war', were already visible. In 1892 Keir Hardie, a Scottish coalminer, entered the House of Commons as an Independent backed by Trade Union funds. He was the first working man to sit as a Member. In 1900 he formed a new party, the Labour Representative Committee, which was soon destined to grow into the Labour Party; and in the election of the same year Hardie and another working man were returned as Members. Their voices were small but the fact that they were raised at all was an indication of what the future held. Besides this, Trade Unionism was growing; and the Fabian Society dominated by Beatrice and Sidney Webb, Graham Wallas and George Bernard Shaw, supported spasmodically by H. G. Wells, was not only educating the public to the meaning of democratic socialism but infusing the Radical politicians of the day with ideas which were to lead Britain forward for the next half century.

Abroad it was not without significance that the friendship between Britain and France kindled by Edward VII's visit to Paris in 1903 was slowly ripening and would soon result in the *entente* of 1904; and it was also significant that the German Kaiser, with a fierce eagle on his shining, spiked helmet, was growing increasingly proud of his efficient, goose-stepping army, and that he was toying with the idea of producing a strong navy as well. These were the threads; but in 1901 only a few Members of Parliament attached much importance to them.

*

One might have expected Winston Churchill to be among the few. During the years he spent as a back-bencher he provided the House of Commons with incident, drama and excitement. He sparkled and shone in his new surroundings. His language was colourful, his personality compelling, and his polished, memorized orations seldom failed to hold the attention of the House. He was master of the unexpected phrase and the unexpected action.

Yet what was surprising about this high-spirited, independent young man, who revelled in unusual tactics, was the fact that his ideas were of a most orthodox and conventional kind. Far from anticipating the new forces of the new century his energies were bent on turning the clock back to the generation before, when Victorian conceptions were in the full bloom of maturity. He preached all the fading doctrines of a fading age: he stood for Isolationism from Europe and for a small Army; for Imperialism; strict economy; Free Trade; no further increases in the income tax. These were the ideas of the past, and as the new century progressed every one of them was to perish.

What curious and paradoxical qualities prompted Churchill to proffer unoriginal ideas with striking originality? Someone once remarked that the politician brings to politics what he is. At twenty-six Churchill was a master of English prose and a trained observer of military events. He knew nothing of finance or economics and possessed only a superficial grasp of history and philosophy which he had acquired by a smattering of reading on the hot Indian afternoons when his fellow subalterns were sleeping. He had not had the benefit of a university education where ideas are constantly explored and challenged; and although his five years in the Army had brought him into contact with many men of outstanding character he had mixed with few men of outstanding intellect.

Churchill's mind was neither philosophic nor profound. He was a man of action rather than thought. He did not feel compelled to examine accepted principles and value them for himself. By nature he was romantic and sentimental. He liked to picture events in simple, bold and vivid colours; and he preferred to follow his emotions rather than his logic. Indeed when he found the path of logic leading him away from the course to which his instincts inclined he often abandoned the logic. For instance, when he was in India he grappled with the subject of religion. He found that although he wished to believe in a Higher Being his mind refused to accept much of the dogma. This might have worried some men but Churchill found an easy, almost feminine solution. 'I adopted quite early in life,' he wrote, 'a system of believing what I wanted to believe, while at the same time leaving reason to pursue unfettered whatever paths she was capable of treading.'[44]

Churchill entered the House of Commons because he believed it would provide him with an exciting occupation. At twenty-six he was less concerned with the political contribution he had to offer than with the political prizes that might await him. He was bursting with energy and ambition. The only thing he lacked was a political theme, but this was easily remedied. He turned to his father's writings for guidance. 'The greatest and most powerful influence in my early life,' he explained many years later, 'was, of course, my father. Although I talked to him so seldom and never for a moment on equal terms I conceived an intense admiration and affection for him; and after his early death, for his memory. I read industriously almost every word he had ever spoken and learnt by heart large portions of his speeches. I took my politics unquestioningly from him. He seemed to me to have possessed the key alike to popular oratory and political action.'[45]

The reader may find it strange that a father who had concerned himself so little with his son should have exercised such a hold over the latter's imagination long after his death. Here the conservatism bred into Winston, with its emphasis on continuity and tradition, asserted itself. Just as he drew strength from the fact that the great

---

[44] *My Early Life*: Winston S. Churchill.

[45] *Thoughts and Adventures*: Winston S. Churchill.

Duke of Marlborough's blood ran in his veins, he likewise enjoyed picturing himself as a projection of his father whose exciting career appealed to his adventurous instincts. He remembered as a child seeing people take off their hats in the street as Lord Randolph passed; he remembered the buzz of excitement and the talk of great orations; the endless columns in the newspapers, the photographs, the cartoons, the thrill of importance his father's presence cast over the household. It is only natural he should have turned to his father's speeches for inspiration. And when he read them he was fascinated by their vivid imagery, their sarcasm and rich irony.

He resolved to write his father's biography. It was possible to combine the task with his political duties, for in 1901 Parliamentary business was so regulated that the House only sat six months of the year. His literary labours were not only an act of filial devotion but a means of earning his living and they occupied him the whole five years he spent as a backbencher. They had a profound effect upon his political career. As he became immersed in his writing he fell more and more deeply under the spell of Lord Randolph's example. This influence was further strengthened by research which threw him into contact with many of his father's old colleagues; and one of these, Sir Francis Mowatt, the head of the Civil Service, exerted a decisive influence upon him.

Sir Francis had served in the Treasury during Lord Randolph's brief tenure as Chancellor of the Exchequer. He held Winston enthralled by stories of his father and won the young man's confidence by his genuine and wholehearted admiration. 'He was one of the friends I inherited from my father,' wrote Churchill. 'Tall, spare with a noble brow, bright eyes and strong jaws, this faithful servant of the Crown, self-effacing but self-respecting, resolute, convinced, sure of himself, sure of his theme, dwelt modestly and frugally for nearly fifty years at or near the centre of the British governing machine ... He represented the complete triumphant Victorian view of economics and finance; strict parsimony; exact accounting; free imports whatever the rest of the world might do; suave steady government; no wars; no flag-waving; just paying of debts and reducing taxation and keeping out of scrapes; and for the rest ... for trade, industry, agriculture, social life ... *laissez-faire* and *laissez-aller*. Let the Government reduce itself and its demands upon the public to a minimum; let the nation live of its own; let social and industrial organization take whatever course it pleased, subject to the law of the land and the Ten Commandments. Let the money fructify in the pockets of the people.'[46]

Winston was looking for a political theme. Mowatt's views on finance seemed to be a faithful reflection of Lord Randolph's views on finance. For the next five years Winston adopted them as his own.

*

Winston Churchill entered Parliament as a celebrity. Although many of the politicians did not know him by sight they all knew him by name. His escape from the Boers, only the year before, was still fresh in the public mind. Members had followed his adventures in the newspapers, read his books, and heard of the huge sum he had been paid for his American tour. But what whetted their curiosity most of all was the fact that he was Lord Randolph's son.

In the six years since Lord Randolph's death the setting and the actors on the Parliamentary stage had changed surprisingly little. Many of the present Members had served as Lord Randolph's colleagues and some of them had heard him at the summit of his powers. The drama was further heightened by the fact that the Conservative Party was more tightly than ever in the grip of the Cecil family. Lord Salisbury, who had broken Lord Randolph's career, was still Prime Minister. His nephew, Arthur Balfour, was Leader of the House of Commons. Another nephew, Lord Balfour of Burleigh, and a cousin, Mr. Gerald Balfour, were in the Cabinet. His son, Lord Cranborne, was Under-Secretary of State for Foreign Affairs. Two more sons, Lord Hugh Cecil and Lord Robert Cecil, were back benchers, and a relative, Lord Selborne, was a member of the Government. It was not surprising that wits often referred to the House as 'The Hotel Cecil'.

It is perhaps opportune to say something about Arthur Balfour here. Before the year had ended he succeeded his uncle as Prime Minister and before three years were out Churchill had crossed swords with him as decisively as his father had with Salisbury. But in 1901, Balfour welcomed Winston into the House with almost paternal warmth. He had once been a member of Lord Randolph's 'Fourth Party' and had met his son when he was a boy of eighteen. Balfour was an enigmatic character. He was a country gentleman and an intellectual, charming, courteous, unemotional and unhurried. He gave the impression, so attractive to English people, of having no

---

[46] *Thoughts and Adventures*: Winston S. Churchill.

political ambitions but of merely seeking to do his duty. He presided over the House with almost astonishing detachment. The newspaper columnists dubbed him 'Prince Arthur' and the cartoonists depicted him with an air of elegant indolence. And yet Balfour was a master of debate and often shrewd and witty. Once, when Churchill told him that he kept a book of press cuttings because every now and then he came across something of special interest, Balfour replied disdainfully that he did not see the point of rummaging through a rubbish heap on the problematical chance of finding a cigar butt.

While the Cecils, fortified by that formidable character, the ex-Radical, ex-mayor of Birmingham, Joseph Chamberlain, dominated the Conservative scene, the Liberal benches sparkled with names that were to go into the history books. There was Asquith, stiff, brilliant and self-confident; there was the erudite pacifist, John Morley, who had written a scholarly life of Gladstone; Haldane who was to lay the foundations for the modern British Army; Sir Edward Grey who was to declare in 1914 'The lights are going out all over Europe'; and Lloyd George, the brilliant, silver-tongued Welsh Radical who was to revolutionize British social thought and lead the country through a war as well.

*

These were some of the men who awaited Winston Churchill's debut with interest and expectancy. He made his maiden speech on 18 February, three days after the opening of the Parliamentary session. The stage was well set. The great issue was the Boer War, and passions ran high. In the King's Speech His Majesty said: 'The war in South Africa has not yet entirely terminated; but the capitals of the enemy and his principal lines of communication are in my possession, and measures have been taken which will, I trust, enable my troops to deal effectually with the forces by which they are still opposed. I greatly regret the loss of life and the expenditure of treasure due to the fruitless guerrilla warfare maintained by the Boer partisans ...'[47]

This was stating the case both mildly and optimistically. The Boer War was proving a bugbear. When it began the Government thought it would last only a few weeks. Yet it had dragged on for a year and was destined to continue for still another. Worse than that, it was making Britain a laughing stock to the rest of the world. The Boers only had fifty thousand fighting men, many of whom were untrained

---

[47] *Hansard*: 14 February, 1901.

farmers armed with shotguns. Yet the British Army now almost two hundred and fifty thousand men strong still failed to subdue them. The reason was that the Boers, familiar with every inch of the terrain, had turned themselves into guerrilla bands and spread out across the country. The British soldiers were not experienced in this kind of warfare. In desperate attempts to rout out the hidden enemy, orders were given that whenever treachery was suspected Boer farms should be burnt to the ground.

This action aroused a storm of protest from the radical element in the House of Commons. To begin with, the Liberal Party was split in half over the dubious justness of the war itself. The Conservatives, supported by the Liberal Imperialists, believed in its righteousness, but the radical and pacifist Liberals bitterly denounced it. John Morley described it as 'a hateful war, and a war innate and infatuated, a war of uncompensated mischief and irreparable wrong'. The Conservatives dubbed members of the anti-war party 'Little Englanders' and decried them as 'traitors to their country'. The latter struck back hotly accusing the Government not only of evil motives but of shocking mismanagement. In this atmosphere of passion and recrimination, Winston Churchill made his maiden speech.

He spoke after dinner to a crowded House. One can picture the scene of 1901; the hansom cabs and carriages clattering across the pavement of New Palace Yard and pulling up in front of the entrance to Westminster Hall; the lobbies lit by flickering gas jets; the Strangers' Dining Room filled with men and women in evening dress; the Chamber itself with Members elegantly attired in striped trousers and frock coats, some of them half reclining on the benches with their silk hats tipped over their foreheads; the wives and daughters, in voluminous, rustling skirts, taking their seats in the gallery and gazing earnestly at the crowded floor.

Lloyd George preceded Winston. He was one of the young Radicals who opposed the war hotly. 'One satisfactory feature in connection with the debate on South Africa,' he began sarcastically, 'is that no one seems to have a good word to say for the Government. Whether they approve of or condemn the war they are all agreed on that point; that the Government have made every possible blunder they could make from any and every point of view ... Though they have the resources of the wealthiest Empire which the world has ever seen to draw upon they have so directed their operations that their own soldiers have been half-starved, stricken by disease and have died by the thousands from sheer lack of the simplest appliances. Who could say a good word for a Government responsible for such a terrible state of affairs?'

Lloyd George then went on to a blistering attack on the Conservatives for not stating specific terms of peace. 'Does anyone think the Boers will lay down their arms merely to be governed from Downing Street?' Then on to farm burning. 'It is not a war against men but against women and children … I appeal to honourable Members opposite.' Then on to the military situation. 'Not a third of the men we sent to South Africa are now in the line of battle. There have been fifty-five thousand casualties; thirty thousand men are in hospital.'[48]

When Lloyd George sat down, dozens of Members rose to their feet in the hope of being called, including the honourable and gallant Member for Oldham. 'Mr. Churchill,' said the Speaker; and thus began the most remarkable parliamentary career of the century. According to the columnist in *Punch* Winston was 'fortunate in the circumstances attending his début,' for Lloyd George's denunciations had aroused the 'frantic cheers of Irish sympathizers' and had drawn in 'loungers from the lobby, students from the library, philosophers from the smoking-room. A constant stream of diners-out flowed in. When young Winston rose from the corner seat of the bench behind Ministers … he faced, and was surrounded by an audience that filled the Chamber. No friendly cheer greeted his rising. To three-quarters of the audience he was personally unknown. Before he concluded his third sentence he fixed attention, growing keener and kinder when, in reply to a whispered question, answer went around that this was Randolph Churchill's son.'[49]

Winston was nervous. He stammered over his opening remark but he had learned his speech by heart and soon regained his composure. He referred to Lloyd George's oration. 'I do not believe that Boers will attach much importance to the utterances of the honourable Member. No people in the world receive so much verbal sympathy and so little political support as the Boers. If I were a Boer fighting in the field … and if I were a Boer I hope I should be fighting in the field …' Here there was a stir on the Conservative front bench as Joseph Chamberlain, the leading Imperialist and Secretary of State for the

---

[48] *Hansard*: 18 February, 1901.

[49] *Punch*: 27 February, 1901.

Colonies, whispered to a colleague, 'That's the way to lose seats!' But Churchill continued unruffled: 'If I were a Boer fighting in the field I should not allow myself to be taken in by any message of sympathy not even if it were signed by a hundred honourable Members. The honourable Member dwelt at great length upon the question of farm burning. I do not propose to discuss the ethics of farm burning now; but honourable Members should, I think, cast their eyes back to the fact that no considerations of humanity prevented the German Army from throwing its shells into the dwelling houses of Paris and starving the inhabitants of that great city to the extent that they had to live upon rats and like atrocious foods in order to compel the garrison to surrender. I venture to think His Majesty's Government would not have been justified in restricting their commanders in the field from any methods of warfare which are justified by precedent set by European or American generals during the last fifty or sixty years. I do not agree very fully with the charges of treachery on the one side and barbarity on the other. From what I saw of the war … and I sometimes saw something of it … I believe that as compared with other wars, especially those in which a civilian population took part, this war in South Africa has been on the whole carried on with unusual humanity and generosity.'

Churchill then went on to make the point that it was impossible to give the Boers self-government as soon as the war ended as a large number of the population had fled. 'What could be more dangerous, ridiculous or futile than to throw the responsible government of a ruined country on that … particular section of the population which is actively hostile to the fundamental institutions of the State?'

The question, he continued, was what sort of interim Government should be set up: military or civil?

'A military government is irksome. I have often myself been very much ashamed to see respectable old Boer farmers … the Boer is a curious combination of the squire and the peasant, and under the rough coat of the peasant there are very often to be found the instincts of the squire … I have been ashamed to see such men ordered about peremptorily by young subaltern officers as though they were private soldiers.'

Churchill suggested that some wise administrator such as Sir Alfred Milner should be set at the head of a civil administration, and ended his speech by stating that the Government should make 'it easy for the Boers to surrender and painful and perilous for them to continue.' Many more troops should be sent to South Africa and the military effort should be redoubled. 'At the same time I earnestly hope that the right honourable Gentleman, the Colonial Secretary, will leave nothing undone to bring home to these brave and unhappy men who are fighting in the field that whenever they are prepared to recognize that their small independence must be merged in the larger liberties of the British Empire there will be a full guarantee for the security of their property and religion, an assurance of equal right, a promise of all representative institutions, and last of all, but not least of all, what the British Army would most readily accord to a brave and enduring foe … all the honours of war.'

Before Churchill sat down he thanked the House for the kindness and patience with which it had heard him. 'It has been extended to me, I know, not on my own account, but because of a splendid memory which many honourable Members still preserve.'[50]

*

Churchill's speech was a triumph. He had steered a delicate course between the two extreme factions in the House. He had supported the Government in its prosecution of the war which pleased the Conservatives; and he had extolled the virtue of the enemy which pleased the pro-Boers. As a result he was praised by both sides of the House. *Punch* commented that the 'high expectations' of his debut were fully justified and that he had his father's 'command of pointed phrase'. 'Instantly commanding attention of the House, he maintained it to end of discourse wisely brief.'[51] Other observers were particularly impressed by the 'parliamentary manner' he had acquired in the brief three days since he had taken his seat. 'Ten minutes after Winston had been sworn,' wrote the *Daily Mail*, 'he was leaning back comfortably on the bench, his silk hat well down over his forehead, his figure crouched up in the doubled-up attitude assumed by Mr. Balfour and other Ministers, both hands deep in his pockets, eyeing the place and its inmates critically as if they were all parliamentary novices.'[52]

When Churchill had finished his speech he went into the smoking-room where he was introduced to Lloyd George. 'Judging from your sentiments,' said the Welsh Radical, 'you are standing against the

---

[50] *Hansard*: 18 February, 1901.

[51] 27 February, 1901.

[52] 7 June, 1901.

Light.' To which Winston retorted: 'You take a singularly detached view of the British Empire.' Thus began a friendship which was to dominate the political life of the next two decades.

*

Although Winston's maiden speech had made a lively impression, Members awaited the development of his career with curiosity and even reservation. Would arrogance and ambition lead him to repeat his father's mistakes? Or was his temperament calmer and his judgment surer? By what means would he attempt to advance his career?

The path of the ambitious young back-bencher, particularly if his own Government is in power, is fraught with peril. He is expected to obey the Party Whips and loyally advance the cause of his own leaders; but if he is young, eager and critical his patience may not be equal to the restraint demanded of him. He is perpetually in a dilemma. If he is silent or merely acquiescent he probably will not be noticed, but, equally, if he is aggressive and rebellious he probably will not be promoted. Back-benchers who flaunt the authority of their leaders unwisely are not easily forgiven.

This is understandable considering that a Prime Minister and his Cabinet only retain their positions so long as they command a majority in the House itself. Party loyalty is the very linchpin of the British parliamentary system. And as a result it is regarded as a cardinal virtue. This of course adds to the problems of the back-bencher who soon finds himself trying to strike as delicate a balance as a tight-rope walker between loyalty to his Party and loyalty to his own opinions. If he disagrees with his leaders he can use all his influence behind the scenes to make them change their course; but if he fails he must search his conscience and decide whether the issue is important enough to endanger the life of his Government or whether he can honourably compromise in view of the larger principles at stake. If he clashes violently with his own side he can cross the floor of the House and join the Opposition, or he can continue within the ranks of his own Party (unless he is expelled) as a 'rebel'.

There are always rebels in Parliament and they add to the liveliness of the debates. But the rebels are rarely serious politicians. They are regarded as unreliable eccentrics and soon resign themselves to the back-benches. Therefore when a determined, ambitious young politician becomes an acknowledged rebel he faces an anxious future. He can only force his way to the top by gathering such a powerful following in Parliament and the country that the Government dares not ignore him and offers him a Ministerial appointment to enlist his support rather than face his opposition. To achieve success by this method the back-bencher must possess dazzling gifts. He must be a man of outstanding personality, a brilliant debater who can command and hold the attention of the House whenever he chooses. Very few back-benchers have the qualities to enable them to reach the heights by this path. Lord Randolph Churchill was one of the few but even he failed to hold his power for long; one false step and the Prime Minister, Lord Salisbury, seized the initiative and smashed his career.

It was only natural that Members watched Lord Randolph's son with curiosity and speculated about his future. Some believed that he possessed his father's temperament and would be incapable of remaining in the Party harness; others insisted that he had profited by his father's mistakes and would move with caution. In support of this assertion they pointed out that only fourteen months previously Winston had dedicated his book, *The River War*, to Lord Salisbury 'under whose wise direction the Conservative Party has long enjoyed power and the nation prosperity'. They also noticed that when Winston took his place in the House he did not sit, as his father had, on the bench below the gangway, the traditional place for those with independent views, but squarely behind the Ministerial front bench.

Winston did not keep the honourable Members in suspense for long. Only four months after he made his maiden speech he delivered a slashing attack on the Government for the size of its peace-time military expenditure. This was the virgin step along a path which was to lead him through angry, stormy scenes with his Conservative colleagues and finally across the floor to the Liberal Opposition.

*

It is interesting to reflect that Winston Churchill, destined to become one of Britain's greatest war leaders, took the first decisive political stand of his career as an Isolationist. His attack on the Government was unexpected, emotional and histrionic. It was an astonishing effort to vindicate his father's political failure. Lord Randolph had resigned as Chancellor of the Exchequer because the War Office refused to cut its expenditure. Lord Randolph was an Isolationist in a peaceful age, believing that Britain's security depended less on her fighting services than on a wise foreign policy designed to keep her aloof from continental wars.

Now the son had come down to the House to preach the same doctrine. But the setting was different. Members of the Government of 1901 were aware that a young, powerful and aggressive Germany was watching the British setback in South Africa with marked interest. They stirred uneasily and decided that something must be done, and the result was a new and higher military budget. They listened to Winston's attack on their efforts with surprise and irritation. What was the fellow up to anyway?

His ideas on Isolation and 'strict economy' were inherited, of course, from his father. Lord Randolph had resigned from the Government when his son was twelve. On innumerable occasions the boy must have heard his mother and his aunts going over the ground and threshing out the subject in an effort to justify Lord Randolph's resignation. In *The Malakand Field Force*, published in 1897, Winston had begun his argument that the British Army must not be constructed with the idea of fighting on the continent. His speech in Parliament was a continuation of the same theme. 'I was so untutored as to suppose that all I had to do was to think out what was right and express it fearlessly,' he explained many years later. 'I thought that loyalty in this outweighed all other loyalties. I did not understand the importance of party discipline and unity, and the sacrifices of opinion which may lawfully be made in their cause.'[53]

Churchill's political naïveté was undoubtedly genuine, but in view of the fact that he continued to pursue an independent course many years after his innocence had been shed, it is fair to assume that other elements entered into the picture as well. He was impatient for success and eager to create a stir. His father's struggles loomed large in his thoughts and the resignation issue appealed to his pugnacious instincts. Besides, the same Mr. Brodrick who had been Under-Secretary at the War Office at the time of his father's quarrel was now the Minister for War. It was too good an opportunity to miss. And last, but not least, Sir Francis Mowatt was standing by with help and encouragement. 'Presently I began to criticize Mr. Brodrick's Army expansion and to plead the cause of economy in Parliament,' wrote Winston. 'Old Mowatt ... said a word to me now and then and put me in touch with some younger officials, afterwards themselves eminent, with whom it was very helpful to talk ... not secrets, for those were never divulged, but published facts set in their true proportion and with their proper emphasis.'[54]

---

[53] *My Early Life*: Winston S. Churchill.

[54] *Thoughts and Adventures*: Winston S. Churchill.

Winston delivered his speech on 13 May. Once again the House was crowded to hear him. The cartoonists of the day evidently saw in his appearance no sign of the John Bull he was to become for they depict him as a small, slim, rather elegant figure with a puckish smile. Some saw a likeness to his father, others not. *Punch* declared that 'nothing either in voice or manner' recalled Lord Randolph, while the *Daily Mail* asserted: 'There is a startling resemblance between the son of the late Lord Randolph Churchill and that brilliant statesman. He has the square forehead and the full bold eye of his father; his hurried stride through the lobby is another point of resemblance; and when something amuses him in the course of a debate he has his parent's trick of throwing his head well back and laughing loudly and heartily.'

What most observers agreed upon was the extreme boyishness of his appearance, which seemed to be exaggerated by the red hair and pink and white complexion, and accentuated by the dignified frock coat and wing collar. 'Sitting in the corner seat from which his father delivered his last speech in the House of Commons, he follows every important speech delivered from the Opposition with an alertness, a mental agility, which develops itself in various ways,' the *Daily Mail* correspondent went on to add. 'Occasionally a sort of mischievous, schoolboy grin settles over his chubby face as he listens to some ridiculous argument; now and then he becomes thoughtful and scribbles down a rebutting fact or a fresh argument and passes the note to a Minister below who is going to speak next; at other times Mr. Gibson Bowles, sitting by his side, whispers some caustic and amusing comment into his ear, and the long strong fingers, which clutch each other so frequently in nervous excitement, are held over the lower part of his face so as to conceal the smile or laugh.'[55]

When Churchill began to speak, however, youth vanished, for his words and manner were those of the elder statesman. He used the polished, rolling language of the Victorians. Only two years before, G. W. Steevens had commented: 'At dinner he talks and talks, and you can hardly tell when he leaves off quoting his one idol Macaulay, and begins his other, Winston Churchill.'

The speech of 13 May is not only historic because it marked a decisive step in his career but is a remarkable example of his early mastery of a style he was soon to make his own. 'If I might be allowed to revive a half-forgotten episode,' he began quietly, '… it is half

---

[55] 7 June, 1901.

forgotten because it has passed into that period of twilight which intervenes between the bright glare of newspaper controversy and the calm rays of the lamp of history … I would recall that once upon a time a Conservative and Unionist Administration came into power supported by a large majority, nearly as powerful and much more cohesive, than that which now supports His Majesty's Government. And when the time came around to consider the Estimates the usual struggle took place between the great spending departments and the Treasury. I say "usual"; at least it used to be so, I do not know whether it is now. The Government of the day threw their weight on the side of the great spending departments and the Chancellor of the Exchequer resigned. The controversy was bitter, the struggle uncertain, but in the end the Government triumphed, and the Chancellor of the Exchequer went down forever, and with him, as it now seems, there fell also the cause of retrenchment and economy, so that the very memory thereof seems to have perished, and the words themselves have a curiously old-fashioned ring about them. I suppose that was a lesson which Chancellors of the Exchequer were not likely to forget in a hurry.'

Winston then picked up a slip of paper and read a few lines from Lord Randolph's letter of resignation to Lord Salisbury. Lord Randolph pointed out that a very sharp sword often offered an irresistible temptation to demonstrate its efficiency in a practical manner. Winston put the slip of paper down and continued to quote the rest of the letter from memory. 'Wise words,' he cried, 'stand the test of time. And I am very glad that the House has allowed me, after an interval of fifteen years, to lift the tattered flag of retrenchment and economy. But what was the amount of the annual Estimates on which the desperate battle was fought? It may be difficult for the House to realize it, though it is within the memory of so many honourable members. "The estimates for the year," said the Chancellor of the Exchequer in resigning, "for the two services amount to no less than £31,000,000 and I cannot consent to that." What are the estimates we are asked to vote now? We are asked to vote, quite irrespective of the drainage of a costly war still in progress, something more than £59,000,000 for the ordinary service of the year …

'What has happened in the meantime to explain this astonishing increase? Has the wealth of the country doubled? Has the population of the Empire doubled? Have the armies of Europe doubled? Is the commercial competition of foreign nations so much reduced? Are we become the undisputed masters in the markets of the world? Is there no poverty at home? Has the English Channel dried up and are we no longer an island? Is the revenue so easily raised that we do not know how to spend it? Are the Treasury buildings pulled down, and all our financiers fled? During the few weeks I have been a member of this House I have heard honourable Members opposite advocate many causes but no voice is raised in the cause of economy ... I think it is about time a voice was heard from this side of the House pleading that unpopular cause; that someone not on the bench opposite, but a Conservative by tradition, whose fortunes are linked indissolubly to the Tory Party, who knows something of the majesty and power of Britain beyond the seas, upon whom rests no taint of cosmopolitanism, should stand forward and say what he can to protest against the policy of daily increasing the public burden. If such a one is to stand forward in such a cause, then, I say humbly, but I hope with becoming pride, no one has a better right than I have, for this is a cause for which the late Lord Randolph Churchill made the greatest sacrifice of any Minister in modern times.'

Churchill wound up his speech with an appeal to the House to place their trust in a strong Navy, adequate for defensive purposes, and to keep clear of continental wars. 'Now, when mighty populations are impelled against each other, each individual severely embittered and inflamed, when the resources of science and civilization sweep away everything that might mitigate their fury, a European war can only end in the ruin of the vanquished and the scarcely less fatal commercial dislocation and exhaustion of the conquerors ... The Secretary of War knows ... that if we went to war with any great Power his three Army corps would scarcely serve as a vanguard. If we are hated they will not make us loved, if we are in danger they will not make us safe. They are enough to irritate; they are not enough to overawe. Yet while they cannot make us invulnerable, they may very likely make us venturesome ... We shall make a fatal bargain if we allow the moral force which this country has so long exerted to become diminished, or perhaps even destroyed for the sake of this costly, trumpery, dangerous military plaything on which the Secretary of State has set his heart.'

Mr. Churchill's friend and fellow war correspondent, J. B. Atkins, sat in the Press Gallery and listened to him make this speech. 'He was a lonely but self-possessed figure as he stood there reproducing the sentiments which caused the dramatic resignation of his father,' he wrote in the *Manchester Guardian*. 'His metaphors were bold and a trifle too ornate here and there, but they were always original and striking. His voice is not really a defect, for it is a distinguishing possession that makes him unlike anyone else to listen to.' *Punch* also commented joyfully on the occasion. 'With the modesty of youth he undertook to challenge the scheme of Army reorganization put forward from the War Office … speech evidently carefully prepared, but wasn't embarrassed by his notes; turned aside from them now and then to make capital debating point out of speeches delivered earlier in evening … Sark[56] complains that his utterance is too rapid, and hopes he won't make fatal mistake of speaking too often. But he'll learn and he'll do …'[57]

*

Once again, Churchill's speech was a minor sensation. The Liberal pacifists were delighted with his sentiments and the Liberal Imperialists were delighted with his attack on his Tory leaders. H. W. Massingham, a well-known Liberal journalist, wrote ecstatically that Churchill's speech 'should long ago have been delivered from our own benches', and prophesied that its author would be 'Prime Minister … I hope Liberal Prime Minister of England.'

The Conservatives were divided in their reactions. Some of them admired the young man for his family loyalty while others regarded his performance merely as a stunt to attract publicity. When the debate was resumed the following day Mr. Arthur Lee, later Lord Lee of Fareham, said acidly: 'It is not well to confuse filial piety with public duty. This is not the time to parade or pursue family traditions …' And Mr. Brodrick, Winston's main target, hit back scornfully. 'I confidently expect,' he said, 'that Parliament, which was not afraid to part company with a brilliant statesman in 1886, will not sleep the less soundly because of the financial heroics of my hon. friend the Member for Oldham. Those of us who disagree with him can only hope that the time will come when his judgment will grow up to his ability, when he will look back with regret to the day when he came down to the House to preach Imperialism without being able to bear the burden of Imperialism, and when the hereditary qualities he possesses of eloquence and courage may be tempered also by discarding the hereditary desire to run Imperialism on the cheap.'

---

[56] The Member for Sark was an imaginary character created by the writer of the political column to give voice to his own *obiter dicta*.

[57] 22 May, 1901.

Thus began the breach between Winston and his leaders which two years later was to widen into an irreparable gap. And thus the ghost of Lord Randolph asserted itself with a vengeance. It is arguable that if Winston had not revived the issue of his father's resignation he would have remained in the Tory fold and become Prime Minister instead of Baldwin after World War I. In that case World War II might not have taken place. However, if all this had happened, it is also possible that Winston would not have emerged as a great man. Great men are judged for the wars they win, not the wars they prevent.

Chapter Seven — Backbencher: Liberal

THE DOMINATION that Lord Randolph Churchill exerted from the grave over a son in whom he had never confided stands out as the most fascinating and remarkable aspect of Winston's career as a back-bencher. As the months passed this strange spell increased rather than diminished. It is not unusual for a son to revere his father's memory, but Winston carried his devotion to such exaggerated lengths that his early Parliamentary life was based on an almost slavish imitation. He not only borrowed his father's views and clung to them no matter what spent forces they had become, but he copied his manner and gestures, sought out his friends and marked down his opponents, memorized his speeches in an effort to catch their flavour, adopted his tactics and finally followed his strategy.

In view of Winston's originality and audaciousness this seems astonishing, but the explanation partly lies in his work on his father's biography. His romantic and forceful mind dramatized whatever subject it centred upon, a quality which had already made him a highly successful journalist. And the fact that his emotions were now keenly involved only served to heighten his powerful sense of theatre. He became increasingly enthralled by the scene he was reconstructing and began to live in it with himself as the chief actor. He identified himself so completely with his father that he told all his friends he was certain he would die at the same early age as Lord Randolph. He was determined to repeat his father's triumphs and since time was short he must repeat them in the same meteoric fashion.

From the very first day Winston entered the House he was openly and unashamedly ambitious, and he made it plain to all who would listen that he regarded the rapid fulfilment of his aims as a matter of the gravest urgency. He decided that only one of two courses was open to him: either to win the leadership of the Tory Party, or to abandon the Tories and make his way with the Liberals. He toyed with the second idea as early as 1901, when he had been in Parliament less than a year. Lady Warwick tells of a conversation she had with him at this time at Cecil Rhodes' house in Scotland. 'On the visit to Loch Rannoch of which I write, Winston Churchill discussed quite openly his political position. He had just been on a visit to Lord Rosebery, and he said he was inclined to leave the leadership to Mr. Balfour and proclaim himself a Liberal. He wanted power and the Tory road to power was blocked by the Cecils and other brilliant young

Conservatives, whereas the Liberal path was open. Cecil Rhodes was all in favour of his turning Liberal.'[58]

Winston evidently decided against this course and began to plan the day when he would head the Conservatives. According to Mr. J. L. Wanklyn, a Tory M.P., Mr. Churchill played with the notion of wresting the leadership from Arthur Balfour in 1902, when he had been a backbencher for only eighteen months. Winston denied this charge, and the controversy which took place in the columns of *The Times* makes highly amusing reading:

The Times. 6 March, 1905. 'On Saturday night Mr. J. L. Wanklyn, M.P. for Central Bradford, addressed a meeting in that city. Mr. Wanklyn said that … at an interview with Mr. Churchill sought with him in that month (November 1902) he was invited to assist Mr. Churchill and others in overthrowing the Conservative Unionist Ministry in order to let in a weak Radical Ministry, which in its turn was to be overthrown, and then Mr. Churchill and others were to lead back to place and power a rejuvenated Conservative Unionist Party. The main argument was that the Duke of Devonshire, Lord George Hamilton, Mr. Ritchie and Mr. Chamber-lain were all too old at sixty, while Mr. Balfour and Mr. Brodrick could easily be overthrown upon the public inquiry after the war. Lord Hugh Cecil and Mr. Ernest Beckett were mentioned as prospective Ministers in the Cabinet to be formed by Mr. Churchill …'

The Times. 7 March. 'Mr. Churchill last night issued the following disclaimer. "Mr. Wanklyn's statement is devoid of the slightest foundation. I have never sought an interview with him on any subject. I have never had any conversation with him on such a subject. The whole story from beginning to end is a pure invention of his own, and, if not a hallucination, can only be described as a wilful and malicious falsehood."'

The Times. 8 March. 'The editor of a Bradford evening paper yesterday telegraphed to Lord Hugh Cecil, M.P., asking whether he had seen the charges made by Mr. Wanklyn, M.P. and whether they were true. The reply received was: "Statement untrue. Hugh Cecil". After Lord Hugh Cecil's disclaimer was received a telegram was sent to Mr. Wanklyn, M.P., who replied as follows: "I did not say that Hugh Cecil knew of conspiracy, but Winston Churchill used his name

---

[58] *Life's Ebb and Flow*: Frances, Countess of Warwick.

to me as probable Education Minister with or without his approval and also Lord Kitchener and Ernest Beckett for War Office. Wanklyn".'

The Times. 11 March. 'Mr. J. L. Wanklyn, M.P., attended last night the annual general meeting of the Leeds Licensed Victuallers. Referring to his controversy with Mr. Churchill he said the latter had been driven into a corner. He denied point blank his (Mr. Wanklyn's) statements but let him refresh his memory for he kept a diary and a day book ... He had tried vague and curt denial but let him come out into the open. Let him issue a writ and let him know that his (Mr. Wanklyn's) solicitor was Mr. Soames. He (Mr. Wanklyn) should like to be at the elbow of the counsel who cross-examined him. Let him refer the matter to the arbitration of Mr. Balfour, or Sir Henry Campbell-Bannerman, or three members of the House of Commons. He made the offer and if Mr. Churchill refused it they could draw their own conclusions.'

Here the correspondence ended; and what probably was a drama in 1905 seems a comic episode in 1953.

*

As a back-bencher Winston was one of the most hard-working young men in England. He had an astonishing capacity for sustained concentration. Although he shared a flat in Mayfair with his brother Jack, he had no time for frivolity and rarely made a social engagement. Sometimes friends persuaded him to visit them for a week-end, but even on these occasions they seldom derived companionship from his presence. He merely brought his work with him and organized his time as he would at home. The American writer, George Smalley, was once a co-visitor with Winston at Dunrobin, the vast mansion of the Duke and Duchess of Sutherland. Winston invited the journalist into his room and the latter was astonished at the sight that greeted him. 'His bedroom had been turned into a literary workshop, strewn with books and papers and all the apparatus of the writer. He had brought with him a tin box, some three feet square, divided into closed compartments. This was his travelling companion on journeys of pleasure. Like his father he wanted ample room for his materials, and his hostess had provided him with a large writing-table. This was covered with papers, loose and in docketed bundles, but all in exact order for ready reference ... When we left Dunrobin we found that Winston had reserved a compartment in the railway train for himself and for his big tin case of papers. He shut himself up there, and during that long long journey read and wrote and worked as if a Highland railway train were the natural and convenient laboratory in which literature of a high order was to be distilled.'[59]

Despite Winston's flexibility he preferred to work at home. His study contained his father's huge writing-desk, his large brass inkwell and his carved oak chair. He hung the walls with pictures of Lord Randolph and even a picture of Lord Randolph's prize-winning horse *Abbesse de Jouarre*, which the jockeys used to call 'Abscess of the Jaw', and he decorated the entrance hall with cartoons of Lord Randolph from *Punch* and *Vanity Fair*.

He spoke in the House of Commons at least once and frequently twice a month. He took infinite pains with his speeches, sometimes working on them for as long as six weeks. He always wrote them out and learnt them by heart. 'In those days, and indeed for many years,' he wrote, 'I was unable to say anything (except a sentence in rejoinder) that I had not written out and committed to memory beforehand.' Besides this, he often practised his speeches by reciting them aloud, a habit which he evidently followed for many years, for in 1908 a well-known newspaper editor wrote: 'I have been told by one who was in Scotland with him when he was campaigning that he never appears at his hostess's table until tea-time. All day he might be heard booming away in his bedroom, rehearsing his facts and his flourishes to the accompaniment of resounding knocks on the furniture.'[60] Once a speech was ready to be delivered he took care that the newspapers received a copy in advance, and editors often were surprised to see that the author had confidently punctuated his script with 'cheers'.

During the first three years of his Parliamentary life he spoke almost exclusively on two themes: military matters, of which he had a wide knowledge, and financial affairs, in which he was guided by his father's ideas, interpreted by Sir Francis Mowatt. It was in the military field that he made his most constructive contribution. Mr. Brodrick's scheme for the reorganization of the Army was technically unsound and unworkable. Winston seized every opportunity and attacked him with tireless repetition, branding the scheme as the months passed with increasing vehemence as 'The Great English Fraud', a 'total, costly, ghastly failure', as a 'humbug and a sham'. Finally the plan was abandoned, Mr. Brodrick was moved to the India Office, and a new

[59] *Anglo-American Memories*: George Smalley.

[60] *Prophets*, *Priests and Kings*: A. G. Gardiner.

Minister was appointed to produce a more sensible proposal. This was a great triumph for the young back-bencher.

His crusade for 'economy', however, was not so successful. The British Army slowly expanded and the Army Estimates slowly rose. On 18 March, 1903, a Conservative M.P., Mr. Elliot, said in the House: 'Does anyone really suppose that the circumstances of the old days are absolutely past, and that in future all that would happen in the case of war with a Continental Power would be our magnificent fleet pursuing an inferior fleet? Such a state of things is unthinkable and I cannot imagine a war between Britain and a Continental Power in which the British Army would not be required.' 'Not in Europe,' interrupted Churchill.

Needless to say Churchill's isolationism was not so much intellectual conviction as an inevitable outcome of championing his father's unborn budget. No matter into what strange waters his cause led him he clung to it stubbornly, and as a result one finds him attacking the Admiralty's proposals to lay down eight new dreadnoughts, ships which proved indispensable to Britain right up until 1912.

During his first four years as a back-bencher Winston took almost no interest in purely domestic matters. He spoke once in favour of the Conservative Education Bill and once in opposition to a Bill to allow a man to marry his dead wife's sister. He was led into this last, he declares, against his better judgment, by the persuasion of his friend, Lord Hugh Cecil, who felt strongly that the sanctity of the home was somehow involved. Although Churchill often raised his father's old cry of 'Tory Democracy' on the public platforms, the words had an empty ring. He offered no proposals with which to bring them to life and once defined the slogan vaguely as 'the association of us all through the leadership of the past'.

It is not surprising that Winston at the age of twenty-six lacked his father's insight and interest in the social problems of the day. But it is an interesting comparison that whereas Lord Randolph predicted the rise of the Labour Party eight years before the Labour Party was even formed, Winston appears to have been completely unaware of the social changes towards which Britain was rapidly moving. 'I like the British working man,' he declared to an interviewer in 1900, 'and so did my father before me.' He had a deep faith in the sterling qualities of the working class, unaccompanied by any knowledge of the conditions in which they lived.

The truth was that he was absorbed by ideas, and knew very little about people; and his ideas as a back-bencher, mainly financial, were simple and old-fashioned. All the great reforms that were to engulf the nation during the next fifty years meant an entirely new approach to the nation's fiscal policy; even if Winston had wished to introduce new reforms it would have been impossible for him to do so without completely altering his Victorian approach to Government expenditure. As it was he believed that an income tax of 1s. 3d. in the pound[61] was the limit which could be imposed. He put his faith in a *laissez-faire* economy which produced the rich at one end who, as good Christians, were expected to help the poor at the other. In 1902 the question of a subsidy for the West Indian sugar trade was discussed in the House of Commons. It was argued that when the world price fell too low thousands of native workers found themselves in desperate conditions. Churchill opposed the subsidy: 'I object on principle,' he said, 'to doing by legislation what properly belongs to charity'.[62]

*

As the months passed Winston became increasingly rebellious. Early in 1903 he organized a group of back-benchers known as 'The Hughlighans', in imitation of Lord Randolph's famous Fourth Party. Among the members were Lord Hugh Cecil, Major Jack Seely, Mr. Gibson Bowles, and Winston's cousins, Ivor and Freddy Guest. All were high-spirited young politicians who agreed with Winston that good food and good brandy were essential to good talk. They discussed their burning questions over the best dinner that could be procured. Winston laid down the policy: 'We shall dine first and consider our position afterwards. It shall be High Imperialism nourished by a devilled sardine.'

Winston led his small group into spirited attacks against the Government's Army scheme. Sir James Fergusson, a loyal Tory, wrote indignantly to the *Daily Telegraph* that he had never known 'an attack upon a Government so organized, and pressed with so much

---

[61] In 1901 and 1902 income tax was raised from one shilling to one shilling and twopence and one shilling and threepence to pay the debts of the Boer War. In 1903 it dropped to elevenpence.

[62] *Hansard*: 31 July.

bitterness and apparent determination by members elected to support it.'

The Government, however, apparently remained unruffled. Arthur Balfour continued to smile upon Winston in a paternal fashion, and Chamberlain evidently took the line that 'boys will be boys'. The reason the breach did not become serious was clear. Whereas Lord Randolph's leadership of the Fourth Party had made him such a power in the land that the Prime Minister had been forced to give him office, Winston's leadership of the Hughlighans merely made him a diversion. The difference was that Lord Randolph's attack on the Opposition aroused popular interest and finally led his party to victory, while Winston's criticisms almost passed unnoticed with the general public.

Suddenly Joseph Chamberlain raised a matter which started a national controversy. This was the chance for which Churchill was waiting. He plunged into the fray and overnight became the storm centre of the House of Commons. The twelve months from May 1903 to May 1904 stand out even to-day as the most turbulent and tempestuous year of his political career; at the end of it he crossed the floor and joined the Liberal Opposition.

*

The issue that generated all the heat was Protection versus Free Trade. It arose because Joseph Chamberlain, the Conservative Colonial Secretary, wished to establish a system of Imperial Preferences which would allow imports from the Colonies and Dominions to receive special financial concessions. In order to do this, however, it was necessary first to establish tariffs on goods from foreign countries. To-day when the policy of Imperial Preference has been in operation for twenty years it is difficult to recapture the feeling it aroused at the beginning of the century; a large section of the public regarded it as straight heresy.

Free Trade had been the corner-stone of British policy for fifty prosperous trading years. To the majority of British people it was not only sound economics but almost a religion. Free Trade, they said, meant freedom and peaceful relations with the rest of the world while tariffs led to wars. The Liberal Party was astonished that anyone should dare to challenge a faith so well established and entered into the fight with passionate conviction. Even the Conservative Party was split in half. Three members of Balfour's Cabinet resigned and Sir Henry Campbell-Bannerman, the Opposition Leader, wrote to a friend: 'This reckless criminal escapade of Joe's is the great event of our time. It is playing Old Harry with all Party relations.'

Gradually Balfour pulled the Conservative Parliamentary Party together again until ninety-five per cent were once more following their leaders through the lobby. But Winston was not among them. This was an issue after his own heart. First of all he was sure that his father would have been with him in fighting Protection. 'Everything I know suggests to me that he would ... have been one of its chief opponents.'[63] Secondly, Sir Francis Mowatt was standing by with his customary advice. 'Mowatt, going far beyond the ordinary limits of a Civil Servant, making no secret of his views, courting dismissal, challenging the administration in admirable State papers, carried on the struggle himself. He armed me with facts and arguments of a general character and equipped me with a knowledge of economics, very necessary to a young man who, at twenty-eight, is called upon to take a prominent part in the controversy.'[64]

A few days after Chamberlain outlined his tariff policy to his Birmingham constituents Churchill made a fighting speech in the House of Commons. 'The new fiscal policy,' he declared, 'means a change, not only in the historic English Parties but in the conditions of our public life. The old Conservative Party with its religious convictions and constitutional principles will disappear and a new party will arise ... like perhaps the Republican Party in the United States of America ... rigid, materialist and secular, whose opinions will turn on tariffs and who will cause the lobbies to be crowded with the touts of protected industries ... Not for the last hundred years has a more surprising departure been suggested.'[65]

It was obvious that Churchill was prepared to be a formidable adversary. This was the psychological moment for Arthur Balfour, in the traditional manner of Prime Ministers with powerful rebels, to silence him by inviting him to join the Government. Winston had carefully smoothed the way by announcing that although he was an opponent of Tariff Reform he was not an opponent of his Party. But Balfour remained adamant. He reshuffled his Cabinet, he invited new

---

[63] *My Early Life*: Winston S. Churchill.

[64] *Thoughts and Adventures*: Winston S. Churchill.

[65] *Hansard*: 28 May, 1903.

Ministers to take the place of old Ministers, but Churchill was not one of them. Arthur Balfour had strict ideas on Parliamentary behaviour. He refused to promote rebels over the heads of loyal party supporters. And perhaps, too, he remembered what his uncle, Lord Salisbury, had replied when someone asked him if he would not like to have Lord Randolph Churchill in his Government again. 'When you have got rid of a boil on your neck, you don't want it back.' Many years later Lord Birkenhead, one of Winston's closest friends, wrote: '"He can wait" has always been the Tory formula which has chilled the hopes of young and able men ... And so chance after chance of modest promotion went by ... Winston characteristically jumped the whole fence.'[66]

*

There is no doubt that although Churchill was genuinely opposed to Protection, he was not slow to see the political possibilities that the issue raised. He had sat on the back benches for two years now, and he felt it was far too long. After all, the Boer War had lifted him to prominence and in the election of 1900 both Balfour and Chamberlain had asked him to address audiences of five thousand people. They knew he had the ability. Why were they holding him back? Because of his youth? He would show them that he was not prepared to spend the best, and perhaps the only, years of his life in parliamentary obscurity. If he could rally enough public and parliamentary support against Chamberlain's Protection scheme he might be able to force the Prime Minister to dissociate himself from it, in which case Winston almost certainly would be invited to step into the Cabinet. This was the way his father had attained office and he would play the same game for the same stakes. 'Politics are everything to you?' a journalist asked him as his new and dangerous course became clear. 'Politics,' he answered, 'are almost as exciting as war and quite as dangerous.' 'Even with the new rifle?' his questioner continued. 'Well, in war,' he replied, 'you can only be killed once, but in politics many times.'

So Churchill buoyantly travelled further along the path of opposition. Joseph Chamberlain spent the summer campaigning throughout the country for his plan, and Winston spent the summer campaigning against it. The battle lifted him to the forefront of political life and he was now regarded as one of the most controversial

---

[66] *Sunday Times*: 27 May, 1924.

figures in the House of Commons. And like all controversial figures he aroused intense emotion.

The personal impression he made on those who met him varies so greatly that the only common denominator appears to be the fact that no one could overlook him. Some idea of the range of opinions may be seen from the following extracts from contemporary diaries. Mrs. Beatrice Webb, the straitlaced, serious-minded Socialist, wrote on 8 July, 1903: 'Went into dinner with Winston Churchill. First impressions: restless ... almost intolerably so, without capacity for sustained and unexciting labour ... egotistical, bumptious, shallow-minded and reactionary, but with a certain personal magnetism, great pluck and some originality ... not of intellect but of character. More of the American speculator than the English aristocrat. Talked exclusively about himself and his electioneering plans ... wanted me to tell him of someone who would get up statistics for him. "I never do any brain work that anyone else can do for me" ... an axiom which shows organizing but not thinking capacity. Replete with dodges for winning Oldham against the Labour and Liberal candidates. But I daresay he has a better side ... which the ordinary cheap cynicism of his position and career covers up to a casual dinner acquaintance ...'[67]

Three months later, on 31 October, Wilfrid Blunt, poet, traveller and humanitarian, wrote in his diary: 'I stopped to luncheon with Victor and Pamela and met there for the first time young Winston Churchill. He is a little square-headed fellow of no very striking appearance, but of wit, intelligence and originality. In mind and manner he is a strange replica of his father, with all his father's suddenness and assurance, and I should say more than his father's ability. There is just the same *gaminerie* and contempt of the conventional and the same engaging plainspokenness and readiness to understand ... He has a power of writing Randolph never had, who was a schoolboy with his pen, and he has education and a political tradition. He interested me immensely.'[68]

*

In the autumn Churchill recklessly began to burn his boats. In December he wrote the Liberal candidate at the Ludlow by-election and wished him success against his Conservative opponent, declaring

---

[67] *Our Partnership*: Beatrice Webb.

[68] *My Diaries*: W. S. Blunt.

that 'the time has now come when Free Traders of all parties should form one line of battle against a common foe': and at a Free Trade Meeting at Halifax two days later he ended his speech with the cry: 'Thank God we have a Liberal Party.'

His local constituency party called him to account, informing him coldly that he could no longer depend on their support. Churchill defended himself by saying that it was the Government, not he, who was betraying the people who voted for him. 'When Mr. Balfour succeeded Lord Salisbury,' he stated, 'he solemnly pledged himself at the Carlton Club that the policy of the Party should be unchanged. And yet at Sheffield,[69] only a year afterwards, he declared for a "fundamental reversal of the policy of the last fifty years". Therefore it is not against me that any charge of breaking pledges can be preferred!'

In the House of Commons Churchill moved to an independent seat below the gangway. He continued to call himself a supporter of the Conservative Party but redoubled his attacks on Chamberlain's tariff policy. There was no doubt that the idea of tariffs was unpopular in the country, and Churchill still felt he might be able to force Balfour to reject it. However, he was aware that anger and dislike were mounting against him in his own Party, and he accepted the fact that if things were pushed too far he must be prepared to cross the floor of the House. There already were persistent rumours that this was what he intended to do, but he remained silent on the subject. The Pall Mall Gazette came out with an article emphatically denying that any such idea had crossed his mind. 'Few people we think realize the intensity of his devotion to Toryism … and yet this is one of the most striking characteristics of the member for Oldham. He is a Tory by birth and inheritance. Toryism possesses him … It is with him something of a religion. He once talked to me — concerning Toryism — of "our spiritual ideals" … "Some of us," he once said, "were born in the Tory Party and we are not going to let any aliens turn us out." I referred to the Radical journalist and the gorgeous future he had mapped out for

---

[69] At the Sheffield Party Conference to which Churchill referred, it became plain that a large majority favoured Protection with an almost idealistic fervour as a means of binding the Empire closer together.

Winston Churchill. "Oh, absurd. I am a Tory and must always remain a Tory".'[70]

Meanwhile the lobby correspondents watched Winston's tactics with amused interest. They could not help referring repeatedly to the resemblance between father and son. 'Less in face than in figure, in gesture and manner of speech. When the young Member for Oldham addresses the House, with hands on hips, head bent forward, right foot stretched forth, memories of days that are no more flood the brain. Like father is son in his habit of independent view of current topics, the unexpectedness of his conclusions, his disregard for authority, his contempt of the conventions, his perfect phrasing of disagreeable remarks.

'His special enmity to Chamberlain and all his works is hereditary. He does not forget and can never forgive the rebuff that seared his father's proud heart when Birmingham clamoured for him to represent them in the House of Commons and Chamberlain peremptorily said "no" ... Winston is a convinced Free Trader. But he enters with lighter, more fully gladdened heart into the conflict, since Protection is championed by his father's ancient adversary.'[71]

It was becoming apparent that the Conservative Party was steadily losing its popularity in the country. The Opposition was able to whip up criticism of the Government on several grounds; first its inept handling of the Boer War; second its employment of indentured Chinese labour in the African gold mines which the Liberals branded as 'slave labour' and were turning into an important moral issue; third its interest in Protective Tariffs which the public suspected would mean 'dearer food'. It was obvious that Conservative election prospects were declining. 'From 1903 onwards,' writes D. C. Somervell, the historian, 'it seemed certain, and not only to those who wished it, that Balfour's Government would be defeated at the next election.'[72]

Winston's repeated attacks in the face of this decline infuriated his colleagues. Instead of trying to retrieve the position he was contributing to the rot, and, incidentally, dashing the political hopes

---

[70] *Pall Mall Gazette*: September 1903.

[71] *Punch*: 8 June, 1904.

[72] *British Politics Since 1900*: D. C. Somervell.

of his associates as well. Although many of them had reservations about the tariff policy they were willing to bury their differences at critical moments and were incensed that Churchill refused to play the game in what they called a 'gentlemanly' fashion. They might have forgiven him had they believed in his sincerity but they thought he was influenced mainly by ambition, and began to denounce him as 'wickedly hypocritical'. One of his contemporaries, Mr. MacCallum Scott, wrote that 'the followers of Mr. Chamberlain repaid his hostility with a passionate personal hatred over which they vainly endeavoured to throw a mask of contempt. There was no better hated man in the House of Commons.'[73]

Some idea of the fury he aroused was demonstrated in March 1904 when an unprecedented scene took place in the House. A week before the incident, Major Jack Seely, a close friend of Churchill, announced his resignation from the Conservative Party on the question of 'Chinese slavery' in South Africa. Emotions ran so high and there was such an uproar in the House Major Seely scarcely could make himself heard. Churchill shouted above the din: 'Mr. Speaker, I rise on a point of order. I am quite unable to hear what my honourable Friend is saying owing to the vulgar clamour maintained by the Conservative Party.' With this a Conservative M.P. jumped up pointing to Winston and screaming angrily that 'the vulgarest expression came from this honourable Gentleman'. Amid the hubbub the Speaker tried to explain that he was not so much concerned with the vulgarity of the expressions as the loudness with which they were delivered.

This was the prelude. A week later the English public picked up the morning edition of the *Daily Mail* to read the following headlines:

CHILLING REBUKE
UNIONISTS REFUSE TO HEAR MR. CHURCHILL
STRANGE SCENE IN THE COMMONS

The reporter then gave the following account: 'The rank and file of the Unionist Party who are still loyal to their leaders took a singular and striking step in the House of Commons yesterday to mark their disapproval of Mr. Winston Churchill's attitude.

'For a considerable time his speeches have been almost without exception directed against the policy of the Government. They have been clever, severe, biting in their sarcasm, full of sneers and scorn for Mr. Balfour and his Ministers. Last week in the incident over

---

[73] *Winston Spencer Churchill*: A. MacCallum Scott.

Major Seely's resignation Mr. Churchill came into sharp collision with his former party friends, when he characterized their interjections as "vulgar clamour".

'The insult was resented at the moment and it rankled. The Unionists apparently resolved that he would not have cause to complain again of "vulgar clamour". Yesterday when he rose to follow Mr. Lloyd George in the debate on the adjournment at five o'clock, there was a general movement to the tea rooms.

'Mr. Balfour at this juncture had risen and met Mr. Austen Chamberlain beyond the glass door behind the Speaker's chair. Mr. Churchill objected to the departure of the Prime Minister when he was about to speak. He was astonished at such a lack of deference and respect. The Unionists who remained then got up and also left the House. Some turned back at the doors and looked in to see how many were left. Less than a dozen members, mostly Free Traders, sat on the Government side.

'The merry jest, the sparkling epigram and the ironical sally departed likewise from Mr. Churchill's oration. He never speaks unless there is a full House. The full House had melted away under his spell. It was a chilling rebuke, crushing, unanswerable. He complained bitterly at the slight, and murmured some phrases about a shifty policy of shifty evasion. There were only the crowded benches of the Liberals to cheer. Behind him was silence and desolation.'[74]

This episode was the breaking point. Churchill at once began making arrangements to stand as a Liberal candidate at the next election. Until his plans were completed he continued to sit, belligerently, on the Conservative benches; but three weeks later, on 22 April, he delivered a speech on the Trade Disputes Bill which left the action he was contemplating in no further doubt. It was the first left-wing speech of his career and was described by the *Daily Mail* as 'Radicalism of the reddest type'. But the speech was not only sensational for its content; it was sensational because its author lost the thread of his argument three-quarters of the way through and was unable to finish it. 'MR. CHURCHILL BREAKS DOWN,' cried the headlines of the *Daily Mail*, 'DRAMATIC SCENE IN TILE HOUSE OF COMMONS'.

Churchill began his oration by calling the Conservative Party a 'sham' and accusing it of being afraid to deal with the problems of the

---

[74] *Daily Mail*: 30 March, 1904.

working classes. 'I do not think it can be said,' he continued, 'that Labour bulks too largely in English politics at the present time. When one considers the gigantic powers which by the consent of both Parties have been given to the working classes; when on the other hand, one considers the influence in this House of company directors, the learned professions, the service members, the railway, the landed and liquor interests; it will surely be admitted that the influence of Labour on the course of legislation is even ludicrously small.'[75]

'It lies with the Government,' he cried, 'to satisfy the working classes that there is no justification ...' He paused, hesitated, then began the sentence again. But the words would not come. According to the *Daily Mail* reporter: 'A few Members murmured a cheer. Mr. Churchill looked confused in his boyish way, and smiled at the awkwardness, the absurdity of the position ... "It lies with them ... What?" he ejaculated, as someone suggested a word which was not the right word. He lifted a slip of paper from the bench but the cue was not there. He searched the deep pockets of his frock-coat but found no help. Major Seely picked torn scraps from the floor, and the words were not there ... It was all over. He sat down murmuring thanks to the House for its kindness. The Conservative Party looked silently on wondering what had overtaken him so suddenly, so dramatically.'[76]

These Members remembered how Lord Randolph had broken down in the House a few months before his death. Was Winston ill? Would he, too, go the way of his father? Rumours swept the lobbies and gossip reached a crescendo of excitement. But Winston was far from a physical collapse. He had merely begun trying to change his methods of speaking. Instead of learning his orations by heart he was attempting to deliver them from paragraph headings. This was an effort to limber up so that Arthur Balfour could not jeer at him for having powerful artillery that was 'not very mobile'. He never broke down again, and continued to arrange his speeches in headings; but he also reverted to memorizing them.

*

Controversy continued to rage about Churchill and it seems to have extended to conflicting views even about his appearance. This was due to his quick, changing moods which sometimes turned from

---

[75] *Hansard*: 22 April, 1904.

[76] *Daily Mail*: 23 April, 1904.

loquaciousness to a silence that was almost sulky. When he was animated he reminded his audience of a young fighting cock, but when his face was in repose he struck them as old and tired. For this reason one finds completely contradictory descriptions of him in the contemporary journals. While the *Daily Mail* correspondent describes the 'unmistakably schoolboy grin' that suddenly lights up Mr. Churchill's face in the middle of a stormy scene, 'not the assumed smile so often seen in Parliament, but the real grin of one who is alive to all the fun of things … I saw it in Mr. Churchill's face when Sir Trout Bartley was rebuking him for vulgarity' — the *Pall Mall Gazette* is assuring its readers that 'in appearance there is nothing of "the Boy" left in the white, nervous, washed-out face of the Member for Oldham. He walks with a stoop, his head thrust forward. His mouth expresses bitterness, the light eyes strained watchfulness. It is a tired face, white, worn, harassed … There is, indeed, little of youth left to the Member for Oldham.'

However, despite these claims there was plenty of energy left. At Easter time Churchill was adopted as Liberal candidate for Northeast Manchester. On 16 May he made what proved to be his farewell speech from the Conservative benches, declaring that extravagant finance would drag the Government to the ground and 'be written on the head of its tombstone'.

On 31 May, he crossed the floor and took his seat on the Liberal benches. 'House resumed to-day after Whitsun holidays,' commented Punch. 'Attendance small; benches mostly empty. Winston, entering with all the world before him where to choose, strides down to his father's old quarters on the front bench below the gangway to the left of the Speaker, and sits among the ghosts of the old Fourth Party. "He's gone over at last, and good riddance," say honest hacks munching their corn in well-padded stalls of the Government stables. They don't like young horses that kick out afore and ahint, and cannot safely be counted upon to run in double harness. "Winston's gone over at last," they repeat whinnying with decorous delight.'[77]

Some years later Joseph Chamberlain confided to Margot Asquith: 'He was the cleverest of all the young men. The mistake Arthur [Balfour] made was letting him go.'[78]

---

[77] *Punch*: 8 June, 1904.

[78] *The Autobiography of Margot Asquith.*

*

Winston found himself in strange company on the Liberal benches. There were, of course, the Liberal Imperialists, known as the 'respectable Liberals', made up of well-to-do sober, conservative aristocrats such as Lord Rosebery and Sir Edward Grey. Then there was the radical group led by Lloyd George which was composed of radicals, pacifists, teetotallers and nonconformists, offering a marked contrast to the robust young soldier-politician who had joined their ranks. These were the people that Winston had once jeered at as 'prigs, prudes and faddists', and they still treated him with a certain amount of suspicion. They remembered that only a few years before, at Oxford in 1901, he had declaimed: 'The Radical Party is not dead ... it is hiding from the public view like a toad in a hole; but when it stands forth in all its hideousness the Tories will have to hew the filthy object limb from limb.' Indeed, shortly after Winston joined the Liberals an anonymous pamphlet was printed quoting many of his anti-Radical sayings, with the heading:

Mr. Winston Churchill on the Radical Party
Before he donned their Every and
Accepted their Pay.

Churchill paid little attention to these rearguard attacks and flung himself into the battle. He was welcomed warmly by Lloyd George, John Morley and Herbert Asquith, all of whom were shrewd enough to know the value of their new recruit. He did not make any more radical speeches in Parliament but continued along his well-worn path of Army reform and financial expenditure. But he added one new target for his guns, and that was the Prime Minister, Arthur Balfour.

Balfour was having a difficult time in holding his Party together over tariffs and the method he chose was to sit firmly on the fence. He skilfully evaded all attempts to raise the matter in Parliament and was often absent from the Chamber during fiscal debates when awkward questions might have been asked him.

This gave Churchill the opportunity for one of the most spirited and hard-hitting attacks the House has ever known. He jibed and jeered at Balfour for his 'miserable and disreputable shifts', for 'his gross and flagrant ignorance'. 'Queens never abdicate,' he announced sarcastically, and he told the House that 'to keep in office for a few more weeks and months there is no principle which the Government is not prepared to abandon, no friend or colleague they are not prepared to betray, and no quantity of dust and filth they are not prepared to eat.'[79]

Once again *Punch* called attention to the similarity between father and son, recalling Lord Randolph's onslaught against Sir Stafford Northcote in 1880. 'The same direct hitting out from the shoulder; the same lack of deference to age and authority; the same pained silence on the side where the assailed Ministers sit; the same cheers and laughter in enemy's camp as cleverly-planned, skilfully-directed blow follows blow ... Prince Arthur [Balfour] lolls on the Treasury Bench looking straight before him, with studious air of indifference betrayed by countenance clouded by rare anger.'[80]

Mr. Balfour seldom deigned to answer Winston's attacks, but sometimes he was provoked too far. On 24 July Winston said in an insolent voice: 'We have been told ad nauseam of the sacrifices which the Prime Minister makes. I do not deny that there have been sacrifices. The House ought not to underrate or deny those sacrifices. Some of them must be very galling to a proud man. There were first sacrifices of leisure and then sacrifices of dignity ... Then there was the sacrifice of reputation ... For some years the right hon. Gentleman has led the House by the respect and affection with which he was regarded in all quarters. In future he will not lead the House by the respect and affection of the Opposition at least ... It has been written that the right honourable Gentleman stands between pride and duty. Pride says "go" but duty says "stay". The right honourable Gentleman always observes the maxim of a certain writer that whenever an Englishman takes or keeps anything he wants, it is always from a high sense of duty.'[81]

This was too much for Balfour and he replied to Winston in icy tones:

'As for the junior Member for Oldham his speech was certainly not remarkable for good taste, and as I have always taken an interest in that honourable Gentleman's career, I should certainly, if I thought it in the least good, offer him some advice on that particular subject. But I take it that good taste is not a tiling that can be acquired by industry,

---

[79] *Hansard*: 28 March, 1905.

[80] *Punch*: 22 March, 1905.

[81] *Hansard*: 24 July, 1905.

and that even advice of a most heartfelt and genuine description would entirely fail in its effect were I to offer it to him. But on another point I think I may give him some advice which may be useful to him in the course of what I hope will be a long and distinguished career. It is not, on the whole, desirable to come down to this House with invective which is both prepared and violent. The House will tolerate, and very rightly tolerate, almost anything within the rule of order which evidently springs from genuine indignation aroused by the collision of debate; but to come down with these prepared phrases is not usually successful, and at all events, I do not think it was very successful on the present occasion. If there is preparation there should be more finish, and if there is so much violence there should certainly be more veracity of feeling.'[82]

It is perhaps only in England that friendship could survive these heated duels. Although the relationship of Balfour and Churchill went through its chilly periods, each time it moved again into the sunshine. And when Balfour died many years later, Winston wrote a warm and generous estimate of his work and character. In tills essay he remarked: 'He was never excited and in the House of Commons very hard to provoke. I tried often and often, and only on a very few occasions, which I prefer to forget, succeeded in seriously annoying him in public.'[83]

*

The General Election took place in January 1906. Everyone expected the Liberals to win, but no one imagined such a sweeping victory. It was the greatest electoral landslide since 1833. The Liberals won 401 seats and the Conservatives were reduced to 157. The new era of social democracy had begun.

---

[82] *Hansard*: 27 July, 1905.

[83] *Great Contemporaries*: Winston S. Churchill.

Chapter Eight — The Radical Minister

IT IS an odd twist of Fate that Winston Churchill's Victorian views on finance should have led him into a Party which, under the leadership of Lloyd George as Chancellor of the Exchequer, was destined to revolutionize British financial thought.

The years from 1906 to 1914 are a milestone in English history. They were the stormy, bitter, spectacular years which swept Britain along the path of social democracy, a course which she once again began to pursue in 1945. A flood of legislation was added to the statute books: old age pensions, national health insurance, workmen's compensation, minimum wages, trade boards, labour exchanges, and many other social measures. But it was not only a period of reform, it was a period of fundamental change. For the first time in history the Budget was used as a political instrument to redress the vastly uneven balance of wealth. For the last time in history the landed aristocracy exerted its rule; the Parliament Bill stripped the House of Lords of the power to block the legislation of the Commons, and transformed it at a stroke of the pen into a useful but innocuous revising Chamber.

Needless to say, the rich and powerful fought for their money and their privileges with all their might. 'Party animosity,' wrote Lord Campion in 1952, 'reached a degree of virulence which is hardly conceivable in the present generation.'[84] And the animosity was concentrated on the two brilliant, glittering platform speakers who emerged as the Radical leaders of the day: Lloyd George and Winston Churchill.

They were an oddly contrasting pair. One was the grandson of a Duke, a Tory aristocrat, who had made the most of the advantages that position and privilege could offer. The other was a poor Welsh boy, brought up by a widowed mother and a shoe-maker uncle, articled to a solicitor at the age of sixteen, who began his career by defending poachers in the County Courts.

And yet these two had much in common. In their natures ran an unusual mixture of emotionalism, impulsiveness and hard-headed ambition. Each possessed the spark of genius that lifted him above his more erudite contemporaries. Each was an adventurer who loved the

---

[84] *Parliament: A Survey*: Lord Campion (formerly Sir Gilbert Campion, Clerk of the House of Commons).

thrill and uncertainty of the political battle. And each had enough generosity to fight his way through the years as friends first and rivals second.

By 1908 they shared a common platform which stood apart from the rostrum of the more conservative Liberals in the Cabinet. 'Both were opposed,' wrote Halévy, 'to a policy of heavy expenditure on the Army and the Navy, both advocates of a policy of social reform which, they maintained, the Liberal Party must pursue with an unprecedented daring, if the Labour Party were not to grow strong on its left. They came forward as the two leaders of the radical group of pacifists and advanced social reformers as opposed to the three Imperialists Asquith, Grey and Haldane.'[85]

It is easy enough to understand the rise of Lloyd George as a great Radical and pacifist leader. Lloyd George entered Parliament as a Welsh nationalist. He was not interested in foreign affairs and regarded the army and navy almost as the stage props of Tory Imperialism to which he was bitterly opposed. At the root of his thinking was strong nonconformism mixed with a deep hatred of the land-owning class which had been bred in his bones by a hard childhood where he saw many examples of the victimization of the poor by the squirearchy.

It is not so easy to picture Winston Churchill, the aristocrat and the soldier, fitting himself to the Radical-pacifist mould. If Winston seemed a slightly incongruous figure on the Liberal benches in 1904 sitting among the 'prigs, prudes and faddists', he seemed even more out of place after the election of 1906. Of the 401 Liberal candidates who were returned, over 200 belonged to the League of Liberals Against Aggression and Militarism, who were commonly known as the LLAMS. Nearly all of these 'lambs' were nonconformists. The aristocratic, landowning Liberal was almost a tiling of the past. The new blood was drawn largely from the professional classes; lawyers, journalists, university professors, and 'champions of all those eccentric causes which arouse the enthusiasm of British philanthropy.'[86]

Winston was not born with the nature of a reformer. His sense of justice was not outraged by the great inequality of wealth, nor by the

---

[85] *A History of the English People in 1905-1915*: Elie Halévy.

[86] Ibid.

hangover of feudal privileges. He did not burn with that indignation at the lot of one section of the community which must always be the main spring of the true Radical. His interest was far less concerned with the individuals who made up the nation than with the nation itself. From the earliest Iris outlook was the outlook of the historian. He saw Britain in her most attractive perspective, as a strong, rich, law-abiding power spreading her enlightened ideas across the world as she moved steadily forward by a wonderful chain of continuous and progressive action. A feeling of continuity was bred in his bones, a feeling as strong as Lloyd George's dislike of the squirearchy. It satisfied his romantic nature. Just as he liked to think of himself as the product of great men he liked to think of the nation as the product of great episodes.

This strong and conservative traditionalism was recognized by most of Winston's closest friends as a fundamental part of his make-up. 'Whereas I am a Conservative by conviction,' a Tory colleague once remarked, 'Winston is one by prejudice.' Sir Ian Hamilton who saw much of Winston during his soldiering days remarked along the same line: 'I have always felt that Winston's coat of many colours was originally dipped in a vat of blue; a good fast natural Tory background, none of your synthetic dyes.' And Lord Birkenhead, who was Churchill's closest friend for twenty years, testified in 1924: 'Fundamentally he has always been of our generation the most sincere and fervid believer in the stately continuity of English life.'[87]

How, then, did Winston become a Radical? He certainly was not one when he joined the Liberal Party in 1904. It is worth noting that he did not deliver a single Radical speech until his relations with his own Party were at breaking point. And in the last speech he made from the Conservative benches he pointed out, almost sadly: 'Since my quarrel with the Government has become serious, I would like to say that it has been solely and entirely on the question of finance. It was on finance that I was drawn to attack the Army scheme of 1900; it has been mainly on finance that I have been drawn to oppose the fiscal proposals of the right honourable Gentleman …'[88]

Winston's Radicalism was fashioned by Conservative animosity. He was not only provoked by Tory wrath but, unexpectedly, surprised

---

[87] *Sunday Times*: 24 March, 1924.

[88] *Hansard*: 16 May, 1904.

and wounded by it as well. He suddenly came to the conclusion that he had been badly treated. First of all, the Tory leaders had refused to give him office although they admitted his ability and did not hesitate to make use of it at election time; secondly, although ultimately fifty Conservatives withdrew their support from the Government over Protection, he was the only one singled out for attack; thirdly, it was not he, but they, who had changed their views on Free Trade. 'Change with a Party, however consistent, is at least defended by the power of numbers,' he wrote many years later. 'To remain constant when a Party changes is to excite invidious comparison.'[89]

However, Winston's picture of himself as an outspoken young man martyred for the consistency of his political opinions was not shared by the Conservatives. First and foremost, they did not believe in his sincerity. To them he was ambitious and unscrupulous, making wildly disloyal speeches in a bold bid for power. And of course the fact that he was brilliant and effective as well did nothing to soften their anger. These were the two sides of the story and the truth probably lay somewhere in the middle.

Once Winston became a Liberal, his powerful and imaginative mind explored the possibilities of the Party creed. He grasped the strongest threads of Liberalism and at once wove them into an exciting theme. He made the Liberal idea sparkle and shine as he linked with it, exclusively, the future glory of Britain.

However, the most interesting aspect of his change of Party lay in the effect it had on the biography of his father. He did not finish it for a year after he joined the Liberals. Lord Randolph was still his great inspiration and Lord Randolph had said: 'No power on earth would make me join the other side.' It was then obviously essential to Winston's peace of mind that he should feel that his father would have approved of his action. First he convinced himself that his father had been treated very badly by the Conservatives. When people heckled him at the General Election of 1906 and called him a turn-coat he replied solemnly and almost embarrassingly: 'I admit that I have changed my Party. I don't deny it. I am proud of it. When I think of all the labours which Lord Randolph Churchill gave to the fortunes of the Conservative Party and the ungrateful way in which he was treated by them when they obtained the power they would never have had but for him I am delighted that circumstances have enabled me to break

---

[89] *Thoughts and Adventures*: Winston S. Churchill.

with them while I am still young and still have the first energies of my life to give to the popular cause.'[90]

Thus Winston built up the figure of Lord Randolph as the hero of the piece and the Tory Party as the villain. If it had not been for Lord Randolph the Tory Party might have disappeared for ever. 'But for a narrow chance they might have slipped down the gulf of departed systems. The forces of wealth and rank, of land and Church, must always have exerted vast influence in whatever confederacy they had been locked. Alliances or fusions with Whigs and moderate Liberals must from time to time have secured them spells of office. But the Tory Party might easily have failed to gain any support among the masses. They might have lost their hold upon the new foundations of power; and the cleavage in British politics must have become a social, not a political division — upon a line horizontal, not oblique.'[91]

Lord Randolph had saved the Tory Party which had repaid him by casting him aside. Would he have become a 'Tory-Socialist' in the new century? his son asked. Or, 'would he, under the many riddles the future had reserved for such as he, have snapped the tie of sentiment that bound him to his party, resolved at last to "shake the yoke of inauspicious stars" …?'[92] Winston decided that his father would have done what he himself had done: become a Progressive.

The fact that Winston painted the picture high-lighting the differences between Lord Randolph and the Conservative Party, which he could scarcely have done so vividly had he remained a Tory, made the book a fascinating drama. It was beautifully written and carefully assembled. The issues of the day became alive and the House of Commons stands forth as 'the best club in the world'.

The reviewers praised the book as a 'literary masterpiece', but politically maintained their reservations. The *Review of Reviews*, one of the leading periodicals of the day, devoted thirteen pages to its analysis, under the heading *Book of the Month*. It called the biography 'shrewd', 'acute' and 'brilliant' but when it dealt with the author's interpretation of Lord Randolph's character and contribution the tone

---

[90] Extract from speech delivered at Manchester quoted in *World*, 16 January, 1906.

[91] *Lord Randolph Churchill*: Winston S. Churchill.

[92] Ibid.

grew ironical. 'Mr. Winston's Lord Randolph dawns upon us as a kind of demi-god transcending all his contemporaries by his piercing insight and demonic energy. In the midst of the clash of parties, and even while he was apparently engaged in the fiercest strife, he stands aloof, alone and apart. More Liberal than the Liberals, he was nevertheless the idolized gladiator of the militant Tories; but for him the Tory Party, that great instrument which had governed Britain for the last twenty years, would have perished miserably. To his genius, to his prescience, to his statesmanlike grasp of the great verities of the situation, is due the realization of the great ideal of a Tory democracy, Primrose-leagued around an Imperial crown. Such a concept of Lord Randolph Churchill may be true: it is certainly new, but it is put forward with such sincerity of conviction, and such plausible and persistent arguments, that it is certain to win much more acceptance than anyone could have believed to be possible before Mr. Winston Churchill took in hand the apotheosis of his father ... I will only say that it is difficult to account for Lord Randolph's resignation on any other theory than that of a swelled head, manifesting itself in an impatient determination to force the hand of Lord Salisbury and constitute himself master of the Cabinet. Mr. Winston disguises, excuses and extenuates the supreme miscalculation of his father's lifetime. But beneath all the excuses due to filial respect the fact stands out clearly that Lord Randolph believed the time had come when he could dictate to Lord Salisbury. It was a fatal miscalculation.'[93]

*

The political battle did not reach its full force for over two years. When the Liberals formed their new Government in 1906, Campbell-Bannerman, a good-natured Scot of upright character but no startling ability, became Prime Minister for the simple reason that he had fewer enemies than other likely contenders. Mr. Asquith became Chancellor of the Exchequer, Sir Edward Grey went to the Foreign Office, and Winston Churchill, aged thirty-one, became Under-Secretary of State for the Colonies.

Churchill was first offered the job of Financial Secretary to the Treasury but he preferred the Colonies, first because the Colonial Office would handle the settlement with the South African Republics, and second, and probably more important, because his chief, Lord

---

[93] *Review of Reviews*: January 1906.

Elgin, sat in the Lords, which gave his Under-Secretary more scope in the Commons.

Winston found plenty of opportunity for his talents. The Liberal Government soon made the daring and enlightened decision to give immediate and complete self-government to the Transvaal and the Orange Free State, and the Conservatives opposed it. Although the Treaty of Peace had stated that 'as soon as circumstances permit, representative institutions leading up to self-government will be introduced', the Tories insisted that the right conditions did not yet prevail. Mr. Balfour viewed with 'alarm and distrust' what he referred to as 'this most reckless development of a great colonial policy'; and in the Upper House Lord Milner and Lord Lansdowne, the Tory leaders, painted dark forecasts of the poor harvest such precipitous action would reap.

Winston was wholeheartedly in favour of the Bill which became his responsibility to pilot through the Commons. In his maiden speech five years before, he had pleaded for a vigorous finish to the war with a humane and just settlement to follow. Now his emotions were involved as well. The reader will remember that Winston was taken prisoner after the armoured train was wrecked, by a Boer horseman who came galloping up and covered him with his rifle. In 1902, shortly after the war had drawn to a close, several Boer generals visited London to ask for assistance for their devastated country, and Winston was introduced at a luncheon to their leader, General Botha. They talked about the war and Churchill told him the story of his capture. 'Botha listened in silence; then he said, "Don't you recognize me? I was that man. It was I who took you prisoner. I, myself," and his bright eyes twinkled with pleasure.'[94] In 1906, shortly after Winston was appointed Under-Secretary, Louis Botha became the first Prime Minister of the Transvaal. He came to London to attend the Imperial Conference and was present at a great banquet given to the Dominion Prime Ministers in Westminster Hall. As Botha strode through the hall to his place at the banquet table he passed Churchill who was accompanied by his mother. He paused and said to Lady Randolph with a twinkle: 'He and I have been out in all weathers.'

Churchill's friendship with Louis Botha, whom he later described as 'one of the most interesting men I have ever met', strengthened his already firm faith in the Boers. He answered the Conservatives in

---

[94] *My Early Life*: Winston S. Churchill.

uncompromising language. 'We do not ask honourable Gentlemen opposite to share our responsibility,' he said in his closing speech. 'If by chance our counsels of conciliation should come to nothing, if our policy should end in mocking disaster, then the resulting evil would not be confined to South Africa. Our unfortunate experience would be trumpeted forth all over the world wherever despotism wanted a good argument for bayonets, wherever an arbitrary government wished to deny or curtail the liberties of imprisoned nationalities.

'But if, on the other hand, as we hope and profoundly believe, better days are in store for South Africa, if the long lane it has been travelling has reached its turning at last, if the near future should unfold to our eyes a tranquil, prosperous, consolidated Afrikander nation under the protecting aegis of the British Crown, then I say, the cause of the poor and the weak all over the world will have been sustained, and everywhere small peoples will get more room to breathe, and everywhere great empires will be encouraged by our example to step forward — it only means a step — into the sunshine of a more gentle and a more generous age.'[95]

The result of this bold experiment was entirely successful. Louis Botha remained Prime Minister of the Transvaal until 1910. During that year the four colonies were federated and Botha became the first Prime Minister of the Union of South Africa. When he died in 1918 his second-in-command, Jan Smuts, succeeded him. Both men were life-long friends of Churchill; and it is perhaps worth reminding the reader that when Britain went to war in 1914 Louis Botha and Smuts also declared war on Germany and attacked German Southwest Africa. It is also worth recording that at home, as soon as the Conservatives saw that the Constitution Bill transformed the Boer Republics into staunch supporters of the British Commonwealth, they changed their tune. Three years later Mr. Balfour swallowed his words of criticism and described it in the House of Commons as 'one of the most important events in the history of the Empire, one of the great landmarks of Imperial policy ... the most wonderful issue out of all those divisions, controversies, battles and outbreaks, the devastations and horrors of war, the difficulties of peace. I do not believe the world shows anything like it in its whole history!'[96]

---

[95] *Hansard*: 17 December, 1906.

[96] *Hansard*, 16 August, 1909.

*

South Africa was not the only subject that occupied Mr. Churchill during the first two years of the Liberal Government. Although he was serving in the comparatively humble capacity of an Under-Secretary, he was regarded as one of the leading figures in the Government. In 1907 he was made a Privy Councillor, an honour rarely accorded to a politician below the rank of a full Minister, a certain indication that as soon as he had served his apprenticeship he would step into the Cabinet. He already had the approach of a Cabinet Minister. His ideas were not confined to his departmental duties but were on a national, policy-making scale. Although 1906 and 1907 are regarded by present-day historians as 'the lull before the storm', Mr. Churchill made several strong Radical speeches during this period which fanned Conservative emotions into bright, angry flames.

One of these speeches, given at Glasgow in October 1906, might have been delivered by Clement Attlee in 1951. It attacked Marxist Socialism but praised the solid ranks of Labour. It defended private enterprise but spoke in favour of further collectivization. It was in fact the doctrine of the middle course; of a mixture of competition and co-operation, of public ownership and private initiative, which has been accepted as the Labour Party's 'democratic Socialism' of to-day.

'No view of society can possibly be complete,' he declared, 'which does not comprise within its scope both collective organization and individual incentive. The whole tendency of civilization is, however, toward the multiplication of the collective functions of society. The evergrowing complications of civilization create for us new services which have to be undertaken by the State, and create for us an expansion of the existing services. There is a growing feeling, which I entirely share, against allowing those services which are in the nature of monopolies to pass into private hands. There is a pretty steady determination, which I am convinced will become effective in the present Parliament, to intercept all future unearned increment which may arise from the increase in the speculative value of the land. There will be an ever-widening area of municipal enterprise. I go farther: I should like to see the State embark on various novel and adventuresome experiments. I am delighted to see that Mr. Burns is now interesting himself in afforestation. I am of the opinion that the State should increasingly assume the position of the reserve employer of labour. I am very sorry we have not got the railways of this country in our hands. We may do something better with the canals, and we are all agreed, everyone in this hall who belongs to the Progressive Party, that the State must increasingly and earnestly concern itself with the care of the sick and the aged and, above all, of the children.

'I look forward to the universal establishment of minimum standards of life and labour, and their progressive elevation as the increasing energies of production may permit. I do not think that Liberalism in any circumstances can cut itself off from this fertile field of social effort, and I would recommend you not to be scared in discussing any of these proposals, just because some old woman comes along and tells you they are Socialistic. If you take my advice, you will judge each case on its merits. Where you find that State enterprise is likely to be ineffective, then utilize private enterprise, and do not grudge them their profits.'[97]

*

Despite the Government's huge Liberal majority in the Commons, it soon became clear that trouble was brewing. The House of Lords, which was overwhelmingly Conservative, coolly began to reject the Government's legislation. First they butchered the Education Bill by amending so many clauses that it was almost unrecognizable and finally had to be dropped. When Augustine Birrell, the Minister, received it back in its massacred condition he told the Commons that he felt like Macduff after the slaughter of his children: 'All gone? All my pretty ones?'

Liberal anger began to rise. No one had forgotten Arthur Balfour's arrogant declaration after the Election that 'whether in power or opposition the Unionist [Conservative] Party will continue to control the destinies of the Empire.' Sir Henry Campbell-Bannerman, the Prime Minister, put down a motion[98] in the House 'that in order to give effect to the will of the people as expressed by their elected representatives' it was necessary that the power of the Lords to alter or reject Bills passed by the Commons 'should be so restricted by law as to secure that within the Emits of a single Parliament the final decision of the Commons shall prevail'. And Winston at once plunged into the attack: 'Has the House of Lords ever been right?' he asked the Commons. 'Has it ever been right in any of the great settled controversies which are now beyond the reach of Party argument? Was it right in delaying Catholic emancipation and the removal of

---

[97] *Liberalism and the Social Problem*: Winston S. Churchill.

[98] In the session of 1907.

Jewish disabilities? Was it right in driving this country to the verge of revolution in its effort to defeat the passage of reform? Was it right in passing the Ballot Bill? Was it right in the almost innumerable efforts it made to prevent this House dealing with the purity of its own electoral machinery? Was it right in endeavouring to prevent the abolition of purchase in the Army? Was it right in 1880 when it rejected the Compensation for Disturbance Bill? I defy the Party opposite to produce a single instance of a settled controversy in which the House of Lords was right.'[99]

However, the Liberal Government decided that the time was not ripe to 'fight it out' with the Lords, and Sir Henry Campbell-Bannerman's motion died a quiet little death. Winston Churchill seized the opportunity to tour East Africa in his official capacity, and came back full of praise for the beauties of Uganda butterflies. He published a book about his trip entitled *My East African Journey*. Shortly after his return to London, Sir Henry Campbell-Bannerman died. The year was 1908. Mr. Henry Asquith succeeded him as Prime Minister; Lloyd George succeeded Asquith as Chancellor of the Exchequer; and Churchill succeeded Lloyd George as President of the Board of Trade. At the age of thirty-four Winston had reached the Cabinet.

*

In those days entry into the Cabinet necessitated fighting a by-election. This gave the Conservatives a chance to demonstrate that they still considered Winston Churchill as Enemy No. 1. They talked of him not only as an 'opportunist' and a 'bounder', but what was even worse in their eyes, as 'a traitor to his class'. The very fact that these unpraiseworthy qualities had led him to the dizzy heights of the Cabinet was more than they could bear. They flung themselves into the campaign against him with eager hostility, enlisting the support of every formidable Conservative speaker they could find. From the beginning it was obvious it was going to be a stiff fight. Northwest Manchester was traditionally a Tory seat which had been won by the Liberals for the first time two years before. However, Winston was now a national figure and a brilliant platform speaker and many people believed he would hold his own.

If he had his detractors, he also had his admirers. Henry Massingham, the Liberal journalist who had predicted in 1901 that Winston would one day be Prime Minister, wrote an article for the

---

[99] *Hansard*: 29 June, 1907.

Daily Mail which appeared under the heading: *A Character Sketch of the Man of the Hour*. 'He is without the baser faults of politicians. There is not an atom of malice in his composition. Mature as is his intellect in many of its aspects he is still a boy, high spirited, friendly, delighting to get his blow in, but abstaining from poisoned weapons, from speech barbed with the cruelty that the hard, fierce warfare of politics so often engenders. Depth he still wants; only experience brings that. And in taste he sometimes fails, as do most young men who are not prigs.'[100]

Winston flung himself into the campaign with characteristic zeal. He worked nearly eighteen hours a day organizing canvassers, receiving deputations, mustering speakers, and writing letters. The motor car in which he toured his constituency was fitted with a small ladder by which he climbed to the roof and addressed open-air meetings. His opponent, Mr. Joynson-Hicks, was a man of personality and ability and Churchill did not make the mistake of underrating him. Besides, a new element soon entered the contest which added to Winston's difficulties.

The Suffragettes' Campaign was entering a violent phase and Churchill was singled out as a target: the reason being that Manchester happened to be the home of the celebrated feminist leader, Mrs. Pankhurst, and her two daughters Christabel and Sylvia. Winston's assurances that he, personally, was converted to the Suffragette Cause were not sufficient; they demanded the official support of the Prime Minister which, of course, he was unable to give. As a result they tried to break up his meetings. 'Painful scenes were witnessed in the Free Trade Hall,' wrote Mr. Churchill, 'when Miss Christabel Pankhurst, tragical and dishevelled, was finally ejected after having thrown the meeting into pandemonium. This was the beginning of a systematic interruption of public speeches and the breaking up and throwing into confusion of all Liberal meetings. Indeed, it was most provoking to anyone who cared about the style and form of his speech to be assailed by the continued, calculated, shrill interruptions. Just as you were reaching the most moving part of your peroration or the most intricate point in your argument, when things were going well and the audience was gripped, a high-pitched voice would ring out, "What about the women?" "When are you going to give women the vote?" and so on. No sooner was one interrupter removed than another in a different part

---

[100] 21 April, 1908.

of the hall took up the task. It became extremely difficult to pursue connected arguments.'[101]

The result was that Churchill was beaten by his Conservative opponent. Mr. Joynson-Hicks polled 5,517 votes and Winston 4,988. As he left the Town Hall after a count a Suffragette seized his arm and cried: 'It's the women who have done this, Mr. Churchill. Now you will understand that we must have our vote.'

The joy of the Conservatives at Winston's defeat was reflected by the *Morning Post* which almost became abandoned in tone. 'At this moment Mr. Joynson-Hicks is the member for Northwest Manchester, and Mr. Winston Churchill, though a Cabinet Minister, is a political Ishmaelite wandering around as an object of compassion and commiseration. Manchester has washed its hands of him. The juveniles have for days past been singing to a popular air "Good-bye, Winnie, you must leave us", and "Winnie" has gone. On the whole Manchester appears to be taking the sorrowful parting with composure.'[102]

Winston did not escape criticism from his own leaders. Some believed that the odds had been stacked against him too heavily for he not only had the Suffragettes to contend with but a strong anti-Liberal tide due to bad trade. Others were inclined to think that if he had conducted his campaign differently he might have won. They felt that the boyish enthusiasm which Massingham praised gave the electorate the impression of a young man willing to employ any stunt and make any promise in order to win his seat. Mr. John Morley, Winston's colleague and close friend, wrote in his diary: 'The belief among competent observers in the place is that the resounding defeat of Winston at Manchester was due to wrath at rather too naked tactics of making deals with this, that, and the other group without too severe a scrutiny in his own political conscience of the terms that they were exacting from him. It is believed that he lost three hundred to four hundred of these honourably fastidious electors.'[103]

However, the joy of the Conservatives was short-lived. Exactly seven minutes after Churchill's defeat he received a telegram asking

---

[101] *Thoughts and Adventures*: Winston S. Churchill.

[102] *Morning Post*: 25 April, 1908.

[103] *Recollections*: Viscount Morley.

him to contest Dundee, one of the great Liberal strongholds in the country. This time victory was certain.

At the Kinnaird Hall in Dundee Mr. Churchill delivered a speech which many years later he described as the most successful election speech of his career. First he attacked Marxist Socialists and appealed to the sound, sober-minded Radicals; second, he attacked the reactionary Conservatives and appealed to the tolerant, sensible Progressives. 'An inconclusive verdict from Dundee, the home of Scottish Radicalism — an inconclusive, or still more, a disastrous verdict — would carry a message of despair to everyone in all parts of our island and in our sister island who is working for the essential influences and truths of Liberalism and progress. Down, down, down would fall the high hopes of the social reformer. The constructive plans now forming in so many brains would melt into air. The old regime would be reinstated, reinstalled. Like the Bourbons, they have learned nothing and will have forgotten nothing. We shall step out of the period of adventurous hope in which we have lived for a brief spell; we shall step back to the period of obstinate and prejudiced negotiations. For Ireland — ten years of resolute government; for England — dear food and cheaper gin; and for Scotland — the superior wisdom of the House of Lords! Is that the work you want to do, men of Dundee?'

Then he moved to the other flank. 'I turn to the rich and the powerful, the Unionist and Conservative elements, who, nevertheless, upon Free Trade, upon Temperance, and upon other questions of moral enlightenment, feel a considerable sympathy with the Liberal Party ... I turn to those among them who complain that we are too Radical in this and that, and that we are moving too quickly, and I say to them: Look at this political situation, not as Party men, but as Britons; look at it in the light of history; look at it in the light of philosophy; and look at it in the light of broad-minded, Christian charity.

'Why is it that life and property are more secure in Britain than in any other country in the world? ... The security arises from the continuation of that very class struggle which they lament and of which they complain, which goes on ceaselessly in our country, which goes on tirelessly, with perpetual friction, a struggle between class and class which never sinks into lethargy, and never breaks into violence, but which from year to year makes possible a steady and constant advance. It is on the nature of that class struggle in Britain that the security of life and property is fundamentally reposed. We are always changing; like nature, we change a great deal, although we change very slowly. We are always reaching a higher level after each change, but yet with the harmony of our life unbroken and unimpaired. And I say also to those persons here, to whom I now make my appeal: Wealthy men, men of light and leading, have never been all on one side in our country. There have always been men of power and position who have sacrificed and exerted themselves in the popular cause; and that is why there is so little class hatred here, in spite of all the squalor and misery which we see around us. There, gentlemen, lies the true evolution of democracy. That is how we have preserved the golden thread of historical continuity, when so many other nations have lost it forever.'[104]

The Dundee campaign did not escape the attention of the Suffragettes. They followed him from Manchester and one of them, a Miss Malony, assiduously attended Churchill's meetings and tried to drown his words with a huge dinner bell. Once he gave up the struggle, sat down, lit a cigar and announced: 'I won't attempt to compete with a young and pretty lady in a high state of excitement.' However, this time the feminists were unable to score a triumph. Churchill was elected by a margin of three thousand votes which, in those days, was considered a huge majority. *The Times* described him as 'the greatest platform asset possessed by the Liberal Party'.

Despite Winston's oratorical successes the political battle was never easy for a man constantly attacked as a 'political renegade'. The Conservatives continued to hate him and Liberals continued to regard him with reservation. Was he really a Radical or, as the Tories insisted, merely an adventurer ready to use any means to take him to the top? They were not certain. A. G. Gardiner, the Editor of the Liberal *Daily News*, expressed this wondering attitude in a character sketch published in his paper in 1908.

'What of his future? At thirty-four he stands before the country as the most interesting figure in politics, his life a crowded drama of action, his courage high, his vision unclouded, his boats burned. "I love Churchill, and trust him," said one of his colleagues to me. "He has the passion of democracy more than any man I know. But don't forget that the aristocrat is still there — latent and submerged, but there — nevertheless. The occasion may come when the two

---

[104] *Liberalism and the Social Problem*: Winston S. Churchill.

Churchills will come into sharp conflict, and I should not like to prophesy the result."

'Has he staying power? Can one who has devoured life with such feverish haste retain his zest to the end of the feast? How will forty find him? — that fatal forty when the youth of roselight and romance has faded into the light of common day and the horizon of life has shrunk incalculably, and when the flagging spirit no longer answers to the spur of external things, but must find its motive and energy from within, or find them not at all.

'That is the question that gives us pause. For with all his rare qualities, Mr. Churchill is the type of "the gentlemen of fortune". He is out for adventure. He follows politics as he would follow the hounds. He has no animus against the fox but he wants to be in "at the kill". It is recorded that, when a fiery headed boy at Harrow, he was asked what profession he thought of taking up, he replied, "The Army, of course, so long as there's fighting to be had. When that's over I shall have a 'shot at politics'" — not so much concerned about who the enemy may be or about the merits of the quarrel as about being in the thick of the fight and having a good time. With the facility of the Churchill mind he feels the pulse of Liberalism with astonishing sureness and interprets it with extraordinary ability. But the sense of high purpose is not yet apparent through the fierce joy of battle that possesses him. The passion for humanity, the resolve to see justice done though the heavens fall and he be buried in the ruins, the surrender of himself to the cause — these things have yet to come. His eye is less on the fixed stars than on the wayward meteors of the night. And when the exhilaration of youth is gone, and the gallop of high spirits has run its course, it may be that this deficiency of abiding and high-compelling purpose will be a heavy handicap. Then it will be seen how far courage and intellectual address, a mind acutely responsive to noble impulses, and a quick and apprehensive political instinct will carry him in the leadership of men.'[105]

One can only smile at this writer asking so earnestly in 1908 whether Winston had 'staying power'. How surprised he would have been to know that forty-five years later Churchill would still be in the race, and what is more, leading the field.

---

[105] *Prophets, Priests and Kings*: A. G. Gardiner.

Chapter Nine — In the thick of the fight

THE THREE years from 1908 to 1911 mark the phase in Mr. Churchill's life when he reached his zenith as a Radical, a reformer, and an Isolationist. During this period Lloyd George and Winston were the two most controversial and publicized figures on the political stage. Both were loyal friends, both were men of genius, both were possible and probable Prime Ministers. Which of these two colleagues and rivals would reach the highest office first? Max Beerbohm drew a cartoon showing the pair standing on the terrace of the House of Commons fingering a coin.

Mr. Churchill: 'Come, suppose we toss for it, Davey.'

Mr. Lloyd George: 'Ah, but, Winsie, would either of us as loser abide by the result?'

Although the public saw the two friends as men of almost equal stature, behind the scenes the relationship was that of the master and the pupil. Lloyd George was the dominating force and wielded an unquestioned authority. First of all he was eleven years older which gave him a natural advantage. Secondly, he knew how to enthral the younger man with his humour and sparkling personality. Winston not only admired the Welshman's spell-binding, facile oratory but he was fascinated by the provocative, radical ideas which had not been assimilated from books but were part of Lloyd George's very being. Now that Winston had convinced himself that Lord Randolph Churchill's liberal mind had saved the hopelessly reactionary Tories from political extinction, and that if Lord Randolph had lived he would undoubtedly have been a Radical like Winston himself, he was willing to turn from the guidance of his father's memory and accept a new leader. And Lloyd George was the man he chose to follow.

This exciting friendship aroused all his competitive instincts. The idea of social reform caught his imagination and dominated his thoughts. Characteristically, once his enthusiasm had been aroused, he could talk of nothing else. Charles Masterman, a close friend and a Liberal colleague, wrote to his wife on 12 February, 1908: 'Winston swept me off to his cousin's house and I lay on the bed while he dressed and marched about the room gesticulating and impetuous, pouring out all his hopes and plans and ambitions. He is full of the poor whom he has just discovered. He thinks he is called by providence — to do something for diem. "Why have I always been kept safe within a hair's breadth of death," he asked, "except to do something like this? I'm not going to live long," was also his refrain. He is getting impatient; although he says he can wait. I challenged him once on his exposition of his desire to do something for the people. "You can't deny that you enjoy it all immensely — the speeches — the crowds, the sense of increasing power." "Of course I do," he said. "Thou shalt not muzzle the ox when he treadeth out the corn. That shall be my plea at the day of judgment." He is just an extraordinarily gifted boy, with genius and astonishing energy. I always feel of immense age when I am with him — though he's only a year younger than I am. "Sometimes I feel as though I could lift the whole world on my shoulders," he said last night.'[106]

Lloyd George was Winston's inspiration, but at the same time the young man was eager to impress the Welshman with his own originality and ability and show him in friendly rivalry that he could outdo him at his own game. When he took over the Board of Trade from Lloyd George in 1908 he is said to have remarked: 'I have got this pie too late. L.G. has pulled out all the plums.' It was true that Lloyd George had made a great reputation for himself during the preceding two years. He had put the Patents Act on the statute books; he had pushed through the Merchant Shipping Bill which raised standards of food and accommodation for the seamen; he had nationalized London's chaotic private dock companies and welded them together into the Port of London Authority; and he had successfully intervened in a railway dispute and averted a national strike. His actions had won applause from both sides of the House.

Winston was not the sort of man to sit back and sigh for triumphs that had been won by someone else. He set about looking for his own plums, even if they happened to be in other people's pies. He fastened on two important reforms. One was in the 'sweated industries'. There had been much talk about these industries in which slum dwellers, mostly women, worked fantastically long hours for little pay, unprotected by Trade Unions or Factory Acts. Charles Booth had printed unpleasant statistics on the subject in his *Life and Labour in London*, and Sir Charles Dilke, a Radical M.P., had suggested the establishment of 'trade boards' composed of an impartial committee to determine minimum wages and hours in each industry. But the Home Office, to whom the subject belonged, refused to do anything about it. Winston saw his chance, grabbed the idea and drove a Trade

---

[106] *C. F. G. Masterman*: Lucy Masterman.

Boards Act through Parliament. The system proved a great success and was steadily expanded.

His second reform was in the field of unemployment. Beatrice and Sidney Webb, the Fabian leaders, had suggested some time before that a system of Labour Exchanges should be established so that people out of work could find new jobs. The Local Government Board to whom they appealed was not interested and once again Churchill saw his chance. He borrowed the idea and established Labour Exchanges.

It seems strange to-day to think of Winston working in close co-operation with Beatrice and Sidney Webb, those astonishing, statistically-minded, super-intellectuals who converted the Trade Unions to their own particular brand of Fabian Socialism and thus fashioned the soul of the present Labour Party. Beatrice was a tall, handsome blue-stocking and Sidney was a little man with a huge head and small, tapering body which his wife said was the 'delight of caricaturists'. The letters they exchanged during their courtship are famous for their solemn comments on social investigation; and they appropriately spent their honeymoon in Glasgow looking up Trade Union records.

The Webbs were the great experts on social reform. They wrote the standard works on Trade Unionism, Industrial Democracy and the Cooperative Movement. They scintillated with ideas for new reforms which they gladly proffered to progressive politicians and which progressive politicians gladly accepted. They were not the sort of people, however, whom one would single out for a jolly evening. When Asquith suggested that Winston should take charge of the Local Government Board he is said to have declined, announcing that he did not wish 'to be shut up in a soup kitchen with Mrs. Sidney Webb'. Nevertheless he recognized the Webbs as experts; and for experts he had a high regard. Evidence of his respect for Mrs. Webb may be gleaned from the latter's diary. On 3 October, 1908, she wrote: 'Winston and his wife dined here the other night to meet a party of young Fabians. He is taking on the look of the mature statesman — bon vivant and orator, somewhat in love with his own phrases ... In the course of the evening he took a fancy to my organizing secretary, Colegate, and told him to apply to the Board of Trade ... Winston Churchill said that anyone, if really recommended "on my honour", he would take on.'[107]

---

[107] *Our Partnership*: Beatrice Webb.

Thus with Lloyd George supplying the inspiration and the Webbs the guidance Winston threw all his energies into the field of social reform. Mrs. Webb's opinion of this energetic and overpowering young man had changed greatly since she first met him in 1903. No doubt she was influenced by the fact that now he was a Radical. 'He is brilliantly able — not a phrase-monger, I think …' she wrote. And although she conceded that Lloyd George was a 'clever fellow' she thought that he had 'less intellect than Winston, and not such an attractive personality — more of the preacher, less of the statesman.'[108]

Winston's activities did not stop with the Board of Trade. In 1910 he was transferred to the Home Office where he at once interested himself in prison reform. He believed that prisoners should have libraries, lectures and entertainments. He succeeded in establishing his ideas and thus started a ball rolling which has continued to roll far. His humane attitude towards prisoners sprang from first-hand knowledge of what confinement was like. 'I certainly hated every minute of my captivity more than I have ever hated any other period in my whole life,' he wrote in *My Early Life*. 'Looking back on those days I have always felt the keenest pity for prisoners and captives. What it must mean for any man, especially an educated man, to be confined for years in a modern convict prison strains my imagination. Each day exactly like the one before, with the barren ashes of wasted life behind, and all the long years of bondage stretching out ahead. Therefore in after years, when I was Home Secretary and had all the prisons of England in my charge, I did my utmost, consistent with public policy, to introduce some sort of variety and indulgence into the life of their inmates, to give to educated minds books to feed on, to give to all periodical entertainments of some sort to look forward to and to look back upon, and to mitigate as far as is reasonable the hard lot which, if they have deserved, they must none the less endure.'

Winston's magnanimous and warm-hearted nature was often deeply stirred by the prisoners under his control. The fact that the Home Secretary had the authority to quash or confirm a death sentence was a torment to him. He was always torn with pity. He told Wilfrid Blunt how 'it had become a nightmare to him the having to exercise his power of life and death in the case of condemned criminals, on an average of one case a fortnight … The Home Secretary can go into a

[108] *Our Partnership*: Beatrice Webb.

prison and on his sole authority can order a release, which if once notified to a prisoner cannot be changed afterwards by any power in England. He had several times done this, and just before leaving the office he had ordered a number of remissions of sentences, notwithstanding the protests of the judges in the case. He spoke of these cases with emotion, and giving us all particulars.'[109]

The vibration of Winston's energy shook the Home Office as it had the Board of Trade before, and was so far reaching that it penetrated to the most obscure civil servants of the Department. Everyone was aware that a new master had arrived. Some of Winston's ideas were good and some were bad, but there was never a shortage of them. Sir E. Troup, the Permanent Secretary of the Home Office, wrote: 'There is no period of my time at the Home Office of which I have pleasanter recollections than when Mr. Churchill was my chief and Mr. (Charles) Masterman his parliamentary lieutenant. Once a week, or oftener, Mr. Churchill came down to the office bringing with him some adventurous and impossible projects: but after half an hour's discussion something was evolved which was still adventurous, but no longer impossible.'[110]

However, some of Winston's colleagues found his constant flood of opinions, and his obsession with whatever he himself was doing, annoyingly egotistical. Mrs. Lucy Masterman recorded in her diary as early as March 1908 a conversation which she had with Sir Edward Grey, the Foreign Secretary, and Augustine Birrell, the Minister of Education, 'I forget whose the phrase was, but they agreed that the tendency in him to see first the rhetorical potentialities of any policy was growing and becoming a real intellectual and moral danger. "I think we are a very forbearing Cabinet to his chatter," Birrell said ... "First time I met him we didn't know each other. We were early for a dinner party, he picked up a book and said "Matthew Arnold's poems — who's Matthew Arnold — do you know anything about Matthew Arnold?" I said yes, he wrote poetry, etc., etc. "Oh," said Winston (shaking his fist), "this public school education. If I ever get my chance at it!" Contrast a remark he made the other evening after he had been lecturing Sir Edward on foreign politics: "The longer I live, the more certain I am I know all there is to be known." Sir Edward

---

[109] *My Diaries*: W. S. Blunt.

[110] *Evening Standard*, 22 April, 1925.

said: "Winston, very soon, will become incapable, from sheer activity of mind, of being anything in a Cabinet but Prime Minister."'[111]

*

While Churchill was pushing through his departmental reforms, he was also playing an even more important role on the great, national, centre-stage where the real drama of the years 1908 to 1911 was taking place. The scenery was floodlit, the play well-advertised and public attention was soon captured. Lloyd George was not only author of the play but the star as well, and Winston took the part of the bright young support who occasionally stole the show.

The drama began when Lloyd George succeeded Asquith as Chancellor of the Exchequer in 1908. Asquith had instituted Old Age Pensions, but Lloyd George was left to find the money for them. Besides this, more money was needed for building new dreadnoughts in the armaments race against Germany. Lloyd George's pacifism and Churchill's faithful adherence to his father's views led them both to resist the proposed increase. While the Welshman ridiculed the idea of building ships 'against nightmares', Winston assured a gathering that Germany had 'nothing to fight about, no prize to fight for, and no place to fight in'.[112] However, it was plain that Conservative alarm, expressed by the cry: 'We want eight, and we won't wait', was arousing widespread public support. Mr. McKenna, the First Lord of the Admiralty, fought Lloyd George and Churchill in the Cabinet and told them if he could not have his ships he was prepared to resign. He won the battle and the building of the dreadnoughts began.

Since Lloyd George regarded the Navy as a Tory stage prop, and believed that it was mainly 'the rich' who were agitating for more ships, he decided that they would have to pay for them; and pay for the Old Age Pensions as well. The conception of the Budget not only as a means of redressing the balance of wealth at the expense of the ruling class was a brilliant new idea which fully appealed to his Radical instincts. And there is no doubt that the scales needed tipping. 'The inequalities in those days were glaring enough and attention was being focused on them,' writes one historian. 'A popular writer on economic subjects had recently published a widely read little book comparing the distribution of wealth in the United Kingdom and

---

[111] *C. F. G. Masterman*: Lucy Masterman.

[112] *Lloyd George*: E. T. Raymond.

France, from which it appeared, according to official statistics in both countries, that in France there were twice as many small estates ranging from £500 to £10,000 as in the United Kingdom, but in the United Kingdom three times as many estates over £50,000 and four times as many over £250,000, the population of the two countries being approximately the same. The redressing of such inequalities was, from Lloyd George's point of view, the most obvious method of securing popular support.'[113]

This was not the only reason that prompted Lloyd George to produce a budget aimed at the upper classes. Looming large on the horizon was the increasing hostility between the Liberals and the Lords. Lord Lansdowne, the Conservative Leader in the Lords, was working in close concert with Arthur Balfour, the Conservative Leader in the Commons. Since the Upper House was overwhelmingly Tory, and all legislation had to win the approval of both Houses before becoming law, the Lords were able to block whatever Liberal Bills they wished, despite a huge Liberal majority. In two and a half years they had wrecked three Education Bills; a Licensing Bill; and a Scottish Land Valuation Bill. Churchill had burst out vehemently against them and Lloyd George had declared that the House of Lords had 'ceased to be the watch-dog of the Constitution, and had become "Mr. Balfour's poodle"; it barks for him; it fetches and carries for him; it bites anybody that he sets it on to.'

Lloyd George convinced Churchill that the time had come to have a show-down with the Upper House. But they must be careful of their issue for it was apparent from the by-elections that Liberal popularity was slumping badly because of the war scare. Churchill paid a long visit to Lloyd George at his home in Criccieth in September 1908, and most historians assume that they planned their strategy at this time. If they could publicize the Budget and make it appear really ferocious, they might succeed in provoking the Lords to fall into the trap of rejecting it.

Although Lloyd George and Winston both denied that they had ever devised any such ingenious plan, contemporary diaries reveal that at least the possibilities occurred to them. Mrs. Lucy Masterman describes Lloyd George discussing the prospects of the Budget in the Lords and quotes him as saying: 'I'm not sure we ought to pray for it to go through. I'm not sure we ought not to hope for its rejection. It

---

[113] *British Politics Since 1900*: D. C. Somervell.

138

would give us such a chance as we will never have again.'[114] Another prominent figure of the day, Wilfrid Blunt, quotes Churchill talking along the same lines. 'Winston gave us a very full account of what his policy in the Budget dispute with the Lords would be. He began by saying that his hope and prayer was that they would throw out the Bill, as it would save the Government from a certain defeat if the elections were put off ...'[115]

The thoughts of the two men were not only revealed in private conversations but were hinted at in public speeches. In December 1908 Lloyd George declared: 'We cannot consent to accept the present humiliating conditions of legislating by the sufferance of Lord Lansdowne. This nobleman has arrogated to himself a position he has usurped — a sovereignty no King has claimed since the ominous days of Charles I. Decrees are issued from Lansdowne House that Buckingham Palace would not dream of sending forth. We are not going to stand any longer the usurpation of King Lansdowne and his Royal consort in the Commons.'[116] Winston Churchill spoke even more plainly: 'For my part, I should be quite content to see the battle joined as speedily as possible upon the plain issue of aristocratic rule against representative government, between the reversion to Protection and the maintenance of Free Trade, between a tax on bread and a tax on — well, never mind.'[117]

At last the great day came. Lloyd George took four hours to deliver his Budget speech to the House of Commons. Churchill watched him like an anxious nannie; there was a short break half-way through and he took him out for refreshments. Judged by to-day's standards the Budget was a small affair. It showed an increase of only eleven per cent on the revenue of the previous year. The fact that it had to be approved by a Cabinet which did not have a Radical majority must be some indication that even at the time it was not regarded by law makers as revolutionary. Income-tax was steepened on incomes over £3,000 a year from 1s. to 1s. 2d. in the pound; whisky was raised from

---

[114] *C. F. G. Masterman*: Lucy Masterman.

[115] *My Diaries*: W. S. Blunt.

[116] Liverpool, 21 December.

[117] Birmingham, 13 January.

3s. 6d. to 4s. a bottle; a tax was imposed for the first time on petrol and motor cars; and there was a tax on licensed premises. The particular tax designed to hit the rich was the introduction of super-tax which amounted to 6d. in the pound on incomes over £5,000 a year. This measure affected only 11,500 people. But it meant that the highest incomes in the country were now subject to a full tax of 1s. 8d. in the pound. To-day this seems a modest demand, yet it amounted to an increase of 66% over the rate of the previous year. Besides this, death duties were raised, there was a tax on undeveloped land, and another tax on 'the unearned increment of land' — or, in other words, on the increase in the value of land.

*

At first the Budget did not provoke any great remonstrance. But since Lloyd George wished to provoke the House of Lords he soon began making violent public speeches in which he drew a sharp distinction between the wealthy business men and the wealthy landowners. The wealthy business men were all right. They worked for their money, while the wealthy landowners merely sat back and demanded it. The landowners, he declared, squeezed everyone, whether for coal royalties, building developments, or household rents. They were the enemies of the entire nation; of artisans and manufacturers, of engineers and merchants alike.

The reason why Lloyd George concentrated on the landowners was obvious; first, he had learned to hate them from childhood, and second, they composed the largest element in the House of Lords. He singled out peers for special attack on every possible occasion. Lord Rothschild made a speech protesting against the Budget at a meeting in the City of London. 'We are having too much of Lord Rothschild,' retorted Lloyd George the following day. 'We are not to have temperance reform in this country. Why? Because Lord Rothschild has sent a circular to the Peers to say so. We must have more dreadnoughts. Why? Because Lord Rothschild has told us so at a meeting in the City. We must not pay for them when we have got them. Why? Because Lord Rothschild says no. You must not have an estate duty and a super-tax. Why? Because Lord Rothschild has sent a protest on behalf of the bankers to say he won't stand it. You must not have a tax on reversions. Why? Because Lord Rothschild as chairman of an insurance company said he wouldn't stand it. You must not have a tax on undeveloped land. Why? Because Lord Rothschild is chairman of an industrial housing company. You must not have Old Age Pensions. Why? Because Lord Rothschild was a member of a

Committee that said it couldn't be done. Are we really to have all the ways of reform, financial and social, blocked by a notice board: "No thoroughfare: By order of Nathaniel Rothschild"?'

However, it was on the dukes that Lloyd George concentrated the full fury of his attack. The dukes were not merely the heads of the peerage; they were the largest landowners in Britain. To critics who accused him of driving capital out of the country, he answered that it was a lie and pointed to figures which proved that imports and exports were steadily increasing. 'Only one stock has gone down badly; there has been a great slump in dukes.' 'A fully-equipped duke,' he declared, 'costs as much to keep up as two dreadnoughts; and dukes are just as great a terror and they last longer.' Lloyd George delighted his audience by describing a nobleman's son as 'the first of the litter' and by attacking the nobleman because 'he has one man to fix his collar and adjust his tie in the morning, a couple of men to carry a boiled egg to him at breakfast, a fourth man to open the door for him, a fifth man to show him in and out of his carriage, and a sixth and seventh to drive him.'

Meantime Winston Churchill was not idle. He too was touring the country making speeches and arousing as much feeling as possible. It is interesting to compare his technique with that of Lloyd George. Lloyd George's shafts were bubbling with humour; comic, vulgar, with the sure mass appeal of the variety turn. Winston's were more solemn, more reasoned, more dignified. Lloyd George was the demagogue and Winston was the statesman. Here are some excerpts from Churchill's speeches during the year 1909.

House of Commons, 4 May. 'The chief burden of taxation is placed upon the main body of the wealthy classes of this country, a class which in number and in wealth is much greater than in any other community, if not, indeed, in any other modern State in the world; and that is a class which, in opportunities of pleasure, in all the amenities of life, and in freedom from penalties, obligations and dangers, is more fortunate than any other equally numerous class of citizens in any age or in any country. That class has more to gain than any other class of His Majesty's subjects from dwelling amid a healthy and contented people, and in a safely guarded land.'

Edinburgh, 17 July. 'We say that the State and the municipality should jointly levy a toll upon the future unearned increment of the land. A toll of what? Of the whole? No. Of a half? No. Of a quarter? No. Of a fifth — that is the proposal of the Budget. And that is robbery, that is plunder, that is communism and spoliation, that is the social revolution at last, that is the overturn of civilized society, that is the end of the world foretold in the Apocalypse. Such is the increment tax about which so much chatter and outcry are raised at the present time, and upon which I will say that no more fair, considerate, or salutary proposal for taxation has ever been made in the House of Commons.'

Norwich, 26 July. 'Is it not an extraordinary thing that upon the Budget we should even be discussing at all the action of the House of Lords? The House of Lords is an institution absolutely foreign to the spirit of the age and to the whole movement of society. It is not perhaps surprising in a country so fond of tradition, so proud of continuity as ourselves, that a feudal assembly of titled persons, with so long a history and so many famous names, should have survived to exert an influence upon public affairs at the present time. We see how often in England the old forms are reverently preserved after the forces by which they are sustained and the uses to which they are put and the dangers against which they were designed have passed away. A state of gradual decline was what the average Englishman had come to associate with the House of Lords. Little by little, we might have expected, it would have ceased to take a controversial part in practical politics. Year by year it would have faded more completely into the past to which it belongs, until, like Jack-in-the-Green or Punch and Judy, only a picturesque and fitfully lingering memory would have remained.

'And during the last ten years of Conservative government this was actually the case. But now we see the House of Lords flushed with the wealth of the modern age, armed with a party caucus, fortified, revived, resuscitated, asserting its claims in the harshest and in the crudest manner, claiming to veto or destroy even without discussion any legislation, however important, sent to them by any majority, however large, from any House of Commons, however newly elected. We see these unconscionable claims exercised with a frank and undisguised regard to party interest, to class interest, and to personal interest. We see the House of Lords using the power which they should not hold at all, which if they hold at all, they should hold in trust for all, to play a shrewd, fierce, aggressive Party game of electioneering and casting their votes according to the interest of the particular political Party to which, body and soul, they belong.'

Leicester, 5 September. 'Formerly the only question asked of the tax-gatherer was "How much have you got?" We ask that question still, and there is a general feeling, recognized as just by all parties, that the rate of taxation should be greater for large incomes than for small. As to how much greater, parties are no doubt in dispute. But now a new question has arisen. We do not only ask to-day, "How much have you got?" we also ask, "How did you get it? Did you earn it by yourself, or has it just been left you by others? Was it gained by processes which are in themselves beneficial to the community in general or was it gained by processes which have done no good to anyone, but only harm? Was it gained by the enterprise and capacity necessary to found a business, or merely by squeezing and bleeding the owner and founder of the business? Was it gained by supplying the capital which industry needs, or by denying, except at an extortionate price, the land which industry requires? Was it derived from active reproductive processes, or merely by squatting on some piece of necessary land till enterprise and labour, and national interests and municipal interests, had to buy you out at fifty times the agricultural value? Was it gained from opening new minerals to the services of man, or by drawing a mining royalty from the toil and adventure of others? Was it gained by the curious process of using political influence to convert an annual licence into a practical freehold and thereby pocketing a monopoly value which properly belongs to the State — how did you get it?" That is the new question which has been postulated and which is vibrating in penetrating repetition through the land.'

In this last speech, Churchill made some opening remarks which roused the Tory press to a storm of anger. The *Daily Express* printed a few of them under a heading 'HIS OWN RECORD FOR ABUSE OUTDONE'. Churchill had begun by complaining that the Tories had no effective speakers to answer the Liberal charges. He referred to 'the small fry of the Tory party splashing actively about in their proper puddles', then to Mr. Balfour 'who aims to lead — who has been meaning to lead for six years if he only could find out where on earth to lead to ... ' then finally to the fact that in lieu of anything else the Tory Party was forced 'to fall back on their dukes. These unfortunate individuals,' he continued, 'who ought to lead quiet, delicate, sheltered lives, far from the madding crowd's ignoble strife, have been dragged into the football scrimmage, and they have got rather roughly mauled in the process ... Do not let us be too hard on them. It is poor sport — almost like teasing goldfish. These ornamental creatures blunder on every hook they see, and there is no sport whatever in trying to catch them (Laughter). It would be barbarous to leave them gasping upon the bank of public ridicule upon which they have landed themselves. Let us put them back gently, tenderly in their fountains;

and if a few bright gold scales have been rubbed off in what the Prime Minister calls the variegated handling they have received they will soon get over it. They have got plenty more.'[118]

Although this was very mild comment in comparison with Lloyd George's attacks, the very fact that Churchill, member of a ducal family himself, had dared to cast aspersions caused widespread indignation. Councillor Howell, Tory candidate for one of the Manchester seats, declared with great pomposity that what was 'neither excusable nor permissible was the lack of common decency shown by vulgar abuse of the dukes on the part of a man who was the grandson of one duke, the nephew of another, and the cousin of a third; who belonged to a family which had produced nine dukes; who figured in Debrett as boasting a dozen titled relatives; and who owed every advantage he possessed over those whom he contemptuously called "the small fry of public life" to his ducal and aristocratic connections.'[119]

Councillor Howell was not the only opponent who hit back. During the years 1908 to 1911 Winston was subjected to a steady stream of personal abuse. Tories described him as 'utterly contemptible'. Here he was, they said, betraying his class and belittling the institutions that had made his country great, merely to gain a sordid political advantage. Of course, they went on, it was not really surprising, for the Churchills were noted for their bad blood; indeed they were one of the few powerful families in England who had never produced 'a gentleman'. Everyone knew that the first Duke was a blackguard, and that Lord Randolph was a cad and a bounder. Winston had inherited the worst qualities of both.

It is difficult for the present generation to understand the furious resentment Mr. Churchill aroused. But many English people in their late fifties remember hearing their Conservative mothers and fathers refer to him as an 'evil' man. One by one the doors of Society closed against him, for in those days the fashionable world was controlled by the Tory aristocracy. He was not invited anywhere, and when he attended public functions many people, some of them old family friends, were careful to look the other way. One duke publicly announced that he would like to put Lloyd George and Winston

---

[118] *The Times*: 6 September, 1909.

[119] *Daily Express*: 6 September, 1909.

Churchill 'in the middle of twenty couple of fox hounds'. But although Lloyd George was cordially disliked he did not arouse nearly so much animosity as his colleague. George Smalley, the American journalist who moved in London Society, explained this in a quaintly Conservative way. 'Mr. Lloyd George,' he says, 'was from the beginning an unregenerate Radical in whom all the natural and acquired vices of Radicalism were fully developed at an early age. Nothing, therefore, but Radicalism in its most extreme, socialistic form, was ever expected of him. But Mr. Churchill was born into the world a Conservative, and a Conservative he remained till Mr. Balfour, then Prime Minister, rejected his application for Cabinet office. Then he crossed the floor of the House and has ever since acted with the Liberals, who knew the value of their recruit and gave him what Mr. Balfour had denied. That is what the Conservatives tell you, and that is why their dislike of Mr. Churchill is so extreme. It does not stop short of something like social ostracism.'

So Winston became the chief target of the Opposition, and in the House of Commons was attacked tirelessly as a cynical careerist. Here are a few samples of the repetitious phrases used by Members of Parliament to describe him during the year 1909.

16 January: Austen Chamberlain declared that 'his conversion to Radicalism coincided with his personal interests.'

13 February: Alfred Lyttelton said: 'One might as well try to rebuke a brass band. He trims his sails to every passing air.'

14 September: Evelyn Cecil said: 'He has an entire lack of principle', and 'He is ready to follow any short cut to the Prime Ministership'.

10 December: Keir Hardie declared he 'well knew how to trim his sails to catch votes.'

14 June, 1910: A. B. Markham said: 'Whenever the Churchills "ratted" they thought it was going to be of benefit to themselves'.

The House of Commons was not the only place in which he was abused. Their lordships went for him as well. The following item, rather comic in its seriousness, printed in *The Times* on 4 November, 1909, is the sort of report which frequently appeared. 'Lord St. Oswald, in opening a Conservative Bazaar yesterday afternoon at Golcar, in the Colne Valley, said he belonged to a House which had got into very bad repute lately in some quarters. "We may be blackguards," continued Lord St. Oswald, "but I don't think we are ... We have got men just as good as Mr. Lloyd George, Mr. Winston Churchill and a lot more Ministers like them (Cheers). I have known

Mr. Winston Churchill since he was so high, and I don't think he has improved since then, and I think many people think the same as I do. The longer he lives the more he will go back, in my opinion. In a few years the people of this country will realize what an "outsider" he is.'

*

The outcome of the quarrel with the Lords long ago became part of history. They fell into Lloyd George's trap and rejected the Budget. To-day, historians are almost unanimous in declaring it one of the most stupid and inept political acts of the century. Ever since 1860 when all the taxes of the year, for the first time, were centred in a single Finance Bill, it had been an understood practice that the Lords did not amend or reject it. King Edward VII foresaw the crisis such an action would provoke and strongly urged Lord Lansdowne to secure the passage of the Budget, but the latter was too weak to stand up against the hot-headed reactionaries in the Party. Peers from all over Britain, known as 'the backwoods men' because they lived on their country estates and rarely attended the House of Lords, arrived on the great day to register their votes. The story soon circulated that most of them had to ask their way to Parliament.

The Liberals promptly went to the country on the slogan of 'the People versus the Peers'. Without this cry there is no doubt that the Liberals would have been soundly beaten. The middle classes were worried by 'socialist' talk. Perhaps Lloyd George was trying to establish a one-Chamber Government, perhaps even a dictatorship. The Budget was not too severe but maybe it was only a beginning; first taxes on the land and then, who knows, maybe gradual confiscation of the land. Besides this, there was still a German menace. Could this party of Radicals and pacifists be trusted to make Britain safe? These were some of the doubts and fears. 'The People versus the Peers' was strong enough to return the Liberals to power, but with a majority reduced by a hundred seats and a majority that was now dependent on the Irish nationalists.

The new Liberal Government set about drafting a Bill for the reform of the Upper House. Then King Edward died. Since the issue was a constitutional one, and the new King was bound to be involved, a moratorium was declared and both parties agreed to sit on a committee in an attempt to work out a compromise. The months dragged on, however, and the committee could not agree; finally the Liberals came out with their own solution. First, the Lords' veto was to be abolished on bills certified by the Speaker as money bills; second, any Bill passed by the House of Commons in three successive sessions was to become law despite the Lords' veto. The Liberals went to the country again to ask for a mandate for this reform. It was the second election in the same year and the result was almost the same as the first.

There was no doubt now that the Parliament Bill asking for a reform of the Upper House was 'the will of the people'. However, the Lords were still obstinate and resentful. The term 'die-hard', a regimental nickname, came into currency for the first time to describe their attitude. They drastically amended the House of Commons Parliament Bill and returned it triumphantly in its emasculated form. But the Prime Minister, Mr. Asquith, had a trump card up his sleeve. He wrote a letter to Mr. Balfour making it known that the King had agreed, if the Lords refused to pass the Bill, to swamp the Upper House by creating two hundred and fifty new Peers who would out-vote the present Conservative majority. This knowledge finally forced the Lords to capitulate, but even so it was a close call. The Bill was passed by only 131 against 114.

*

During these tempestuous years two important events took place in Winston's personal life. The first was the beginning of his friendship with F. E. Smith, later Lord Birkenhead, Lord Chancellor of England.

Mr. F. E. Smith was a Tory who began his political career as a dark horse. He had neither connections nor wealth to help him. His grandfather was a miner and his grandmother was a gypsy. The miner would not allow his son to go into the pits and consequently F.E.'s father became a barrister. He died when F.E. was only sixteen, leaving the boy to make his own way in life. The latter won a scholarship to Oxford, took his bar examinations, and five years later was earning six thousand pounds a year.

He entered Parliament in 1906 and decided to stake everything on his opening speech. Most maiden speeches are modest and uncontroversial, but F.E.'s was a fierce attack on the Government, full of lightning shafts and humorous but stinging invective. When he rose to speak Members looked at the tall, languid figure with the black patent-leather hair and the sallow unsmiling face, and asked who he was. An hour later the lobbies were ringing with his name. Never before had a newcomer scored such a triumph with a single speech. He was acknowledged at once as one of the new forces within the Tory Party. His merits continued to be recognized and soon he was famous throughout the country for his brilliant repartee and merciless wit.

At first F.E. refused to meet Winston. He did not like what he had heard of him and disapproved strongly of his desertion from the Tory Party. But one night, in 1906, the two men were introduced in the smoking-room of the House of Commons. 'From that hour our friendship was perfect,' wrote Winston. 'It was one of my most precious possessions. It was never disturbed by the fiercest Party fighting. It was never marred by the slightest personal difference or misunderstanding. It grew stronger as nearly a quarter of a century slipped by, and it lasted until his untimely death.'[120]

This friendship was perhaps even more remarkable than Churchill's relationship with Lloyd George, for it had to stand the stress and strain of bitter Party strife, with the two men facing each other from opposite camps and doing battle on almost every important issue of the time. Both men, however, possessed the rare capacity to divorce politics from personal feelings. They argued hotly, but they never allowed their differences to hinder the mutual enjoyment derived from each other's company. Often they treated the House of Commons to a fierce verbal dual which their enemies liked to suggest had been carefully rehearsed beforehand. Once F.E. remarked that Winston 'had devoted the best years of his life to his impromptu speeches.'

On another occasion Churchill showed F.E. a cartoon in which both of them appeared. The artist had drawn his characters comically, but so cleverly that there was no mistaking them. F.E. was dressed in a bearskin hat with a slightly sardonic expression on his face; Winston was short and round like a happy bulldog. 'What a wonderful caricaturist!' said Winston cheerfully. 'He gets you to a nicety. It's astonishing how like you are to your cartoons.' F.E. gazed at the picture a moment then handed it back, saying solemnly: 'You seem to be the only one who's flattered.'[121]

The Conservatives disapproved of F.E.'s friendship with Winston and warned him that it would do his career no good. But F.E. paid no attention. The two men met regularly; they spent week-ends together; they went on summer cruises; they served together in the Oxfordshire Hussars; they even founded a dining club, known as 'The Other Club', to enable politicians of opposite Parties to meet and exchange views.

---

[120] *Great Contemporaries*: Winston S. Churchill.

[121] *Great Contemporaries*: Winston S. Churchill.

'Never did I separate from him without having learnt something, and enjoyed myself besides,'[122] wrote Winston.

Many years later these two men sat in the same Cabinet together.

*

The second personal event of these memorable years was the greatest happening of Winston's life. In 1908 he was married. He met his bride, appropriately enough, in the smoke of an election battle. When he went to Scotland in 1908 to contest Dundee he was introduced to a beautiful young lady, Miss Clementine Hozier. She was the daughter of the late Colonel H. M. Hozier and Lady Blanche Hozier, and a granddaughter of the Countess of Airlie, a staunch and powerful Liberal supporter.

Miss Hozier was just twenty-three. The pictures of her published at this time show a charming oval face, hair parted in the middle, finely cut classic features and large wide-set eyes. As far as Winston was concerned it was love at first sight. Miss Hozier was not only beautiful but she was high spirited, intelligent, liberal minded, and passionately interested and amused by politics herself. Up to this time Winston had taken little interest in the female sex. Once or twice he had fancied himself enamoured but the spell had been of short duration; politics were so much more exciting than women. Besides, Winston was hard to please. Mr. George Smalley described the visit he made to New York when he was twenty-six years old and when the matchmakers had their eyes on him. 'He met everybody, but would sit in the midst of the most delightful people, absorbed in his own thoughts. He would not admire the women he was expected to admire. They must have not only beauty and intelligence, but the particular kind of beauty and intelligence which appealed to him; if otherwise, he knew how to be silent without meaning to be rude ... It was useless to remonstrate with him. He answered: "She is beautiful to you, but not to me".'[123]

Miss Hozier's mother approved of Winston as a future son-in-law. 'He is gentle and tender, and affectionate to those he loves, much hated by those who have not come under his personal charm,' she wrote to Wilfrid Blunt.[124] The wedding took place at St. Margaret's,

---

[122] Ibid.

[123] *Anglo-American Memoires*: George Smalley.

[124] *My Diaries*: W. S. Blunt.

Westminster; Lord Hugh Cecil, the ardent Tory, was best man; wedding presents were received from Winston's three most formidable opponents, Balfour and the two Chamberlains; the church was packed; the newspapers interested; and Wilfrid Blunt wrote in his diary: 'The bride was pale, as was the bridegroom. He has gained in appearance since I saw him last, and has a powerful if ugly face. Winston's responses were clearly made in a pleasant voice, Clementine's inaudible.'[125]

The marriage, as everyone knows, proved to be one of the great marriages of the century. The bride was not a *partie*. Indeed, Mrs. Sidney Webb wrote approvingly in her diary: 'On Sunday we lunched with Winston Churchill and his bride — a charming lady, well-bred and pretty, and earnest withal — but not rich, by no means a good match, which is to Winston's credit.' It was also to Winston's enduring advantage for Clementine Churchill will go down in history as a wife who loyally shared her husband's political vicissitudes and enjoyed his complete devotion for over forty years. She is a woman of courage, character and shrewd political judgment. Winston always carefully considers her opinions, and if he does not always follow her advice he is at least very much aware of what the advice was. Although Mrs. Churchill would never allow any disagreement to arise between herself and her husband in public, she does not hesitate to argue with him at home. Often her attitude towards him is protective, like a mother with a precocious, unruly child; his towards her is attentive and devoted.

The first years of their marriage were not easy for a young, gay and beautiful bride. Mrs. Churchill was not only taking on a husband, but the wrath of Society as well. Docility, however, was not part of her character and far from regretting the circumstances she welcomed them as a challenge. By instinct she was more of a Liberal than Winston. She had been brought up to distrust Tory politics, and she had a natural interest in reform. She regarded Conservative ostracism as something of a compliment and soon had created an agreeable existence for herself and her husband among a small circle of intimate friends. Blenheim was the only Tory house open to them, and in order to please Winston who was deeply sentimental about his family ties, she occasionally accompanied him on a visit. Although Churchill was censored by the Tories for being disrespectful to the dukes, his cousin,

---

[125] Ibid.

the Duke of Marlborough, managed to overlook his jibes. Consequently Churchill was criticized by his own side for seeing too much of his relative. 'The fact that Mr. Churchill thoughtlessly went to Blenheim for Christmas [1910],' writes E. T. Raymond, one of Lloyd George's biographers, 'somewhat diminished the effects of his comrade's oratory.' However, on one occasion, when the Duke of Marlborough made disobliging remarks about Mr. Asquith, Mrs. Churchill packed her bags and left; and she could not be induced to go there for many months.

The fact that the Churchills began their life together cut off from Society and dependent on their own resources, gave their marriage a sure foundation.

*

Although Winston was hated more than Lloyd George, the Welshman was the undisputed master. As Chancellor of the Exchequer he held the Radical leadership firmly in his hands; he made the decisions; he conceived the strategy; he played the trump cards. While Winston was almost as great a figure in the public eye, behind the scenes he acknowledged Lloyd George as his leader. People who remember them together say that Lloyd George was the only man to whom Churchill ever deferred. The quick-witted Welshman knew how to charm and control his high-spirited subordinate as nobody else had ever succeeded in doing. Indeed the relationship of the master and the pupil continued throughout the years, long after Churchill ceased to be under Lloyd George's political influence in any way. Robert Boothby, a Tory M.P., who was Winston's Parliamentary Private Secretary when the latter became Chancellor of the Exchequer in the Conservative Government of 1924, says that for a time Churchill and Lloyd George drifted apart. Then one day Winston asked Boothby to make an appointment for him to see L.G. 'Lloyd George,' writes Mr. Boothby, 'came to his room in the evening, and remained there for about half an hour. When he had gone, I waited for the summons. None came, so I went in and found the Chancellor sitting in his armchair before the fire, in a brown study. "It is a remarkable tiling," he observed, "but L.G. hadn't been in this room for three minutes before the old relationship was completely re-established." I was delighted. He then looked up with a twinkle in his eye, and added: "The relationship of master and servant".'[126]

---

[126] *I Fight to Live*: Robert Boothby.

What was unusual about the association of these two titans was an almost total lack of jealousy. Once Lloyd George remarked: 'Sometimes when I see Winston making these speeches I get a flash of jealousy and I have to say to myself, "Don't be a fool. What's the use of getting jealous of Winston?"' And occasionally Winston felt a twinge of envy over the limelight Lloyd George won with the Budget. When he was not asked to speak in the Commons on the third reading of the Bill lie was annoyed but made up for it by airing his views on the public platform. 'You see,' he said to Lloyd George, 'in spite of your trying to keep me out of the Budget, I made a show after all.' 'I like that,' said Lloyd George. 'I offered to hand you over the whole of Part II, the income tax.' 'Oh, that's detail,' said Winston scornfully, 'I'm not going to do detail.'[127]

Mrs. Masterman goes on to tell how amusing they were together 'with their different weaknesses and their different childishnesses'. She describes them one night at dinner. 'At one point Winston said "I am all for the social order." George, who had had a glass of champagne, which excites him without in the least confusing him, sat up in his chair and said: "No! I'm against it. Listen. There were six hundred men turned off by the G.W. works last week. Those men had to go out into the streets to starve. There is not a man in that works who does not live in terror of the day when his turn will come to go. Well, I'm against a social order that admits that kind of thing." And he made a beckoning gesture I have seen him use once or twice. "Yeth, yeth," said Winston, hurriedly, subdued for a moment, and then rather mournfully: "I suppose that was what lost us Cricklade." "Yes, and Swindon," said George. Winston cocked his nose in a way he does when he knows he's going to be impertinent. "That's just what I say," he answered, "you are not against the social order, but against those parts of it that get in your way," and George crumpled up with amusement.'[128]

*

Although Churchill was constantly attacked, in conjunction with Lloyd George, as the wicked inspiration of the 'class war' — and nobody would deny that his speeches were formidable assaults against the fortress of privilege — behind the scenes he was a moderating

---

[127] *C. F. G. Masterman*: Lucy Masterman.

[128] *C. F. G. Masterman*: Lucy Masterman.

influence. Indeed, it is obvious from reading the memoirs and diaries of the time that from the middle of 1910 onwards, Churchill's Radicalism began to diminish. Mrs. Masterman quotes Lloyd George as declaring that Winston was not in favour of the heatedly controversial Land Tax which probably encouraged the Lords to reject the Budget more than any other item. Winston was eager for reform but did not want to impose any unnecessary penalties on the ruling class. What he called 'revolutionary talk' upset him, and Mrs. Masterman describes an evening she spent with Winston, Lloyd George and her husband. When the last two began talking in fun 'of the revolutionary measures they were proposing next: the guillotine in Trafalgar Square; the nominating for the first tumbril,' Winston became more and more indignant and alarmed, 'until they suggested that this would give him a splendid opportunity of figuring as the second Napoleon of the revolutionary forces, when, still perfectly serious, Winston, as George put it, seemed to think there was something in it. "It is extraordinary," said George, "I had no idea anyone could have so little humour."'[129] That night Winston walked home with Masterman. He was still very much perturbed by the conversation. "If this is what it leads to," he said solemnly, "you must be prepared for me to leave you!"'

Winston, it appears from this diary, was not in favour of abolishing the Lords' Veto. He was willing to reform the Upper House but he did not wish to lessen their powers, and on more than one occasion he had heated arguments with Lloyd George on the subject. Mrs. Masterman describes a dinner which she and her husband had with Lloyd George, in the course of which the latter said: 'Winston was up here last night and he got just as he did that time in the spring. You remember, Masterman, he began to fume and kick up the hearth rug, and became very offensive, saying: "You can go to Hell your own way, I won't interfere. I'll have nothing to do with your ——policy," and was almost threatening until I reminded him that no man can rat twice.' Mrs. Masterman commented on this by writing: 'Winston, of course, is not a democrat, or at least, he is a Tory democrat. He cursed Charlie one night when they dined together *à deux*, swearing he would resign sooner than accept a Veto policy again and spend four years with Sir Ernest Cassel, getting rich: then again and again repeating: "No, no, no; I won't follow George if he goes back to that d——d Veto." Three

---

[129] Ibid.

weeks afterwards he was making passionate speeches in favour of the Veto policy. He became cantankerous and very difficult, and, said George, "for three weeks while he is at a thing, he is very persistent, but he always comes to heel in the end," which is a very true description.

'Once in the spring he made a quite excellent speech on the Veto in the House of Commons, although that very morning he had been abusing the Government policy up hill and down dale to Charlie. "If we," said George, "put a special clause in the Budget exempting 'Sonny' (the Duke of Marlborough) from taxation, Winston would let us do what we liked."'

Although Winston argued and fought with Lloyd George behind the scenes, in public he presented an absolutely united front. He never stooped to intrigue, or allowed himself to belittle his leader in any way. He was completely loyal; and the reward of this loyalty was a friendship unique among politicians.

*

Winston's deflection from the Radical and Isolationist line he had adopted for four years began with his appointment as Home Secretary in 1910, and was completed by the time he was appointed First Lord of the Admiralty in 1911. During the year he spent as Home Secretary he accomplished important prison reforms. But he also took actions which were most bitterly resented by the Leftist and Labour circles and are held against him to this day.

As Home Secretary Winston was responsible for the maintenance of law and order. The years 1910 to 1911 heralded an epidemic of serious strikes, and his task was neither easy nor enviable. First came a bitter coal strike in South Wales in which his actions were misunderstood and deeply resented by the miners. As recently as the 1950 General Election Welsh Socialists revived the events of that time, now generally grouped together and referred to as 'Tonypandy', declaring that he had sent soldiers to attack the miners. Churchill hotly denied the charge, and informed a Cardiff audience that the allegation was a 'cruel lie'.[130]

Here are the facts. The coal strike broke out during the first week in November. There were riots and a number of mines were partially flooded. On the morning of 8 November Churchill received a telegram from the Chief Constable of Glamorgan declaring that the local police

---

[130] *Daily Mail*: 9 February, 1950.

were incapable of maintaining order and that he had applied for troops from Southern Command. The Liberal Party was facing a General Election and Winston at once realized the undesirability of using the military against miners. He prevented the War Office from sending troops on a large scale, and quickly made plans to reinforce the Welsh police with 850 Metropolitan police. At the same time, however, after a consultation with Mr. Haldane, the Secretary of State for War, Churchill agreed to send a limited number of troops as a safeguard.[131] Churchill asked that both soldiers and police be placed under the command of a high Army officer, General Macready, and made it clear that the latter must be responsible, not to the War Office, but to himself as Home Secretary.[132]

On that same morning, 8 November, he sent a telegram to the Chief Constable of Glamorgan, informing him that 250 constables of the London Metropolitan Police would arrive at Pontypridd that evening. 'Expect these forces will be sufficient,' his telegram read, 'but as further precautionary measure, 200 cavalry will be moved into district to-night and remain there pending the cessation of trouble. General Macready will command the military, and will act in conjunction with civil authorities as circumstances may require. Military will not, however, be available, unless it is clear that police reinforcements are unable to cope with the situation.'[133]

In relating the events to the House of Commons on 11 February, 1911, Churchill said that shortly after this message was sent he was able to get into telephonic communication with the Chief Constable who told him that he believed the Metropolitan Police would be sufficient, and that there was very little accommodation for soldiers as well as police at Pontypridd. Churchill then sent a message, through the War Office, for the cavalry to detrain at Cardiff. 'But orders were also sent to General Macready,' he continued in his speech to the House of Commons, 'who was also travelling to Cardiff, that if any

---

[131] When Keir Hardie asked in the House of Commons on 15 November, 1910, 'at whose instance' the troops had been sent to Wales, Haldane replied: 'they were sent at my instance after careful consultation with my rt. hon. Friend, the Home Secretary.'

[132] *Annals of an Active Life*: General Sir Nevil Macready.

[133] *Hansard*: 11 February, 1911.

further request of special emergency reached him from the Chief Constable on the spot he could use his own discretion about going forward with the cavalry that night ... About eight o'clock telephonic communication was received that there was rioting in progress, and we immediately telegraphed to General Macready to move into the district with his squadrons, only one of which had up to that time arrived at Cardiff. He had already received authority to do so, and had, in fact, acted in anticipation of that message half an hour earlier.'[134]

Macready had strict instructions that the soldiers were to be kept apart from the strikers, and used only to guard mine premises in conjunction with the police, unless the latter found themselves unable to deal with the situation. He meticulously observed his orders, and in most cases police proved equal to the task, and troops were not brought into direct contact with the miners.

On two or three occasions, however, he found it necessary to call out the military to prevent the police from being heavily stoned. 'In order to counter these tactics on the part of the strikers on the next occasion when trouble was afoot,' wrote General Macready, 'small bodies of infantry on the higher ground, keeping level with the police on the main road, moved slowly down the side tracks, and by a little gentle persuasion with the bayonet drove the stone-throwers into the arms of the police on the lower road. The effect was excellent; no casualties were reported, though it was rumoured that many young men of the valley found that sitting down was accompanied by a certain amount of discomfort for many days. As a general instruction the soldiers had been warned that if obliged to use their bayonets they

---

[134] One of the riots that took place on the evening of 8 November was in Tonypandy Square. The strikers attempted to attack the colliery in protest against the owners' lock-out notices, and were driven away by the local police. On their way back they smashed and looted the shops in Tonypandy Square in what *The Times* described as 'an orgy of naked anarchy'. In view of the many erroneous accounts given of this well-known incident it is necessary to emphasize that neither London police nor troops arrived in the district in time to take any part in the scene. Order was restored by the local police. (See *Hansard*, 7 February, 1911, p. 231.)

should only be applied to that portion of the body traditionally held by trainers of youth to be reserved for punishment.'[135]

No matter how 'gentle' the 'persuasion' of the bayonet the very fact that this weapon was used, and men were hurt by it, aroused the miners to fury. Wild and exaggerated stories spread throughout South Wales. And thus Mr. Churchill fell between two stools. His desire to avoid the use of the military, successful in 99% of the instances, was not appreciated. As a result for nearly forty years he has been accused of sending troops 'to attack the miners'. Keir Hardie, one of the founders of the Labour Party and a Member of Parliament, contributed to this interpretation by publishing a powerful little booklet entitled Killing No Murder in which he wrote: 'Once more the Liberals are in office and Asquith is Prime Minister, and troops are let loose upon the people to shoot down if need be whilst they are fighting for their legitimate rights. They will give you Insurance Bills, they will give you all kinds of soothing syrups to keep you quiet, but in the end your Liberal Party, just like your Tory Party, is the Party of the rich and exists to protect the rich when Labour and Capital come into conflict.'

In the House of Commons Winston took full responsibility for the presence of troops in the Welsh valleys, declaring that they would be withdrawn when he decided they were 'no longer necessary'.[136] In the light of after events it seems clear that it would have been wiser if Churchill had not stationed them in South Wales at all, but had held them in reserve in a neighbouring county. However, the ironical part of the story is the fact that Churchill was strongly criticized in the House of Commons for exactly the opposite reason by the powerful Conservative Opposition, which was eager to prove Liberal inefficiency at the imminent General Election. The Tories argued that he should have sent troops a week earlier to take charge of the situation, and if this had been done all damage to property would have been prevented. But General Macready in a fair and unbiased account praises Churchill for having sent the London police. 'It was entirely due to Mr. Churchill's foresight in sending a strong force of Metropolitan Police directly he was aware of the state of affairs in the valleys that bloodshed was avoided, for had the police not been in

---

[135] *Annals of an Active Life*: General Sir Nevil Macready.

[136] *Hansard*: 24 November, 1910, p. 426.

strength sufficient to cope with the rioters there would have been no alternative but to bring the military into action.'[137]

Next came the dock strikes and railway strikes of August 1911. The anger 'Tonypandy' had aroused among the working people had not fully impressed itself on Churchill, for this time he did not hesitate to call upon the military in force. He declared that the nation was on the brink of a national railway strike and dispatched troops in all directions without even waiting for the local authorities to ask for them.

Once again he was furiously attacked by Labour Members in the House, and defended himself by saying: 'The task which was entrusted to the military forces was to keep the railways running, to safeguard the railways, to protect the railwaymen who were at work, to keep the railways running for the transportation of food supplies and raw materials. And it was necessary, if they were to discharge that task, that the General commanding each area into which the country is divided, the General responsible for each of the different strike areas, should have full liberty to send troops to any point on the line so that communications should not be interrupted. That is how it arose, of course, that on Saturday the soldiers arrived at places to protect railway stations and signal boxes, goods yards, and other points on the line without their having been requisitioned by the local authorities.'[138]

There was a feeling in Parliament, however, that Churchill revelled in strong measures; that in this case instead of using troops as a last resort his first instinct has been to turn to the military. Ramsay MacDonald reminded him in biting tones that these were not the sort of methods that the average Englishman liked, whether his party was Liberal, Tory or Socialist.

'This is not a mediaeval State, and it is not Russia. It is not even Germany. We have discovered a secret which very few countries have hitherto discovered. The secret this nation has discovered is that the way to maintain law and order is to trust the ordinary operations of a law-abiding and orderly-inclined people … If the Home Secretary had just a little more knowledge of how to handle masses of men in these critical times, if he had a somewhat better instinct of what civil liberty

---

[137] *Annals of an Active Life*: General Sir Nevil Macready.

[138] *Hansard*: 22 August, 1911.

does mean, and if he had a somewhat better capacity to use the powers which he has got as Home Secretary, we should have had much less difficulty in the last four or five days in facing and finally settling the very difficult problem we have had before us.'[139]

Indeed, the sending of troops was so deeply resented by the labour ranks it nearly resulted in a General Strike. 'This military intervention,' wrote Elie Halévy, 'was not always successful. If in London the dispute was peaceably settled by an agreement concluded on August 11, it was not so at Liverpool where the presence of the Irish element no doubt gave the strike a peculiarly violent character. One day the offices of the Shipping Federation were burnt down. Another day the soldiers used their rifles and there were casualties. They were, to be sure, local disturbances. But by the indignation they aroused throughout the working class they provoked, or came within an ace of provoking, another social crisis of a more formidable character.'[140]

At this point Lloyd George stepped in with permission from the Cabinet to act as a negotiator. He was completely successful. He not only brought the railway strike to an end, but left the impression that if his tact and persuasiveness had been employed sooner labour relations would never have reached such a pitch. Winston on the other hand had merely widened the deep antagonism which was now firmly established between himself and the working class.

*

In January, before the railway strike and after the Welsh coal stoppage, an incident took place which provided the country with a certain amount of comic relief, but at the same time gave further ammunition to Churchill's enemies. It was known as 'The Siege of Sidney Street'. In January 1911 the police telephoned the Home Secretary and informed him that they had cornered a gang of desperadoes, among whom was 'Peter the Painter', an anarchist responsible for recent murders of the police in Houndsditch. The men were entrenched in a house in Sidney Street in Stepney. No one knew how many there were but they appeared to have plenty of ammunition and probably some home-made bombs. Churchill could not resist the excitement. Dressed in a top-hat and a fur-lined overcoat with an astrakhan collar, and

---

[139] Ibid.

[140] *A History of the English People*: Elie Halévy.

accompanied by the Chief of the C.I.D., the Commissioner of the City Police and the head of the political section of Scotland Yard, he hurried to the scene. The house was surrounded by several hundred armed police reinforced by a small file of Scots Guards, equipped with a Maxim gun, who had been summoned from the Tower. The Guards were firing on the house and occasionally from the broken windows a bullet answered back. One policeman had been wounded.

Hugh Martin, a journalist who was present at the scene, described Mr. Churchill as 'altogether an imposing figure'. 'Peeping round corners he exposed himself with the Scots Guards to the random fire of the besieged burglars, or consulted with his "staff" in tones of utmost gravity ... He agreed that it might be an excellent thing to have in reserve a couple of field guns from the Royal Horse Artillery depot at St. John's Wood, and that a party of Royal Engineers from Chatham might be useful if mining operations had to be undertaken against the citadel. He even suggested that casualties might be avoided if steel plates were brought from Woolwich to form a portable cover for the military sharpshooters — an early version of one of his ideas in the Great War.'[141]

Soon wisps of smoke began to rise from the windows, and half an hour later the house was burning fiercely. Fire engines arrived and quickly got to work. When the police finally entered the ruins, instead of a formidable gang, they found only two charred bodies; and neither belonged to Peter the Painter.

The Conservatives made as much of the story as they could. They ridiculed Churchill for the troops and the field gun, for the false excitement and self-advertisement. Arthur Balfour commented sarcastically in the House: 'We are concerned to observe photographs in the Illustrated Papers of the Home Secretary in the danger zone. I can understand what the photographer was doing but not the Home Secretary.'

Winston's Liberal colleagues were also sarcastic. The soldier seemed to be much more prominent these days than the Radical. Were the Tories right? Was he purely an adventurer at heart? In 1912 A. G. Gardiner published a character sketch in the *Daily News* which showed how far Liberal feeling had changed towards him:

'He is always unconsciously playing a part — an heroic part. And he is himself his most astonished spectator. He sees himself moving

---

[141] *Battle: The Life Story of Winston Churchill*: Hugh Martin.

through the smoke of battle — triumphant, terrible, his brow clothed with thunder, his legions looking to him for victory, and not looking in vain. He thinks of Napoleon; he thinks of his great ancestor. Thus did they bear themselves; thus in this rugged and awful crisis, will he bear himself. It is not make-believe, it is not insincerity; it is that in this fervid and picturesque imagination there are always great deeds afoot, with himself cast by destiny in the Agamemnon role. Hence that portentous gravity that sits on his youthful shoulders so oddly, those impressive postures and tremendous silences, the body flung wearily in the chair, the head resting gloomily in the hand, the abstracted look, the knitted brow. Hence that tendency to exaggerate a situation which is so characteristic of him — the tendency that sent artillery down to Sidney Street and during the railway strike dispatched the military hither and thither as though Armageddon was upon us. "You've mistaken a coffee-stall row for the social revolution," said one of his colleagues to him as he pored with knitted and portentous brows over a huge map of the country on which he was making his military dispositions.'[142]

This paragraph was often gleefully quoted by Winston's Tory opponents during the next few years. But once World War I had begun, they found it convenient to omit the three sentences that followed. Gardiner had gone on to say: 'Hence his horrific picture of the German menace. He believes it all because his mind once seized with an idea works with enormous velocity round it, intensifies it, makes it shadow the whole sky. In the theatre of his mind it is always the hour of fate and the crack of doom.'

Alas, that fate was not only in Winston's imagination.

---

[142] Reprinted in *Pillars of Society*: A. G. Gardiner.

Part Four
World War I

Chapter Ten — Prologue at the Admiralty

THE YEAR 1911 marked a turning point in Winston Churchill's life. On 1 July, a German gunboat, the *Panther*, suddenly stationed itself off the obscure Atlantic port of Agadir on the North African coast. This was a direct threat to French expansion in the Mediterranean. The Chancelleries of Europe were electrified and for three months the western world hovered on the brink of war. Churchill's eyes opened with a start as he at last became conscious of the peril that threatened England. For eleven years he had followed first in his father's footsteps, and then in Lloyd George's, as an apostle of 'Peace, Retrenchment and Reform'. The championing of these ideas had cast him in the strangely incongruous role of 'The Little Englander'; the opponent of a strong Army and Navy; the darling of the pacifists; the provincial reformer so engrossed in tidying up his house that he could not see the approaching tornado.

Overnight he abandoned retrenchment. His ardour for prison reform died as his powerful mind swung on to world affairs. For the first time since he had become a Member of Parliament he began to think independently. And although neither he nor anyone else realized it at the time, he had finally veered on to his true course, as a champion of the might and right of Britain.

The Agadir incident, as it became known, was a highlight in a series of events which began at the beginning of the century when Germany decided to build a large Navy. Germany was young and virile. She was already the strongest military power on the Continent. This fact had worried the French for some time, but it had not aroused much concern among the English who believed they could remain safely aloof in their island fortress with their Navy the undisputed ruler of the sea lanes of the world. But when Germany published a new Fleet Law in 1900 revealing that the Emperor not only wished to control the greatest army in Europe but to rival English sea power as well, the British Foreign Office became alarmed. The preamble of the Fleet Law stated: 'In order to protect German trade and commerce under existing conditions, only one thing will suffice, namely, Germany must possess a battle fleet of such strength that, even for the most powerful naval adversary, a war would involve such risks as to make that Power's own supremacy doubtful.'

Why did Germany want this vast Navy? Against whom was it intended? The British could find only one answer: and that was the beginning of the fear that led to protective alliances; and the alliances that involved them in war. Throughout her history Britain had always allied herself with the second strongest power on the Continent, gathering to her banner small states eager to maintain their independence. It therefore seemed natural to the English that in 1904, when the Kaiser in a flamboyant speech was proclaiming himself 'The Admiral of the Atlantic', that Britain should be making an entente with France.

The *entente* proved of mutual advantage to both countries. The French agreed to give the British a free hand in Egypt and the British agreed to help France round off her North African Empire by the acquisition of Morocco. In the minds of both nations was the belief that it would be a good thing to keep Germany out of the Mediterranean. The Kaiser was indignant. In 1905 he paid a visit to Tangier, in Morocco, and made a speech declaring that his friend, the Sultan, must remain absolutely independent. The result was a twelve months' 'cold war', but Britain stood steadfastly by France and in the end the Germans sulkily backed down.

It is well to remind the reader that in those days diplomacy was for the few and the very few. The British public had little say in Foreign Affairs. And when one speaks of 'the Government' deciding this or that, one means the Prime Minister, the Foreign Secretary, and perhaps one or two other leading Ministers, but by no means the whole of the Cabinet. With this in mind it does not seem so strange that while 'the Government' was strengthening its relations with France and keeping an anxious eye on Germany, the Cabinet also decided, in 1906, to cut down Britain's shipbuilding programme. Winston Churchill and Lloyd George led the attack on naval armaments, while Sir Edward Grey, the Foreign Secretary, quietly went on his way building up a diplomatic bulwark against Germany.

In 1907 Sir Edward made an alliance with France's ally, Russia, which led to another 'cold war' scare in 1908. Germany's ally, Austria, stole a march on Russia by proclaiming the annexation of Bosnia, a Turkish province which Russia regarded as within her 'sphere of influence'. Russia was compelled to forgo her authority, but British public opinion was stirred; and that was the year that the clamour for eight new warships reached its height.

Meantime France went ahead with her conquest of Morocco, offering Germany as compensation a part of French Equatorial Africa. When the German gunboat was sent to Agadir in 1911 to enforce French generosity the situation reached its third climax. Once again the Anglo-French *entente* held firm and once again Germany retreated from her stand. Lloyd George played a sudden and surprising part in the crisis, making it clear that Britain was in no mood to be bullied.

Up to this time there had been a cleavage between Sir Edward Grey as leader of the Liberal Imperialists and Lloyd George as leader of the Liberal pacifists. Churchill relates in *The World Crisis* how he met Lloyd George several weeks after Germany had shown her mailed fist. Lloyd George was due to make a speech to the City bankers that evening, at an annual dinner at the Mansion House. 'He saw quite clearly the course to take ... He pointed out that Germany was acting as if England did not count in the matter in any way; that she had completely ignored our strong representation; that she was proceeding to put the most severe pressure on France; that a catastrophe might ensue; and that if it was to be averted we must speak with great decision and act at once.'

Consequently Lloyd George's speech contained a passage that fell on German ears like a thunderbolt. 'If a situation were forced upon us,' he said, 'in which peace could only be preserved by the surrender of the great and beneficent position Britain has won by centuries of heroism and achievement, by allowing Britain to be treated where her interests were vitally affected as if she were of no account in the Cabinet of nations, then I say emphatically that peace at that price would be a humiliation intolerable for a great country like ours to endure.'

The Germans were not only astonished but furious. The German Ambassador was recalled in disgrace for portraying Lloyd George as a 'pacifist'; and once again after three agitated months, the crisis passed. 'People think,' complained Lloyd George, 'that because I was a pro-Boer I am anti-war in general, and that I should faint at the mention of a cannon.'

*

The Agadir episode was a turning point in Churchill's life. Some men are so exhilarated by a sense of danger that a sudden surge of new power seems to rise within them. Winston was one of these. The prospect of a great conflict obsessed him and he could think of little else. How could he keep his mind on Home Office matters when life and death were in the balance? How could he interest himself in strikes and Suffragettes when at any moment Germany might strike at Britain? He had always believed himself to be a Man of Destiny. His colossal self-confidence, which some people unkindly referred to as egotism, and his almost superstitious attitude towards life had led him to analyse his position a hundred times. He often dwelt on the chance encounters, the narrow escapes, the impulsive decisions that had carried him so far along the road to power. It must all be for some definite purpose. First he had thought his destiny lay in avenging his father; then in helping the poor; now he was certain his mission was to save England. In the middle of August, a few weeks after the Agadir incident, he went to the country and sat on a hilltop looking over the beautiful green fields and meditating about the perils of war. The words of Housman's *A Shropshire Lad* kept running through his head:

> *On the idle hill of summer,*
> *Sleepy with the sound of streams,*
> *Far I hear the distant drummer*
> *Drumming like a noise in dreams.*
> *Far and near and low and louder,*
> *On the roads of earth go by,*
> *Dear to friends and food for powder,*
> *Soldiers marching, all to die.*

With the gathering storm 'fiercely illuminated' in his mind, he set out to learn all he could of military and foreign affairs. Parliament was not sitting, but he remained in London throughout the hot weeks of August devouring documents and picking the brains of General Wilson, the Director of Military Operations, and Sir Edward Grey, the Foreign Secretary. Grey and Churchill often met in the late afternoon, and strolled across the park together to the Royal Automobile Club for a swim.

Churchill did not suffer from timidity and before a fortnight had passed he was offering advice to both Wilson and Grey. He began to bombard the Cabinet with suggestions and directives signed 'W.S.C.' The first of these was entitled *Military Aspects of the Continental Problem* — Memorandum by Mr. Churchill. This outline suggested that the War Office took too sanguine a view of the potential resistance of the French Army. Winston prophesied that by the twentieth day the French would be 'driven from the line of the Meuse and will be falling back on Paris and the South'. He then went on to say that he believed by the fortieth day the Germans would be extended at full strength both internally and on their war fronts, and that if the French Army had not been squandered the Allies should be able to execute their main counterstroke. General Wilson referred to the document as 'ridiculous and fantastic — a silly memorandum', but events proved Churchill right; the Battle of the Marne was lost by Germany on the forty-second day.

Winston's passionate concern with the German menace induced the Prime Minister to invite him to join the Committee of Imperial Defence. This was virtually an Inner Cabinet. Its members consisted of the Prime Minister, the Foreign Secretary, the Chancellor of the Exchequer and the War Minister, Lord Haldane. The Committee met on 23 August to consider what action Britain would take if France were attacked. And at this particular meeting it was disclosed that a vital and astonishing difference of opinion existed between the War Office and the Admiralty. Lord Haldane, as War Minister, had built up an Expeditionary Force to go abroad as soon as war started. Plans had been drawn up in conjunction with French staff officers for British troops to strengthen the French left wing as rapidly as possible.

Incredible as it may seem, there had been no joint consultation with the Navy, and the Admiralty had made no plans for conveying the Force across the Channel. In fact, the Admiralty did not want an army sent across the Channel. The sailors were certain that the Navy could handle the situation alone. They would sink the German Fleet, and blockade the German ports, and soon the whole conflict would be over. This was the gist of the remarks made at the meeting by the Admiralty spokesman who urged that Lord Haldane's Expeditionary Force be abandoned and that the Army concentrate its attention on small raids on the German coast in conjunction with the Navy.

Needless to say Lord Haldane left the meeting greatly perturbed. He could expect no help from his colleague, Reginald McKenna, the First Lord of the Admiralty, for although McKenna had courageously pressed for a full-blooded naval programme, he supported the Admiralty view as far as strategy was concerned. It was clear to Haldane that McKenna must be removed to another office and a new First Lord appointed. He wrote the Prime Minister a strong letter: 'I have after mature consideration come to the conclusion that this, in the existing state of Europe, is the gravest problem which confronts the Government to-day; and that, unless it is tackled resolutely, I cannot remain in office. Five years' experience of the War Office has taught me how to handle the Generals and how to get the best out of them; and I believe that the experience makes me the best person to go to the Admiralty and carry through as thorough a reorganization there as I have carried out at the War Office. In any event, I am determined that things at the Admiralty shall not remain any longer as they are.'[143]

Haldane was a man of intellect and broad vision. He had done a brilliant job in reorganizing the Army along modern lines. He was admired by his colleagues and respected by his opponents. He was a lifelong Liberal and a close friend of Asquith. He was eager to take on the Admiralty job. What made Asquith choose Churchill instead?

There is no doubt that Asquith was deeply impressed by Winston's dynamic ability. He always read his memoranda carefully; they were unfailingly concise and well-written, which appealed to his legal mind. 'I believe I owed the repeated advancements to great offices which he accorded me,' wrote Winston, 'more to my secret writing on Government business than to any impressions produced by conversations or speeches on the platform or in Parliament.'[144] Besides, Asquith was amused by Winston whom he often referred to as 'my right honourable and picturesque colleague'. There were several strong arguments in Churchill's favour; firstly, the Admiralty might be induced to accept the policy of the War Office if someone other than the War Minister took on the job; secondly, it would be an advantage to keep the First Lord in the Commons; thirdly, Asquith undoubtedly felt that it was wise to keep the rebellious Churchill fully occupied and using his energies constructively. Lloyd George urged Asquith strongly to appoint Churchill.

The Prime Minister invited the two Ministers to join him on a holiday in Scotland. Winston arrived two days before Haldane and on the second afternoon, as they were leaving the golf course, Asquith suddenly asked him if he would like to go to the Admiralty. 'Indeed I would,' replied Winston. The Prime Minister then said they must discuss the matter with Haldane when he arrived the following day. It must have been an extraordinary meeting, with Asquith sitting as the imperturbable judge, and Haldane and Churchill advancing with all their skill and forensic ability the reasons why each considered himself the right man for the job. Haldane gave an account of it in a letter to Sir Edward Grey: 'Asquith asked me to see him first alone and then with Winston. I did so without mincing matters. Winston was very good, reasoned that if he went there [the Admiralty] he would work

---

[143] *Haldane*: Sir Frederick Maurice.

[144] *Great Contemporaries*: Winston S. Churchill.

closely with me at the War Office, in the spirit of his father, who had always said that there ought to be a common administration. I felt, however, that, full of energy as he is, he does not know his problem or the vast field of thought that has to be covered. Moreover, though I did not say this to him, I feel that it was only a year since he had been doing his best to cut down mechanized armies, and that the Admiralty would receive the news of his advent with dismay; for they would think, wrongly or rightly, that as soon as the financial pinch begins to come eighteen months from now, he would want to cut down. He is too apt to act first and think afterwards, though of his energy and courage one cannot speak too highly.'[145]

Several days later the Prime Minister wrote to Haldane that he had decided in favour of Churchill. 'The main and, in the longer run, the deciding factor with me in a different sense, has been the absolute necessity for keeping the First Lord in the Commons.'[146]

Churchill was overjoyed with the appointment. Now he was sure of his mission. When he was undressing for bed, on the night Asquith had first suggested the Admiralty to him, he picked up the, Bible from his table and opened it at random. His eyes fell on the following passage: 'Hear, O Israel, Thou art to pass over Jordan this day, to go in to possess nations greater and mightier than thyself, cities great and fenced up to heaven.

'A people great and tall, and children of the Anakims, whom thou knowest, and of whom thou hast heard say, Who can stand before the children of Anak!

'Understand therefore this day, that the Lord thy God is he which goeth over before thee; as a consuming fire he shall destroy them, and he shall bring them down before thy face; so shalt thou drive them out, and destroy them quickly, as the Lord has said unto thee.'

To Churchill's strangely superstitious mind it seemed 'a message full of reassurance'.[147]

*

Churchill threw himself into his new job heart and soul. Like the other Government departments which he had controlled, the Admiralty at

---

[145] *Haldane*: Sir Frederick Maurice.

[146] *Haldane*: Sir Frederick Maurice.

[147] *The World Crisis*: Winston S. Churchill.

once felt the impact of his powerful personality. He began by heightening the drama of an already dramatic situation. First of all he ordered that Naval Officers, as well as resident clerks, must remain on duty all night at the Admiralty so that if a surprise attack came not a moment would be lost in giving the alarm. Secondly, he gave instructions for a huge chart of the North Sea to be hung on the wall of his room. Every day a staff officer marked the positions of the German Fleet with flags. 'I made a rule to look at this chart once every day when I first entered my room. I did this less to keep myself informed, for there were many other channels of information, than in order to inculcate in myself and those working with me a sense of ever present danger. In this spirit we all worked.'[148]

Churchill's overall commission was to put the Fleet into 'a state of instant and constant readiness for war in case we are attacked by Germany.' Behind these broad instructions two immediate tasks confronted him: first, to set up a Naval War Staff, such as the Army possessed, which would give all its time to the study of strategy and tactics; second, to maintain close co-operation with the War Office and concert the fighting plans of the two services.

Churchill at once put himself in touch with Lord Fisher, that brilliant, explosive, astonishing old man of seventy-one, who had recently retired as First Sea Lord and was regarded by many as 'the greatest sailor since Nelson'. Fisher was living in retirement in Italy. He had burning black eyes, a rugged face and a fiery temperament. The passion of his life was the Navy, and in this field he was a genius. When he first joined the service in 1854 the Navy's ships still carried sails, many had no auxiliary steam and none had armour. He grew up in a period of change and was fascinated by the amazing new developments. When he became First Sea Lord himself the changes came fast and furiously and soon the British Fleet was far ahead of all others in modern and efficient design. Fisher scrapped dozens of ships which he declared could 'neither fight nor run away'. He reorganized the Navy's educational system, introduced the submarine, and replaced the Battle Fleet's twelve-inch guns with thirteen point fives, the biggest ever tried.

In carrying out these changes 'Jackie' Fisher made many enemies. 'Ruthless, relentless and remorseless' were words that he often repeated proudly to describe himself. With his terrific drive and his

---

[148] Ibid.

pig-headedness he struck at his opponents savagely. He branded as traitors those who opposed him either secretly or openly, and boasted childishly that 'their wives should be widows, their children fatherless, and their homes a dunghill'. This threat was not altogether meaningless for he ruined the professional career of more than one officer who opposed his policies. Those in Fisher's favour were described as being 'in the Fish-pond', and woe betide those who were not. Needless to say, Fisher's enemies grew in number. His chief adversary was Lord Charles Beresford, the Commander-in-Chief of the Channel, or principal, Fleet. Soon the Navy was divided into two camps — Fisher's men and Beresford's men — and every sort of intrigue and warfare was carried on between the two rival sections. The final result was Fisher's resignation. Nevertheless when 1914 came it was the ships that Fisher and the First Lord, McKenna, had built between the years 1906 and 1911, in the face of Winston Churchill's powerful opposition, that were ready to face the enemy.

Winston had first met Sir John Fisher, as he was then, in Biarritz in 1907. They had talked far into the night and although the young man did not agree with the old man's belief in the necessity for a large Navy, they recognized each other as kindred spirits; they were unconventional, forceful and daring. They both liked a storm. Churchill now sent for Fisher who came home from Italy and the two men spent three days discussing naval problems. Fisher's ideas were as vehement, as brilliant and stimulating as ever. He impressed Churchill so deeply that the latter toyed with the idea of reappointing him First Sea Lord then and there. If Fisher had dropped the slightest hint, Churchill would have spoken, but for the moment the thought passed.

Nevertheless, Lord Fisher became Churchill's inspiration and ally. From then on the old man bombarded the young First Lord with dozens of forceful, amusing and valuable letters which arrived at the Admiralty fastened together, sometimes with a ribbon, sometimes with a pearl pin. The letters began breezily: 'My beloved Winston' and ended 'Yours to a cinder', 'Yours till hell freezes', or 'Till charcoal sprouts'. 'Alas,' wrote Winston in *The World Crisis*, 'there was a day when hell froze and charcoal sprouted and friendship was reduced to cinders; when "My beloved Winston" had given place to "First Lord: I can no longer be your colleague".' But that belongs to another chapter.

Meanwhile, with Lord Fisher's unofficial aid and backing, Winston set about to learn his business and do his job. Out of two years and nine months that remained before war was to begin, he spent nearly eight months afloat in the Admiralty yacht *Enchantress*. He visited every important ship. At the end he knew 'what everything looked like and where everything was, and how one thing fitted into another. I could put my hand on anything that was wanted and knew the current state of our naval affairs.' He not only worked for the Navy, he lived for it. His sense of drama was deeply stirred, for he saw beyond the ships themselves to the broad horizon. The following extract from *The World Crisis* reveals how romantically he visualized the charge that had been entrusted to him. 'Consider these ships, so vast in themselves, yet so small, so easily lost to sight on the surface of the waters. Sufficient at the moment, we trusted, for their task, but yet only a score or so. They were all we had. On them, as we conceived, floated the might, majesty, dominion and power of the British Empire. All our long history built up century after century, all our great affairs in every part of the globe, all the means of livelihood and safety for our faithful, industrious, active population depended upon them. Open the sea-cocks and let them sink beneath the surface as another Fleet was one day to do in another British harbour far to the North, and in a few minutes — half an hour at the most — the whole outlook of the world would be changed. The British Empire would dissolve like a dream; each isolated community struggling forward by itself; the central power of union broken; mighty provinces, whole Empires in themselves, drifting hopelessly out of control, and falling a prey to strangers; and Europe after one sudden convulsion passing into the iron grip of the Teuton and of all that the Teutonic system meant.'

*

With this conception of the Navy's great role it is not surprising that Churchill was thrilled by his task. He kept his promise to Haldane and worked in the closest co-operation with the military experts. The War Minister quickly overcame his disappointment at not being appointed to the Admiralty himself, and soon wrote to his mother: 'Winston and L.G. dined with me last night, and we had a very useful talk. This is now a very harmonious Cabinet. It is odd to think that three years ago I had to fight these two for every penny for my Army Reform. Winston is full of enthusiasm about the Admiralty, and just as keen as I am on the war staff. It is delightful to work with him. L.G. has too quite changed his attitude and now is very friendly to your bear, whom he used to call the Minister of Civil Slaughter.'[149]

Lloyd George, however, did not share Winston's emotional excitement over the danger of Germany. Winston thrived on the drama. He flung himself into the preparations with grim determination but at the same time with a certain exhilaration. Lloyd George, on the other hand, was not convinced that war was inevitable. He insisted that every effort should be made to placate Germany; to remove her grievances, and to try to arrive at a sensible understanding about armaments. He impressed Sir Edward Grey with his arguments and an unofficial emissary was sent to Berlin to contact the Kaiser and pave the way for serious conversations. The basis of the British point of view was quite simple: Britain had no objection to German military strength or German colonial expansion; but if Germany insisted on rivalling British sea-power, on which the whole security of the British Island depended, a clash would indeed come. The Kaiser sent word that he would be glad to discuss the problem with the British Government, and consequently Lord Haldane was sent to Berlin.

While Haldane was on his mission Churchill went to Glasgow to inspect some shipbuilding works on the Clyde. He picked up an evening newspaper and read a speech by the Kaiser to the Reichstag announcing large increases both in the Army and the Navy. Once again Churchill felt a sensation of approaching danger. A sentence which particularly struck him was this: 'It is my constant duty and care to maintain and to strengthen on land and water, the power of defence of German people, *which has no lack of young men fit to hear arms*.'

Churchill's ire was roused. He decided that someone should speak publicly, speak plainly and speak now. Consequently he spoke himself in Glasgow the following day. 'This island,' he declared, 'has never been, and never will be, lacking in trained and hardy marines bred from their boyhood up to the service of the sea.' The Germans did not object to this warning; after all it was tit for tat. But what enraged them was the opening paragraph of Winston's address: 'The purposes of British naval power are essentially defensive. We have no thoughts, and we have never had any thoughts of aggression, and we attribute no such thoughts to other great Powers. There is, however, this difference between the British naval power and the naval power of the great and friendly Empire — of Germany. The British Navy is to us a

---

[149] *Haldane*: Sir Frederick Maurice.

necessity and, from some points of view, the German Navy is to them more in the nature of a luxury. Our naval power involves British existence. It is existence to us; it is expansion to them …'[150]

The word 'luxury', it appeared, had an unfortunate significance when translated into German. 'The *luxus Flotte*,' wrote Churchill, 'became an expression passed angrily from lip to lip.' But the Germans were not only angry; they were shocked. The Kaiser regarded young Churchill as a personal friend. After all, the latter had twice been the monarch's guest at manoeuvres in 1906 and 1909; besides, the Crown Prince had been a fellow visitor with Winston at a week-end house party and they had even had a pillow fight together. Winston had been one of the leaders of the pacifist wing in England, and had always spoken kindly of Germany. The Kaiser had been delighted when he read of the appointment and had interpreted it as a triumph for the pro-German element in England. It was as rude an awakening as Lloyd George's Mansion House speech. The English were unpredictable indeed.

Churchill's speech was not only criticized in Germany but at home. The Government considered it precipitous and rash, and the Tories went around saying, 'What can you expect from a fellow like that?' Haldane, however, returned from Germany and declared that it had helped rather than hindered. It had emphasized the very points he had been making. However, as far as the Germans were concerned, it failed to produce the desired result. Germany continued her naval programme and in March Churchill declared that Britain would build two more ships than she had the previous year. He made one more conciliatory gesture. 'Suppose we were both to take a naval holiday in 1913 and introduce a blank page into the book of misunderstanding.' This proposal was received by Germany in icy silence. Churchill returned his attention to preparations for war.

*

One of Winston's first tasks at the Admiralty was to create a Naval War Staff in the face of stiff naval opposition. The professional sailors declared that a War Staff would undermine and divide the all-powerful authority of the First Sea Lord, diminishing rather than increasing efficiency. Fisher wrote to a friend on 7 November, 1911: 'The argument for a War Staff is that you *may* have a d——d fool as First Sea Lord, and so you put him in commission, as it were.' Churchill,

---

[150] *The Times*: 10 February, 1912.

however, had agreed to set up the new Staff and he pushed ahead with his task despite the fact that the First Sea Lord resigned, and the Second and Third Sea Lords had to be replaced.

Haldane helped him to work out the plans for the organization but when Winston announced his startling intention of bringing the Naval War Staff directly under himself, a politician, rather than under the First Sea Lord, a sailor, Haldane objected stoutly and won his point.

Despite this concession, many admirals were still far from satisfied. Even though the new body was under the direction of the First Sea Lord they felt that the Chief of the Naval Staff was bound to clash in authority with his superior. Lord Fisher advised Winston to overcome the difficulty by declaring that the First Sea Lord would automatically become Chief of the Naval Staff, but Churchill did not accept his suggestion. Time proved Fisher right but it was not until Winston had left the Admiralty and Jellicoe had become First Sea Lord that the two offices were combined.

Since Lord Fisher's position was completely unofficial he had no power to alter decisions of high policy. He therefore concerned himself with influencing appointments. Who, for instance, was to command the principal Fleet when war broke out? Fisher was an ardent supporter of Jellicoe and argued his case strongly with Winston. The latter acted on his recommendation and some idea of Fisher's triumphant satisfaction may be gleaned from a letter he wrote to a friend: 'My two private visits to Winston were fruitful. I'll tell you the whole secret of the changes — to get Jellicoe Commander-in-Chief of the Home Fleet prior to October 1914, which is the date of the battle of Armageddon. He will succeed Callaghan automatically in two years from December 1911, so will have all well in hand by the before-mentioned date. Nunc Dimittis. Every thing revolved around Jellicoe!'[151] Fisher's forecast of the beginning of the war, correct within two months, gives some idea of the shrewd judgment of the old man.

About the same time that Churchill appointed Jellicoe he picked the youngest Flag Officer in the Fleet for his private secretary. This was the same young man who had moved his gunboat up the Nile in support of the Lancers in their charge against the Dervishes at Omdurman, and the same young man who had thrown the soldiers a

---

[151] *The Life of Lord Fisher*: Admiral Sir R. H. Bacon.

bottle of champagne. His name was David Beatty and before World War I had ended he succeeded to Jellicoe's command.

Fisher approved of Beatty, but he did not approve of several other important appointments that Churchill made on his own initiative. In fact, he was furious. He wrote to Winston in heated indignation and announced that their relations were at an end. 'I consider,' he said, 'you have betrayed the Navy by these three appointments, and what the pressure could have been to induce you to betray your trust is beyond my comprehension.'[152] With that he packed his bags and left for Naples.

Winston behaved almost like a love-lorn suitor, sending a stream of letters begging Fisher to return. Then he badgered him with requests for his advice on this matter and that, and got other people to do the same. Fisher remained obdurate. Finally Churchill went after him. It so happened that the Prime Minister had agreed to accompany Winston through the Mediterranean in the Admiralty yacht with the object of visiting Kitchener in Egypt, where the latter was serving as British Agent and Consul-General, and talking over problems of strategy. When the conversations finished Churchill headed for Naples, and Asquith reinforced Churchill's pleas for the old man to return. Still Lord Fisher remained adamant. Then Churchill employed feminine subtlety. On Sunday morning they all went to the English service. In the middle of the sermon the chaplain looked at Fisher and said solemnly: 'No man possessing all his powers and full of vitality has any right to say: "I am now going to rest, as I have had a hard life," for he owes a duty to his country and fellow men!' Fisher relented and returned to England; and the powerful, unofficial combination once more went into action. Considering the fact that both men were pugnacious, opinionated and autocratic, quarrels were to be expected; what is surprising is the fact that the alliance worked as well as it did.

The two most formidable decisions taken by the Churchill-Fisher combination were first, to advance from the thirteen-point-five-inch gun to the fifteen-inch, and second, to change the entire Navy over from coal to oil. These innovations took place during 1912-13. At this time a fifteen-inch gun had not even been designed. Yet there was no time to test it. A valuable year would be lost. On the other hand if the ships would not stand the stress the Navy might become a ghastly fiasco. However, the experts all assured Churchill that the gun would

---

[152] *The Life of Lord Fisher*: Admiral Sir R. H. Bacon.

work and declared that they were ready to stake their professional careers upon it; and Lord Fisher urged Churchill forward with passionate insistence. 'What was it that enabled Jack Johnson to knock out his opponents?' he argued. 'It was the Big Punch.' Winston went ahead; and as the Germans were soon to learn, the result was more than satisfactory.

The new guns led to the change-over from coal to oil. Striking power, Fisher declared, was not enough. Speed was absolutely essential, and ships run by oil gave a large excess of speed over coal. Furthermore they had another advantage; they could be refuelled, if necessary, at sea. The obvious drawback to the whole idea was the fact that Britain produced coal and not oil. Churchill pondered over the difficulties, while once again Lord Fisher pressed him furiously on. Winston set up a Royal Commission on Oil Supply and appointed the old man as chairman. The final outcome was a long term contract with the Anglo-Persian Oil Company which, for an initial investment of £2,000,000, later increased to £5,000,000, secured the necessary oil and gave the Government a controlling share in oil properties which increased their value many hundred per cent. In 1951 this same British interest became the subject of dangerous controversy.

The new guns and the change-over to oil involved enormous expense. Churchill's Naval Estimates presented to the Cabinet at the end of 1913 were the highest in British history, and the highest in the world. The figure was over £50,000,000. The Cabinet gasped; and for the first time since Lloyd George and Churchill had been colleagues in the same Government they found themselves desperately opposed to one another. Each threatened to resign unless the other gave way.

*

The relationship between Lloyd George and Churchill altered during the years 1911 and 1912. The two men remained staunch friends but the political affinity ended. No longer did they fasten on their armour and walk out to do battle on the same ground. They stood firmly together over the Agadir incident but when the crisis faded Churchill was a different man. He could not turn back to domestic affairs. His interest in reform had evaporated and he no longer found it amusing to bait rich landlords.

Lloyd George had the opposite reaction. As soon as the scare had passed he returned eagerly to the battle on the home front. How could the destruction of war compare for excitement with the construction of peace? As Chancellor of the Exchequer he had a finger in every pie, and 1911-12 were full years. They were the years of the stormy

Parliament Bill; of the railway strike, the dock strike and the coal strike; of growing violence in the suffrage movement; of a new Home Rule Bill and a Welsh Disestablishment Bill; and most important of all, the years of Lloyd George's greatest triumph — the National Health Insurance Act. This was the first step towards the Health Service that exists in Britain to-day and its initiation aroused as much furious opposition among the doctors and the Tories as its successor did in 1946. The Insurance Act operated by both employers and employees contributing to weekly stamps. *Punch* ran a cartoon with an angry Duchess exclaiming: 'What! Me lick stamps!' and a correspondent, in a letter to the *Daily Mail*, declared: 'If the Insurance Bill becomes law it will be advisable for us to leave England.'

Lloyd George was puzzled and a little irritated that Winston was unable to arouse any enthusiasm over these exciting measures. He told Mrs. Masterman that Churchill was taking 'less and less part in home politics, and getting more and more absorbed in boilers'. It was true that Winston could never take up a subject without overflowing, a fact to which some of his colleagues objected strongly. Lloyd George complained that he would bear down on him saying: 'Look here, David, I want to talk to you,' and then he would 'declaim for the rest of the morning about his blasted ships!'[153] 'You have become a water creature,' Lloyd George once told him in a reproving voice. 'You think we all live in the sea, and all your thoughts are devoted to sea life, fishes and other aquatic creatures. You forget that most of us live on land.'[154]

Thus the friendship survived while each man marched along his own particular path. Lloyd George still regarded the landed proprietors as enemies of society. 'The land,' he declared, 'is still shackled with the chains of feudalism;' and he began to formulate a Land Act that would revive agriculture; fix rents and tenures; tackle housing and slum clearance. 'The squire is God,' he announced, 'the parson, the agent, the gamekeeper — these are his priests; the pheasants, the hares — these are the sacred birds and beasts of the tabernacle.' Lloyd George was just getting under way when the 'Marconi scandal' broke, which, as it turned out, proved no scandal at all. The Tories claimed that Lloyd George and two other Liberal Ministers had used inside

[153] *C. F. G. Masterman*: Lucy Masterman.

[154] *More Pages from My Diary*: Lord Riddell.

knowledge to gamble in Marconi shares. The House of Commons set up an inquiry which found that (a) the Ministers held very few shares, (b) they had made a loss and not a profit. They had done nothing dishonourable; the worst they could be accused of was indiscretion. During the ordeal Winston stood by Lloyd George firmly. When it was over the National Liberal Club gave a dinner in honour of the three pilloried Ministers. Winston arrived at the club late, found the door locked, and climbed through the pantry window. He made a rousing speech declaring that these men 'had been vilely and damnably ill-treated in our cause for our sakes'. The agitation, he continued, had been concocted 'by the pole-cats of politics'.

Thus the friendship between these two rivals continued steadfastly in spite of vicissitudes and differing opinions. Then came Winston's huge Naval Estimates, and for the first time loyalty underwent a severe strain. Lloyd George needed all the revenue he could raise for his social reforms. Besides, he did not believe in big ships. He took the view, which had some important naval support, that destroyers and light cruisers were just as effective as dreadnoughts and far less costly. Also, Winston had made a bargain with him over expenditure and had not kept it. Winston, on the other hand, refused to budge. 'L.G. is accustomed to deal with people who can be bluffed and frightened, but I am not to be bluffed and frightened!' he told a friend. 'He says that some of the Cabinet will resign. Let them resign!'[155]

As the weeks passed the situation became more and more critical for neither man would give way. Each said he would rather resign. Early in January Lloyd George gave an astonishing interview to the *Daily Chronicle* calling for a reduction in armaments on the grounds that the international sky had never been 'more perfectly blue'. Lord Riddell, a newspaper proprietor who was a close friend of both, recorded the following excerpts in his *Diary*:

17 January, 1913: Lloyd George said: 'The P.M. must choose between Winston and me … We now ascertain for the first time that Winston has exceeded the estimates by no less than £5,000,000. That is gross extravagance … I am not a "little Navy" man. I don't want to reduce the Navy. I only want reasonable economy. I am not fighting about that. Winston says he can make no more reductions. The truth is he is not a Liberal. He does not understand Liberal sentiment.'

---

[155] *More Pages from My Diary*: Lord Riddell.

18 January: Churchill said: 'I don't know how long I shall be here [at the Admiralty]. The position is acute. I cannot make further economies. I cannot go back on my public declarations. L.G. will find the Cabinet with me. The P.M. is committed to the expenditure up to the hilt. I can make no further concessions. I cannot agree to the concealment of the actual figures. I think I know the English people. The old Cromwellian spirit still survives. I believe I am watched over. Think of the perils I have escaped.' Lord Riddell then inserted in the diary: '(L.G., as I have already recorded, believes the same about himself. If there is a row it will be interesting to see which guardian angel is stronger.)'[156]

Churchill played every card he possessed. He let it be known that his resignation would be accompanied by that of all four Sea Lords; he allowed a rumour to spread that he was considering rejoining the Conservative Party; he hinted at a compromise with the Tories over Home Rule. The Liberals took fright and a few weeks later Winston and Lloyd George reached a compromise which, although it saved L.G.'s face, was, in fact, a triumph for Winston. The latter agreed to knock £1,000,000 off his £52,000,000 Bill; and Lloyd George agreed to remain in the Government.

A politician can afford to be hated by the Opposition; but he cannot run the risk of alienating too many members of his own side. Churchill was still vehemently distrusted by the Tories. Although they approved of his naval programme they continued to regard him as unscrupulous and dangerous. Until the moment he had become First Lord of the Admiralty he had opposed the Naval Estimates; now, they said, when he thought he could reap personal glory he was in favour of them. The *World* called him a 'boneless wonder' for his change of policy, an epithet which Winston was to employ effectively against Ramsay MacDonald some years later.

*

Churchill ignored the Tory attack but lie regarded the rising feeling against him among the Radical section of his own party with concern. The Radicals objected strongly to his increased naval expenditure. More and more it was being said that he was 'not a Liberal'. Largely to appease Radical sentiment Winston decided to fling himself into the Irish controversy. The Asquith Government was dependent on the votes of the eighty-four Irish Nationalist Members of Parliament for

---

[156] Ibid.

its majority; consequently it had pledged itself to introduce a Home Rule Bill. This Bill was popular with the Radicals, so Churchill took up the cause.

For over thirty years the passionate affairs of Ireland, with their almost insuperable difficulties, had occupied the attention of successive British Governments. The Catholic South did not wish to be ruled from Westminster despite the fact that they were represented in the Westminster Parliament by their eighty-four Members; they insisted that Dublin should have its own Parliament, and furthermore, and here the insoluble element came in, that Dublin should rule a united Ireland including the Protestants of the North. Ulster rebelled furiously. 'Home Rule,' they declared, was 'Rome rule.' They loudly emphasized their 'loyalty' to British authority.

In the latter years of his life Gladstone twice attempted to bring in a Home Rule Bill, but on both occasions it was defeated. Lord Randolph Churchill played a leading part in the opposition, declaring that 'Ulster will fight; and Ulster will be right.' For some years the sleeping dog slept fitfully; then came the elections of 1910 which gave Asquith's Liberals a majority only with the votes of the eighty-four Irish Nationalists. The price demanded of him was a third attempt at a Home Rule Bill. At once the Irish question was brought into the arena of Party politics. The Liberals drew up the Bill: the Conservatives opposed it to a man.

Churchill played a leading part in the controversy and in one of the most brilliant performances of his career, piloted the second reading of the Bill through the House of Commons. When Lord Randolph's dictum was flung at him he denounced it as one from which 'every street bully with a brickbat and every crazy fanatic fumbling with a pistol may draw inspiration.'

In February 1912 he plunged into the hornets' nest itself by making a daring speech in Belfast, the capital of Ulster. The Irishmen refused to let him speak in the Ulster Hall, saying they would smash up the meeting, so he hired a marquee and addressed a huge open air meeting. Ten thousand troops were sent out to keep order, and the story was circulated that if Mrs. Churchill had not accompanied her husband the Orangemen would have thrown Churchill into the river.

The House of Commons was also the scene of wild confusion. Once a debate grew so stormy that an Ulsterman picked up the Speaker's manual on parliamentary procedure and flung it at Winston's head. It reached its target and Churchill had to be restrained by force from returning the blow. The next day the offender apologized handsomely and Winston assured him that 'I have not, nor have I at any time, any personal feelings in the matter, and if I had any personal feelings the observations he has thought proper to address to the House would have effectually removed them.'

The strife of party politics in Westminster was steadily fanning the flames of Irish discord. In the middle of 1912 Bonar Law, the Conservative leader, made an astonishing declaration which amounted to an incitement to civil war. 'Ireland is two nations,' he said. 'The Ulster people will submit to no ascendancy, and I can imagine no lengths of resistance to which they might go in which they would not be supported by the overwhelming majority of the British people.' Meanwhile, Sir Edward Carson, a former Conservative Minister and now the accepted leader of the Northern Irish, was making fiery speeches in Belfast. In the summer of 1913, Carson held a monster rally and opened enlistments for the 'Ulster volunteers'; by the end of the year the volunteers had grown to one hundred thousand men. Gun running, in defiance of the law, began to take place. Before the winter was over rifles and ammunition were being supplied only too willingly by Germany.

One of the most extraordinary aspects of this turmoil was that while Churchill was playing a leading role on the Home Rule side, his most intimate friend, F. E. Smith, was a prominent figure on the Ulster front. F.E. was Sir Edward Carson's right hand man and he was making vehement speeches to the Northerners to hold their ground whatever the price. How the friendship of the two men survived such a crisis is perplexing; one is driven to the conclusion that neither was emotionally involved in the affair but both were playing politics. However, Winston secured his main objective. In the heat of the controversy his Naval Estimates were passed by the House with surprisingly little opposition.

In March 1914 Irish events began to move towards a climax. Asquith forced the Irish Nationalists in the House of Commons to agree to a plan which would enable the Northern Counties to vote themselves out of the Home Rule Bill until two British General Elections had taken place. If the Conservatives won either of these they could amend the Bill to their liking. The Tories, however, turned down the idea flatly, and a few days later Churchill, who had worked hard for the Clause excluding Ulster, made a speech at Bradford in which he said: 'There are worse things than bloodshed ... We are not going to have the realm of Britain sunk to the condition of the Republic of Mexico.'[157]

Then he made a move which nearly had fatal and terrible consequences. In collaboration with his friend and colleague, Colonel Seely, who had succeeded Haldane as Secretary of State for War, he worked out a plan by which the British Army would occupy all munition dumps and arsenals, and all strategic positions in Ulster. A flotilla was ordered to Lamlash where it lay ready to transport troops to Belfast if the railways refused to carry them.

Churchill declares in *The World Crisis* that this scheme was evolved to protect the Army stores in Northern Ireland in case civil war broke out at the same time that war with Germany was declared. However, the most eminent historians do not accept this version any more than the Tories did at the time. Halévy describes the move as 'nothing less than a plan of campaign against Northern Ireland'. Needless to say, the action aroused a storm of fury. The British Army contained many officers and men of Ulster origin. General Gough, in command of a cavalry brigade at the Curragh in Ireland, resigned rather than carry out the order, and was immediately replaced. The following day Lloyd George spoke warningly: 'We are confronted with the gravest issue raised in this country since the days of the Stuarts. Representative government in this land is at stake ... I am here this afternoon on behalf of the British Government to say this to you — that they mean to confront this defiance of popular liberties with a most resolute, unwavering determination whatever the hazard may be.'

But during the twenty-four hours following Gough's resignation nearly all the British officers of the two cavalry brigades at the Curragh had resigned in sympathy with the General. Asquith saw that the Government was facing a large-scale mutiny unless an immediate retraction was made. He announced in Parliament that a military campaign against Ulster had never been intended. General Gough was hurriedly reinstated and given a written assurance by War Minister Seely that Ulster would not be coerced by force.

These actions were described in the Unionist Press as a 'complete surrender' and, although they pacified the Conservatives, they threw the Liberal Party into a storm of anger. Northern Ireland, declared the Liberals furiously, must be made to comply. The Prime Minister had now jumped from the frying pan into the fire. In a prevaricating speech

---

[157] 14 March, 1914.

he told the House of Commons that the pledge given to Gough had not received the assent of the Cabinet. Then, in order to produce a scapegoat, he accepted Colonel Seely's resignation and took over the War Office himself.

Asquith's parliamentary statement about Gough was, in effect, a repudiation of the promise that Seely had given to the General, but the latter was not 'officially' informed of what had happened and calmly remained at his post. Thus the almost unbelievably muddled events of March 1914 dragged on. A month later forty thousand rifles and a million cartridges were distributed throughout Northern Ireland. They had come from Hamburg and the rifles were Mausers. 'Was it astonishing,' wrote Churchill, 'that German agents reported, and German statesmen believed, that England was paralysed by faction and drifting into civil war, and need not be taken into account as a factor in the European situation?'[158]

The King summoned a conference of the leaders of the two factions at Buckingham Palace but after three days an *impasse* was reached. Rioting broke out in Dublin where thousands of men were flocking to join the Irish Nationalist Volunteers. Then suddenly an event occurred which swung British attention from the anxieties of Ireland and riveted it permanently on the European scene. Four weeks previously a Serbian peasant had assassinated the heir to the Austrian throne. Now on 24 July the Austrians had sent Serbia an ultimatum which amounted to annexation. The curtain was rising on World War I. The pistol shot at Sarajevo gave the Germans their pretext for war. Serbia refused to accept the harsh ultimatum flung at her and the next day Austria declared war. The day after, the Russians began to mobilize on the Austrian frontier; three days later Germany sent an ultimatum to Russia to disperse her troops, then declared war. On 3 August, this time without any declaration, Germany invaded Belgium and France.

Ten tense and fearful days had passed between the Austrian ultimatum and the German invasion. During this time the British Cabinet was overwhelmingly pacifist. Every attempt was made to stop the conflagration from spreading, every hope was sustained, and every argument advanced, why Britain could remain aloof. However, England had guaranteed Belgian neutrality; and when the news was received that German troops were pouring through Flanders all thought of peace vanished. An ultimatum was sent to Germany

---

[158] *The World Crisis*: Winston S. Churchill.

demanding her withdrawal from Belgium within twenty-four hours. When the chimes of Big Ben struck eleven on the warm summer evening of 4 August, Britain was at war.

Winston had played his part well. Lord Fisher had prophesied repeatedly that 1914 was the crucial year. As a result the Fleet was not sent on its usual manoeuvres to the North Sea. Instead, Churchill ordered a mobilization exercise, which meant putting not only the main Fleet but the ships and men of the Second and Third Reserve Fleets, on active service footing. This exercise took place in the middle of July. It ended on 17 and 18 July in a grand review of the Fleet by the King at Spithead.

After this the normal course would have been dispersal. Instead, on 20 July, the newspapers carried an Admiralty notice: 'Orders have been given to the First Fleet, which is concentrated at Portland, not to disperse for naval leave for the present. All vessels of the Second Fleet are remaining at their home ports in proximity to their balance crews.'

The following week when Austria attacked Serbia, Winston acted quickly. With the assent of Sir Edward Grey he gave instructions for the Fleet to take up its station in Scottish waters, at Scapa Flow, opposite the German Fleet, in order to prevent it being bottled up in the face of a surprise attack. The operation was carried out in the greatest secrecy; the ships moved through the Straits of Dover at night with their fires banked.

During the ten days that the Government debated the terrible issue of war and peace, Churchill was the strongest force for intervention in the Cabinet. While his colleagues hesitated, worried and uncertain, Churchill was longing to act. Asquith describes him in his memoirs as 'very bellicose, demanding instant mobilization'. On Friday, 31 July, Churchill asked his friend, F. E. Smith, to sound his Conservative leaders on the question of coalition in case the Liberal Government remained hopelessly divided. Bonar Law refused to consider coalition unless he was approached by the Prime Minister himself, but made it clear that the Administration could count on loyal Conservative support.

On Saturday, 1 August, Germany declared war on Russia. Churchill, on his own authority and without the sanction of the Cabinet (which he received the following morning), ordered the full mobilization of the Fleet. Lord Beaverbrook describes Churchill's reactions when he heard the news of the fateful act. Beaverbrook had been invited with Mr. F. E. Smith to Admiralty House for dinner and bridge. 'Suddenly an immense dispatch box was brought into the room. Churchill produced his skeleton key from his pocket, opened the box and took out of it a single sheet of paper ... On that sheet was written the words "Germany has declared war against Russia".

'He rang for a servant and asking for a lounge coat, stripped his dress coat from his back, saying no further word ... He left the room quickly ... He was not depressed; he was not elated; he was not surprised ... Certainly he exhibited no fear or uneasiness. Neither did he show any signs of joy. He went straight out like a man going to a well-accustomed job. In fact, he had foreseen everything that was going to happen so far that his temperament was in no way upset by the realization of his forecast. We have suffered at times from Mr. Churchill's bellicosity. But what profit the nation derived at that crucial moment from the capacity of the First Lord of the Admiralty for grasping and dealing with the war situation.'[159]

Not many months later, in one of the bleakest periods of his career, Lord Kitchener was to say to him: 'There is one thing they cannot take from you: the Fleet was ready.'

---

[159] *Politicians and the War*: Lord Beaverbrook.

Chapter Eleven — Antwerp

WINSTON CHURCHILL'S star had. been rising steadily for eight years, and when war broke out he stood as one of the three most powerful men in Britain. He was only thirty-nine years old, yet he was head of the greatest fighting service of the greatest Empire in the world. Fortune was smiling as far as his own opportunities were concerned and the path ahead seemed straight and sure. He was a forceful orator, an accomplished writer and an able administrator. He was blessed with boundless energy. He enjoyed the close friendship of the Chancellor of the Exchequer and the admiration of the Prime Minister. With his dazzling gifts and his pugnacious spirit it seemed certain that he would play a leading role in the great struggle against Germany, and even his enemies began to reckon on him as a probable successor to Asquith.

But Fortune is a fickle mistress. Only ten months later he was dismissed from the Admiralty and five months after that he was excluded from the War Cabinet. His power was broken; he had no further voice in the conduct of the war. Even though Lloyd George brought him back into the Government in 1917 he never regained the great position he held at the outset. He was given a purely administrative job, while questions of high policy were carefully shielded from his influence. His contribution to World War I, therefore, was sensational but brief. What brought about his downfall?

The answer undoubtedly lay in Churchill's personality. The Tories still hated and mistrusted him and lost no opportunity to discredit him; but leaving politics aside, Churchill was not popular as a man. His parliamentary colleagues recognized his genius but they did not warm to him for the simple reason that he offended their *amour propre*. Ideas, not people, interested him, and his absorption with his own affairs and his own opinions at times could be almost childlike in its vanity and intensity. He treated his colleagues to brilliant monologues but the fact that he seldom wanted to hear their views in exchange often left them ruffled and offended while he, in turn, was completely oblivious to their reactions. His was the insensibility of the headstrong child, warm-hearted, and generous when taken to task, but too utterly engrossed in his own pursuits to have much heed for others. This insensibility was a serious defect in a democratic statesman whose task it was not only to expand ideas but to persuade others to follow them. As a result Churchill was unable to command the personal sympathy and loyalty necessary to sustain him through precarious times.

But let the events of the day unfold the story. At the outbreak of hostilities Churchill's Navy was more than ready. Its main task was to ensure the safe transport of the British Expeditionary Force to France, which it did without the loss of a single life. Winston was eager and bellicose. He was brimming over with ideas and longed for a showdown. The Grand Fleet patrolled the North Sea majestically, challenging the German Navy to come out and fight. But why wait for them, asked Churchill? What about a raid on the German ships in the Heligoland Bight? As a result a plan was drawn up and put into operation with brilliant success. Two flotillas of British destroyers and cruisers made a sudden drive near the island of Sylt, sank one cruiser, smashed two others and crippled three more. They also sank a destroyer. Churchill declared triumphantly that 'the nose of the bulldog has been slanted backwards so that he can breathe without letting go'.

The Army was not having such a successful time. The Germans had thrown their whole strength into the attack against France, and were staking everything on one conclusive gamble: the complete destruction of French military power. At the end of three weeks a million men of the French Army were falling back on Paris, leaving the Channel ports dangerously exposed. Surprise and alarm swept through England, but Churchill was not dismayed. In order to reassure his colleagues he reprinted the memorandum lie had written in 1911 which predicted these very happenings, but went on to declare confidently that by the fortieth day the Germans would be fully extended, which would allow the Allies to stage a counterstroke. He sent a copy of the memorandum to Sir John French, the Commander of the British Expeditionary Force, who replied in a letter on 10 September: 'What a wonderful forecast you made in 1911. I don't remember the paper, but it has turned out almost as you said. I have shown it to a few of my staff.'

Lord Kitchener, the Secretary of State for War, was worried. As the Allied line fell back in France he began to fear that the Germans might strike at London by zeppelin raid. Three-quarters of the planes the English possessed were under the control of the War Office and were being used in support of the retreating armies. The other quarter, planes that Churchill himself had scraped together in 1912 and 1913 to form a 'Naval Air Service', were under the jurisdiction of the Navy and lying idle. Consequently Lord Kitchener asked Winston if he would undertake the aerial defence of Great Britain, and the latter eagerly assented. This led to a series of unusual events, some comic, some tragic, which contributed to Churchill's final downfall. It also led to an invention destined to revolutionize modern warfare — the birth of the Tank.

This is how the tank idea came into being. Churchill knew that if the German zeppelins were to be destroyed they must be attacked in their hangars. In those days aeroplane engines were not strong enough to reach the height at which zeppelins flew in the necessary time. Aviation was in its infancy, night flying was only beginning, and location of aircraft by sound was not then known. Churchill, therefore, set up air bases at Dunkirk and Calais, as near to the enemy lines as possible. From then on intrepid pilots in uncertain machines conducted innumerable sweeps over Cologne, Dusseldorf, Friedrichshaven and Cuxhaven; and before twelve months had passed the Royal Naval Air Service could claim to have destroyed no less than six of the great gas-filled monsters.

However, it soon became apparent that Churchill's new air bases were in danger of direct attack from German patrols. Winston immediately ordered a hastily improvised armoured car equipped with a machine gun; next he ordered the formation of armoured car squadrons under the Admiralty. But once again difficulties arose. German cavalry units succeeded in warding off these mobile attacks by digging themselves in behind trenches. And as the days passed the trenches stretched out further and further until they finally reached the sea. There was no way for the cars to get round them.

Winston refused to bow to such an obstacle. Something must be done at once to 'beat the trench'. On 23 September, he wrote a letter to Admiral Bacon, the General Manager of a large ordnance works, asking for a design of an armoured car that could cross trenches by means of a folding, portable bridge. 'The air was the first cause that took us to Dunkirk,' he explains in *The World Crisis*. 'The armoured car was the child of the air: and the tank its grandchild.'

Admiral Bacon produced the design, but the armoured car with the portable bridge was never manufactured; for, a month later, the Admiral showed Churchill a caterpillar tractor which he decided was more suitable. This, too, had a folding bridge. He ordered several of these machines to be made but when the first one was tested in May 1915 the Admiralty perversely rejected it because it could not descend a four-foot bank or go through three feet of water.

However, Winston had other irons in the fire. Some idea of his persistence may be gathered from a letter which he wrote in January 1915 to the Director of the Air Division: 'I wish the following experiment made at once: Two ordinary steam-rollers are to be fastened together side by side by very strong steel connections, so that they are to all intents and purposes one roller covering a breadth of at least twelve to fourteen feet. If convenient, one of the back inside wheels might be removed and the other axle joined up to it. Some trenches are to be dug on the latest principles somewhere near London in lengths of at least 100 yards, the earth taken out of the trenches being thrown on each side, as is done in France. The roller is to be driven along these trenches one outer rolling wheel on each side, and the inner rolling wheel just clear of the trench itself. The object is to ascertain what amount of weight is necessary in the roller to smash the trench in. For this purpose as much weight as they can possibly draw should be piled on to the steam-rollers and on the framework buckling them together. The ultimate object is to run along a line of trenches, crushing them all flat and burying the people in them.'[160]

This experiment also failed. The steam-rollers merely bogged down in the centre and refused to budge.

But Winston persevered. The following month he talked to an Army major who suggested the creation of huge 'land battleships'. This idea led to the formation of the Landships Committee of the Admiralty under whose auspices two designs were finally produced, one on large wheels, the other on a caterpillar tractor. He ordered eighteen of these machines to be built at a cost of £70,000. The money was not authorized by the Treasury but he assumed the responsibility himself. When he was dismissed from the Admiralty a few months later his successor cut down the order to one. This one was the exact prototype of the tank used for the first time in the Battle of the Somme in 1916.

*

Churchill began the war as Asquith's blue-eyed boy, but his triumphs were short-lived. Before eight weeks had passed his position with the Prime Minister had begun to deteriorate. According to Lord Beaverbrook, who was a close friend of the most powerful political figures of the day, the thing which first attracted Asquith's attention and made him doubt in the long run whether Churchill was a 'wise war counsellor' was the Dunkirk Circus. This project was born from

---

[160] *The World Crisis*: Winston S. Churchill.

the fear, which persisted for many months, that the Germans might capture the Channel ports. On 16 September, Marshal Joffre asked Lord Kitchener if a brigade of Marines could be sent to Dunkirk to reinforce the garrison and give the enemy the idea that British, as well as French troops, were operating in the area. Once again Kitchener turned to Churchill, and once again Churchill assented.

The Marines were sent across the Channel and Winston requisitioned fifty motor omnibuses from the streets of London to give them the necessary mobility. Soon British detachments were showing themselves in Ypres, Lille, Tournai and Douai. The Marines suffered no casualties and had a good deal of fun; so did the First Lord of the Admiralty. Winston began to spend a good deal of time in France inspecting his air bases and thinking up new escapades for his Circus.

It is not difficult to understand the criticism that began to arise. Why wasn't the fellow at his desk in the Admiralty where he belonged, the Tories began to growl, instead of racing off to France poking his nose into other people's business, and making himself ridiculous? Armoured cars and London buses; what on earth did they have to do with the Navy? Even his colleagues in the Government began to be annoyed. 'There were, on more than one occasion,' wrote Lord Beaverbrook, 'unexplained absences on the part of the First Lord of the Admiralty, which were often inconvenient and caused a growing sense of annoyance among other members of the Government. The Prime Minister, who at the outset had approved of the "Circus", found himself tolerating these absences and trying to conceal the whereabouts of his colleague from other Ministers. Subsequently he discovered that he must take charge at the Admiralty during an absence of Churchill. On a later occasion still he could not find the First Lord when the date of the sailing of a New Zealand contingent was at stake so that, Asquith complained, a very serious delay in dispatching this force occurred.'[161] Asquith soon saw that the Dunkirk Circus was wound up.

Then an unfortunate incident occurred. On 21 September Churchill delivered a flamboyant speech in which he made a boastful and unwise observation that was destined to be flung back at him for years to come. 'So far as the Navy is concerned we cannot fight while the enemy remains in port ... If they do not come out and fight they will be dug out like rats from a hole,' he cried. The English public did not

---

[161] *Politicians and the War*: Lord Beaverbrook.

like this sort of talk. They recognized the Germans as a formidable foe and had an uneasy feeling that Winston was tempting fate. Their reaction was swiftly justified, for the very next day three British ships, the *Aboukir*, the *Hogue* and the *Cressy*, which were steaming along on patrol duty off the Dutch coast, were torpedoed and sunk. Churchill had ordered the withdrawal of this 'live-bait' squadron three days before and if his order had been carried out promptly the loss would have been avoided; but this could not be known. His speech had been a political *gaffe* and disaster following it so promptly placed him in a ridiculous light. His opponents had every right to seize on the incident and discredit him, but one Tory M.P., Captain Bowles, circulated an outrageous pamphlet which contained the preposterous statement: 'The loss on 22 September of the *Aboukir*, the *Cressy*, and the *Hogue*, with 1,459 officers and men killed, occurred because, despite the warnings of the admirals, commodores and captains, Mr. Churchill refused, until it was too late, to recall them from a patrol so carried on as to make them certain to fall victims to the torpedoes of an active enemy.'

Shortly after this sensation, the Antwerp episode damaged Churchill still further. Once again he undertook a mission at Lord Kitchener's request. 'I seem to have been too ready to undertake tasks which were hazardous or even forlorn,' he wrote many years later in *The World Crisis.* 'I believed, however, that the special knowledge which I possessed and the great authority which I wielded at this time of improvisation, would enable me to offer less unsatisfactory solutions of these problems than could be furnished in the emergency by others in less commanding positions.' Thus Churchill was driven on by his supreme self-assurance, into positions which wiser statesmen might have avoided. The circumstances were these; the Battle of the Marne, fought between 6 and 16 September over a 180-mile front, had flung the Germans back from the Marne to the Aisne and severely damaged their hope of a speedy victory. There was one more chance: the immediate capture of Antwerp. This would enable them to sweep to the Channel ports and perhaps roll up the Allied line in total defeat. Consequently the Kaiser gave an imperative order for the capture of Antwerp, regardless of cost, and on 28 September the German 17-inch howitzers began their bombardment. The heavy fortifications were destroyed with astonishing case and four days later the King of the Belgians sent out an urgent call for aid; if reinforcements did not arrive at once the Belgian Army might be captured intact. Plans to evacuate the city were already in hand.

Churchill was on his way to Dunkirk when this desperate news was received. He raced back to London and attended a conference at Lord Kitchener's house. Kitchener explained that reinforcements would not be ready for three or four days; could Churchill hurry to Antwerp, explain the position to the King and Prime Minister, and urge them to hold on with the help of a brigade of Marines until further aid arrived? Once again Churchill said yes, and departed.

Asquith was not in London when this decision was taken but made the following entry in his diary. 'I was away but Grey, Kitchener and Winston held a late meeting and, I fancy, with Grey's rather reluctant consent, the intrepid Winston set off at midnight and ought to have reached Antwerp about nine o'clock. He will straight away see the Belgian Ministers. Sir J. French is making preparations to send assistance by way of Lille. I had a talk with K. this morning and we are both anxiously awaiting Winston's report. I do not know how fluent his French is, but if he is able to do justice to himself in a foreign tongue the Belges will have to listen to a discourse the like of which they have never heard before. I cannot but think that he will stiffen them up.'[162]

The Prime Minister was correct in his opinion. Winston's arrival at Belgian Headquarters in the uniform of an Elder Brother of Trinity House had a slightly comic flavour about it, but his force and his eloquence put new heart into the Belgians. 'At one o'clock in the afternoon,' wrote an American correspondent, 'a big drab-coloured touring-car filled with British Naval officers drove down the Place de Mer, its horn sounding a hoarse warning, took the turn into the March-aux-Souliers on two wheels, and drew up in front of the hotel. Before the car had fairly come to a stop the door of the tonneau was thrown violently open and out jumped a smooth-faced, sandy-haired, stoop-shouldered, youthful-looking man in undress Trinity House uniform.

'As he darted into the crowded lobby which, as usual in the luncheon hour, was filled with Belgian, French and British staff officers, diplomatists, Cabinet Ministers, and correspondents, he flung his arms out in a nervous characteristic gesture, as though pushing his way through a crowd. It 'was a most spectacular entrance, and reminded me for all the world of a scene in a melodrama where the hero dashes up bare-headed on a foam-flecked horse, and saves the heroine, or the old homestead, or the family fortune as the case may be ...

---

[162] *Memories and Reflections*: The Earl of Oxford and Asquith.

'The Burgomaster stopped him, introduced himself, and expressed his anxiety regarding the fate of the city. Before he had finished Churchill was part way up the stairs. "I think everything will be all right now, Mr. Burgomaster," he called in a voice which could be distinctly heard throughout the lobby. "You needn't worry. We're going to save the city."'[163]

Although the outer defences of Antwerp had been smashed, the water supply cut, and guns, ammunition and entrenching materials were running low, Winston succeeded in convincing the Belgian staff that with the help that was arriving it was possible to hang on for some time yet. When Jack Seely, the ex-Secretary of State for War, arrived from Sir John French's Headquarters to report on the situation, he wrote: 'From the moment I arrived it was apparent that the whole business was in Winston's hands. He dominated the whole place — the King, Ministers, soldiers, sailors. So great was his influence that I am convinced that with twenty thousand British troops he could have held Antwerp against almost any onslaught.'[164]

Winston had the same belief himself. If only he were in command he was certain the city could be saved. He was thrilled by the situation and, as with all things that captured his imagination, absorbed in it to the exclusion of all else. Consequently he sent a message to the Prime Minister which seemed sensible to him but struck his colleagues as extraordinary. He asked Asquith to relieve him of his post at the Admiralty and give him the proper rank so that he could take over the military command himself. 'I am sure this arrangement will afford the best prospects of a victorious result to an enterprise in which I am deeply involved,' he added confidently.

Asquith gasped at the impertinence of an ex-subaltern of cavalry asking to command major-generals, and so did most of the Cabinet. However, it is interesting to note that Kitchener had a more open mind on the subject. 'I will make him a major-general if you will give him the command,' he told Asquith.

The Prime Minister remained obdurate. That night he wrote in his diary: 'I at once telegraphed to him warm appreciation of his mission and his offer, with a most decided negative saying that we could not spare him at the Admiralty. I had not meant to read it at the Cabinet

---

[163] *Fighting in Flanders*: E. Alexander Powell.

[164] *Adventure*: Major-General the Rt. Hon. J. E. B. Seely.

but, as everybody, including K., began to ask how soon he was going to return, I was at last obliged to do so. Winston is an ex-Lieutenant of Hussars and would, if his proposal had been accepted, have been in command of two distinguished major-generals not to mention brigadiers, colonels, etc., while the Navy are only contributing their light brigade.'[165]

In the meantime Winston had wired Kitchener to send two Naval brigades, which he knew could be dispatched at once. This detachment amounted to about six thousand men, inexperienced, ill-equipped and only partially trained. They fought stubbornly and well and played a vital part in prolonging the resistance, but before the battle ended nine hundred were taken prisoner, and another two and a half battalions crossed into Holland by mistake and were interned.

Antwerp fell only five days after Winston's arrival. But according to the British official history of the war these five days were of incalculable value. 'Until Antwerp had fallen, the troops of the investing force were not available to move forward on Ypres and the coast; and though, when they did, they secured Zeebrugge and Ostend without struggle, they were too late to secure Nieuport and Dunkirk and turn the Northern flank of the Allies, as was intended.' What seems incredible is that Kitchener failed to grasp the strategic significance of Antwerp. Military historians declare that it could have been held if he had sent even one division of Territorials which were available, but, apart from his lack of understanding, like many other professional soldiers of his day he had a disdain for the Territorials; so, incongruously enough, he allowed Winston to try his luck with his half-trained Naval brigades.

At the time it was impossible for the public to gauge the full significance of the five days of added resistance. People only saw the obvious facts. Churchill had dashed over to Belgium in an effort to save a city and a few days later the city had capitulated. Furthermore, to the layman it seemed an act of incredible folly to fling raw and badly equipped recruits into the battle. Even the Prime Minister's son, Brigadier-General Asquith, who took part in the Antwerp fighting, condemned Winston on this account. 'I had a long talk with him (my son) after midnight,' wrote the Prime Minister in his diary, 'in the course of which he gave a full and vivid account of the expedition to Antwerp and the retirement. Marines, of course, are splendid troops

---

[165] *Memories and Reflections*: The Earl of Oxford and Asquith.

and can go anywhere and do anything, but Winston ought never to have sent the two Naval brigades. I was assured that all the recruits were being left behind and that the main body at any rate consisted of seasoned Naval Reserve men. As a matter of fact, only about a quarter were Reservists and the rest were a callow crowd of the most raw recruits most of whom had never fired off a rifle while none of them had ever even handled an entrenching tool.'[166]

The Antwerp expedition damaged Winston's reputation badly. The Conservative Press was beginning to attack him savagely: 'Mr. Churchill's characteristics make him in his present position a danger and an anxiety to the nation,' stated the *Morning Post* on 15 October.

It was apparent that even the Prime Minister was losing confidence in him. Although Mr. Asquith was still amused by the latter's highly original approach to matters, a derisory note was now creeping into his diary. Even so, it is difficult to suppress a smile when one reads the Prime Minister's account of an interview with Churchill shortly after his return from Belgium. 'I have had a long call from Winston who, after dilating in great detail on the actual situation, became suddenly very confidential and implored me not to take a conventional view of his future.

'Having, as he says, tasted blood these last few days he is beginning like a tiger to raven for more and begs that sooner or later, and the sooner the better, he may be relieved of his present office and put in some kind of military command. I told him that he could not be spared from the Admiralty. He scoffed at that, alleging that the naval part of the business is practically over as our superiority will grow greater and greater every month.

'His mouth waters at the thought of Kitchener's Armies. Are these glittering commands to be entrusted to dug-out trash, bred on the obsolete tactics of twenty-five years ago, mediocrities who have led a sheltered life, mouldering in military routine?

'For about an hour he poured forth a ceaseless invective and appeal and I much regretted that there was no shorthand writer within hearing as some of his unpremeditated phrases were quite priceless. He was, however, three parts serious and declared that a political career was nothing to him in comparison with military glory.'[167]

---

[166] *Memories and Reflections*: The Earl of Oxford and Asquith.

[167] *Memories and Reflections*: The Earl of Oxford and Asquith.

*

As the reader has seen, Churchill's prestige had declined sharply during the first three months of the war in which the events I have related took place. Much of the blame was unfair. The truth was that he had rendered valuable service to his country. His small but gallant Naval Air Force was busy scouting for enemy Zeppelins; his Dunkirk Circus had fooled the Germans into believing that their flank was threatened by forty thousand men and finally stimulated a German retreat; the prolongation of the resistance of Antwerp delayed the enemy's movement towards Ypres and prevented the capture of Dunkirk.

The mounting criticism against Churchill was almost entirely due to his self-assured manner. All his life he had irritated people by his belief in his own importance. But now that he was in a position of great power, his exuberance of spirit and his supreme self-confidence had become almost overwhelming, and he seemed to be indulging in a form of exhibitionism which his colleagues watched not only with annoyance but growing alarm. Many of them, including the Prime Minister, genuinely began to doubt his suitability as a Cabinet Minister. He seemed so rash and unstable. First there was the speech about 'digging the Germans out of their holes' the day before three British ships were sunk, then the spectacle of the First Lord rushing back and forth from Dunkirk like an excited schoolboy instead of leaving the direction of his Circus to someone else.

Even at the Admiralty things were not going too well. It was felt that Churchill was wielding far too much authority over the Navy for a civilian, largely due to the indulgent attitude of the First Sea Lord, Prince Louis of Battenberg, father of the present Lord Mountbatten. Prince Louis, it was believed, lacked the necessary vigour and decision to control the dynamic politicians, and Churchill was now dubbed 'the amateur Commander-in-Chief'.

As the problems confronting the Navy increased, criticism mounted. The *Emden* and *Königsberg* were sinking Allied ships in the Indian Ocean; the *Goeben* and *Breslau* had successfully slipped into the Sea of Marmora; and the *Gneisenau* and *Scharnhorst* were menacing Allied shipping off the west coast of Africa.

Winston was hotly attacked and for the first time realized that his position at the Admiralty was far from secure. Besides this, criticism of Prince Louis was mounting; not, however, because of the latter's work as First Sea Lord, but for the cruel reason that he was of German origin.

Winston knew that he could not defend Prince Louis much longer against the rising tide of anti-German feeling; he knew, also, that it was imperative to bolster his own position. He therefore sent for Lord Fisher. 'Churchill co-opted Fisher to relieve pressure against himself,' wrote Lord Beaverbrook, 'but he had no intention of letting anyone else rule the roost. Here, then, were two strong men of incompatible temper both bent on autocracy. It only required a difference of opinion on policy to produce a clash, and this cause of dissension was not long wanting.'[168]

However, at first the Churchill-Fisher combination proved a distinct success. Within a few weeks of swinging into action it scored a notable victory. Lord Fisher took over as First Sea Lord just as the British Navy was sustaining a sharp defeat. A cruiser squadron was attacked in overwhelming force off the coast of Chile, by five German warships under the brilliant command of Admiral von Spee. The British Admiralty was blamed for having sent as a reinforcement an old battleship capable of steaming only thirteen knots.

Lord Fisher acted with characteristic force, dispatching the *Invincible* and the *Inflexible* to the scene of action although this meant seriously weakening the Grand Fleet. Some idea of Fisher's drive may be gathered from the fact that these two ships were undergoing repairs when their sailing orders arrived. Word came back to the First Sea Lord that the date of their departure would have to be delayed, to which the old Admiral replied that they could sail with the workmen if necessary, but sail they would.

These two magnificent battle-cruisers went straight to the Falklands, and ran into von Spee by a brilliant stroke of luck. His famous squadron, including the *Gneisenau* and the *Scharnhorst*, was annihilated and von Spee and his two sons were killed. Fisher's triumph was complete. The country was ringing with his praise and Winston wrote to him: 'My dear, This was your show and your luck. I should have sent only one "Greyhound" and "Defence". These would have done the trick. But it was a great *coup*. Your flair was quite true. Let us have some more victories together and confound all our enemies abroad — and (don't forget) at home.'[169]

---

[168] *Politicians and War*: Lord Beaverbrook.

[169] *The Life of Lord Fisher*: Admiral Sir R. H. Bacon.

At about this time Fisher wrote to a friend: 'I am working hard … It is long and arduous to get back to a good position with a consummate good player for an enemy. But *I'm trying*. Let him not that putteth his armour on boast himself like him that taketh it off.'[170]

Churchill and Fisher agreed not to take any action without each other's knowledge. They manned the Admiralty almost the twenty-four hours around, forming what they called a 'perpetual clock'. Fisher rose at four in the morning and finished his work in the early afternoon; Winston began in the late morning and worked through the night. Winston wrote his minutes in red ink, and Fisher in green, and both referred to them as the Port and Starboard Lights.

Lord Fisher had strong ideas on strategy. He believed that the fighting in France would prove a fatal deadlock. The proper way to end the war, he argued, was to carry out a huge combined naval and military operation in the Baltic and place an army behind the enemy's lines. An enormous naval programme had been authorized by the Chancellor of the Exchequer. Fisher now extended it, and began to concentrate on the design of special ships for his Baltic plan. Churchill supported him and the two men agreed that the operation should take place some time in 1915.

Thus, for the first two months, the old Admiral and the young politician worked in close harmony. Then suddenly a fly appeared in the ointment. Turkey had entered the war on Germany's side two months previously. On 2 January, 1915, an urgent appeal was received from the Grand Duke Nicholas of Russia for the Allies to take some action in the Middle East that would draw off Turkish pressure from the Caucasus. Lord Kitchener pondered over the request but said that he could not spare troops from France. He wrote to Winston: 'I do not see that we can do anything that will seriously help the Russians in the Caucasus … The only place where a demonstration might have some effect on stopping reinforcements going East would be the Dardanelles. We shall not be ready for anything big for some months.'[171]

Churchill at once seized upon the idea of forcing the fortresses that flanked the narrow Straits of the Dardanelles by a naval operation alone. This idea had been contemplated more than once in the past but

---

[170] Ibid.

[171] *The World Crisis*: Winston S. Churchill.

had always been abandoned because it was considered too risky. Although Lord Fisher consented to the plan his instincts were against it and the quarrel that gradually developed between himself and Winston was the greatest political sensation of World War I. It brought Asquith's Liberal Government tumbling down; it ended Lord Fisher's naval career; and it resulted in the curt dismissal of Churchill from the Admiralty.

Chapter Twelve — Downfall over the Dardanelles

THE FAILURE of the attack on the Dardanelles was the most tragic episode of the First World War. And blame for the failure, fastened on Winston, pursued him all the way to World War II. Shortly after he became Prime Minister in 1940, a Conservative politician who had fought at Gallipoli, remarked to me grimly: 'Whatever Winston does, he does on a colossal scale; he'll either pull us through in a colossal way, or we'll have a colossal muck-up — like the Dardanelles.'

What makes the failure seem even more tragic to-day is the fact that when the first war ended, and evidence from both sides was available, most experts came to the conclusion that if a combined military and naval attack had been launched against the Dardanelles it would have succeeded. As a result Turkey would have capitulated, Bulgaria would have been prevented from joining Germany, Russia would not have collapsed, and in all probability World War I would have ended in 1915, saving millions of lives.

What is the truth of this bitter, half-forgotten story? Was Churchill really responsible or merely the scapegoat for the mistakes of others? The root of the trouble lay in the haphazard, almost amateurish way in which high political decisions were reached in the opening period of the war. 'During the first two months ... there was no established War Council,'[172] wrote Lloyd George in his *Memoirs*. 'There were sporadic and irregular consultations from time to time between the Secretary of State for War and the First Lord, between each of them individually and the Prime Minister and, now and again, between the two War Lords and the Prime Minister sitting together. The Foreign Secretary was occasionally brought in. I was not summoned to these conferences except when there were matters to be decided that directly affected finance.'

This irregular method of consultation was remarkable enough; but even more remarkable was the fact that, although Churchill had encouraged a spirit of co-operation with the War Office, there was no machinery for consultation between chiefs of staff of the two great services; no committee of military and naval experts to study joint

---

[172] The War Council was not set up until 25 November, and it replaced the Committee of Imperial Defence, an Advisory body composed of the Prime Minister and five or six other Ministers.

planning or review joint strategy. The two services operated, from a technical point of view, in water-tight compartments, while questions of strategy became an open tussle between all those who held strong views. In the autumn of 1914 Winston was in favour of a combined attack on Turkey; Lord Fisher was pressing his plan for an amphibious attack in the Baltic; Lloyd George was loudly in favour of an offensive in the Balkans; and Lord Kitchener believed the decisive theatre was in France.

Lord Kitchener dominated the scene. He was admired, feared, and respected. As a professional soldier raised to the office of Secretary of State for War, he was virtually a Commander-in-Chief and a Cabinet Minister rolled into one. Besides this, he had an immense following in the country. He was the hero of the British public and no government would have dared to oppose him and face his resignation. As a result, even when a War Council was set up by the Prime Minister, his voice predominated. Although the Council included such eminent men as Sir Edward Grey, the Foreign Secretary, Lloyd George, Chancellor of the Exchequer, Arthur Balfour, the Leader of the Conservative Opposition, and the Marquis of Crewe, Secretary of State for India, the only two members who could talk to Kitchener with authority were the Prime Minister, Mr. Asquith, and the First Lord of the Admiralty, Mr. Churchill. Thus the main responsibility for the war rested in effect with these three men.

But despite the fact that Winston was on an equal political footing with Kitchener he was well aware that he lacked the War Minister's prestige and authority. Not only did the great soldier have the backing of the British public, but the fact that he was a famous general in Egypt when Churchill was an unknown subaltern gave him an automatic ascendancy. Kitchener remembered how young Winston Churchill had begged to join his army in 1898; how, as Commander-in-Chief, he had said 'no' and Winston had come anyway; and how when the campaign was over Winston had criticized him for 'desecrating the Mahdi's tomb'. But all these incidents were respectably buried in the past and both men now regarded each other with genuine good will and esteem. Nevertheless, Kitchener could not help thinking of Winston as a subordinate and as a result did not encourage any real equality or intimacy. Besides, he was cold and reserved and did not make friends easily. Naturally silent, he disliked communicating his views to anyone save his own military staff. Winston on the other hand was a born talker, warm and volatile, bubbling over with political and strategic ideas which he liked to develop in conversation. Neither man was attracted to the personality of the other, and the barrier of temperament added one more obstacle in the way of close co-operation between the two fighting services.

This was the background of the story that opened on 2 January, 1915, when the Grand Duke Nicholas of Russia asked for a diversion in the Middle East to ease Turkish pressure on Russian troops in the Caucasus. Kitchener wrote Churchill a memorandum suggesting a Naval 'demonstration' at the Dardanelles. But Lord Fisher at once came forward with a plan for a combined operation which called for seventy-five thousand troops. This scheme was promptly rejected, for Kitchener repeated emphatically that no divisions could be spared from the European theatre; every British soldier must be held in reserve in case of an early spring offensive.

Winston began to study the possibilities of a purely naval assault. He had always believed that an attack on Turkey was the right strategy. But there seemed so little hope of persuading Kitchener to consider it that he had lately given his support to Lord Fisher's project for a combined offensive in the Baltic. Now it seemed as though events were playing into his hands, and he returned to the idea of an operation in the Middle East with high enthusiasm.

Lord Fisher's discarded scheme for the Dardanelles had included a naval attack on the outer fortresses of the long, curving straits which led into the Sea of Marmora, on the far shores of which rose Constantinople, the Turkish capital. The strategic advantages of a successful assault at once became illuminated in Winston's mind. If the fleet could get past the many fortresses that dotted the steep banks of the Straits and force its way into the Sea of Marmora, Constantinople might capitulate, and the Allies would be able to join hands with their Russian Allies. Arms could be shipped in and wheat sent out. Besides, the whole Balkan area would be neutralized, leaving Germany and Austria fighting alone.

The more Winston thought of the project the more enthusiastic he became. On 3 January he wired Admiral Carden, commanding at the Dardanelles: 'Do you think that it is a practicable operation to force the Dardanelles by the use of ships alone? It is assumed that older battleships would be employed, that they would be furnished with minesweepers and that they would be preceded by colliers or other merchant vessels as sweepers and bumpers. The importance of the results would justify severe loss. Let me know what your views are.'[173] Two days later Carden replied: 'I do not think that the Dardanelles can be rushed but they might be forced by extended operations with a large number of ships.'[174] This was not a particularly enthusiastic answer, but it was sufficiently encouraging for Churchill. He wired back asking the Admiral to draw up a plan of attack, which he received a week later.

Carden's outline was divided into four parts; first the destruction of the outer defences; second, the intermediary defences; third, the defences of the Narrows; and fourth, the sweeping of a clear channel through the minefields and into the Sea of Marmora. From this moment on, Winston was wholeheartedly in favour of an attack by ships alone, and set out determinedly to put the plan into operation. Mr. Lloyd George wrote in his Memoirs: 'Mr. Winston Churchill has been in constant touch with Lord Kitchener and when the former has a scheme agitating his powerful mind, as everyone who is acquainted with his method knows quite well, he is indefatigable in pressing it upon the acceptance of everyone who matters in the decision … he was prepared to act without waiting for an immediate dispatch of troops. His proposal was a purely naval operation in its initial stages.'

On 13 January the War Council met. Winston put forward his project and all the members, with the exception of Lloyd George, agreed to it. Lord Fisher and Admiral of the Fleet Sir Arthur Wilson were present and made no comment. The conclusions of the Ministers resulted in the following directive: 'The Admiralty should prepare for a naval expedition in February to bombard and take the Gallipoli Peninsula with Constantinople as its objective.'

This meeting of the 13th is now famous for both the importance and the confusion of its decisions. At that time there was no Cabinet Secretary, and Cabinet Minutes were not taken.[175] As a result neither Lord Fisher nor Admiral Wilson was aware that any decision had been taken. 'Very likely the Prime Minister went and wrote it down when the meeting was over,' Lord Fisher commented caustically some time

---

[173] Report of the Dardanelles Commission.

[174] Ibid.

[175] It was not until Lloyd George became Prime Minister that a Secretariat was established.

later.[176] The Prime Minister, however, claimed that he read it out before the meeting adjourned, but that perhaps Lord Fisher and Admiral Wilson had already left. The next point of confusion was the fact that half the members of the Council were under the impression that the Navy had been ordered merely to prepare for an expedition, while the other half, including Mr. Churchill, assumed that definite approval had been given. The third point of confusion concerned the directive itself. The instructions given to the Admiralty to bombard and take the Gallipoli Peninsula with Constantinople as its objective, 'were odd to the point of grotesqueness if a purely Naval expedition was envisaged ... it was obviously an impossible task for a fleet acting by itself,' comments Cruttwell in a standard History of the Great War.[177]

Winston, however, speculated that if the Fleet could force its way into the Sea of Marmora, the Greek Army might join the Allies; furthermore, that a revolution might take place in Constantinople. He told the War Cabinet that he believed victory could be won without military aid; the Army, he declared, would only come in to 'reap the fruits'.

The Sea Lords, on the other hand, regarded the project in an entirely different light. In the Naval Staff conferences that were held at the Admiralty between 3 and 13 January, not a single Naval expert favoured the attack by ships alone. All of them expressed a strong preference for a combined operation; and on the very day that Churchill first wired Carden, Admiral Sir Henry Jackson, a high authority at the Admiralty, wrote a memorandum in which he stated: 'Assuming the enemy squadrons destroyed and the batteries rushed, they would be open to the fire of field artillery and infantry and to torpedo attack at night, with no store ships with ammunition, and with no retreat without re-engaging the shore batteries, unless these had been destroyed while forcing the passage. Though they might dominate the city and inflict enormous damage, their position would not be an enviable one, unless there were a large military force to occupy the town ...'[178]

---

[176] Report of the Dardanelles Commission.

[177] *A History of the Great War*: C. R. M. F. Cruttwell.

[178] Report of the Dardanelles Commission.

How, then, did Winston persuade the Admirals to agree to the Naval operation? He swung them over on the grounds, first, that it was vital to take some action that would help the Russians; second, that the strength of the Grand Fleet would be unimpaired, for only old battleships unfit for service in the North Sea would be used; and third, and most important, that if the operation did not prove successful the Navy could withdraw at any time. On these conditions the Admirals consented, without enthusiasm. But at the same time that Winston was assuring the Sea Lords that they could break off the bombardment whenever they wished, he sent the Grand Duke Nicholas of Russia a telegram (19 January) saying: 'It is our intention to press the matter to a conclusion.' Thus from the very beginning the politician and the Admirals were at cross purposes; and the rift made itself more and more apparent as each week passed.

First of all, soon after the meeting on 13 January, Lord Fisher's lukewarm consent began to harden into opposition. He strongly urged Churchill not to proceed with the Naval plan unless the Army agreed to send troops and make it a joint operation. He could not say that the Naval bombardment would fail, but he had little faith in it: and now he began to fear that the expedition might interfere with his own pet project — amphibious operations in the Baltic. He wrote to the Prime Minister that he did not want to attend any more War Councils, and in a private meeting with Asquith and Churchill on 28 January, he told them both that he was becoming increasingly opposed to the Dardanelles. Since he did not base his objections on the technical difficulties involved but on his preference for his Baltic operation, the two men finally persuaded him to attend the War Council meeting which was being held the same morning. However, when the old Sea Lord saw that the Dardanelles expedition was receiving its final blessing, he rose from the table and walked over to the window on the verge of resignation. Lord Kitchener followed him and persuaded him to remain at his post. That same afternoon Churchill and Fisher thrashed the subject out again, and the young politician finally secured the old sailor's support on the grounds, emphasized again, that the Navy could break off the operation when it liked. Thus the struggle between the two men continued, with one buoyant and confident and the other doubtful and disapproving.

Two and a half weeks later Lord Kitchener made an announcement which changed the whole complexion of the operation. Early in February he told the War Council that the situation in France had altered and he felt he might be able to send troops to aid the Naval attack after all. Lord Fisher at once took heart and weighed in eagerly with a letter to Winston. 'I hope you were successful with Kitchener,' he wrote on the evening of 16 February, 'in getting divisions sent to Lemnos *to-morrow*! Not a grain of wheat will come from the Black Sea unless there is military occupation of the Dardanelles, and it will be the wonder of the ages that no troops were sent to co-operate with the Fleet with half a million soldiers in England. *The war of lost opportunities!!! Why did Antwerp fall?* The Haslar boats might go at once to Lemnos, as somebody will land at Gallipoli some time or another.'[179] Churchill comments on this letter in *The World Crisis*: 'I still adhered to the integrity of the Naval plan.'

The rest of the story is well known. For a week Kitchener vacillated, then finally decided to commit troops to the operation, and on 24 February informed the War Council that 'if the Fleet did not get through the Army would see the business through.' The effect of a defeat in the Orient would be very serious, he added, and there could be no turning back; and this, of course, altered the whole basis on which the Admiralty had consented to the proposition.

Kitchener sent General Birdwood and, a few weeks later, Sir Ian Hamilton, to the scene of action to report on developments. The Fleet had opened its bombardment of the fortresses on 19 February. For the first ten days all went well, the outer fortresses fell and the attention of the world became riveted on the action. Then suddenly progress stopped. The Turks were putting up a much stiffer resistance and the mine-sweeping trawlers were unable to stand the fire. General Birdwood telegraphed to Kitchener: 'I am very doubtful if the Navy can force the passage unassisted.' The following day he sent another telegram: 'I have already informed you that I consider the Admiral's forecast is too sanguine, and ... I doubt his ability to force the passage unaided.'

However, on 18 March, Admiral de Robeck, who had assumed the Command of the Fleet from Admiral Carden, who was suddenly taken ill, massed all his ships for a decisive attempt. The forts were subjected to an intense bombardment which lasted nearly all day, and by 4 p.m. such damage had been inflicted the enemy had practically ceased firing. As the ships steamed forward victory seemed in sight, but suddenly the vessels struck a row of mines, three were sunk and four put out of action. This meant that nearly half the Fleet was crippled.

---

[179] *The World Crisis*: Winston S. Churchill.

Admiral de Robeck wired the Admiralty that the plan of attack must be reconsidered and means found to deal with floating mines, but that he hoped to renew the operations in a few days' time.

But during the course of the next four days he changed his mind. At a conference on the 22nd he told General Sir Ian Hamilton that 'he was now quite clear' he could not get through without a large military force. In order to maintain communications when the Fleet penetrated the Sea of Marmora all gun positions guarding the Straits must be destroyed, and he had come to the conclusion that only a small percentage could be rendered useless by attack from ships. Hamilton had already formed a similar impression himself and wired Kitchener three days earlier, 'I am being most reluctantly driven to the conclusion that the Straits are not likely to be forced by battleships as at one time seemed probable ...'[180]

Churchill received de Robeck's decision with consternation. He drew up a telegram ordering de Robeck to continue the attack but Lord Fisher and the other Admirals refused to send it, declaring that they were not willing to overrule the Commander on the spot. Naval operations were never resumed, and from then on the attack became a purely military affair. As everyone knows, it ended in heart-breaking failure.

First of all, five long precious weeks were allowed to lapse between the breaking off of Naval operations and the initial assault of the Army; and during these weeks, while rumours spread that a military force was gathering, the Turks feverishly strengthened their defences. When troops finally stormed the Gallipoli beaches on 25 April the precious element of surprise was gone, and they were unable to capture vital key points. Then, a week or so later, German submarines began to appear in the Mediterranean, and the Admiralty ordered its most valuable and powerful battleship home. Gradually the Navy pulled out and left the whole task to the Army, which struggled on the rocky beaches, overlooked by high cliffs in the hands of the enemy, for eight desperate months with an ever-mounting death roll. In December 1915 Gallipoli was evacuated with a cost of a quarter of a million French and British casualties.[181]

---

[180] *Gallipoli Diary*: Sir Ian Hamilton.

[181] This figure includes sick.

But long before the final evacuation, the British public was aware that something was wrong. People saw the Naval attack had failed and assumed that the Army had been called in to pull the Navy's chestnuts out of the fire. If troops were available why hadn't they been sent earlier? Who was responsible for the whole blundering idea of an attack by ships alone?

Churchill makes a powerful case for himself in *The World Crisis*. This brilliant and fascinating book is half history and half autobiography. Sometimes the narrative sweeps forward on a tide of facts, sometimes on a long swell of argument and opinion. The book was written not only to present the events of the time, but to silence the author's critics and vindicate his statesmanship.

Winston's account of the Dardanelles reaches an impressive climax, for after the war facts and figures were collected from the enemy, and it became known for certain that the Turkish gunners in the Dardanelles forts had only enough ammunition to fight one, or possibly two, more actions such as that on 18 March. 'The Turkish Commander in the Dardanelles was weighed down by a premonition of defeat,' writes the official historian. 'More than half the ammunition had been expended, and it could not be replaced. The antiquated means of fire control had been seriously interrupted. The Turkish gun crews were demoralized and even the German officers present had, apparently, little hope of successful resistance if the Fleet attacked the next day ... A German journalist describes the great astonishment of the defenders of the coastal forts when the attack suddenly ceased. He records that the German Naval gunners who were manning the batteries at Chanak told him later that they had made up their minds that the Fleet would win, and that they themselves could not have held out much longer.'[182]

But even if the Fleet, or what was left of the Fleet, had forced the Straits and sailed into the Sea of Marmora, what would have happened then? Would Constantinople have fallen? Could the Navy have sustained its position?

The greatest authority on the subject, General Liman von Sanders, the German Commander-in-Chief of the Dardanelles defence, who is usually quoted by the historians and whom Mr. Churchill himself quotes in other contexts, did not believe that a break-through would

---

[182] *Military Operations Gallipoli*: Compiled by Brig.-General C. F. Aspinwall-Oglander.

have been decisive. 'In my opinion even if the Allied Fleet had been successful in breaking through the Dardanelles and victorious in a sea-fight in the Sea of Marmora, its position would have been scarcely tenable unless the entire shore of the Straits of the Dardanelles were strongly occupied by enemy forces. Should the Turkish troops be successful in holding their positions along the shores of the Straits, or should they be successful in recapturing these, then the necessary flow of supplies [*Nachschub*] through ships and coaliers would be rendered impossible. Measures of defence taken rendered a landing by troops near Constantinople, who might have lived on the country, almost without prospect of success.

'A decisive success could only be gained by the enemy if a landing by troops upon a great scale occurred either simultaneously with the breakthrough by the Fleet or if it preceded this. A landing by troops following the break-through would have been obliged to renounce artillery support by the Fleet which would have had to occupy itself with other tasks.'[183]

However, the argument as to whether or not the ships could have got through, and if they had got through whether or not Constantinople would have fallen, must always remain in the realms of speculation. No one will ever know the answer. But this is not the main point. Experts agree that a combined operation against the Dardanelles would have succeeded. If Winston had not been captivated by the idea of a Naval attack alone, and had exercised more patience in working out the scheme, would a co-ordinated plan have emerged? 'I have asked myself in these later years,' he writes in *The World Crisis*, 'what would have happened if I had taken Lord Fisher's advice and refused point blank to take any action at the Dardanelles unless or until the War Office produced on their responsibility an adequate army to storm the Gallipoli Peninsula? Should we by holding out in this way have secured a sufficient army and a good plan? Should we have had all the advantages of the Dardanelles policy without the mistakes and misfortunes for which we had to pay so dearly?' He goes on to say that although no one can probe this 'imaginary situation' he does not think that anything less than the 'oracular demonstration and practical proof of the strategic meaning of the Dardanelles' would have made men sufficiently conscious of the importance of an attack on Turkey, to agree to send troops.

---

[183] *Five Years in Turkey*: Liman von Sanders.

This, however, is a weak defence, for it must be remembered that on 16 February, only two and a half weeks after the Naval operation had received sanction from the War Council, and three days before the bombardment actually began, Kitchener declared that the possibility of sending troops was opening up. If Winston had paused then, as both Lord Fisher and Sir Henry Jackson begged him to do, there is every reason to believe that a combined operation might have been planned and put into operation.

In 1916, Parliament authorized the setting up of a Royal Commission, composed of ten of the ablest and most distinguished men in public life, 'for the purposes of inquiring into the origin, inception, and conduct of operations of war in the Dardanelles and Gallipoli.' Lord Kitchener died before he could give evidence, but the Commissioners made it clear that the three most responsible members of the War Council were the Prime Minister, the War Minister and the First Lord of the Admiralty. They then went on to say: 'We do not think that the War Council were justified in coming to a decision without much fuller investigation of the proposition which had been suggested to them that "the Admiralty should ... bombard and take Gallipoli Peninsula with Constantinople as its objective". We do not consider that the urgency was such as to preclude a short adjournment to enable the Naval and military advisers of the Government to make a thorough examination of the question. We hold that the possibility of making a surprise amphibious attack on the Gallipoli Peninsula offered such great military and political advantages that it was mistaken and ill-advised to sacrifice this possibility by hastily deciding to undertake a purely Naval attack which from its nature could not attain completely the object set out in the terms of the decision.'[184]

The Royal Commission declared that Churchill had not been guilty of any 'incorrect' behaviour, and had always acted with the concurrence, unwilling though it may have been, of his naval advisers. Their final judgment was that although he bore a heavy responsibility he did not bear it alone. Asquith and Kitchener were just as much to blame. But the judgment of his colleagues in the House of Commons was more severe. They knew that Winston was the most dynamic member of the trio. They also knew that he possessed formidable powers of persuasion. This, coupled with his impetuosity, made him a

---

[184] Report of the Dardanelles Commission.

danger to the country. He may not have been solely responsible, but without him, they argued, the whole disastrous operation would never have taken place. As far as strategy was concerned, he was right. Tactically, he blundered. Thirty years later he wrote: 'I was ruined for the time being over the Dardanelles, and a supreme enterprise was cast away, through my trying to carry out a major and cardinal operation of war from a subordinate position. Men are ill-advised to try such ventures.'[185]

*

Now we must return to the events that led to Lord Fisher's sensational resignation on 15 May which brought down the Government. Ten days previously the Army had stormed the rocky beaches on the Gallipoli Peninsula at a cost of twenty thousand men, and secured only a precarious foothold. Fisher regarded the situation with alarm. The combined operation was taking place too late. The vital element of surprise was gone, the Turks had had time to fortify their defences, and it was obvious that military operations would be long and costly.

In Naval circles two conflicting opinions were gathering strength. The first was that the Navy should once again attempt to force the Straits because of the severe losses the Army was sustaining; the second was that the Navy should on no account attempt an operation until the Army had effectively occupied the shores. Churchill stood between the two views. He was in favour of a limited operation. He wanted the Fleet to engage the forts of the Narrows and test their supposed shortage of ammunition. At the same time he believed that the minefields could be swept.

Lord Fisher was adamant. He was strongly against Naval action until the Army had secured the shores, and he was determined, this time, that his view would prevail. He distrusted Winston's plan, for he felt that if the operation were successful the latter would insist on penetrating the Sea of Marmora. The old Admiral was under an added strain because of the increasing German submarine menace in home waters; and he also had received intelligence that these submarines would soon make their appearance in the Mediterranean. Then the *Lusitania* was sunk, which heightened his anxieties.

Consequently, on 12 May Lord Fisher declared that he was no longer prepared to risk the *Queen Elizabeth* at the Dardanelles and demanded her return to the Grand Fleet. Lord Kitchener was furious.

---

[185] *Their Finest Hour*: Winston S. Churchill.

In a stormy meeting he accused the Navy of deserting the Army. Lord Fisher announced flatly that 'either the *Queen Elizabeth* left the Dardanelles that afternoon or he left the Admiralty that night'. Lord Fisher won his point and was proved right; a dummy ship equipped to represent the *Queen Elizabeth* was left at the Dardanelles while the real vessel came home. Two weeks later the dummy was torpedoed and sunk.

On the same day that Lord Fisher had his altercation with Kitchener he sent a memorandum to Winston and the Prime Minister stating his reasons for refusing to allow a Naval attack to take place until the Army was in occupation of the shores. He enclosed the following covering letter to the Prime Minister:

'My dear Prime Minister,

'It will be within your recollection that you saw me and the First Lord of the Admiralty in your private room, prior to a meeting of the War Council (28 January, 1915), to consider my protest against the Dardanelles undertaking when it was first mooted. With extreme reluctance, and largely due to the earnest words spoken to me by Kitchener, I by not resigning (as I now see I should have done) remained a most unwilling beholder (and, indeed, a participator) of the gradual draining of our Naval resources from the decisive theatre of the war. The absence, especially at this moment, of destroyers, submarines, and mine-sweepers (which are now) at the Dardanelles most materially lessens our power of dealing with the submarine menace in home waters — a menace daily becoming greater as foreshadowed in the print I submitted to you six months before the war.

'I have sent the enclosed memorandum to the First Lord, and I ask for it to be circulated to the War Council.'[186]

Churchill and Lord Fisher talked things over that evening and as a result the latter seemed more content. But on the next day the quarrel flared up again. Lord Fisher wrote the Prime Minister once more.

'My dear Prime Minister,

'Thank you for your letter of yesterday, in which you state that you had been given to understand that an arrangement had been come to between the First Lord and myself, and you kindly added that you were very glad. But I regret to say that within four hours of the pact being concluded, the First Lord said to Kitchener "that in the event of

---

[186] *The Life of Lord Fisher*: Admiral Sir. R. H. Bacon.

the Army's failure, the Fleet would endeavour to force its way through", or words to that effect. However, for the moment, with your kind assurance of no such action being permitted, I remain to do my best to help the Prime Minister in the very biggest task any Prime Minister ever had — not excepting Pitt and his Austerlitz! Still, I desire to convey to you that I honestly feel that I cannot remain where I am much longer, as there is an inevitable drain daily (almost hourly) on the resources in the decisive theatre of the war. But that is not the worst. Instead of the whole time of the whole of the Admiralty being concentrated on the daily increasing submarine menace in home waters, we are all diverted to the Dardanelles, and the unceasing activities of the First Lord, both by day and night, are engaged in ceaseless prodding of everyone in every department afloat and ashore in the interest of the Dardanelles Fleet, with the result of the huge Armada now there, whose size is sufficiently indicated by their having as many battleships out there as in the German High Seas Fleet! Therefore this purely private and personal letter, intended for your eye alone and not to be quoted, as there is no use threatening without acting, is to mention to one person who I feel *ought* to know *that I feel that my time is short*. 13 May, 1915.'[187]

The quarrel between the two men had now reached its climax. Each had his toes dug in. Churchill was determined that the Navy should continue to take part in the Dardanelles operation, and Fisher was determined that it should not. Both were ready to get rid of the other if it proved necessary. On 14 May the War Council met and Fisher reiterated his views, declaring that he had been against the Dardanelles from the start. That afternoon Winston wrote to the Prime Minister:

'I must ask you to take note of Fisher's statement to-day that he "was against the Dardanelles and had been all along" or words to that effect. The First Sea Lord has agreed in writing to every executive telegram on which the operations have been conducted; and had they been immediately successful, the credit would have been his. But I make no complaint of that. I am attached to the old boy and it is a great pleasure to me to work with him. I think he reciprocates these feelings. My point is that a moment will probably arise in these operations when the Admiral and General on the spot will wish and require to run a risk with the Fleet for a great and decisive effort. If I agree with them, I shall sanction it, and I cannot undertake to be paralysed by the veto of

---

[187] *The Life of Lord Fisher*: Admiral Sir R. H. Bacon.

a friend who whatever the result will certainly say: "I was always against the Dardanelles."

'You will see that in a matter of this kind *someone* has to take the responsibility. I will do so — provided that my decision is the one that rules — and not otherwise …

'But I wish now to make it clear to you that a man who says, "I disclaim responsibility for failure," cannot be the final arbiter of the measures which may be found to be vital to success.

'This requires no answer and I am quite contented with the course of affairs.'[188]

That evening Churchill and Fisher had another long interview, and once again appeared to have settled their differences. Fisher was adamant that no more reinforcements should go to the Dardanelles, and Churchill apparently agreed. When the old Admiral returned to his room he called his Naval Assistant. 'You need not pack up just yet,' he told him. He went on to say that the matter of reinforcements was not settled with the First Lord and added: 'But I suppose he will soon be at me again.'

That night, however, Winston sent the Admiral a long minute. Paragraph 6 contained a fatal sentence. 'In view of the request of the Vice-Admiral, I consider that two more "E" boats should be sent to the Dardanelles.' When Churchill's secretary brought the minute to Fisher's Naval Assistant he asked, 'How do you think the old man will take it?' The Naval Assistant said that he had no doubt whatever that Lord Fisher would resign instantly if he received it. Churchill's secretary took it away, then came back and said that the First Lord was certain that Lord Fisher would not object to his proposals, but that, in any case, it was necessary that they should be made. Lord Fisher resigned his office of First Sea Lord the following morning.[189]

*

Lord Fisher's resignation caused a sensation. First he went to Lloyd George who was just leaving Downing Street for the week-end. 'I want to speak to you,' he said. 'I have resigned. I can stand it no longer. Our ships are being sunk, while we have a Fleet in the Dardanelles which is bigger than the German Navy. Both our Army and Navy are being bled for the benefit of the Dardanelles.' Then the

---

[188] *The World Crisis*: Winston S. Churchill.

[189] See *The Life of Lord Fisher*: Admiral Sir R. H. Bacon.

old Admiral, smouldering and indignant, retired to his official residence which adjoined the Admiralty. He pulled down the blinds and refused to admit anyone. Mr. McKenna, who had preceded Churchill as First Lord, forced his way in and tried to argue with him, but Fisher was adamant.

Winston now began to realize the political storm he would have to face if the First Sea Lord remained obdurate and he wrote him a long and persuasive letter, which gives some idea of the pressure Churchill was willing to apply. 'In order to bring you back to the Admiralty I took my political life in my hands — as you well know,' the letter began. This assertion was something of an exaggeration, for Winston had brought Fisher back largely to fortify his own position. 'You then promised to stand by me and see me through,' he continued. 'If you now go at this bad moment and therefore let loose on me the spite and malice of those who are your enemies even more than they are mine, it will be a melancholy ending to our six months of successful war and administration. The discussions that will arise will strike a cruel blow at the fortunes of the Army now struggling on the Gallipoli Peninsula and cannot fail to invest with an air of disaster a mighty enterprise which with patience can, and will, certainly be carried to success.

'Many of the anxieties of the winter are past. The harbours are protected, the great flow of new construction is arriving. We are far stronger at home than we have ever been, and the great reinforcement is now at hand.

'I hope you will come and see me to-morrow afternoon. I have a proposition to make to you, with the assent of the Prime Minister, which may remove some of the anxieties and difficulties which you feel about the measures necessary to support the Army at the Dardanelles.

'Though I stand at my post until relieved, it will be a very great grief to me to part from you; and our rupture will be profoundly injurious to every public interest.'[190]

Lord Fisher wrote Winston the following reply:

'YOU ARE BENT ON FORCING THE DARDANELLES AND NOTHING WILL TURN YOU FROM IT — NOTHING. I know you so well. I could give you no better proof of my desire to stand by you than my having remained by you in this Dardanelles business up to the last moment against the strongest conviction of my life.

---

[190] *The World Crisis*: Winston S. Churchill.

'YOU WILL REMAIN AND I SHALL GO — it is better so. Your splendid stand on my behalf I can never forget when you took your political life in your hands, and I have really worked very hard for you in return — my utmost; but there is a question beyond all personal obligations. I assure you it is only painful to have further conversations. I have told the Prime Minister I will not remain. I have absolutely decided to stick to that decision. Nothing will turn me from it. You say with much feeling that *it will be a very great grief to you to part from me* — I am certain that you know in your heart no one has ever been more faithful to you than I have since I joined you last October. *I have worked my very hardest.*'[191]

It is well known that people seldom see themselves as others see them. Winston knew that he had many political enemies but he did not seem to understand the intensity of the feeling against him. This was curious in view of the savage attack which the Tory Press had launched during the previous few weeks, largely inspired by high ranking Army officers in France who were violently opposed to what they called 'side-shows'. The Conservatives had been hostile ever since Antwerp, but now the *Morning Post* outdid itself. Almost daily they struck out at Winston under a series of headlines: 'The Amazing Amateur', 'The Amateur Admiral', 'Politician versus Expert', 'Too Much Churchill'. Some idea of the virulence of their campaign may be seen from an extract printed on 30 April: 'Mr. Churchill is still his own Party, and the chief of the partisans. He still sees himself as the only digit in the sum of things, all other men as mere cyphers, whose function it is to follow after and multiply his personal value a million-fold … He has not ceased to be the showman of a one-man show. He is none the less true to himself because, indulged by the larger opportunities of world-wide war, his instinct for the melodramatic has blossomed into megalomania.'

Winston discounted these attacks as ordinary Tory propaganda. But he lived so much in a world of his own, the world of great and stirring events, that he made the mistake of forgetting he was a politician and, as such, dependent on the confidence of his Parliamentary colleagues.

He attended the House of Commons infrequently and only as a matter of form. 'He failed in 1915,' wrote Lord Beaverbrook, 'because

---

[191] *The Life of Lord Fisher*: Admiral Sir R. H. Bacon.

he showed himself too confident to be prudent. He neither tied the Liberals to him nor conciliated the Tories.'[192]

The day after Fisher's resignation Winston dined with the Prime Minister. He told the latter that Admiral Sir Arthur Wilson had agreed to serve under him as First Sea Lord, and showed him the list he had drawn up of the new Board of Admiralty. Asquith approved the names and assured Winston of his support.

But in the meanwhile, other events were taking place. Bonar Law, the Leader of the Conservative Opposition, had learned of Lord Fisher's departure and at once went to see Lloyd George at 11 Downing Street. He told him bluntly that the Conservatives were not willing to continue to support the Government unless Churchill left the Admiralty. Lord Fisher was the darling of the Tory Party; Winston was its *bête noire*. Why should they allow a man they admired to be sacrificed for a man they utterly distrusted? He said flatly he would be unable to control the storm in the House of Commons. 'Of course,' replied Lloyd George, 'we must have a Coalition, for the alternative is impossible.' He took him by the arm and led him through the private passage to 10 Downing Street where they had an interview with Mr. Asquith.

Winston was ignorant of these proceedings and on Monday appeared at the House ready to announce his new Board. The next forty-eight hours were filled with bitter disappointments for him. First of all, Asquith and Lloyd George informed him that a Coalition Government was being formed and that, as part of the bargain the Tories had demanded his removal from the Admiralty. Just as they were breaking this news to him a message came asking him to return to his office at once on urgent business. He hurried back to learn that the German High Seas Fleet was emerging. Was the great battle in the North Sea at last to be fought? Churchill gave orders for every available ship to be dispatched to the scene of action. Perhaps he would return to the House to announce a great victory. If so, could they let him go? One can imagine the anxious and tense hours he passed; but by morning it was clear that the Germans were not looking for a fight; they had returned to their bases.

On Tuesday it was certain that nothing could save Churchill's position, yet he still clung to hope. Lord Beaverbrook called on him at the Admiralty with F. E. Smith, and later wrote: 'One felt rather as if

---

[192] *Politicians and the War*: Lord Beaverbrook.

one had been invited "to come and look at fallen Antony" … What a creature of strange moods he is — always at the top of the wheel of confidence or at the bottom of an intense depression … That Tuesday night he was clinging to the desire of retaining the Admiralty as though the salvation of England depended on it. I believe he would even have made it up with Lord Fisher if that had been the price of remaining there. None the less, so little did he realize the inwardness of the whole situation that he still hoped.'[193]

As well as hoping, he wrote a long and pleading letter to Bonar Law. This was a strange act, for Bonar Law was more implacable in his dislike and distrust of Winston than almost any other Tory. A melancholy, humdrum, unimaginative man, Law was utterly devoid of gaiety or exuberance. Winston's flamboyant personality was anathema to him. He regarded him as a boastful buccaneer upon whom no reliance could ever be placed. Besides, he found it hard to forgive Winston's patronizing airs. Lord Beaverbrook, who, as Max Aitken, was Bonar Law's closest friend and confidant, gives a sample of the interchanges that took place between the two men when Churchill was at the height of his power as First Lord and Law was merely the Leader of the Opposition.

'The words which you now tell me you employed,' wrote Churchill in a letter to Law, 'and which purport to be a paraphrase, if not an actual quotation, are separated by a small degree of inaccuracy and misrepresentation from the inaccuracy and misrepresentation of the condensed report.' And on another occasion: 'I resist all temptation to say, "I told you so!"' Lord Beaverbrook goes on to say that he never heard Bonar Law use but one kind of language about Churchill: 'I consider Churchill a formidable antagonist. None the less, I would rather have him in opposition to me than on my side.'

It was obvious to everybody but Winston that Bonar Law was immovable. Nevertheless, Winston sent him a letter containing the following extracts:

'Admiralty,
'Whitehall.
'17 May, 1915.

'My dear Bonar Law,

The rule to follow is what is best calculated to beat the enemy and not what is most likely to please the newspapers. The question of the

---

[193] *Politicians and the War*: Lord Beaverbrook.

Dardanelles operations and my differences with Fisher ought to be settled by people who know the facts and not by those who cannot know them. Now you and your friends, except Mr. Balfour, do not know the facts. On our side only the Prime Minister knows them. The policy and conduct of the Dardanelles operations should be reviewed by the new Cabinet. Every fact should be laid before them. They should decide and on their

'My lips are sealed in public, but in a few days all the facts can be placed before you and your friends under official secrecy. I am sure those with whom I hope to work as colleagues and comrades in this great struggle will not allow a newspaper campaign — necessarily conducted in ignorance and not untinged with prejudice — to be the deciding factor in matters of such terrible import.

'Personal interests and sympathies ought to be strictly subordinated. It does not matter whether a Minister receives exact and meticulous justice. But what is vital is that from the outset of this new effort we are to make together we should be fearless of outside influences and straight with each other. We are coming together not to work on public opinion but to wage war: and by waging successful war we shall dominate public opinion.

'I would like you to bring this letter to the notice of those with whom I expect soon to act: and I wish to add the following: I was sent to the Admiralty four years ago. I have always been supported by high professional advice; but partly through circumstances and partly no doubt through my own methods and inclinations, an exceptional burden has been borne by me. I had to procure the money, the men, the ships and ammunition; to recase with expert advice the war plans; to complete in every detail that could be foreseen the organization of the Navy ...

'Many Sea Lords have come and gone, but during all these four years (nearly) I have been according to my patent "solely responsible to Crown and Parliament" and have borne the blame for every failure; and now I present to you an absolutely secure Naval position; a Fleet constantly and rapidly growing in strength, and abundantly supplied with munitions of every kind, an organization working with perfect smoothness and efficiency, and the seas upon which no enemy's flag is flown.

'Therefore I ask to be judged justly, deliberately and with knowledge. I do not ask for anything else.'[194]

Lord Beaverbrook tried to use his influence with Bonar Law on Churchill's behalf but to no purpose. The following reply came from the Conservative leader: 'My dear Churchill, I thank you for your letter which I shall show to my friends beginning with Austen Chamberlain; but, believe me, what I said to you last night is inevitable.'[195]

Once again Lloyd George proved a staunch friend. He begged Asquith to offer Winston an important office such as the Colonies or the India Office, but Asquith insisted that the Conservatives would not hear of anything but a minor post and that the Duchy of Lancaster was the best he could do. 'It was a cruel and unjust degradation,' wrote Lloyd George. 'It was quite unnecessary in order to propitiate them to fling him from the masthead whence he had been directing the fire, down to the lower deck to polish the brass.'[196]

Just before Winston moved out of the Admiralty Lord Riddell called on him and found him harassed and worn. 'I am the victim of a political intrigue. I am finished,' he said. Riddell replied: 'Not finished at forty, with your remarkable powers!' 'Yes,' he said. 'Finished in respect of all I care for — the waging of war: the defeat of the Germans. I have had a high place offered to me — a position which has been occupied by many distinguished men, and which carries with it a high salary. But all that goes for nothing. This is what I live for. I have prepared a statement of my case, but cannot use it.' Riddell then asked him if he thought Asquith had been weak in the conduct of the war. 'Terribly weak,' said Winston. 'Supinely weak. His weakness will be the death of him.'[197]

*

Lord Fisher was not recalled as First Sea Lord. He might have been had he not made an astonishing mistake. While the Prime Minister was looking for a successor to Churchill Fisher suddenly took up his

---

[194] *Politicians and the War*: Lord Beaverbrook.

[195] Ibid.

[196] *War Memoirs of David Lloyd George*.

[197] *Lord Riddell's War Diary*.

pen and wrote him an extraordinary memorandum: 'If the following six conditions are agreed to, I can guarantee the successful termination of the war, and the total abolition of the submarine.' Fisher then laid down a series of preposterously dictatorial terms; that 'Winston Churchill is not in the Cabinet to be always circumventing me. Nor will I serve under Mr. Balfour'; that Sir Arthur Wilson left the Admiralty as 'his policy is totally opposed to mine, and he accepted the position of First Sea Lord in succession to me ... that there should be a new Board of Admiralty and so forth. The memorandum ended with a P.S. 'The 60 per cent of my time and energy which I have exhausted on nine First Lords in the past I wish in the future to devote to the successful prosecution of the war. This is the sole reason for these six conditions. These six conditions must be published verbatim so the Fleet will know my position.'[198]

Needless to say Lord Fisher's resignation was accepted. And thus the quarrel between two brilliant, impulsive and autocratic men of genius came to its sorry end.

*

Churchill accepted the sinecure office of the Duchy of Lancaster, which carried no departmental work, in order that he could remain a member of the War Council and press for the continuance of the Gallipoli campaign. He believed, and believed rightly, that Turkey was the key to the war, and he wanted the Government to persevere with courage. In November, however, the military losses were so heavy and hope of success so limited, the Council decided on a final evacuation. The tragic story had ended, and Churchill was not to be included in the new War Committee which was being formed to replace the War Council. He decided that he could no longer remain in 'well-paid inactivity' and that the time had come for him to join his regiment in France. He resigned his office and on 15 November made a farewell speech to the House of Commons which filled twenty-two columns of Hansard. He began by telling his listeners that he was entering upon 'an alternative form of service to which no exception can be taken, and with which I am perfectly content'. Then he went on to offer a vindication of his record over the previous fourteen months, mainly centred on the Dardanelles. 'I have gone through this story in detail in order to show and to convince the House that the Naval attack on the Dardanelles was a Naval plan, made by Naval

---

[198] *The Life of Lord Fisher*: Admiral Sir R. H. Bacon.

authorities on the spot, approved by Naval experts in the Admiralty, assented to by the First Sea Lord, and executed on the spot by Admirals who at every stage believed in the operation … I will not have it said that this was a civilian plan, foisted by a political amateur upon reluctant officers and experts.'

The speech was warmly received and Churchill sat down amid a hubbub of congratulations and 'Hear hears' that might almost be described as cheers. But as so often happens after dramatic occasions, a cool and critical reaction set in. As Members reflected on what he said their doubts came creeping back. They felt he had spoken the truth but not the whole truth, and a week later *The Times* ran a four-column letter by the foremost correspondent of the day, Ashmead Bartlett, with the headline: 'Mr. Churchill's Defence — A Criticism'. The letter pointed out a number of discrepancies in Winston's explanation, and restored to many readers the same opinions they had held before his vindication.

Three days after the speech, on 18 November, 1915, Major Churchill of the Oxfordshire Yeomanry was on the eve of his departure for France. 'The whole household was upside down while the soldier-statesman was buckling on his sword,' wrote Lord Beaverbrook who had dropped in to pay his farewell respects. 'Downstairs Mr. "Eddie" Marsh his faithful secretary was in tears … Upstairs, Lady Randolph was in a state of despair at the thought of her brilliant son being relegated to the trenches. Mrs. Churchill seemed to be the only person who remained calm, collected, and efficient.'[199]

The next day Winston landed at Boulogne.

---

[199] *Politicians and the War*: Lord Beaverbrook.

Chapter Thirteen — Soldiering, Painting, Munitions

THE NEXT twenty months stand out as the most disappointing, frustrating, unproductive and unhappy period of Churchill's life. The Great War was raging; the future of the Empire was at stake; history was being made; and British statesmen were making it. Yet the creative, dynamic Winston, confident of his ability to lead his country to victory, was banished from the political scene. For him it was a tragedy.

It required all the strength of character he possessed to turn his attention from high policy to the battlefields of France, which he believed was the only honourable course left to him. He plunged into his new life with determination and at first things went well. When he reached Boulogne he was told that Sir John French's car was waiting for him, and he was whirled off to the Commander-in-Chief's headquarters near St. Omer. French was a loyal friend. He provided Churchill with an excellent dinner and accorded him the same ceremony and courtesy as though he were still First Lord of the Admiralty. The next morning he asked him what he would like to do. 'Whatever I am told,' replied Winston. Sir John then confided that his own position was far from secure and that he might soon be replaced by a new Commander-in-Chief. 'I am, as it were, riding at single anchor. But it still counts for something. Will you take a brigade?' A Brigade Commander had the rank of Brigadier-General and the control of four thousand men. Winston assented gladly, stipulated that he must first have a month's training in trench warfare, and suggested that the Guards Division would give him the best experience. A few days later he was attached to one of the Grenadier Battalions due to move into the line at once.

The Guards received Major Churchill with reserve. Why was this politician being foisted upon them? True, he had been a soldier once, but what did he know about modern conditions? The Grenadiers had a proud and exacting tradition; if Major Churchill thought he was to be accorded any special privileges because he had been a Cabinet Minister he was very much mistaken. The Colonel greeted him coldly, and after half an hour's silence, as the two men jogged along on their horses towards the front, he remarked: 'I think I ought to tell you we were not at all consulted in the matter of your coming to join us.' Winston was not offended. He understood the Colonel's feelings. 'Knowing the professional Army as I did and having led a variegated life, I was infinitely amused at the elaborate pains they took to put me in my place and to make me realize that nothing counted at the front except military rank and behaviour,' he wrote. 'It took about forty-eight hours to wear through their natural prejudice against "politicians" of all kinds, but particularly of the non-Conservative brands.'[200] Winston won the officers over by his good humour, his politeness, and above all, by his determination to lead a soldier's life and his ability to lead it well.

Although the Guards did not undertake any major actions during the few weeks he was with them, the trenches were always disagreeable and dangerous. It was November and the weather alternated between driving rain and hard frost. There was an almost unceasing cannonade; bullets and shells whined and whistled across the faulty parapets, and at night men and officers went out together to mend the wire and strengthen the fortifications. As a result the casualty list mounted steadily. Despite the mud and the noise Winston preferred the trenches to Battalion Headquarters, established in a ruined farm a short distance away. Headquarters was almost as uncomfortable as the fine and with a further serious disadvantage: only tea was allowed. Winston asked to move forward.

Major Churchill was subjected to a constant glare of mass scrutiny. He was a famous figure and the troops wrote home about him as their chief topic of news. Every action he took and almost every word he spoke was noted. The officers were nearly as vigilant as the men in their observations but their interest was more politely masked. However, on one occasion the curiosity of a general saved Winston's life. A week after he joined the Guards he received a message that the Corps Commander would like to see him and would send a car to fetch him at a certain crossroads that afternoon. This order obliged Churchill to walk three miles across muddy and dangerous fields. When he arrived at the rendezvous he found no one; after an hour's wait a staff officer appeared on foot and explained that the car had been sent to the wrong place and it was now too late for the General to see him. It was not important, the officer added airily. The General had merely wished to have a chat with him. Winston made his way back, angrily cursing the Corps Commander, but when he arrived his attitude changed. He was congratulated on his 'luck' and discovered that his

---

[200] *Thoughts and Adventures*: Winston S. Churchill.

dug-out had received a direct hit from a shell a few minutes after he had left, and had been completely demolished.

*

Meanwhile rumours began to reach the House of Commons that Winston was to be given a brigade. It should be remembered that in those days England was very much a land of privilege, and 'gentlemen' automatically became officers. Winston had spent a few years as a professional soldier and Sir John French regarded it as perfectly reasonable to entrust him with a relatively important command. But in Parliament his Tory opponents were indignant, for they looked upon him as a dangerous fraud. They knew his adroitness at string-pulling and thrusting himself into central positions, so with a smugly patriotic air they decided it was their duty to thwart him. They attacked him on the ground of 'privilege' which they, as Conservatives, so gladly defended when it concerned themselves. On 16 December a Tory M.P. asked a question in Parliament which was reported in *The Times* the following day: 'Major Sir C. Hunter (Bath, U.) asked the Under-Secretary of State for War whether Major Winston Churchill had been promised the command of an infantry brigade; whether this officer had ever commanded a battalion of infantry; and for how many weeks he had served at the front as an infantry officer.

'Mr. Tennant: I have no knowledge myself and have not been able to obtain any, of a promise of command of an infantry brigade having been made to my right honourable and gallant Friend referred to in the question. On the second point I have consulted books of reference and other authentic sources of information, and the result of my investigations is that my right honourable and gallant Friend has never commanded a battalion of infantry. No report has been made to the War Office of the movements of Major the Right Honourable Winston L. S. Churchill since he proceeded to France on 19 November. If he has been serving as an infantry officer between that date and to-day the answer to the last part of the question would be about four weeks.' (Laughter.)

'Sir C. Hunter: Will the right honourable Gentleman let me know whether the right honourable and gallant Gentleman has been promised the command of an infantry battalion? (Cries of "Why not?") Sir C. Scott Robertson: Is not the question absurd on the face of it, Major Churchill being under sixty years of age? (Laughter.) Mr. E. Cecil: Is the right honourable Gentleman aware that if this appointment were made it would be thought by many persons inside the House and outside to be a grave scandal? (Cries of "Oh".)'

At the same time that questions were being asked in Parliament, Sir John French paid a visit to London. When he told the Prime Minister that he was giving Winston a brigade, Asquith protested strongly, saying that the House of Commons would not like it. He urged French not to offer him more than a battalion. French was not in a position to insist on having his own way for he knew his days were numbered; less than a month later he was succeeded as Commander-in-Chief by Sir Douglas Haig. As a result, Churchill was made a Lieutenant-Colonel, not a Brigadier-General, and given a battalion of the Sixth Royal Scots Fusiliers, not a brigade.

He was bitterly disappointed and for many months nursed a deep grievance against Asquith. He felt that the Prime Minister had not defended him over the Dardanelles as he should have done, and now he was treacherously interfering with his military life. Although both Bonar Law and Lloyd George believed that Winston should not receive special favours, Lord Beaverbrook shared the latter's indignation. 'A Premier may have to throw a colleague overboard to save the ship,' he wrote, 'but surely he should not jerk from under him the hen-coop on which the victim is trying to sustain himself on the stormy ocean.'[201]

Winston swallowed his chagrin as best he could and turned his attention to his new job. The Scots Fusiliers were in a billeting area, preparing to move into the line near Armentières, at Ploegstreet Village, known to the British as 'Plugstreet'. Battalion Headquarters was in a squalid, filthy farmhouse, half of which was still occupied by French peasants. Colonel Churchill summoned his officers to the orderly room and the peasants, who had got wind that a man of great importance had arrived, clustered around, peering through the door and exclaiming in loud whispers: '*Monsieur le ministre? Ah, c'est lui? C'est votre ministre?*'

The Scots Fusiliers were no more pleased than the Grenadiers to have a politician thrust upon them, but Winston won them over the following day when he gathered the officers together and announced solemnly: 'War is declared, gentlemen, on the lice.' This was followed by an erudite and dramatic lecture on the origin, growth and nature of the louse, with particular emphasis on the decisive role it had played

---

[201] *Politicians and the War*: Lord Beaverbrook.

throughout history as a vital factor in war. The officers were not only amused but impressed; 'Thus,' wrote one of them, 'did the great scion of the House of Marlborough first address his Scottish captains assembled in council.' After that the ice was broken and the battalion set to work to 'delouse' itself with scrubbing brushes and hot irons. The result was completely successful.

Winston was hardworking, cheerful and bursting with new ideas. The spectacle of a great creative mind being focused full strength on the humble needs of a small battalion provided the officers with plenty of excitement. In an amusing little booklet *With Churchill at the Front*, Captain Gibb describes the period under Winston as his 'most treasured war-memory'. This was a high compliment, for Colonel Churchill believed in keeping his men busy. When the battalion reached 'Plugstreet' he set his men to filling sandbags and strengthening and repairing their trenches for hours on end. Yet he was so energetic himself no one could object. Early and late he was in the line. 'On an average he went around three times a day, which was no mean task in itself,' wrote Captain Gibb, 'as he had plenty of other work to do. At least one of these visits was after dark, usually about 1 a.m. In wet weather he would appear in a complete outfit of waterproof stuff, including trousers or overalls, and with his French light-blue helmet he presented a remarkable and unusual figure. He was always in the closest touch with every piece of work that was going on, and, while at times his demands were a little extravagant, his kindliness and the humour that never failed to flash out made everybody only too keen to get on with the work, whether the ideal he pointed out to them was an unattainable one or not.'

Winston not only took an interest in everything that was going on but gave his men long and learned dissertations on all sorts of subjects including bricklaying, the handling of sandbags and master masonry. But some of his ideas, wrote Gibb, were 'too recherchés, too subtle to stand the practical test of everyday fighting'. For instance, he gave an order that when a parapet was hit it was not to be repaired before nightfall so that the enemy would not know what damage he had done. However, bullets came through the gaps, casualties resulted, and the order was ignored. Another time Churchill suddenly declared that all batmen must serve as bodyguards to their officers while they were in the line in order to protect the latter's precious lives; this too was utterly impractical and laughed out of court. On the other hand Churchill devised wonderful schemes for 'shelters and scarps and counterscarps and dugouts and half-moons and ravelins' which made sleep far safer than ever before.

Colonel Churchill believed that an officer should not live in discomfort because he happened to find himself in a trench, and took pains to acquire what amenities he could. He got hold of a tin bath which became the envy of the battalion, and stocked the mess with the best cigars and the best brandy he could find. But at the same time he was making himself comfortable he was also establishing a reputation for complete indifference to danger. Apparently he was a man entirely devoid of fear. 'War is a game to be played with a smiling face,' he often announced, and to Winston the smiles seemed to come naturally. Captain Gibb describes an occasion when Churchill suggested that they look over the parapet to get a better view. They felt the sickening rush of air as shells whined overhead, and then he remembers Churchill saying dreamily: 'Do you like war?' 'At the moment,' wrote Gibb, 'I profoundly hated war. But at that and every moment I believe Winston Churchill revelled in it. There was no such thing as fear in him.'[202] Stories of Winston's bravery had already spread, and on 28 December, 1915, *The Times* printed an interview with Corporal Walter Gilliland, of the Royal Irish Fusiliers, who said: 'Near here Mr. Winston Churchill is stationed and a cooler and braver officer never wore the King's uniform … He moves about among the men in the most exposed positions just as though he was wandering in the lobbies of the House of Commons. During the Ulster business before the war there was no man more detested in Belfast, but after what we have seen of him here we are willing to let bygones be bygones — and that is a big concession for Ulstermen to make. The other night his regiment came in for a rough time … Bullets spluttered around him knocking over his men left and right but he seemed to bear a charmed life and never betrayed the least sign of nervousness. His coolness is the subject of much discussion among us, and everybody admires him.'

*

And yet, despite his success at the front, Winston could not keep his mind on soldiering. At first he enjoyed himself. The danger, the fresh air and the physical exercise, all acted as a tonic after years of strenuous mental effort. But soon the novelty began to pall, and he found that he could not keep his thoughts from questions of high

---

[202] *With Churchill at the Front*: Captain Gibb.

policy. Early in December, at the request of French, he wrote a paper entitled *Variants of the Offensive* in which, among other things, he urged the use of caterpillar tanks to lead and protect infantry assaults. Tanks were at last being produced but they had not yet been employed. Winston stressed that they must not be flung in piece-meal but kept back until they could be used in large numbers to secure both maximum strength and maximum surprise. He sent a copy of his paper to the Committee of Imperial Defence but, as the reader will see, his advice was not heeded.

Meanwhile many distinguished visitors came to Winston's Battalion Headquarters including the regal Lord Curzon, the lion-hearted General Seely, and the indignant F. E. Smith, who was arrested en route by the military authorities for not having a pass. With these political friends Winston unburdened himself and talked far into the night; soon he found himself hankering after Westminster with increasing nostalgia. His buoyancy began to fade and he had long spells of deep dejection. As early as March, when he had only been in France four months, he wrote a letter to Lord Beaverbrook indicating that he was thinking of abandoning his soldiering and returning to England in the hope of exerting some influence on events which he believed were being mishandled. It would be awkward: he had left the House of Commons with a flourish for 'an alternative form of service to which no exception can be taken, and with which I am perfectly content'. It would not be easy to meet the natural criticism that would arise. 'The problem which now faces me is difficult,' he said in his letter. 'My work out here with all its risk and all its honour which I greatly value: on the other hand the increasingly grave situation of the war and the feeling of knowledge and power to help in mending matters which is strong within me: add to this dilemma the awkwardness of changing and the cause of my, I hope, unusual hesitations is obvious. In principle I have no doubts: but as to time and occasion I find very much greater difficulties.'[203]

Churchill could keep away from the political arena no longer, and in March he travelled to London to speak on the Naval Estimates. He made a long and critical speech on the conduct of the Naval war and urged Arthur Balfour, his successor at the Admiralty, to take more vigorous steps against the German U-boat campaign which was taking a heavy toll of merchant shipping. He ended his speech with the

---

[203] *Politicians and the War*: Lord Beaverbrook.

startling advice that Mr. Balfour, the First Lord, should 'vitalize and animate his Board by recalling Lord Fisher as First Sea Lord.'[204] This suggestion was characteristic of Winston's refusal to allow personal rancour to deflect him from a course he believed was right; but the House of Commons did not receive it in the same spirit. They refused to give him credit for magnanimity, suspecting him of some deep game. The following day the *Daily Express* political correspondent wrote: 'So far as one can gather in the lobby to-night, most members, irrespective of Party, are of the opinion that Colonel Churchill has done himself and the State no good. "What I think about the Churchill speech is this," said a leading M.P. to-night. "I think he was merely out to strafe Balfour. It will have no effect." The general interpretation of the speech is "Lord Fisher and I can run the Admiralty fine; have us back." Here are a few representative statements made in the lobby to-night by various Members. "It was a bid for the leadership"; "It was a good sign that the big blow at the enemy is coming off soon"; "It was an attempt to get back into the Cabinet".'[205]

Despite this criticism Churchill began to receive overtures from various public men including Sir Edward Carson and Sir Arthur Markham, both Members of Parliament, and C. P. Scott, the Editor of the *Manchester Guardian*, pressing him to come back to England and take part in a patriotic Opposition. He made up his mind to follow their advice. In the summer his battalion was amalgamated with another and he was without a command. By this time he could probably have had a brigade but he was now firm in the conviction that his duty lay at home. He wrote to the Secretary of State for War asking to be released from the Army. This placed the latter in a difficult position. If he allowed Winston to return, he would be accused of favouritism; if he refused him, he would be told he was trying to avoid opposition. He finally accepted his resignation on the understanding that he would not apply again for military service.

*

Back in London in June 1916, Winston was not much happier than he had been in France. One of his friends described him as 'a character depressed beyond the limits of description … When the Government was deprived of his guidance, he could see no hope anywhere.' He

---

[204] *Hansard*: 7 March, 1916.

[205] *Daily Express*: 8 March, 1916.

hung about Westminster trying to win back his fickle mistress, Power, like a lovelorn suitor. He grew pale and dispirited and complained to all his friends how badly and unjustly he was being treated. 'I am finished,' he told Lord Riddell once again. 'I am banished from the scene of action.'

Meanwhile the Conservatives had not softened towards him. The fact that he had thrown up his commission had not raised their estimate but merely confirmed their view of him as an opportunist. His friends, however, believed that his avidity for office was due to his self-assurance and self-confidence. 'He cared for the Empire profoundly,' wrote Lord Beaverbrook, 'and he was honestly convinced that only by his advice and methods it could be saved. His ambition was in essence disinterested. He suffered tortures when he thought that lesser men were mismanaging the business.'[206]

There was plenty to worry about in 1916. That was the year of the terrible Battle of the Somme in which the British Army was hurled, wave after wave, against the enemy's strongest defences. The conflict raged, off and on, for nearly five months. It cost Britain half a million of her finest soldiers, yet it did not alter the Allied position to any advantage. Winston was horrified by Sir Douglas Haig's strategy. Haig believed that France was the decisive theatre of war; that the only way to defeat the enemy was by frontal attack, or in plain language 'by killing Germans in a war of attrition'. Winston had always opposed this conception. From the first he was convinced that the Allies should open a new theatre and strike where the enemy's defences were weakest, not strongest; an offensive through Turkey, or the Balkans or even the Baltic, would give a better and quicker chance of victory than the bloodbath on the Western Front. As early as June 1915 he had written to the Prime Minister: 'It is a fair general conclusion that the deadlock in the West will continue for some time and the side which risks most to pierce the lines of the other will put itself at a disadvantage.'[207]

Very few military men defend Sir Douglas Haig's strategy to-day; most experts acknowledge that Winston was right. Yet throughout 1916 he was forced to sit back, powerless, and watch the appalling slaughter. At the beginning of August, a month after the Battle of the

---

[206] *Politicians and the War*: Lord Beaverbrook.

[207] *The World Crisis*: Winston S. Churchill.

Somme had opened, he wrote a memorandum which F. E. Smith circulated to the Cabinet, on the terrible futility of these offensives against the enemy's deeply entrenched positions. Already in this one battle alone the British losses were a hundred and fifty thousand men and the German only sixty-five thousand. 'Leaving *personnel* and coming to ground gained, we have not conquered in a month's fighting as much ground as we were expected to gain in the first two hours. We have not advanced three miles in the direct line at any point ...' he wrote. 'In *personnel* the results have been disastrous; in *terrain* they have been absolutely barren. And, although our brave troops on a portion of the front, mocking their losses and ready to make every sacrifice, are at the moment elated by the small advances made and the capture of prisoners and *souvenirs*, the ultimate moral effect will be very disappointing. From every point of view, therefore, the British offensive per se has been a great failure.'[208] A copy of this memorandum found its way to G.H.Q. in France where it was hotly repudiated, and its author severely criticized; to-day no one would deny that the facts were true.

A few months later another event occurred which caused Winston much distress. With the casualty list mounting by leaps and bounds, Haig decided to experiment with caterpillar tanks, now beginning to roll off the stocks. However, instead of using them in strength, in an attempt to achieve a complete break-through, only fifty were thrown in. Churchill pleaded with Asquith to prevent the generals from using the weapon prematurely, but the Prime Minister refused to overrule the military decision. The effect was startling and the enemy flabbergasted. The *Times* correspondent described the tanks as 'huge, shapeless bulks resembling nothing else that was ever seen on earth which wandered hither and thither like some vast antediluvian brutes which Nature had made and forgotten.' Unfortunately, just as Winston had warned, the tanks were too few in number to achieve a decisive result.

*

It is strange to think that Churchill was out of office for twenty months, nearly half of the Great War. As his frustration grew, his thoughts began to centre more and more on himself. He wrote a long report vindicating all that he had done in connection with the Dardanelles operation, and was indignant when the Cabinet refused to

---

[208] Ibid.

allow him to publish it on the grounds of secrecy. He remarked dejectedly to Lord Riddell that it was hard to 'remain under a stigma'. 'Although we are at war,' he added, 'there is no reason why injustice should be done to individuals.'[209] He wrote Asquith to this effect and the Prime Minister finally agreed to appoint a Royal Commission to gather evidence and make a report; but even this judgment was withheld from the public because it 'might give information to the enemy'; and Winston was more morose than ever.

These were his darkest days. The public was still hostile, and the feeling against him in Conservative families still intense. When one reads over the press cuttings of the day, one is struck by the anger that runs through them. Here is an extract from *The World*[210] of 14 November, 1916. 'Mr. Churchill, in his frantic effort to reinstate himself in public esteem, is enlisting the support of some powerful newspaper interests ... But if a serious attempt is being made to foist Winston once more on the British public the matter would assume a different aspect ... Winston Churchill was responsible for the *opéra bouffe* Antwerp expedition which made the British nation ridiculous in the eyes of the world ... He was responsible for the disastrous Dardanelles expedition which ranks with Walcheren as one of the greatest military disasters of our time ...'

*

His chief consolation throughout this difficult period was his happy family life. By 1916 he had three children: Diana, age 7, Randolph, age 5, and Sarah, age 2. He had a house in Cromwell Road, London, and did a good deal of entertaining, mostly of a political nature. The mainspring of his existence was his wife. Mrs. Churchill used all her tact and resourcefulness to take his mind away from his personal worries. She reassured him, gathered interesting people around him, backed up his political views and, above all, remained confident and cheerful.

She encouraged him in his new hobby, painting. He had first begun to paint in the summer of 1915, soon after he left the Admiralty. One Sunday he picked up a box of children's water-colours and experimented with them. The next day he went out and bought an

---

[209] *Lord Riddell's War Diary.*

[210] *The World* was a weekly Society journal which carried a widely read political column.

expensive set of oils. He tells how he made a mark the size of a bean on a canvas, then stood back, brush poised in air, surveying the white expanse with trepidation. He heard a voice behind him. 'Painting? But what are you hesitating about?' It was Lady Lavery, the wife of the well-known artist Sir John Lavery, who had recently completed Winston's portrait. 'Let me have the brush — a big one,' she said.[211] Then she slashed the canvas with fierce, bold strokes. That was the end of Winston's inhibitions. He was living in a farmhouse in Surrey which he had rented for the summer and after that he was seen every day in a long cream-coloured smock which came to his knees; he set up his easel in the garden or along the country lanes, and when it was hot he stuck a huge umbrella in the ground beside him. He became fascinated by his pursuit and told Lord Riddell that painting was his greatest solace. On the rare occasions when he visited friends, he arrived with his painting equipment. Lord Beaverbrook describes such an occasion and tells how, as Winston arranged his easel, he announced that he could not paint and talk too. 'But I have not left you unprovided for,' he remarked, and unloaded from his dispatch case a huge manuscript — his defence of the Dardanelles.

*

In December 1916, the Asquith Government fell, and Lloyd George became Prime Minister. This was brought about by a manoeuvre, that could almost be described as a plot, in which Lord Beaverbrook played a leading part. There was growing dissatisfaction with Asquith's direction of the war. Despite his fine brain he seemed to lack the drive and decision necessary to harness a great effort, and was continually at the mercy of advisers who were often pulling in opposite directions. Lord Northcliffe, the great newspaper magnate who owned the most popular and the most influential papers in England, the *Daily Mail* and *The Times*, detested Asquith. He depicted him to the public as the man of 'Wait and See' and built up Lloyd George as the man of 'Push and Go'.

However, it is not easy to get rid of a Prime Minister. A man in this position is always protected by the loyalty of those who enjoy his favour and fear that they will fall with him. In this situation Bonar Law, the Conservative leader, was the key. No Coalition Government could be controlled by a Liberal Prime Minister who did not have the approval of the Conservatives. Here Lord Beaverbrook stepped into

---

[211] *Thoughts and Adventures*: Winston S. Churchill.

the picture. Beaverbrook was then Sir Max Aitken. He was a fascinating, speculative, even romantic figure, who had arrived from Canada when he was barely thirty, a self-made multi-millionaire. He was the son of a poor Methodist parson and, according to gossip, had made his vast fortune as a company promoter. In 1913 he bought the *Daily Express* which, in the post-war period, eventually rivalled in circulation and finally surpassed the *Daily Mail*.

He was quick, amusing and provocative, and he possessed a rare talent; he could charm whoever he set out to capture. People have found it strange that the dour, humourless, unimaginative Bonar Law should have come under his spell, but the very difference between the two men obviously proved the attraction. Beaverbrook became Law's confidant; the latter asked his advice on every sort of matter, ranging from policy to people, and accepted it often enough for Beaverbrook to be treated with great respect. But besides winning Law's friendship Beaverbrook also became an intimate of Lloyd George, F. E. Smith and Winston Churchill. These men, each a genius in his own way, had much in common. They were all brilliant conversationalists; they were all individualists and adventurers, with a zest for conflict and a marked indifference to convention. They were the most gifted group of friends in public life and all of them, separately and together, were distrusted and disliked by the average Conservative 'gentleman'.

Beaverbrook convinced Bonar Law that Asquith must be removed; and persuaded him to back Lloyd George as Prime Minister. But the upheaval would require careful handling and was well rehearsed. Lloyd George delivered an ultimatum to Asquith designed to remove the direction of the war from the latter's hands and place it with an Inner Cabinet. Asquith refused, as he was intended to do, and Lloyd George resigned. Asquith then was forced to resign himself as he could not continue to govern with his Party split in two. The King followed customary procedure by sending for Bonar Law who declined the offer to form a Government, suggesting that His Majesty entrust the task to Lloyd George instead.

Thus a new Prime Minister took over the reins. Churchill's spirits soared as he thought his chance had come, but once again he was doomed to disappointment. Although Beaverbrook had succeeded in reconciling Bonar Law to Lloyd George's leadership he could not persuade him to accept Churchill. Law flatly refused to support any Government that included Winston. He recognized the latter's brilliance; indeed, he had declared in the House of Commons, on the eve of Churchill's departure for France, that 'in mental power and vital force he is one of the foremost men in the country'; yet he did not believe that brilliance was enough. Lloyd George used every argument he could summon to change his mind. 'The question is, even though you distrust him, would you rather have him FOR you or AGAINST you?' he queried. 'I would rather have him against me every time,' Law replied obdurately.[212]

Winston had no idea of the difficulties Lloyd George was encountering on his behalf, and firmly expected to be a member of the new Government. He regarded office as a certainty when, at Lloyd George's request, F. E. Smith invited him to a small dinner party of close colleagues. But Lloyd George had extended the invitation impulsively and realizing almost at once that Winston's hopes might be raised falsely, asked Beaverbrook, who was also one of the guests, to drop a hint to him that it would not be possible to include him in the Administration at the present time. Lord Beaverbrook did as he was bid, and in the course of the dinner said to Churchill: 'The new Government will be very well disposed towards you. All your friends will be there. You will have a great field of common action with them.'

'Something in the very restraint of my language,' wrote Beaverbrook, 'carried conviction to Churchill's mind. He suddenly felt that he had been duped by his invitation to dinner, and he blazed into righteous anger. I have never known him address his great friend Birkenhead in any other way except as "Fred", or "F.E." On this occasion he said suddenly: "Smith, this man knows that I am not to be included in the new Government." With that Churchill walked out into the street carrying his coat and hat on his arm. Birkenhead pursued him, and endeavoured to persuade him to return, but in vain.'[213]

Lloyd George finally smoothed things over by assuring Winston privately that he would do two things for him. First, he would release the Report of the Dardanelles Royal Commission; second, after publication, he would find him a job. He kept his word. The Report came out in March 1917, and although many people did not consider that its conclusions exonerated Winston, they at least were forced to admit that both Asquith and Kitchener were equally to blame. Then, in May, Churchill made a passionate and moving speech in the House, delivered at a secret session, in which he once again attacked the

---

[212] *War Memoirs*: David Lloyd George.

[213] *Politicians and the War*: Lord Beaverbrook.

principle of the war of attrition. 'I was listened to for an hour and a quarter with strained attention, at first silently but gradually with a growing measure of acceptance and at length approval,' he wrote. 'At the end there was quite a demonstration.'[214] His argument was that Britain and France must not squander the remaining strength of their armies in costly and futile offensives, but wait until American power had made itself felt; in the meantime Britain must concentrate on the anti-submarine war and keep its sea communications intact. His speech made a deep impression but when Lloyd George replied he refused to commit himself against a renewed offensive; Winston learned later that he did not feel able to overrule Haig and Robertson. 'He proceeded to lead a captivated assembly over the whole scene of the war, gaining the sympathy and conviction of his hearers at every stage,' wrote Winston. 'When he sat down the position of the Government was stronger than it had been at any previous moment during his Administration.'[215]

Indeed Lloyd George's stock was so high he now felt strong enough to include Winston in his Government. In July 1917 he offered him the Ministry of Munitions. This did not include a seat in the War Cabinet, but at least it was the end of exile. The Prime Minister knew that he would have to take a barrage of criticism but he had no idea of its intensity. The publication of the Dardanelles Report and Winston's moving speeches had apparently done little to allay the hostility against him. For days the storm raged. Admiral Beresford told a large audience at Queen's Hall: 'The P.M. has no right to make such appointments in opposition to public opinion.'[216] Furious letters appeared in the Conservative newspapers: 'We cannot forget that his name is associated with disaster.' A formal protest was made by the Committee of Conservative Associations; and in the House of Commons an M.P., Mr. Evelyn Cecil, put down a question to Lloyd George: 'Whether, in view of the feeling which exists in many quarters in this House and in the country that the inclusion of Mr. Churchill in the Government and particularly at this time, as Minister

---

[214] *The World Crisis*: Winston S. Churchill.

[215] *The World Crisis*: Winston S. Churchill.

[216] 26 July, 1917.

of Munitions, is a national danger, he will give time for the discussion of the appointment?'[217]

This was not all. Lloyd George was inundated with angry letters from his Cabinet colleagues, and for a time the Government tottered. Why were they so bitter and implacable? Lloyd George attempted to answer this question in his *Memoirs* in a fascinating summary of the feelings and prejudices of Winston's adversaries. 'They admitted he was a man of dazzling talents, that he possessed a forceful and a fascinating personality. They recognized his courage and that he was an indefatigable worker. But they asked why, in spite of that, although he had more admirers, he had fewer followers than any prominent public man in Britain? They pointed to the fact that at the lowest ebb of their fortunes, Joseph Chamberlain in Birmingham and Campbell-Bannerman in Scotland could count on a territorial loyalty which was unshakable in its devotion. On the other hand, Churchill had never attracted, he had certainly never retained, the affection of any section, province or town. His changes of Party were not entirely responsible for this. Some of the greatest figures in British political life had ended in a different Party from that in which they had commenced their political career. That was therefore not an adequate explanation of his position in public confidence. They asked: What then was the reason?

'Here was their explanation. His mind was a powerful machine, but there lay hidden in its material or its make-up some obscure defect which prevented it from always running true. They could not tell what it was. When the mechanism went wrong, its very power made the action disastrous, not only to himself but to the causes in which he was engaged and the men with whom he was co-operating. That was why the latter were nervous in his partnership. He had in their opinion revealed some tragic flaw in the metal. This was urged by Churchill's critics as a reason for not utilizing his great abilities at this juncture. They thought of him not as a contribution to the common stock of activities and ideas in the hours of danger, but as a further danger to be guarded against.

'I took a different view of his possibilities. I felt that his resourceful mind and tireless energy would be invaluable under supervision … I knew something of the feeling against him among his old Conservative friends, and that I would run great risks in promoting Churchill to any position in the Ministry; but the insensate fury they

---

[217] *Hansard*: 20 July, 1917.

displayed when later on the rumour of my intention reached their ears surpassed all my apprehensions, and for some days it swelled to the dimensions of a grave Ministerial crisis which threatened the life of the "Government".'

Lloyd George went so far as to declare that 'some of them were more excited about his appointment than about the war … It was interesting to observe in a concentrated form every phase of the distrust and trepidation with which mediocrity views genius at close quarters. Unfortunately, genius always provides its critics with material for censure — it always has and always will. Churchill is certainly no exception to this rule'.

*

'Not allowed to make the plans,' wrote Winston, 'I was set to make the weapons.' Strictly speaking this was true, but Winston was not one to keep his fingers out of the policy-making pic for long. The Ministry of Munitions gave him the opportunity to increase his exertions in favour of the one idea that gripped and dominated his mind: tanks. For many months he had watched the battle of attrition in France with increasing dislike. War was a great art, but how low it had fallen. Where was the skill, the ingenuity, the surprise? The only method the Allied commanders understood was the repeated hurling of flesh and blood against the strongest fortified positions, arguing that if they could slaughter more Germans than the Germans could slaughter in return they were bound to win in the end. Winston had wanted to leave France in its deadlock and strike through the back door of Turkey. If that was impossible, new methods must be developed to beat the trench, and the methods were obvious: a mechanical blow. But so far the tank had been badly misused. Not only had a mere handful been employed at the Battle of the Somme, but at Passchendaele they had been kept back until all element of surprise had vanished, then 'condemned to wallow in the crater fields under the first blast of German artillery'.

The War Cabinet could not understand the importance of the new weapon. Although Lloyd George, as Minister of Munitions, had ordered the manufacture of several hundred tanks, the military mind still regarded them with a marked lack of enthusiasm. Now Winston redoubled his efforts. On 21 October, 1917, he wrote a memorandum: 'Someone must stop the tiger … It is becoming apparent that the "blasting power" of the artillery is only one of the factors required for a satisfactory method of the offensive. "Moving power" must be developed equally with "blasting power" … When we see these great armies in the West spread out in thin lines hundreds of miles long and organized in depth only at a very few points, it is impossible to doubt that if one side discovered, developed and perfected a definite method of advancing continuously, albeit upon a fairly limited front, a decisive defeat would be inflicted upon the other. If, therefore, we could by organized mechanical processes and equipment impart this faculty to our armies in 1918 or in 1919, it would be an effective substitute for a great numerical preponderance in numbers. What other substitute can we look for? Where else is our superiority coming from?'[218]

Sir Douglas Haig was still unimpressed by the possibilities of tanks. Winston constantly had Passchendaele thrown in his face. 'They cannot cope with mud.' 'The Army doesn't want them any more.' 'General Headquarters does not rank them very high in its priorities.' However, on 20 November, only a few weeks after Churchill's memorandum, General Sir Julian Byng gave the Tank Corps its first great opportunity by employing the new weapon as it was designed to be used. No artillery barrage was laid down until the tanks were actually launched; and nearly five hundred were put into the field. 'The attack,' say the historians of the Tank Corps, 'was a stupendous success. As the tanks moved forward with the infantry following close behind, the enemy completely lost his balance, and those who did fly panic-stricken from the field surrendered with little or no resistance … By 4 p.m. on 20 November one of the most astonishing battles in all history had been won and, as far as the Tank Corps was concerned, tactically finished, for no reserves existing it was not possible to do more.'[219] The German trench system had been penetrated to a depth of six miles; ten thousand prisoners and two hundred guns had been captured; and the British had lost only fifteen hundred men.

'Moving power' now began to have its ardent supporters. Lloyd George stated that tank production must be rapidly increased; recruiting for the Tank Corps was redoubled; training establishments were expanded. Despite the urgency Winston met more obstacles. The Admiralty had first priority on steel plates. These were needed for ship-building but they were also needed for tanks. The only method by which Winston could secure any at all was to gorge the Admiralty

---

[218] *The World Crisis*: Winston S. Churchill.

[219] *The Tank Corps*: Clough and A. Williams-Ellis.

until they held stocks far beyond their most excessive demands; then he took the remainder for his tanks.

At last a programme was in operation that would transform the conflict, should it continue in 1919, into a mobile, mechanical war. Winston's victory was won. Had he been able to convince the Cabinet of the importance of tanks in 1915, he believes the war would have ended in 1917. To-day most people agree with him.

*

The Ministry of Munitions was a huge organization staffed by twelve thousand civil servants and divided into fifty departments. It was operating smoothly when Winston took over, but he tightened it up still further. He combined the fifty groups into less than a dozen new ones; he referred to each group by a letter — F for finance, D for design, P for projectiles, X for explosives; he set up a Council of business men rather like the Board of Admiralty; and over the business men he established a small, powerful 'clamping committee'. The organization was a triumph. 'Instead of struggling through the jungle on foot I rode comfortably on an elephant, whose trunk could pick up a pin or uproot a tree with equal ease, and from whose back a wide scene lay open,'[220] he wrote.

The Ministry of Munitions covered an enormous field. It was not only responsible for guns and shells, but for all sorts of moving and rolling stock, and for the design and production of aircraft as well. 'Owing to the energy which Mr. Winston Churchill threw into the production of munitions,' wrote Lloyd George in his *Memoirs*, 'between 1 March and 1 August the strength of the Tank Corps increased by twenty-seven per cent, and that of the Machine Gun Corps by forty-one per cent, while the number of aeroplanes in France rose by forty per cent.'

On top of this effort came American demands. The United States had declared war in April 1917, three months before Churchill was brought back into the Government. The Americans planned to put forty-eight divisions in the line, which amounted to six armies each requiring twelve thousand guns. But owing to the difficulty of switching peace-time factories to war production they could only produce a small proportion of their needs.

Winston accepted a contract for £100,000,000 to supply the American Army with all its medium artillery. This was done under a

---

[220] *The World Crisis*: Winston S. Churchill.

'gentleman's agreement' by which the United Kingdom promised not to make a profit and the United States promised to make good a loss. The bargain worked to the complete satisfaction of both countries. Indeed, the cordial relations which Winston established with his opposite number in Washington, Mr. Bernard Baruch, whom he had never met, grew into a warm friendship after the war and continues to-day. Mr. Baruch was influential in seeing that Churchill received the United States Distinguished Service Medal which was awarded him at the end of the war by General Pershing.

*

The Ministry of Munitions had large establishments in France which gave Winston the opportunity of crossing the Channel whenever he wished. He seized the excuse to visit the front regularly and often appeared at Sir Douglas Haig's headquarters. Here he studied the flagged maps and talked strategy and tactics to his heart's content. Finally Sir Douglas Haig assigned him his own quarters in a French chateau near Verochocq, and he became almost a daily visitor. He found that he could work at the Ministry of Munitions in the morning, fly to Verochocq at lunchtime, and have a whole afternoon at the front. 'I managed to be present at nearly every important battle during the rest of the war,' he wrote with pride.

These trips probably were not strictly essential to his work as a Minister, but he was blissfully happy. The fact that aeroplanes were uncertain quantities in those days seemed to add to his pleasure. Once when he was over the Channel on his return to London a valve burst, the engine spluttered and the plane descended towards the grey water. The pilot made a gesture indicating that there was nothing he could do, and it seemed as though the end had come. Then the engine coughed, the plane rose unsteadily, and the pilot headed back to France where he managed to land the machine without damage. On another occasion the same pilot had to make a forced landing on English soil. 'He side-slipped artistically between two tall elms, just missing the branches,' wrote Winston in *Thoughts and Adventures*; and later, when someone asked him whether he was not afraid at such moments he replied: 'No, I love life, but I don't fear death.'

*

Winston was at the front when the great and final offensive against the British opened in March 1918. He heard the enemy barrage begin and listened to the Allied guns thunder back in reply. This was Ludendorff's last hope of winning the war. Both Russia and Italy had collapsed and the Germans were free to concentrate most of their force in the West. Although the United States had been in the war for a year it had only two hundred thousand men in the line. Ludendorff knew the Americans would be arriving in strength throughout the summer, and decided to stake everything on a final, knock-out blow before that time.

This offensive was the climax of the war. It lasted forty days and cost Britain three hundred thousand casualties. Everyone knows how the British lines recoiled with the terrific impact; how the French nearly broke contact with their Allies; how for the first time an electric whisper went through England: 'What if the Germans should win, after all?' Winston returned to London three days after the battle had begun and went to 10 Downing Street at once. Lloyd George asked him anxiously: 'If we cannot hold the line we have fortified so carefully, why should we be able to hold positions farther back with troops already defeated?'[221] Winston explained that an offensive was like throwing a bucket of water over the floor; it lost its force as it proceeded.

But during the next days an alarming rumour spread that the French regarded the defeat of the British armies as inevitable and, instead of sending reinforcements, were planning to break contact with them. Lloyd George summoned Winston and asked him to hurry to France and find out what was happening. 'Go and see everybody,' he said. 'Use my authority. See Foch. See Clemenceau. Find out for yourself whether they are making a really big move or not.'[222]

The story of the trip has been recounted dramatically by Churchill himself. Clemenceau greeted him with the message: 'Not only shall Mr. Winston Churchill see everything, but I will myself take him to-morrow to the battle and we will visit all the Commanders of Corps and Armies engaged.'[223]

The next day the two statesmen set forth, accompanied by high officials and staff officers, in a fleet of military cars decorated with satin tricolours. First, they visited Foch who gave them a brilliant exposition of the battle ending emotionally with the assurance that the enemy effort was nearly exhausted. '*Alors, Général, il faut que je vous*

---

[221] *Thoughts and Adventures*: Winston S. Churchill.

[222] Ibid.

[223] *Thoughts and Adventures*: Winston S. Churchill.

embrasse,' said Clemenceau, and the two Frenchmen clasped each other tightly. Next, they went to the headquarters of the British Fourth Army where they had lunch with Sir Douglas Haig. Clemenceau and Haig withdrew to an adjoining room. When they came out Winston noticed that Haig seemed content and the Tiger was smiling. 'It is all right,' he said, 'I have done what you wish. Never mind what was arranged before. If your men are tired and we have fresh men near at hand, our men shall come at once and help you. And now,' he added, 'I shall claim my reward.'

The reward was to see the battle. The Army commanders protested, but Clemenceau insisted on being driven as far forward as possible. Shells whistled overhead, and even Winston finally protested that he ought not to go under fire too often. '*C'est mon grand plaisir*,' replied the old Frenchman.

*

As everyone knows the British lines held, and the British and French armies did not break contact. By the summer the Americans were pouring into France and the Germans no longer had a chance of victory. The war ended on 11 November, 1918. Winston was in his office in the Hotel Metropole when Big Ben struck the hour of eleven, the signal that the worst conflict in history had ended. Mrs. Churchill joined him and together they drove down to Whitehall to see the Prime Minister.

Part Five
The Aftermath

Chapter Fourteen — War and Peace

THE TEN restless years between 1919 and 1929 did little to advance Mr. Churchill's reputation as a statesman. It was a turbulent decade of clashing colours and dark shadows; of booms and slumps, of Bolshevism and a League of Nations, of flappers, cocktail parties and Bright Young People. It was a decade of strikes, unemployment, of the rise of the Labour Party, of civil wars, of pacifism, of demoralization, of a half-hearted belief in collective security. It was a decade that was to usher in a new factor in world politics: the Common Man.

When the First World War ended there was only one statesman in England who counted. That was Lloyd George. The prophecy made by John Morley that 'if there is a war Churchill will beat L.G. hollow' had proved utterly false. Winston was forced to stand in the wings of the political stage while Lloyd George took all the bows. Mr. Churchill had no following from any party or any group. The Liberals were suspicious of him, the Labour leaders opposed him, and the Conservatives disliked him. His only strength lay in his friendship with Lloyd George.

The two men sat together on Armistice night and discussed the great problems that peace would bring. Winston was not a vindictive man, and now that the terrible conflict was over his instinct was to hold out the hand of friendship to Germany. It was essential to the future of Europe, he argued, that Germany should be brought into the democratic family as soon as possible, and he urged Lloyd George to send a dozen food ships to Hamburg. But public opinion was strongly hostile to the idea with the result that nothing was done until Plumer, in command in Germany, threatened to resign if food were not sent, and got his way.

A month after the Armistice Lloyd George's Coalition Government went to the country in what was known as the 'Coupon' Election. All candidates supporting the Coalition, mainly Conservatives, received coupons guaranteeing their loyalty. They were opposed by Labour candidates and Asquithian Liberals over whom they scored a resounding victory, winning five hundred and twenty-six seats which gave them a clear majority of three hundred and fifty-seven over all other parties. But the election was fought on a swelling tide of public opinion symbolized by national slogans: 'Hang the Kaiser' and 'Make the Germans Pay'. No candidate was elected who tried to withstand the pressure. Even Winston was forced to knuckle under, and when the Government returned to Whitehall it found itself committed to a policy of reparations which many regarded with deep misgivings.

A few weeks after the election Lloyd George appointed Winston Minister of War with the Air Ministry amalgamated under him. He wanted a strong man to iron out the demobilization tangle, which Churchill promptly did. Lloyd George recognized his colleague's brilliant qualities and he was also conscious of his headstrong and impetuous nature. He undoubtedly believed that while the War Office would absorb Winston's energies and interests, it also had the advantage of being a 'safe' post, for in peace time a Service Department was not likely to offer much scope for sensational action. Sir Henry Wilson, the Chief of the Imperial General Staff, evidently did not share this view, for when he heard of the appointment he wrote in his diary: 'Whew!'; and at his first meeting with his new boss he asked caustically why the Admiralty had not been thrown in as well. As things turned out the 'whew' was not unreasonable. The world was still in a troubled state, and most troubled of all was Russia, which was torn by civil war, and which still contained British troops.

Russia became Winston's chief preoccupation; and since Lloyd George was fully absorbed by the Paris Peace Conference he had something of a free hand. The gigantic country was in an appalling state of disintegration. The Czar had been overthrown in 1917, and a few months later the Bolsheviks had captured the Central Government. In the spring of 1918 they had signed a separate peace with the Kaiser which had allowed Germany to release a million more men to fight the Allies on the Western Front. Britain had sent troops to Archangel, the Caucasus and Siberia to prevent oil supplies and Allied materials from falling into the enemy's hands. In the meantime White Russian counter-revolutionary forces many hundreds of miles apart — those in the South under the leadership of General Denikin, and those in the East under Admiral Kolchak — had remained faithful to their commitments and continued the war as best they could. Now these forces were fighting the Bolsheviks and desperately begging England for help. Lord Milner, Winston's predecessor at the War Office, had more or less promised aid. Was Britain to abandon them? All Winston's chivalrous instincts bade him send assistance. Besides this, looking at the picture objectively, it would not be in Britain's interests to allow Bolshevik leaders who believed in organized terror and who were preaching world-wide revolution to gain the final power. Germany lay prostrate. What would prevent Russia from overrunning the whole of Europe?

This was the practical argument. But as far as Winston was concerned, the emotional argument was even stronger. He was disgusted by the Bolshevik atrocities. He understood wars between soldiers and nations, but he could not forgive wars between families, neighbours and classes, where thousands of civilians were murdered in the name of humanity. To him the Russian spectacle was sordid and evil. 'For all its horrors,' he wrote many years later, 'a glittering light plays over the scenes and actors of the French Revolution. The careers and personalities of Robespierre, of Danton, even of Marat, gleam luridly across a century. But the dull squalid figures of the Russian Bolsheviks are not redeemed in interest even by the magnitude of their crimes. All form and emphasis is lost in the vast process of Asiatic liquefaction. Even the slaughter of millions and the misery of scores of millions will not attract future generations to their uncouth lineaments and outlandish names.'[224]

It was characteristic of Churchill that when he took up a cause he fought for it wholeheartedly. All his vigour was concentrated on a campaign against the Bolsheviks. In the House of Commons and on the public platform he attacked the Reds in a flow of rich and merciless invective. On 11 April, 1919, speaking at a luncheon at the Aldwych Club in London, he declared: 'Of all the tyrannies in history, the Bolshevist tyranny is the worst, the most destructive, the most degrading. It is sheer humbug to pretend that it is not far worse than German militarism. The miseries of the Russian people under the Bolshevists far surpass anything they suffered even under the Czar. The atrocities of Lenin and Trotsky are incomparably more hideous, on a larger scale and more numerous than any for which the Kaiser is responsible. The Germans at any rate have stuck to their allies. They misled them, they exploited them, but they did not desert or betray them. It may have been honour among thieves, but it is better than dishonour among murderers.'

The next month Winston alluded to 'the foul baboonery of Bolshevism' and came out openly in favour of sending arms and supplies to their adversaries. But there was no action he could take without the approval of the Supreme Council, a body which sat in Paris and represented the five leading Allied powers. He went to

---

[224] *Great Contemporaries*: Winston S. Churchill.

France in February and talked to President Wilson who told him affably that he did not pretend to know the solution to the Russian problem. There were the gravest objections to every course, and yet some course must be taken — sooner or later.

For three months the Allies vacillated. Winston pleaded his cause without ceasing. He argued with members of the British Cabinet, with foreign representatives, with anyone who would listen. He sent a flow of memoranda to every influential quarter. Finally, in May, the Supreme Council came to a decision. It sent a note to Admiral Kolchak informing him that the object of Allied policy was 'to restore peace within Russia by enabling the Russian people to resume control of their own affairs through the agent of a freely elected Constituent Assembly ...' If Kolchak would agree to this, and certain other conditions, the Allies would assist him with munitions, supplies and food, to establish a Government of all Russia; at the same time the Allies made it clear that the time was approaching when they must withdraw their own troops 'to avoid interference in the internal affairs of Russia'.

This note was obviously designed to have the best of two worlds. It was ambiguous and vague, yet Winston seized it eagerly. At last he had the authority to act. For the next eight months he poured ammunition and material worth many millions of pounds into Russia. He also made plans for the evacuation of the British forces. In order to cover the withdrawal it was necessary to stage a diversion; and for this he called for a volunteer army of eight thousand men.

The British public stirred with alarm. They had not forgotten Winston's excursion to Antwerp and his impetuosity over the Dardanelles. Was he trying to plunge them into another war? Apart from this fear, there was a growing dislike of his attitude towards the Soviets. Most people in England believed that Britain should mind her own business and let the Russians settle their own affairs. As to the pros and cons of Bolshevism itself, the country was divided into two distinct camps, Left and Right. The Right shared Winston's dislike of the Reds, but the Left, which was composed of Radical Liberals and Labour Party followers, cast sympathetic glances at the new 'social experiment' which was taking place. The Labour Party, backed by the Trade Unions, was particularly sympathetic for they had recently acquired a new constitution, drafted by Sidney Webb, which committed them to Socialism. True, British socialism was not Marxist, but Fabian, democratic and Christian. Nevertheless, the Labour leaders believed many of the Bolshevik slogans: that war was engineered by capitalist societies; that the ownership of the means of production and distribution would automatically create a new Utopia.

Lloyd George was far from being a Socialist, but his Radical instincts bade him look upon Russia with a tolerant eye. After all, the oppression and tyranny of the Czarist regime had brought about the revolution. One could not blame the people for trying to throw off the yoke. He believed that trade with Russia was economically important, and both he and President Wilson would have liked to recognize the Soviets and establish friendly relations with them but they knew they could not carry Parliament and Congress with them. Lloyd George disliked Winston's passionate denunciations and some years later in his *Memories of the Peace Conference* wrote acidly: 'The most formidable and irresponsible protagonist of an anti-Bolshevik war was Mr. Winston Churchill. He had no doubt a genuine dislike for Communism ... His ducal blood revolted against the wholesale elimination of Grand Dukes in Russia.'

A storm was gathering around Winston's head but in the end it never really broke. Although he was hotly attacked by almost every Labour leader in England, as soon as the Allied forces had been withdrawn in the autumn of 1919 it became apparent that the White Russians were doomed to failure. They fought without conviction and hung on for only a few months. In the spring of 1920 they finally collapsed and Soviet authority was complete. Up to the very end Churchill sustained his attack on the Bolsheviks. In a speech at Sunderland on 3 January, 1921, he said: 'Was there ever a more awful spectacle in the whole history of the world than is unfolded by the agony of Russia? This vast country, this mighty branch of the human family, not only produced enough food for itself, but before the war it was one of the great granaries of the world, from which food was exported to every country. It is now reduced to famine of the most terrible kind, not because there is no food — there is plenty of food — but because the theories of Lenin and Trotsky have fatally, and it may be finally, ruptured the means of intercourse between man and man, between workman and peasant, between town and country; because they have shattered the systems of scientific communication by rail and river on which the life of great cities depends; because they have raised class against class and race against race in fratricidal war; because they have given vast regions which a little while ago were smiling villages and prosperous townships back to the wolves and the bears; because they have driven man from the civilization of the twentieth century into a condition of barbarism worse than the Stone Age, and have left him the most awful and pitiable spectacle in human experience, devoured by vermin, racked by pestilence and deprived of hope.

'And this is progress, this is liberty, this is Utopia! This is what my friend in the gallery would call an interesting experiment in Social Regeneration (Laughter). What a monstrous absurdity and perversion of the truth it is, to represent the Communist theory as a form of progress, when, at every step and at every stage, it is simply marching back into the Dark Ages.'

Winston not only supported the White Armies to the bitter end, but in the early months of 1920 when Poland attacked Russia, in a ridiculous act of aggression, he was instrumental in seeing that British arms were sent to their aid as well. The Russians drove the invaders out, then invaded Poland themselves, and for a few weeks Churchill had visions of his worst fears being realized with all Europe overrun. He sent a memorandum to Lloyd George pleading for the rehabilitation of Germany as the only hope of erecting a barrier against the Russian giant — a line of argument which is again being used to-day.

'Since the Armistice,' he wrote, 'my policy would have been "Peace with the German people, war on the Bolshevik tyranny". Willingly or unavoidably, you have followed something very near the reverse. Knowing the difficulties, and also your great skill and personal force — so much greater than mine — I do not judge your policy and action as if I could have done better, or as if anyone could have done better. But we are face to face with the results. They are terrible. We may well be within measurable distance of universal collapse and anarchy throughout Europe and Asia. Russia has gone into ruin. What is left of her is in the power of these deadly snakes.

'But Germany may perhaps still be saved … You ought to tell France that we will make a defensive alliance with her against Germany if, and only if, she entirely alters her treatment of Germany and loyally accepts a British policy of help and friendship toward Germany.'[225]

The British Left vehemently opposed any aid being given to Poland, and the British Right seemed strangely uninterested. Indeed, many people were more concerned with Winston's activities than with Russia's. In May 1920 a sensation was caused by the publication of a memorandum which was alleged to have fallen into Soviet hands after

---

[225] *The World Crisis*: Winston S. Churchill.

the Allied withdrawal from Archangel, and was brought back to London by a Labour Party deputation. The note claimed to be an account of an interview which Colonel Golvin, a White Russian emissary, had had with Winston, in which the latter had promised the White Russians an indefinite postponement of the evacuation of the British forces, and twelve thousand volunteers to form a new garrison. Winston indignantly declared that the document was a complete travesty of the truth but it caused a Parliamentary storm. Labour Members even went so far as to draft a resolution for Mr. Churchill's arrest, on the grounds that he was using British military resources against the Soviet without the consent or knowledge of Parliament.

The Civil War had come to an end; and Poland, in the inspired Battle of the Vistula, had managed to repel the Russian hordes. For the time being the urgency of the Bolshevik menace subsided. In January 1921 Lloyd George transferred Mr. Churchill from the War Office to the Colonial Office and Mr. Churchill transferred his attention from Europe to the East.

*

Throughout his life Winston had never received any credit as a peacemaker, yet in the brief eighteen months he was at the Colonies he was largely responsible for bringing about two vitally important and lasting peace settlements. The first was in the Middle East. This part of the world was in a state of ferment. Despite the bitter opposition of the Arabs, the Peace Conference had given the mandate of Syria to the French, who then threw out the Emir Feisal from Damascus. As a result Palestine and Egypt were smouldering with discontent, and a bloody uprising had been suppressed in Iraq. The British were obliged to keep forty thousand troops stationed in Iraq to preserve order, which was costing the Government £30,000,000 a year. This was thought to be far too expensive and the Prime Minister asked Winston to see what he could do to restore harmony and save the British taxpayer some money.

Winston set about the matter in his usual independent fashion. First he enlisted on his side that strange and romantic genius, 'Lawrence of Arabia.' This fascinating Englishman was the uncrowned king of the Arab world. He had lived and fought with them throughout the war and now lived and worked to secure them a just peace. He identified his interests with them so completely that he appeared in London and Paris in flowing Arab robes. He even refused a high decoration from the King in order to impress the public with the seriousness of his cause.

Winston called a conference in Cairo, and with Lawrence as his chief adviser and all the experts and authorities of the Middle East at his service he worked out a plan. A month later he sent the following proposals to the Cabinet. First, that the British must repair the injury done to the Arabs by placing the Emir Feisal on the throne of Iraq as King, and transferring to the hands of his brother, the Emir Abdulla, the Government of Transjordan. Secondly, that the troops must be withdrawn from Iraq, and order maintained by the Air Force rather than the Army, which would cut down the cost from £30,000,000 to £5,000,000 a year. And third, that an adjustment must be made in Palestine between the Arabs and the Jews which would serve as a foundation for the future.

It was a brilliant settlement. As soon as the Cabinet accepted it tension in the Arab world subsided. When Lawrence wrote his great classic *Seven Pillars of Wisdom* he sent Winston a copy with the following inscription: 'Winston Churchill who made a happy ending to this show ... And eleven years after we set our hands to making an honest settlement, all our work still stands: the countries have gone forward, our interests having been saved, and nobody killed, either on one side or the other. To have planned for eleven years is statesmanship. I ought to have given you two copies of this work!'[226]

*

During the time that Winston was negotiating a settlement in the Middle East he was also a member of the Cabinet Committee dealing with the problem of Ireland. Since the war, relations between the Irish and the Mother Country had deteriorated badly. In the 1918 'Coupon' Election the Irish Nationalists had been swept away and in their place had arisen a far more extremist group, the Sinn Fein Party (Ourselves Alone). The Sinn Feiners wanted to sever all connection with England and establish a republic, and they were prepared to use any methods to realize their aims. In 1919 they began to burn down houses and murder English officials. The British Government retaliated by sending a special police force manned by ex-officers from the wartime army, who wore dark caps and khaki uniforms and became known as the 'Black and Tans'. They were instructed to take severe reprisals, and as a result punished outrage by still further outrage. By the end of the year Ireland was gripped in a reign of terror.

---

[226] *Great Contemporaries*: Winston S. Churchill.

The situation was intensely complicated. The Northern and Protestant part of Ireland was loyal to the British Empire and determined to stay within it, while Southern and Catholic Ireland, which represented a majority of the population, was bent on gaining complete independence. Should the British crush the rebellion by overwhelming force, or should they partition the country and let the South have its freedom? Winston Churchill was in favour of doing both. He told his colleagues on the Cabinet Committee — Lloyd George, F. E. Smith (later Lord Birkenhead), Austen Chamberlain, Sir Hamar Greenwood and Sir Laming Worthington-Evans — that he believed it was essential to prove to the Irish that Britain was not giving way through weakness and fear; then when they had been soundly beaten he was in favour of granting them Dominion status which would make them independent and self-governing, yet at the same time would preserve a link with the Empire through loyalty to the Crown.

About this time King George V went to Northern Ireland and delivered a speech which had been carefully prepared by his Ministers. In it was a reference to the South and a plea for reconciliation which met with a startlingly large response from the Irish public itself. This started the ball rolling. The Government invited the Irish leaders to London to negotiate, and the leaders accepted. Thus negotiations started before Britain had proved herself the master, as Churchill and his colleagues would have liked.

The tense, charged atmosphere and the protracted discussions which finally led to the signing of the Irish Treaty have provided the theme for many books. 'It would have been possible in 1886,' wrote Winston, 'to have reached a solution on a basis infinitely less perilous both to Ireland and to Great Britain than that to which we were ultimately drawn.'[227] At that time Mr. Gladstone was begging the House of Commons to pass his Home Rule Bill. 'Think, I beseech you — think well, think wisely, think not for a moment but for the years that are to come, before you reject this Bill.' But the Bill was defeated and Winston's father was one of Gladstone's most powerful opponents. Now the son was trying to find a solution to a problem grown fierce and strong on the mistakes of the older generation.

Although Winston did not play a major part in the Treaty negotiations he did much to smooth the relations between the two

---

[227] *Thoughts and Adventures*: Winston S. Churchill.

sides by friendliness alone. 'Our settlement with the Boers,' he wrote, 'with my own vivid experiences in it, was my greatest source of comfort and inspiration in this Irish business. Indeed it was a help to all. I remember one night Mr. Griffith and Mr. Collins [the leading Irish statesmen] came to my house to meet the Prime Minister. It was at a crisis, and the negotiations seemed to hang only by a thread. Griffith went upstairs to parley with Mr. Lloyd George alone. Lord Birkenhead and I were left with Michael Collins meanwhile. He was in his most difficult mood, full of reproaches and defiances, and it was very easy for everyone to lose his temper.

'"You hunted me day and night!" he exclaimed. "You put a price on my head."

'"Wait a minute," I said. "You are not the only one." And I took from my wall the framed copy of the reward offered for my recapture by the Boers. "At any rate it was a good price — £5,000. Look at me — £25 dead or alive. How would you like that?"'[228]

In the end Michael Collins and Arthur Griffith signed the Treaty which gave Ireland Dominion status. But when they returned to Dublin they found the Sinn Fein Party split in two. One half backed the Treaty, but the other half, led by de Valera, declared that Dominion status was not enough; nothing short of recognizing Ireland as a republic would suffice. Members of this faction became known as the Anti-Treatyites and worked fanatically to prevent Griffith and Collins carrying out the agreement made in London. They provoked acts of violence against Northern Ireland and soon began murdering the members of their own party who believed in the Treaty. Only nine months after Collins had put his signature to the document he was killed in an ambush. Before long Ireland was again in the grip of civil war.

It was at this point that Winston Churchill became Colonial Secretary and, as such, Chairman of the Cabinet Committee on Irish affairs. His task was to help Griffith and Collins establish a Provisional Government, and at the same time to protect the integrity of Northern Ireland which had voted for a partition. The world seldom thinks of Churchill in the role of a conciliator and yet in this case he worked tirelessly, patiently and sagaciously to achieve his purpose. He handled innumerable situations with delicacy and tact, writing repeatedly to the various leaders, both North and South, smoothing

---

[228] *Thoughts and Adventures*: Winston S. Churchill.

away misunderstandings, emphasizing good will, minimizing foolish and petty actions, cajoling, praising, encouraging and suggesting. In the end the Treatyites won; the Provisional Government was established, and tragic Ireland settled down to peace, and finally to isolation. From that time on she gradually ceased to be an issue or to play a part in the internal affairs of Great Britain.

*

Mr. Churchill's role as peace-maker was not long remembered. In the middle of 1922 trouble arose with Turkey, and events threw Churchill into the more familiar role of a belligerent 'man of action'. The seeds of the Turkish discord had been sown by Lloyd George. At the Peace Treaty the Prime Minister had come under the spell of the Greek statesman, M. Venizelos, and as a result had sanctioned a Greek occupation of a large part of Anatolia, Turkey's homeland, which was completely Turkish in population save for a few Greek coastal towns. France and Italy objected to this settlement; so did Britain's Foreign Secretary Lord Curzon; so did Winston Churchill; nevertheless Lloyd George pushed it through, signing the Treaty of Sèvres which not only confirmed a Greek occupation of Smyrna but gave Greece most of Turkey's possessions in Europe as well.

Fighting soon broke out. In 1921 the Greeks in an effort to enforce the Treaty advanced on Ankara, the Turkish capital, but were stopped by the Turks fifty miles away. They remained there for a year; then in the summer of 1922 Mustapha Kemal, the head of the Turkish Government, attacked them, routed their armies, and massacred most of the Greek population.

The Western powers were alarmed. Was Kemal planning to recapture Turkey's European possessions? If so, he would have to cross the Straits which were under international protection, guarded by small contingents of British, French and Italian troops. The French and Italians saw trouble coming and immediately withdrew leaving only the British at Chanak on the Asiatic side of the Dardanelles. The situation was electric. Would Turkey move? And if she did, would this mean war with Britain?

Half a dozen men in the British Cabinet decided that firm action must be taken to stop Turkey. They were the same men who had sat together on the Committee for Irish affairs — Lloyd George, Churchill, Birkenhead, Chamberlain, Balfour and Worthington-Evans. 'We made common cause,' declares Churchill in *The Aftermath*. 'The Government might break up, and we might be relieved of our burden. The nation might not support us; they could find others to advise them. The Press might howl; the Allies might bolt. We intended to force the Turk to a negotiated peace before he set foot in Europe.'

Winston then sat down and drafted a bold and determined communique calling on the British Dominions and the Balkan States to co-operate with Great Britain in resisting Turkish aggression, and announcing flatly: 'It is the intention of His Majesty's Government to reinforce immediately … the troops at the disposal of Sir Charles Harington, the Allied Commander-in-Chief at Constantinople, and orders have been given to the British Fleet in the Mediterranean to oppose by every means any infraction of the neutral zones by the Turks or any attempt by them to cross the European shores.'

The uncompromising tone of this statement startled the British public. It also startled the Turk who changed his mind and ordered his troops away from Chanak. Two weeks later Mustapha Kemal signed an armistice. And a year later the grievance was removed by the Treaty of Lausanne which gave Turkey the Straits and Constantinople.

But even though the incident ended peacefully, the public was still unnerved. Anger quickly took the place of fear, and Conservatives and Socialists alike denounced diplomacy 'based on wild and reckless gambles'. Bonar Law declared that Britain could not police the world alone, and the Labour Party attacked Winston with the familiar charge that he was trying to 'dragoon the Empire into war'.

Since that time his action has been appraised more favourably. 'To Mr. Lloyd George and above all to Mr. Churchill,' writes Harold Nicolson in a biography of Curzon, 'is due our gratitude for having at this juncture defied not the whole world merely, but the full hysterical force of British public opinion.'[229] Nevertheless, the two men paid a high price. The Chanak incident brought down the Government.

*

Lloyd George's Coalition Government was three-quarters Tory and one-quarter Liberal. The Tories decided that the wave of public enthusiasm which had given the Government its renewed lease of life at the end of the war had vanished. The inevitable disillusion which awaited any post-war government had at last set in, and the time had come for the Conservatives to march ahead under their own banner.

Besides, the Tories had plenty of quarrels with the Government. When the war ended Lloyd George had become so deeply involved in

---

[229] *Curzon, the Last Phase*: Harold Nicolson.

the Paris Peace Conference that he had practically withdrawn from the House of Commons, leaving Bonar Law to run it for him. Thus he fell into the habit of ignoring Parliament, surrounding himself with personal advisers, dealing with any matter that caught his fancy and deliberately by-passing Secretaries of State whenever it suited him. The Tories were highly critical of this state of affairs and declared that 'Cabinet responsibility' had become a joke.

They were also critical of his handling of the Irish question. They felt it was nothing short of lunacy first to initiate a policy of severe reprisals then to turn around and give the Irish everything they wanted short of a republic. Finally, they were indignant over the Chanak communique. They not only disliked its bluntness but were shocked by the fact that the Foreign Secretary, Lord Curzon, was not even consulted, and that it had been issued to the press before the Dominions had received it. Bonar Law wrote a letter to *The Times* on this subject which was almost a vote of censure.

A few of the leading Conservative Ministers who held office under Lloyd George remained steadfastly loyal. Among these Lord Birkenhead and Austen Chamberlain were the most conspicuous. They did their best to dissuade their Tory colleagues from breaking up the Government but their arguments were unavailing. Largely through the organization of Mr. Leo Amery, who was then Parliamentary and Financial Secretary to the Admiralty, a meeting was held at the Carlton Club on 17 October, 1922, which later became known as the 'Revolt of the Under-secretaries'. Bonar Law, who had resigned the Conservative Party leadership a year earlier on grounds of ill-health, made a strong and telling speech, believed to have been inspired by Lord Beaverbrook, which completely carried the assembly with him. Then Stanley Baldwin, a figure almost unknown to the public but recently appointed President of the Board of Trade by Lloyd George, introduced a resolution to end the Coalition. Baldwin told the meeting that L.G. was a dynamic force but that 'a dynamic force is a very terrible thing'. His resolution was passed by 187 votes to 87.

When Lloyd George heard of the vote he at once resigned and Bonar Law consented to form a Government. The new Prime Minister asked for the dissolution of Parliament and went to the country. The Conservatives scored a sweeping victory. Lloyd George never held office again.

*

Winston Churchill fought the election at Dundee, the great Radical working-class stronghold which had welcomed him joyously in 1908

259

when he had been the formidable antagonist of Tory privilege. 'I stand as a Liberal and a Free Trader, but I make it quite clear that I am not going to desert Lloyd George ...' he announced in his election address.

But Dundee was not at all convinced that Winston really was a Liberal. Ever since he had become First Lord of the Admiralty he had shown practically no interest in domestic matters but concentrated exclusively on military and foreign affairs. During the previous eleven years he had been repeatedly the strongest advocate of Coalition government. On three occasions before the war-time Coalition came into being he had urged that Conservatives and Liberals merge their differences; and in the four years since the close of the war he had floated publicly the idea of a Centre Party composed of moderates from both sides.

Why was Winston so eager to end the traditional warfare between the two great parties? *The Times* ran a series of articles entitled 'Front Bench Figures' and on 15 November, 1920, summed up Mr. Churchill's position as follows: 'Some men hang themselves on their politics, others hang their politics on themselves, and these need to be stout pegs, well screwed into the scheme of things, as indeed Mr. Churchill is. He manages it very well. His first party will still have no good said of him, his second believes him to be hankering after his first love, and latterly he has been advertising for a new Centre Party which is to combine the charms of the other two. But even if this third match came off and then turned out ill, Mr. Churchill would not be greatly embarrassed, for wherever he is there is his party.'

The truth was that Winston disliked wearing a party tag of any description. He could not see that there was any longer a deep, dividing line between Liberals and Conservatives. How much more gratifying from his own personal point of view it would be to heal the old wounds between himself and the Party which was his by birth and inheritance. How much more sensible to receive a mandate from the people to govern, and then to govern to the best of one's ability, untrammelled by stupid Party slogans. However, British politics do not operate in such a free and easy way. The Centre Party came to nothing and Winston was forced to proclaim his colours. The Conservatives would not accept him and besides, he was not prepared to desert his leader. So he stood as a Lloyd George Liberal.

Was there any trace of the Radical left in Winston? In the years since the war had ended there had been much hardship in Britain. In 1922 there were a million and a half unemployed. Housing conditions were appalling and 'Homes fit for heroes' remained only an election slogan. During these four years of booms and slumps Winston had taken practically no interest in the conditions of the great mass of the wage earners. He had no new ideas to offer. His thinking was on conservative lines. *The Times* commented on this orthodox streak, in the article already quoted: 'One could imagine a man of Mr. Churchill's great intellectual power carrying out reforms at the Admiralty that would have made the early Naval history of the war a very different thing, for the Navy was ready for war in everything but that which mattered most, the habit of independent and unconventional thought, and this he might have supplied. At the War Office at the end of the war the same opportunity seemed to offer and again there was the same disappointment. There is tremendous efficiency and business ability, and feats of organization are accomplished, but of the man himself with his sheer intellectual power and his fertility of ideas there is no sign. It may be after all that the fabric of his thinking is conventional, and only its colours and expressions are original; or it may be that his mind does not gear readily to other minds, and that he must either think and act independently for himself, or when that is impossible tumefy the conventions …'

*

Winston fought the election under the most adverse conditions that could be imagined. Three days before the contest opened he was stricken with appendicitis and rushed off to the hospital for an operation. He was unable to appear in Dundee until two days before the poll, and even then was in pain and mounted the platform only with the aid of a walking stick.

All over Britain it was apparent that there was a rising tide of opinion in favour of Conservatism. But it was not so in Dundee. Dundee's Radical heart was beating more strongly than ever. If Winston wished to retain his seat he had to convince the electors that he still retained his reforming zeal and was not leaning towards the Right. He had prepared his speech with great care. He told the audience how important it was to steer a middle course between the extremes of die-hard Toryism on the one hand and Socialism on the other. 'I do not think,' he said, 'that the country is in a fit condition to be torn and harried by savage domestic warfare. What we require now is not a period of turmoil but a period of stability and recuperation. Let us stand together and tread a middle way.'[230]

But in his election address, issued the week before, he had been careful to establish himself as a progressive. He talked about housing, larger unemployment benefits, and an improvement in the public services. He attacked the Tories as the retrograde party. 'Mr. Bonar Law has described his policy as one of negation. Such a message of negation will strike despair in the heart of every earnest social worker and of every striver after social justice. It cannot be accepted by any generous-hearted man or woman ... Over the portals of 10 Downing Street the new Prime Minister has inscribed his words: "All hope abandon ye who enter here".'[231]

But the Dundee electorate was not impressed. They felt that Winston's interest in domestic affairs and his concern with the condition of the working classes were only political opportunism. Besides this, they disapproved of his attitude in foreign affairs. Winston, on the other hand, felt that he had never done so well politically as he had in the post-war years. 'I had in two years,' he wrote, 'successfully conducted the settlement of our affairs in Palestine and Irak, and had carried through the extremely delicate and hazardous arrangements necessitated by the Irish Treaty. I think I may say that the session of 1922 was the most prosperous I have ever had as a Minister in the House of Commons.'[232]

But Dundee had forgotten Palestine and Iraq; and Winston's patient negotiations over the Irish question were overshadowed by the fact that he had been Minister of War in a Government which had instituted the Black and Tans. Most of all they resented his interference in Russia and Poland. The Radicals had a firm belief that nations must be allowed to handle their own affairs and that all interference came under the hated head of Tory Imperialism.

On the evening of 14 November, Winston attempted to address a mass meeting of nine thousand people in the Drill Hall. The hall was packed with opponents, seething with emotion, discontent and ill-will. He was carried on to the platform in an invalid chair. 'I was struck by

---

[230] *The Times*: 13 November, 1922.

[231] *The Times*: 7 November, 1922.

[232] *Thoughts and Adventures*: Winston S. Churchill.

looks of passionate hatred on the faces of some of the younger men and women. Indeed but for my helpless condition I am sure they would have hit me.'

He was unable to deliver his speech. Every time he started the audience burst into song, swelling the hall with the strains of: 'Tell me the old, old story.' And above the din were bitter, hysterical cries of: 'This time we'll do the same as Manchester.'

When the poll was announced Winston and his National Liberal partner, Mr. D. J. MacDonald, were defeated by the two Left-wing candidates, both of whom emerged with the huge majorities of ten thousand each. For the first time since 1900 Winston was out of Parliament. 'In the twinkling of an eye I found myself without an office, without a seat, without a party, and even without an appendix.'[233]

---

[233] Ibid.

Chapter Fifteen — Back to the Tories

AS SOON as the Dundee result of 1922 was known, Mr. and Mrs. Churchill left for the South of France. Winston was still weak from his appendicitis operation and the doctor agreeably recommended the sunshine and sea air of Cannes. Accompanied by a maid, a valet and a secretary, and equipped with plenty of foolscap and his painting kit, he cheerfully set off. Winston loved bright colours and since the dull English sky often prevented him from transmitting them to his canvas he made the most of the brilliant days that stretched out before him. Every afternoon he put up his easel on the beach or along the quiet country lanes and painted to Iris heart's content. 'I agree with Ruskin,' he wrote, 'in his denunciation of that school of painting who "eat slate-pencil and chalk, and assure everybody that they are nicer and purer than strawberries and plums". I cannot pretend to feel impartial about the colours. I rejoice with the brilliant ones, and am genuinely sorry for the poor browns. When I get to heaven I mean to spend a considerable portion of my first million years in painting, and so get to the bottom of the subject. But then I shall require a still gayer palette than I get here below. I expect orange and vermilion will be the darkest, dullest colours upon it, and beyond them will be a whole range of wonderful new colours which will delight the celestial eye.'[234]

To Winston painting was a solace, a relaxation and an infinite pleasure. Although Augustus John found that he had 'extraordinary talent' and Orpen proclaimed that he was 'most promising' he did not attempt to enter the ranks of the professionals. In 1921, however, he exhibited five landscapes in Paris under the name of Charles Morin and sold four of them for £30 each. Yet his head was not turned. He understood enough to appreciate the genius of the great artist and consequently was aware of his own limitations; but this in no way diminished his enjoyment. He found that painting opened out a fascinating new world. He was noticing shadows and lights and colours he had never been aware of before, and even his travels took on an added excitement. He began to feel sorry for the people who rushed around Europe searching for pleasure in 'mammoth hotels', unaware of the priceless gifts they were missing. Once one was

---

[234] *Thoughts and Adventures*: Winston S. Churchill.

interested in painting, 'the vain racket of the tourist gives way to the calm enjoyment of the philosopher, intensified by an enthralling sense of action and endeavour.'

But whereas painting was a pastime, writing was a business. In this field Winston was the true professional for in it he earned his living when politics failed, and took pride in the large sums his work commanded. Although he had not produced a book since the biography of his father appeared sixteen years earlier, when he was out of office in the war he had found no difficulty in providing for his family by newspaper and magazine articles. Now he no longer had to write for a living for in 1919 he inherited a fortune under the will of his great-grandmother, the Marchioness of Londonderry, and he had an income in the region of £5,000 a year. Yet he still regarded the creation of books as his chief occupation after politics, and as soon as he reached the South of France he settled down to work.

For some years he had been carefully filing letters, documents and memoranda for a book on the war. It was to be a major effort, published in four or five volumes and entitled *The World Crisis*. He had already outlined and prepared much of the first two volumes, one of which dealt with the years from 1911 to the outbreak of the war, and the second with the first year of the conflict and his part in the Dardanelles tragedy. The chapters on the Dardanelles had been written during the war and submitted to the Royal Commission appointed to investigate the matter, as a justification of his actions. These went into the book almost as they stood.

He worked every morning dictating to his secretary, often pacing up and down the room chewing a cigar. He could talk a book better than write one and he often got through three or four thousand words a day. The first volume of *The World Crisis* appeared in April 1923 and the second in October of the same year.

The book attracted wide attention. It was a brilliant effort, the argument was lucid and persuasive, the characters stood out boldly, the prose sparkled and flowed, the narrative was compelling, and the theme was presented in the grand manner worthy of a great drama. Yet it was not history. It lacked the purpose of the scholar eager to present his story with scrupulous objectivity, and revealed the purpose of the politician anxious to explain and justify his actions. It was carefully done, for it breathed an air of neutrality, yet by its skilful emphasis was strongly partisan. This was no reflection on Winston. The book was an artistic triumph and he had recorded events as he saw them. He was capable of great generosity, but not of impartiality. He believed in his own ideas and his own powers with such an intensity that he could rarely see the merits of an approach to a problem other than his own.

The reviewers hailed the two volumes as an absorbing contribution, but they all fastened on its personal character. Professor Pollard, professor of English history at London University, reviewed the book in *The Times* under the heading: 'Apologia for the Admiralty — First Class Material for History'. He described it as 'more brilliant and fascinating than the biography of his father', then went on to say: 'Wide vision and a vivid imagination lift alike his matter and his style far above the pedestrian scope of the mere chronicler of naval and military events or the retailer of official information. His book will therefore appeal to a vastly wider public than the more precise and impersonal histories of the naval and military operations of the war. Serious students will not need, and others will not heed, the warning that an apologia may be first-class material for history but cannot be history itself.'[235]

Winston's friends could not refrain from being malicious at his expense. Lord Balfour told someone that he was immersed in Winston's brilliant autobiography disguised as a history of the universe, and another colleague commented: 'Winston has written an enormous book about himself and called it *The World Crisis*.' However, the books netted him £20,000 and he spent the money on buying his country house, Chartwell Manor.

*

Despite his literary triumph, his new country house, his painting and his other countless activities, Winston was not happy. He was a creature of moods, and when lie was out of office his pleasures were disturbed by a hankering for power which increased as the days passed. His thoughts were always on politics. It was some comfort to be able to reconstruct events as he saw them in a political book, but how much more exciting it was to create the events themselves. He followed every debate in the House of Commons, and every move the Government made; and when people came to dine with him he sat at the table until midnight discussing the personalities and questions of the day. The men in power were a mediocre lot; how much better he would handle things, he thought, if only he were given the chance.

---

[235] 10 April, 1923.

But at this point the future looked bleak, for the General Election of 1922, at which he had been defeated, had returned the Conservatives with 344 seats. It had left the Liberals weak, divided and impotent. The Lloyd George Liberals had won only 57 seats and the Asquith Liberals 60. The Labour Party had emerged as the official Opposition with its 142 Members, by far the most they had ever sent to the House of Commons. Did this mean that Liberalism was dead? If so, where did Winston fit in? The Conservatives would have nothing to do with him and he would have nothing to do with the Labour Party. Besides, Labour cordially detested him. There was only one answer: somehow he must make his peace with the Tories.

Winston's friends regarded his future dubiously. Even Lloyd George and Lord Birkenhead, who appreciated his brilliant gifts, predicted that he would make a greater contribution to history as a writer than as a statesman. He was out on a political limb, and it seemed doubtful if he could ever climb back.

*

It was apparent to anyone who took an interest in national affairs that an important change was taking place in English political life. For over a century the two great parties of the State, Liberal and Conservative, had fulfilled opposing but complementary functions. The duty of Conservatives was to 'conserve'. Their hands were seldom off the brake. They defended the *status quo* and resisted most changes until they saw that change was absolutely inevitable, then accepted it with as good a grace as possible. The Liberals, on the other hand, constituted a reforming Party. William Gladstone summed up their outlook when he said: 'I will back the masses against the classes the world over.' The Liberal function was to spread democratic rights, many of which were enjoyed only by the privileged class.

But whereas, to the bulk of the people, the struggle of the working man in the nineteenth century was mainly concerned with political freedoms such as the right to vote, and the right of Trade Unions to organize and expand, in the twentieth century the struggle took on a different aspect. Political freedom was clearly defined and clearly established. The working man was now concerned with economic freedom. Britain was the richest manufacturing country in the world and London the greatest capital city. Yet at the turn of the century in London itself thirty per cent of the population was suffering from malnutrition. Nowhere in the Western world were there greater extremes of riches and poverty. The wealth of the nation lay in the hands of a tiny minority. Even as late as 1936 it was estimated that only one per cent of the population owned fifty-five per cent of the nation's private property.[236]

Lloyd George understood and sympathized with the discontent of the working classes. He made British history by using the budget as an instrument for re-distributing the national income. Taxation of the rich was made to pay for a whole system of social benefits and security. But Lloyd George's legislation was only a first step in satisfying the aspirations of the wage-earning population. During the war progress came to a halt, but when the conflict was over the demands were more pressing than ever. The working classes had been promised 'homes fit for heroes' and they were determined to get them. However, there was little reforming zeal about Lloyd George's Coalition Government, which was mainly dominated by Conservatives. And Lloyd George himself, preoccupied with the Paris Peace Treaty, seemed to have lost his Radical outlook. Up till this time the bulk of the working class had voted Liberal. Now they began to turn towards the Labour Party as their only hope.

But the Labour Party itself had undergone a drastic change. When it was formed in 1900 the idea of its leader, Keir Hardie, was to mould a political organization, backed by the Trade Unions, strong enough to send working men to Parliament to represent the interests of their own class. Hardie resented the fact that the Liberals, despite their progressive ideas, generally refused to accept miners or factory hands as their candidates. He was convinced that the case of the working man would never be placed forcibly before the country until the working man himself had the opportunity to state it.

Until 1918 this remained the simple object of Keir Hardie's party. But when the war ended Labour broadened its aims. A new constitution was drafted by Sidney Webb, designed to end Labour's narrow class appeal by addressing itself to all those who 'produced by hand or brain'. It also adopted Socialism as its faith, but it was not the Socialism of Karl Marx. It was Christian Socialism which rejected revolutionary methods, basing itself firmly on democratic institutions and the theory of 'gradualism'. Its aim, it declared, was by these orthodox methods 'to secure for the producers by hand or by brain the full fruits of their industry and the most equitable distribution thereof that may be possible, upon a basis of common ownership of the means

---

[236] *Public and Private Property in Great Britain*: H. Campion.

of production and the best obtainable system of popular administration and control of each industry and service.'

The widened appeal of the Labour Party attracted new recruits from all walks of life. Professional men from the middle classes and even aristocrats began to flock to its banner. Several leading Liberals such as Mr. Noel Buxton and Sir Charles Trevelyan joined its ranks. The historic division between the English Conservative and the English Radical was now becoming a division between wage earners backed by a large number of professional men and women, and property owners supported by a cross-section of all classes who believed that the well-to-do made the best rulers. The argument between the two parties was the age-old quarrel over money.

If the Liberal Party was dead, and the struggle of the future lay between Labour and Conservatism, Winston had no difficulty in making his choice. Before the war Lloyd George's immense driving power had carried him along the path of Radicalism but now that that impetus had subsided, he reverted instinctively to his natural aristocratic background.

He had a genuine desire to see a minimum standard of living established below which no one would be allowed to fall, and he vigorously held the opinion that compulsory insurance was the answer. But he never had any patience with the idea that the manual labourer, simply because he was in a majority in the country, should rule or dominate it. He felt that the nation's prosperity depended on brains and enterprise, and his Liberalism took the form of denouncing privilege in favour of 'the golden ideal' of 'careers open to talent'. But that is as far as it went. If the working man wanted power and responsibility let him climb up the ladder; but he should not sit at the bottom and demand the prizes by virtue of number rather than ability.

The problem for Winston, therefore, was not in making a choice between the two parties, but in finding a way of installing himself in the good graces of the Conservatives. Only one bridge was possible: an issue that transcended the differences between Liberals and Conservatives and ranged them on the same side. Ever since the war Winston had been a relentless enemy of Bolshevism. If he could convince the electorate that the British Labour Party had an affinity with the tyrants of Russia, no one could blame him for deserting a weakened Liberal Party to lend his strength to the only force capable of real opposition.

It is difficult to judge a man's motives fairly. They are often made up of an elaborate mixture of idealism and calculation. Winston may have had a genuine fear that the Labour Party would prove unconstitutional if it got into power. In those days the Movement contained a good many extremists, and it was even rumoured that the *Daily Herald* was supported by Russian funds. Some of the extremists advocated a General Strike as a basic tenet of policy, and the Government took the threat so seriously that as early as the summer of 1920 preparations were begun to set up a volunteer organization to operate in case of an emergency. On the other hand many people considered these provisions hysterical, for the Labour Party leaders, who represented the majority of their followers, were deeply pledged to democratic methods and repeatedly and publicly had repudiated the 'catastrophic' theories of the Marxists.

Whenever Winston embraced a cause, however, it impressed itself upon him with increasing force and, as a result, he treated the public to a horrific picture of strife and upheaval in the event of Labour reaching full power. But most Liberals and even a large number of Conservatives did not share his belief that the Socialist leaders were such a sinister lot. Many of them were openly embarrassed by his extreme point of view, but this only strengthened his fervour. On 4 May, 1923, he addressed the Aldwych Club in London: 'We see developing a great, vehement, deliberate attack upon the foundations of society ... We see not only Liberals of the Left but Conservatives of the Right, assuring the country that there is no danger of Socialism or of a Socialist Government, that it is a mere bogey or bugbear not worthy of serious attention; that the Labour leaders are very sensible and honest men, who would never think of carrying out their pledges. Finally we are told that in any case we must not resist them or organize effectively against them, because it would not be democratic or modern-minded to oppose Labour. Thus all resistance to violent change is paralysed or reduced to feebleness and futility.'

Winston was only happy when he was fighting a dangerous foe and as a result most of those attacks lost their effect through over-statement, and more than once he received a biting indictment from H. G. Wells. 'He believes quite naïvely,' Wells wrote, 'that he belongs to a peculiarly gifted and privileged class of beings to whom the lives and affairs of common men are given over, the raw material of brilliant careers. His imagination is obsessed by dreams of exploits and a career. It is an imagination closely akin to the d'Annunzio type. In England, d'Annunzio would have been a Churchill; in Italy, Churchill would have been a d'Annunzio. He is a great student and collector of the literature of Napoleon I, that master adventurer. Before all things he desires a dramatic world with villains — and one hero.'

When one reads these scathing vignettes one can only ponder on the narrow line between political failure and success. In those days it was the fashion to ridicule Churchill and if he had died before the age of sixty his obituary notice would not have praised him as a statesman. The political genius was there but the occasion was lacking. When it finally presented itself H. G. Wells, and millions of his countrymen, were thankful that Churchill was there to play the part.

*

In 1923 an event occurred which proved advantageous for Mr. Churchill. Bonar Law, the Conservative Prime Minister and Winston's firm political enemy, resigned and soon afterwards died, and Stanley Baldwin, the Chancellor of the Exchequer, succeeded to the Premiership. Baldwin, a shrewd, kind, stolid Englishman, who liked the countryside, smoked pipes and was a cousin of Rudyard Kipling, was worried by the fact that unemployment still hovered at the million mark. He came to the conclusion that the only way to cure this national disease was by introducing tariffs against foreign goods and thereby stimulating British trade. But in view of pledges given by Bonar Law in the 1922 election he did not feel that he could undertake such a drastic step without having a mandate from the country. Consequently a general election took place.

Baldwin thus picked the only issue capable of uniting all Liberals in one battle-line. Asquith and Lloyd George at once joined forces on the subject of Free Trade. This put Winston in an awkward position. He had no wish to fight against a Conservative candidate when he was trying to re-enter the ranks of the Conservative Party. However, he found a way out of the dilemma. He stood as a Liberal Free Trader at West Leicester where his chief opponent in a three-cornered fight was not a Conservative but a Socialist, Mr. F. W. Pethick-Lawrence.

Winston's campaign was noisy and excited. His violent attacks on the Labour Party raised the temperature to boiling point and drew packed meetings filled with irate hecklers. The Socialists flung up every accusation they could find. Winston's *The World Crisis* had revived the old controversy of Antwerp and the Dardanelles and these subjects were raised so consistently that General Sir Ian Hamilton finally sent a telegram pointing out to the public that the expedition had been 'triumphantly vindicated' at a meeting of the Senior Naval and Army Officers. Winston himself answered his opponents vigorously. 'The Dardanelles might have saved millions of lives. Don't imagine that I run away from the Dardanelles: I glory in it.'

He was so bitterly hated by a large section of the working class, however, that when he spoke in London, at Walthamstow, on 3 December, 1923, the authorities were obliged to send both mounted and foot police to protect him. A brick was hurled at the window of his car, and a man who had shaken his fist in Churchill's face was hustled off to the police station. Winston gave an interview to the *Evening News* describing the hecklers as 'the worst crowd I have ever seen in England in twenty-five years of public life. They were more like Russian wolves than British workmen — if they are British workmen — howling, foaming and spitting, and generally behaving in a way absolutely foreign to the British working classes.' He was defeated by 13,000 votes to 9,000.

The result of the general election was that Conservatives, Liberals and Labour were each returned in numbers that gave no single party a clear majority over the other two. The only way a Government could be carried on was by two parties forming a coalition. It was unthinkable at this period that Conservative and Labour could work together, and the fact that Conservatives and Liberals had opposed each other on the main issue of the election, Protection, made this second combination impossible. The only alternative was a Liberal-Labour Government. And since Labour had more seats than the Liberals it fell to them to form an Administration with Liberal backing. Thus Ramsay MacDonald became Prime Minister of England.

It must have been apparent to Mr. Churchill, as it was to everyone else connected with politics, that a Labour Government held in power by Liberal support could not introduce any drastic changes. It must also have been apparent to him that the Labour leaders, Ramsay MacDonald, J. R. Clynes, Philip Snowden and Arthur Henderson, were not the sort of men for whom revolutionary tactics had any appeal whatsoever. Most of them were nonconformists and all of them were democrats; they were high-minded men whose main purpose was to alleviate the conditions of the poor. There was nothing in Ramsay MacDonald's philosophy that could have prevented him becoming a Liberal; indeed, only a short while previously MacDonald had advocated the dropping of Socialism as a party label 'because there is a sort of bookish association about socialism'.

However, Winston's only hope of a reconciliation with the Conservatives was to keep the Socialist bogey alive and inflate it as much as possible. On 17 January, 1924, he wrote a letter to the press stating the following view: 'The currents of Party warfare are carrying us into dangerous waters. The enthronement in office of a Socialist Government will be a serious national misfortune such as has usually befallen great States only on the morrow of their defeat in war. It will delay the return of prosperity, it will open a period of increasing political confusion and disturbance, it will place both the Liberal and the Labour Parties in a thoroughly false position ... The great central mass of the nation desires to see foreign affairs and social reform dealt with by the new Parliament on their merits without rancour or prejudice, and in a sincere spirit of good-will. All such prospects will be destroyed by the accession to office of a minority party innately pledged to the fundamental subversion of the existing social and economic civilization and organized for that purpose and that purpose alone. Strife and tumults, deepening and darkening, will be the only consequence of minority Socialist rule.'

A month later, in February, a Conservative seat fell vacant in the Abbey Division of Westminster. Winston at once set about trying to get himself adopted as the Conservative candidate. His Tory friends, Lord Birkenhead, Austen Chamberlain and Lord Balfour, all used their influence on his behalf. On 24 March an article about Winston written by Lord Birkenhead was spectacularly displayed in the *Sunday Times*. It dealt with Winston's early career and told how, in the writer's opinion, Winston would never have severed his connections with the Tory Party if the Tory Prime Minister, Arthur Balfour, had encouraged him by offering him a job. Winston had always been a Tory at heart. He was a 'restive young thoroughbred' and his defection had been one of the 'tragedies of modern politics' for no one believed in the 'stately continuity of English life' more thoroughly than he. Birkenhead then went on to say: 'To those who know him well it is very remarkable how complete is the public misconception of the man. He is looked upon as reserved, insolent and even bullying. For these illusions his own demeanour is (unintentionally) much to blame. He has no small talk, and says everything which comes into his mind. Sometimes caustic and disagreeable things come into it though in private life this never happens ... He has indeed, in the intimacy of personal friendship, a quality which is almost feminine in its caressing charm. And he has never in all his life failed a friend, however embarrassing the obligation which he felt it necessary to honour proved at the moment.'

273

Despite the powerful intervention on his behalf the Conservative Association of Westminster turned down Winston's application in favour of Captain Otho Nicholson, a nephew of the retiring Member. Winston, however, was undaunted and on 10 March the press carried his announcement that he was standing as an 'Independent and Anti-Socialist' candidate. 'My candidature,' he explained, 'is in no way hostile to the Conservative Party or its leaders, on the contrary I recognize that the Party must now become the main rallying ground for the opponents of the Socialist Party. In the King's Speech of the late Government the Conservatives leaders have announced a broad progressive policy in social matters and have made declarations which in their main outline might well have served as the King's Speech of a Liberal Government.'

Winston's intervention almost comes under the heading of a schoolboy prank. He often had an irresistible urge to make the 'stuffier element' of the Tory Party sit up and take notice and the Westminster election provided him with a golden opportunity. Conservatives in the House of Commons were divided into two groups; those who regarded his candidature as a glorious knock-about turn and those who decried it as a monstrous act for a man who called himself an 'anti-Socialist'. Westminster was a Conservative seat. The only possible hope of Labour winning the contest lay in dividing the Tory vote, which easily might have been the result of Winston's entry. Several angry letters appeared in *The Times*. One by William Morris, a City Councillor, declared: 'Westminster Conservatives have selected Mr. Nicholson as their anti-Socialist candidate. Mr. Churchill's intrusion is an attempt to spoil his chances — where, therefore, is Mr. Churchill's anti-Socialism?'[237]

Winston answered his critics with an extraordinary piece of political humbug. 'If I thought that the present Conservative candidate,' he said, 'really represented the force of character of the constituency I should not have come forward as a candidate. An important public principle is involved. The days of family preserves and pocket boroughs ought not to be revived. It is not right that the Westminster Abbey Division should be passed on from hand to hand as if it were a

---

[237] 11 March, 1924.

piece of furniture — handed on from father to son, or from uncle to nephew.'[238]

The by-election was an exciting affair and front page news. The Abbey Division was the most colourful seat in England; it included Buckingham Palace, the Houses of Parliament, Soho, Pimlico, the Strand, Covent Garden, a fashionable residential district, a slum area, and a slice of theatre-land. A Conservative M.P. lent Winston a luxurious house in Lord North Street, equipped with priceless Gainsborough pictures, as his headquarters. A bevy of beautiful Society ladies canvassed for him, and the chorus girls at Daly's sat up all night dispatching his election address.

Winston fought the campaign almost entirely against the Socialists. His speeches were woven against a background of blood and thunder, against the ruin and shame that a Labour Government would bring to Britain. The fact that a Labour Government had been in office for three months and was conducting affairs in an orderly and dignified way did not dismay him. 'How well the Socialist Government is doing,' he jeered. 'How moderate, how gentle they are. How patriotic Mr. Thomas's speeches. How lofty Mr. MacDonald's views of his functions. How pious is Mr. Henderson. How prudent is Mr. Snowden, how careful of the State. I say there is no correspondence between this glossy surface, and the turbulent currents that are flowing beneath. These leaders can never restrain their followers.'[239]

Winston soon had a spectacular machine working for him. He had gathered over thirty Conservative M.P.s and a glittering array of peers and peeresses to canvass for him. He also had the support of Lord

---

[238] In February 1944, when Mr. Churchill was Prime Minister, Lord Hartington, the Duke of Devonshire's eldest son, stood as a Government candidate in the by-election at West Derbyshire, which had previously been represented by his uncle. Winston wrote him the following letter of support: 'My dear Hartington, I see that they are attacking you because your family has been identified for about three hundred years with the Parliamentary representation of West Derbyshire. It ought, on the contrary, to be a matter of pride to the constituency to have such a long tradition of such constancy and fidelity through so many changing scenes and circumstances ...'

[239] *The Times*: 12 March, 1924.

Rothermere's *Daily Mail*. Nevertheless he did not feel he had a chance unless he could persuade an important Tory political leader to back his cause. Lord Balfour agreed to support him but Baldwin would not consent unless some other Conservative leader came out in support of Nicholson. This not only seems an extraordinary attitude for a Party leader to adopt towards an official candidate, but the very fact that Baldwin himself delayed issuing an endorsement of Nicholson prompted Mr. Leo Amery to write a letter to *The Times* in his support. At once Balfour's letter was released and broadcast through the constituency. He informed Winston of his strong desire to see him once more in the House of Commons, 'once more able to use your brilliant gifts in the public discussion of the vital problems with which the country is evidently confronted.'

However, the rank and file of the Tory Party had not yet accepted Winston. Many of them resented his intervention against the candidate their Association had adopted. Captain Nicholson plastered the constituency with posters. 'Dundee didn't. West Leicester laughed. Westminster won't.' And Captain Nicholson proved to be right. Despite all the great names, the glamour and glitter, Winston's forceful and spellbinding oratory, the unknown Nicholson defeated him by forty-three votes.[240] The following day *The Times* wrote acidly: 'The features of his late campaign that attracted legitimate criticism were his ill-timed insistence on sheer anti-Socialism as the paramount claim on the electors at this moment, and the impulse that drove him, holding these views, to jeopardize a seat which without him was at least anti-Socialist. It is no new thing, after all, to discover that judgment is not the most conspicuous of Mr. Churchill's remarkable gifts.'[241]

But Winston was far from downcast. His path was now clear. He had severed his connection with the Liberals, he had a number of powerful Conservative friends, he had the good will of the Conservative leader, Mr. Baldwin, and every day he was establishing himself more securely as a Conservative champion against the forces

---

[240] The result was as follows: Captain Nicholson (Conservative) 8,187; Rt. Hon. Winston S. Churchill (Independent and Anti-Socialist) 8,144; Fenner Brockway (Socialist) 6,165; Scott Duckers (Liberal) 291.

[241] 21 March, 1924.

of 'revolution'. Although none of his prophecies about the Labour Government were fulfilled and they remained a Party of restraint and moderation, Winston was determined not to let the public forget that they were there, and merely altered the line of his attack. On 8 May he said at Liverpool: 'The present Government is one vast movement of sham and humbug ... It has deserted with the utmost cynicism the whole of its Socialist principles so far as its present finance, legislation and administration is concerned ...'

*

In the autumn of 1924, only nine months after the Labour Government had taken over, the Liberals withdrew their support and Ramsay MacDonald was forced to go to the country. The election is known in history as 'The Red Letter Election'. A few days before the poll the Foreign Office published a letter, purported to be from Zinovieff, head of the Bolshevik Third International, calling on the British Communist Party to organize an armed revolt in England. This was bitterly denounced by the Labour Government as a forgery, and to this day the truth of the matter is not known. But forgery or not, it secured the Conservatives a huge majority over all parties.

The two years that Winston had been out of Parliament were to prove a turning point in English politics. They were to mark the end of the Liberal Party as a parliamentary power, and the rise of the Labour Party as the official opposition to Toryism; they were also to mark the advent of fifteen years of the most mediocre and incompetent Conservative rule the nation had experienced for a century.

During this period Winston had fought and lost three contests, had severed his connections with the Liberals, and made Ins way once more back to the Conservative ranks. At the Red Letter Election, his fourth in two years, he stood for Epping as a 'constitutionalist' with Conservative support. This time he was successful. A few days after the result was known the country learned that Stanley Baldwin had appointed him Chancellor of the Exchequer.

Chapter Sixteen — Chancellor of the Exchequer

THE CONSERVATIVES were astonished by the news of Winston's appointment. The Chancellorship was a glittering prize to be awarded to a black sheep after nearly twenty years of wandering in heretical fields. Besides, it was only the year before that Winston had stood as an ardent Free Trader against the Tory policy of Protection. And lastly, what did he know of finance? He had no knowledge of economics and no business experience; indeed in the previous thirteen years he had taken less interest in domestic affairs than almost any other leading politician.

Why had Stanley Baldwin made the appointment? Winston's biographers explain unconvincingly that Baldwin was tired of mediocrity and had a particular liking for Winston's buoyant personality. Neither of these reasons was the real one. The truth was that Baldwin feared Churchill, and above all he feared the combination of Churchill and Lloyd George. If he did not include Winston in the Government he was afraid he might join forces again with Lloyd George in a Centre Party, and perhaps take his friend, Lord Birkenhead, along with him. Baldwin had no wish to find himself attacked by the three greatest orators of the day. His first move, therefore, was to detach Churchill from Lloyd George. And while he was doing the detaching he decided to put Winston in a position where Conservative pressure would force him to water down his views on Free Trade. It was a cleverly thought-out manoeuvre by an astute politician.

If the Conservatives were astonished by Winston's appointment, he was apparently even more astonished himself. A story was soon circulating that when Baldwin offered him the Chancellorship he nodded and asked pleasantly: 'Of the Duchy of Lancaster?' His fortunes had changed with a dazzling rapidity. The year before he had been a political outcast with a bleak future; now he was reinstated in the Tory Party and held the second most important position in the State. Once again he was in line for the Premiership.

Winston was delighted by his new position for sentimental reasons as well as political. When his father had resigned from the Chancellorship Lady Randolph Churchill had refused to hand on his robes to his successor, as was the custom in those days, but had packed them away in moth balls, declaring that one day Winston would need them. Although she was no longer alive to see her son's triumph

Winston was immensely proud to think that her prophecy had come true. Yet the victory was soon to have a hollow ring for he was destined to preside over the Treasury for five years of depression, bitterness and strife, accentuated by the gravest industrial crisis the nation had ever known — the General Strike. And many of the difficulties were to be the direct result of his own financial policy: the return to the Gold Standard at the pre-war parity of exchange.

*

Churchill's first Budget, presented to the Commons on 28 April, 1925, was a masterly parliamentary performance. There were the usual crowds outside No. 11 Downing Street waiting to see the Chancellor come out, red dispatch box in hand, on his way to the House; there was the usual air of smiling secrecy; the crowded Chamber; the galleries filled with distinguished visitors. But there was an atmosphere of added excitement for people expected a lively 'show' and Winston did not disappoint them. His long address was not the customary dry exposition but an artistic performance that sparkled and flowed and even managed to amuse. In the middle he broke off, filled a glass in front of him with excisable liquor, and lifting it commented cheerfully: 'It is imperative that I should fortify the revenue, and this I shall now, with the permission of the Commons, proceed to do.'

However, when the first effects of the Chancellor's speech had worn off and Members had had time to reflect upon it they found that it contained nothing very original. It was strait-laced, orthodox Tory finance. Indeed, when Stanley Baldwin congratulated the Chancellor he said that 'one of the reasons why my right honourable Friend's Budget commends itself particularly to me, and will commend itself to our Party — as also, I believe, to the House, and, I am certain, to the country — is because it follows the soundest lines of prudence and Conservative finance.'

The Opposition based its attack on these same grounds. Philip Snowden, the Labour ex-Chancellor, jeered at Churchill, the Free Trader, for the Protectionist duties he had placed on silk. Winston declared that they were not Protectionist but merely revenue duties. Snowden then twitted him for having changed his views on taxing silk imports. 'There is nothing wrong with change, if it is in the right direction,' retorted Churchill. 'You are an authority on that,' said Snowden. 'To improve is to change,' recited Churchill blandly. 'To be perfect is to change often.'

Snowden also attacked the Budget for its partiality. 'There is not one penny of relief for the wage-earning classes,' he declared. 'Shorn of all the glamour of the right honourable Gentleman's eloquence this is his Budget. No more of a rich man's Budget has ever been presented … I congratulate the right honourable Gentleman. It will not take long for the glamour to disappear, and then the great toiling masses of this country will realize the true character of this Budget, and will realize, too, that the Tory Party is still more than ever what Lord George Hamilton declared many years ago: "A party that looks after its own friends, whether it be in office or out of office".'[242]

*

Churchill's Budget will be remembered in history, but not for its duties on silk nor its reduction in taxation for the rich. It is remembered as the Budget that announced Britain's return to the pre-war parity of gold. To-day most economic experts agree that this was a disastrous step. It accentuated the trade depression already in existence and indirectly brought about an industrial upheaval destined to have far-reaching consequences. As a result Churchill's critics like to claim that he was 'the worst Chancellor Britain has ever had' and even to-day remind him angrily of the responsibility he bore. In 1946 Ernest Bevin told the House of Commons: 'Directly the right honourable Gentleman (Baldwin) got into office they (the Government) started to contemplate our return to the Gold Standard. No sooner had the right honourable Gentleman, the Member for Woodford (Churchill) agreed to that course, than Sir Otto Niemeyer left the Treasury to go back to the Bank of England. That was very significant. We were brought back to pre-war parity of gold. No single trade union or industrialist in this country, outside the bank directors, was ever told. There was no notice in the Press that it had ever been discussed and like a bolt from the blue we were suddenly met with the complete upset of the wage structure in this country …'[243]

Bevin's statement implies that sensible people understood the full implications of a return to gold at the pre-war rate, and that Winston's move was deliberately rash and precipitate. This was not the case. Business men and financiers were almost unanimous in their opinion that Britain should take the step in order to re-establish herself as the financial centre of the world, which they believed was essential to her future prosperity. A standing committee of experts appointed by the

---

[242] *Hansard*: 29 April, 1925.

[243] *Hansard*: 13 February, 1946.

Lloyd George Government in 1918 to investigate the position, urged that the decision should be taken, and the majority of politicians of all parties accepted it in principle. Only one clear, emphatic voice was raised against it, and that was the voice of the brilliant young Cambridge don, J. M. Keynes, whose books on economic theory were later to revolutionize the economic thought of the Western world.

The truth of the matter was that in 1925 Britain was midway between two economic concepts of society. The prevailing belief was in the school of 'hard facts' which insisted that wages and prices must be adjusted strictly by the laws of supply and demand. The other school, led by Keynes, preached the idea of a 'managed economy'. But in 1925 Keynes' theories were considered heretical. He had not yet fully developed his ideas and although he could point out the risks and consequences of a return to the Gold Standard, he had no convincing alternative to offer. He had a few disciples among the young Labour Party economists, but the leaders favoured the established view. As a result the Labour Party put down an amendment against the 'timing' of the motion, but not against the principle of it. The motion stated: 'That this House cannot at present assent to the Second Reading of a Bill, which, by providing a return to the Gold Standard with undue precipitancy, may aggravate the existing grave condition of unemployment and trade depression.'

Philip Snowden, however, found even this motion hard to defend for only a few weeks previously he had an article in the *Observer* arguing in favour of a return to the Gold Standard. However, a young Socialist by the name of Hugh Dalton, who was one of Keynes' greatest admirers, and who was himself destined to become Chancellor of the Exchequer in 1945, had no such cramping limitations. 'We on these benches will hold the Chancellor of the Exchequer strictly to account, and strictly responsible,' he told the House of Commons, 'if, as we fear, there should be a further aggravation of unemployment and of the present trade depression as a result of his action, and should it work out, that men who are employed lose their jobs as a result of this deflation. Should that be so we will explain who is to blame.'[244]

After debating the amendment the Labour Opposition let the matter drop. It did not even press a division and the Gold Standard Bill passed through the House in two days. Only Keynes continued the attack. He

---

[244] *Hansard*: 4 May, 1925.

wrote a series of articles for the *Evening Standard* which were published in a pamphlet entitled: *The Economic Consequences of Mr. Churchill*. Why, he asked, had Mr. Churchill made such a silly mistake? 'Partly, perhaps, because he has no instinctive judgment to prevent him from making mistakes; partly, because, lacking this instinctive judgment, he was deafened by the clamorous voice of conventional finance; and most of all, because he was gravely misled by his experts.'

Keynes then went on to refer scathingly to the arguments of the experts as 'vague and *jejune* meditations'. In five brilliant paragraphs which proved a startlingly accurate prophecy, he stated what the experts, if they had any sense, should have told Mr. Churchill. 'Money-wages, the cost of living, and the prices which we are asking for our exports have not adjusted themselves to the improvement in the exchange, which the expectation of your restoring the Gold Standard, in accordance with your repeated declarations, has already brought about. They are about ten per cent too high. If, therefore, you fix the exchange at this gold parity, you must either gamble on a rise in gold prices abroad, which will induce foreigners to pay a higher gold price for our exports, or you are committing yourself to a policy of forcing down money wages and the cost of living to the necessary extent.

'We must warn you that this latter policy is not easy. It is certain to involve unemployment and industrial disputes. If, as some people think, real wages were already too high a year ago, that is all the worse, because the amount of the necessary wage reduction in terms of money will be all the greater.

'The gamble on a rise in gold prices abroad may quite likely succeed. But it is by no means certain, and you must be prepared for the other contingency. If you think that the advantages of the Gold Standard are so significant and so urgent that you are prepared to risk great unpopularity and to take stern administrative action in order to secure them, the course of events will probably be as follows.

'To begin with, there will be great depression in the export industries. This, in itself, will be helpful, since it will produce an atmosphere favourable to the reduction of wages. The cost of living will fall somewhat. This will be helpful too, because it will give you a good argument in favour of reducing wages. Nevertheless, the cost of living will not fall sufficiently and, consequently, the export industries will not be able to reduce their prices sufficiently until wages have fallen in the sheltered industries. Now, wages will not fall in the sheltered industries, merely because there is unemployment in the unsheltered industries. Therefore, you will have to see to it that there is unemployment in the sheltered industries also. The way to do this will be by credit restriction. By means of the restriction of credit by the Bank of England, you can deliberately intensify unemployment to any required degree, until wages *do* fall. When the process is complete the cost of living will have fallen too: and we shall then be, with luck, just where we were before we started.

'We ought to warn you, though perhaps this is going a little outside our proper sphere, that it will not be safe politically to admit that you are intensifying unemployment deliberately in order to reduce wages. Thus you will have to ascribe what is happening to every conceivable cause except the true one. We estimate that about two years may elapse before it will be safe for you to utter in public one single word of truth. By that time you will either be out of office, or the adjustment, somehow or other, will have been carried through.'

*

The just complaint against Churchill's tenure at the Treasury is that he was not a financial genius at a time when a financial genius was desperately needed; that for once in his life he was orthodox when orthodoxy should have been flung to the winds. Keynes' predictions came true and the coal mines were the first to feel the consequences of Churchill's policy. For some time the industry had been in an unhealthy state. By 1919 it was apparent that such a large amount of capital equipment was necessary to make the mines profitable that the Sankey Commission recommended their nationalization. This was not done and by 1925 British coal, faced with a German revival and burdened by an uneconomic organization, was scarcely a paying proposition. Then came the return to the Gold Standard which meant that British goods worth 18s. automatically cost the foreign buyer £1. The coal owners were forced to lower their prices and consequently decided to lower the miners' wages.

The reduction would have made mining one of the worst sweated industries in the country. There was already a deep legacy of bitterness at the coal face for the tragic way the workers had been exploited during the past century. As a result the miners were the most politically conscious group in the country and possessed one of the strongest unions. A miner, Keir Hardie, was the founder of the Labour Party.

The men protested vigorously at the threatened cuts and the Trade Union Congress and the Labour Party protested with them. The Union chiefs declared that if the reductions were put into operation and the miners struck, other unions would strike in sympathy with them. The Government realized that serious trouble lay ahead and Baldwin opened negotiations with the T.U.C. Two days before the cuts were to become effective he declared that the Treasury would subsidize the miners so that they could maintain the wage standard, until a Commission, under the chairmanship of Lord Samuel, could investigate the matter.

The Commission took seven months to issue its report. During the interim period Keynes championed the cause of the miners and tried to make people see that they were the helpless victims of Winston's Gold Standard policy. 'Why should coal miners suffer a lower standard of life than other classes of labour?' he asked. 'They may be lazy, good-for-nothing fellows who do not work so hard or so long as they should. But is there any evidence that they are more lazy or more good-for-nothing than other people?

'On grounds of social justice no case can be made out for reducing the wages of the miners. They are the victims of the economic Juggernaut. They represent in the flesh the "fundamental adjustments" engineered by the Treasury and the Bank of England to satisfy the impatience of the City fathers to bridge the "moderate gap" between 4.40 and 4.86. They (and others to follow) are the "moderate sacrifice" still necessary to ensure the stability of the Gold Standard. The plight of the coal miners is the first, but not — unless we are very lucky — the last, of the Economic Consequences of Mr. Churchill.'[245]

*

The Samuel Report was issued on 11 March, which gave the two sides about six weeks to come to an agreement. It was generally felt that the Report was a sensible and liberal-minded document. It made a mass of practical suggestions for the improvement of the mines, which involved a very large expenditure on the part of the coal owners for re-equipment. But since the mines were not running as an economic proposition, and since the Government was not prepared to continue a subsidy, it was forced to the conclusion that during the period of reorganization the miners should accept a temporary reduction in wages.

Short of nationalizing the mines, or of continuing a subsidy, the Samuel Report was the best compromise that could be hoped for. But

---

[245] *The Economic Consequences of Mr. Churchill*: J. M. Keynes.

instead of grasping it eagerly and urging it wholeheartedly upon the coal owners, Baldwin took no trouble to conceal his distaste for it, then announced unenthusiastically that if the parties to the dispute accepted it, the Government would do likewise. This attitude merely encouraged both sides to tear the recommendations to pieces and finally turn down the Report. The wage cuts were introduced and a coal stoppage began on 30 April.

The next forty-eight hours are now a matter of history. A series of events took place which ended in misunderstanding and recrimination between the Government and the Trade Union leaders, and resulted in a General Strike. Since that time Ernest Bevin, who became the virtual leader of the strike, twice declared on public platforms that Winston Churchill was responsible for the breaking off of negotiations which made the strike inevitable, by a fateful last-minute intervention. What is the truth of the story?

On 1 May, a day after the coal stoppage had begun, the Trade Union General Council held a conference of the executives of its affiliated unions. By an almost unanimous vote the meeting decided to call a National Strike in support of the miners, which would begin at midnight on 3 May. At the same time they sent a letter to the Prime Minister informing him that all affiliated unions, including the miners, had handed over the conduct of the dispute to the General Council of the Congress, which would undertake negotiations and was willing to meet the Government at any time.

That same evening, 1 May, Baldwin sent for the General Council. After a discussion lasting several hours the Prime Minister suggested that the Government might be willing to continue the coal subsidy for another two weeks so that talks could be reopened, if on their part the General Council was 'confident that a settlement could be reached on the basis of the Samuel Report'. Since this implied a reduction in the miners' wages, and since the miners had now developed a burning slogan 'Not a penny off the pay, not a minute on the day,' the General Council replied that it could not give an answer until the miners' leaders were consulted. So Baldwin left to put the proposition before the Cabinet, while the Council sought the miners.

On Sunday morning, however, when the General Council summoned the miners they found that they were not in London, but had returned to their various districts. Telegrams were sent recalling them, but it was not until late Sunday night that they finally assembled in Downing Street.

The General Council arrived at Downing Street first and immediately started discussions with Baldwin and Lord Birkenhead about the exact meaning and wording of the proposition that had been given to them. Lord Birkenhead then presented them with a precise formula drawn up in his own hand. 'We, the Trade Union Council, would urge the miners to authorize us to enter upon discussion with the understanding that they and we accept the Report as a basis of settlement, and we approach it with the knowledge that it may involve some reduction in wages.'[246]

While the Government and Trade Union leaders were discussing this formula, it was announced that the miners' representatives had finally arrived. It was now 11.15 p.m. The General Council immediately withdrew with the miners to a room in Downing Street to explain to them what had transpired and to try and secure their acceptance of the formula. Baldwin and Birkenhead meanwhile went to 11 Downing Street where the Cabinet was gathered to inform their colleagues of what was happening.

About an hour later the Union leaders suddenly had a message that the Prime Minister would like to see them. The members of the General Council Negotiating Committee, Mr. J. H. Thomas and Mr. Arthur Pugh, went down to his room. Mr. Thomas later gave the House of Commons an account of what happened. 'Lord Birkenhead and himself [Baldwin] were present. The right honourable Gentleman said, "Gentlemen, I am sorry to say that our efforts for peace are unavailing. I have a letter to give you, but I feel in honour bound, having regard to all our efforts, at least to say a word to you personally." He said, "Something has happened at the *Daily Mail* and the Cabinet has empowered me to hand you this letter," and he said — and this is very important, because none of us knew what was in the letter he handed to us. We shook hands and he said, "Good-bye; this is the end".'[247]

The Union leaders then learned that the printers of the *Daily Mail* had refused to set up a leader entitled 'For King and Country'. Baldwin told the Commons that when the Cabinet heard of this action members felt that 'the first active overt move in the General Strike was being actually made, by trying to suppress the press. We felt that

---

[246] *Hansard*: p. 412, 5 May, 1926.

[247] *Hansard*: p. 240, 5 May, 1926.

in those circumstances the whole situation was completely changed.'[248]

But since the Government knew that the General Council had nothing to do with the printers' move,[249] which was a spontaneous and impulsive action, why had they taken such a serious view of it? Ernest Bevin placed the blame on Churchill. In 1929 he told his tin-plate workers in Swansea: 'If Mr. Churchill had not come into the Cabinet room on that Sunday night [2 May] with the Daily Mail business, the peace terms would have been in the hands of the Prime Minister and there would have been no National Strike. The two sides were in another room in Downing Street, getting almost to the last clause for handing to the Prime Minister, when Mr. Churchill saw red, walked in and upset the Cabinet, and we had an ultimatum. That is a fact which can be corroborated.'[250] Bevin repeated this same accusation in 1946 in the House of Commons. 'On Sunday, 2 May, we were within five minutes of a settlement … What happened? I am sorry that the right honourable Member for Woodford [Mr. Churchill] is not in his place. He dashed up to Downing Street, ordered a meeting of the Cabinet, rushed Baldwin off his feet — if he was awake — and in a few minutes the ultimatum was given to us and the country was thrown into this terrible turmoil, when within the same few minutes it might have been saved.'[251]

Mr. Churchill was in America when Bevin made this charge, and therefore did not reply to it. But upon examining the facts there appears to be no foundation to the story whatsoever. First of all, because the Trade Unionists were meeting at 10 Downing Street, the Cabinet was held at 11 Downing Street, Mr. Churchill's residence. So there was no question of Winston 'dashing up to Downing Street'. Secondly, according to Mr. Baldwin's statement in the House of

---

[248] *Hansard*: p.345, 5 May, 1926.

[249] Baldwin admitted in the House of Commons on 5 May, 1926: 'I think it is quite likely that he [Mr. Thomas] had no knowledge of the [*Daily Mail*] incident. But that does not affect the fact. He may have repudiated it, but it showed that he had entirely lost control.'

[250] *Bevin*: Trevor Evans.

[251] *Hansard*: 13 February, 1946.

Commons the Cabinet was already in session when news of the *Daily Mail* strike was received; thirdly, the news was not delivered by Mr. Churchill but came through by telephone.'[252]

Apart from this inaccuracy, what truth was there in Mr. Bevin's assertion that the two sides, miners and Union leaders, were within five minutes of agreement? Sir Arthur Pugh, Chairman of the Trade Union Congress in 1925-26, does not believe that this claim can be substantiated in the light of the events that followed. Arthur Pugh was present at Downing Street on the night of 2 May as a member of the Trade Union Negotiating Committee, and in his book *Men of Steel* makes the following comment: 'In view, however, of the subsequent attitude of the miners' leaders, it is fairly certain they would have accepted no formula that would have given the necessary assurance that a return to the *status quo* would result in a settlement on the basis of the Samuel Commission Report ... The miners' leaders had committed their people to a slogan "Not a penny off the pay, not a minute on the day," and this ruled out from their standpoint any negotiations on the basis of compromise on the major questions at issue. The conception of the miners' leaders about the sympathetic strike appeared to be that it was the "big stick" which was to force the implementation of the terms of the slogan, and their mental reasoning that if the threat of the strike and an embargo on the movement of coal could produce a subsidy in 1925, its actual execution in 1926 could hardly fail to give a like reduction.'[253]

The trouble lay in the fact that although the miners had authorized the General Council to negotiate for them, they had not authorized the General Council to compromise for them. Since successful negotiations depended on concessions all round, including an acceptance by the miners of a temporary reduction in wages, it was a blunder for the General Council to accept a negotiating role without full powers to take a final decision.

A second blunder on the part of the T.U.C. was its failure to instruct its affiliated unions to withhold all strike notices while discussions were taking place. All day on Sunday, 2 May, individual unions were

---

[252] *Hansard*: p. 345, 5 May, 1926.

[253] *Men of Steel* is a chronicle of eighty-five years of Trade Unionism in the British Iron and Steel Industry. It was published in 1951 by the Iron and Steel Trades Confederation.

sending out precise instructions for the beginning of the strike. Sir Arthur Pugh states in his book that 'it would perhaps have been better tactics,' and placed the T.U.C. General Council in 'a stronger bargaining position' if the unions 'had delayed the notices for a sympathetic strike for twenty-four hours or so, in order to see the outcome of the negotiations between the T.U.C. and the Government Committee.'[254]

However, the strike notices were not the cause of the breakdown. Although the letter which Baldwin handed to Thomas and Pugh at midnight stated that negotiations could not be continued until the Union leaders repudiated the action of the *Daily Mail* printers and ordered their unions to withdraw their instructions for a General Strike, the Prime Minister knew early on Sunday afternoon that instructions were flowing out and yet was still ready to negotiate.[255] The notices, therefore, were merely used by the Government as a final argument to strengthen their case.

It was impossible for the General Council to comply with the Government's request, for by Sunday evening, with coal pits closing down all over the country, feeling was running so high in the Unions there was little hope that such an order would have been obeyed. The Government obviously was aware of this, for as soon as the letter had been delivered the Cabinet adjourned and Baldwin went to bed. Proof that the General Council was desperately anxious to avoid a breakdown lies in the fact that they drew up a reply repudiating the *Daily Mail* incident and sent a deputation to the Prime Minister requesting him to discuss the matter of the strike notices. 'But when the deputation arrived at that room,' Ramsay MacDonald told the House of Commons, 'they found the door locked and the whole place in darkness.'[256]

As a result of these happenings the Conservatives have always insisted that the Trade Union General Council was not the true master of the situation; that the extremists had control and that there was no use in continuing the discussions until the General Council wielded full authority. On the other hand, the Trade Union leaders have always

---

[254] *Men of Steel*: Sir Arthur Pugh.

[255] See *Hansard*: p. 69, 3 May, 1926.

[256] *Hansard*, 5 May, 1926.

believed that a majority of the Cabinet were not averse to 'teaching the Unions a lesson'.

Undoubtedly there is truth in both these assertions. Many Conservatives were so preoccupied with the fear of Bolshevism they had come to regard the Trade Union leaders as revolutionaries who wished to destroy the parliamentary system. This was far from the truth but the fact that the secretary of the Miners' Federation, Mr. Cook, was a Communist, strengthened their arguments, and was used to discredit the national leaders. There had been the threat of a National Strike in support of the miners in 1921 and again in 1925. Tory opinion was hardening towards the view that it might be a good thing if the matter came to a 'showdown.'

Although the Trade Union leaders made serious blunders, it is difficult to excuse the Conservative Government for their refusal to grapple with the problem of the mines much earlier. It was no secret that for the last century the coal and royalty owners had bled the industry by taking out huge profits instead of re-introducing the necessary capital equipment. Coal was Britain's basic industry. Quite apart from the fact that the Cabinet was pursuing a financial policy bound to depress the coal industry, it is difficult to understand how any Government, either in the interests of humanity or the nation itself, could drift along in such an irresponsible manner, refusing to interfere while the coal owners neglected the mines year after year, until the only solution involved forcing an inadequate standard of living upon the miners.

*

The General Strike began on 4 May, 1926, and lasted for nine days. Everywhere work came to a halt. The press shut down, transport ceased, the gas and electricity works closed, the iron and steel industry and many others came to a standstill. But the Government was prepared. The organization, designed in 1920, was called into action. The country was divided into nine sections, each run by a central controller with semi-military apparatus. The police were fully mobilized and in London Hyde Park became a military camp. The Home Secretary sent out appeals for volunteers and thousands of men and women, mostly from the middle and upper classes, came forward to drive trains, lorries and cabs.

Ernest Bevin emerged as the leader of the General Strike, and once the strike had begun Winston Churchill stood forth as his counterpart on the Government side. These two men who opposed each other so strongly when the country was in a state of upheaval were destined to work together as colleagues and faithful friends when the nation was faced with a far greater danger in 1940. But in 1926 they were formidable antagonists. Winston flung himself into the fight with all his energy. Since there were no newspapers he persuaded the proprietor of the *Morning Post* to lend him his plant, and with the help of several of Lord Beaverbrook's type-setters he published a daily paper called the *British Gazette*.[257] The paper presented the struggle as a constitutional issue: the nation versus a group of revolutionary union leaders who, by trying to force a democratically elected Government to subsidize the miners' wages, were striking at the very roots of the democratic system. 'For King and Country' became Winston's own battle-cry.

Lloyd George looked askance at his old friend and former Liberal colleague. He did not approve of the General Strike but, with his deep, humane outlook, he sympathized with the reasons for it. The day before the strike started he defended the Union leaders in the House of Commons. 'I know a great many of the people responsible. They are as little revolutionaries as any men in this House. They have fought the rebellious ones in their own Party. Therefore, I want to put this to the House of Commons in all earnestness, that this is not a threat by people using it merely for revolutionary propaganda.'[258]

To-day, most people in Britain, including a large section of the Labour Party, agree that the General Strike was unconstitutional and, as such, a reckless act. But that is a far cry from being 'a sinister and revolutionary plot'. If Lloyd George had been in Churchill's shoes it is probable that the whole disaster would have been averted. Winston, on the other hand, flung himself into the fray with unconcealed relish. The British Gazette was a sensation. Labour Members attacked Winston in the House of Commons for falsifying the news, and Lloyd George accused him of deliberately suppressing an attempt by the Council to negotiate a settlement. But Winston gloried in the fight. Why shouldn't a Government put out Government propaganda? At the end of the week the Gazette had a circulation of over two millions.

---

[257] *The Times* issued a one-page typewritten sheet on 5 May, the day the *British Gazette* made its appearance, and the next morning printed a four-page paper which it continued throughout the strike. The Trade Unions also put out a four-page paper, *The British Worker*.

[258] *Hansard*: 3 May, 1926.

The General Strike collapsed on 13 May. Public opinion was strongly against the Unions, and the General Council realized that the Government's policy of attrition was bound to be successful. The Trade Union Movement was treading the path to bankruptcy and in order to prevent its strength and morale from being permanently damaged in a hopeless struggle, the T.U.C. capitulated. The miners' stoppage went on for another six months but in the end they were starved back to work on the owners' terms.

*

This whole period in Churchill's life seems strangely out of tune with his character as a man. He will not be remembered in history as a humanitarian, for his interests have led him to other fields; yet by nature he is warm-hearted and magnanimous. But throughout the nineteen-twenties his attitude towards the working class was hard, narrow and uncompromising. His outlook was influenced by his fear and dislike of Bolshevism, yet his policies and actions were so short-sighted that they did more to strengthen the British Socialist movement than any other single factor.

The truth was that Churchill was out of joint with the times. He did not understand the changing economy, or the reasons why a changing economy was necessary. In two successive elections he had been defeated by the votes of working people in favour of a Labour candidate, facts which did not tend to increase his sympathy with the common man. Then he joined the Conservative Party, which widened the disaffection. For the first time in twenty years he was subjected to all the pressures and influences of die-hard Toryism and like all converts he went to extremes.

At any period Mr. Churchill would have been a doubtful choice as a Chancellor of the Exchequer. Economic theories and industrial statistics bored him. 'He was basically uninterested in the problems of high finance,' writes Mr. Robert Boothby, who served as his Parliamentary Private Secretary at the Treasury. But to have him in charge of the Treasury at a time when his outlook towards the working class was peculiarly rigid and defiant was a calamity both for the nation and himself. Unemployment and poverty, evils against which he championed so fervently under Lloyd George's inspiration, now seemed to awake no indignation in his heart. If he had had a burning desire to protect the lowest wage earners from further hardships it is difficult to believe that his brilliant brain would not have found a solution. It was the sympathy that was missing, not the ability. A single spark of his old-time Radicalism would have driven him to discover what powerful weapons the Chancellor of the Exchequer held in his hands.

Instead, when the General Strike ended and the Prime Minister calmly left for his annual holiday at Aix-les-Bains, Churchill contented himself merely in trying to persuade the miners to accept the owners' terms, with some slight modifications, and go back to work. But by this time the owners, flushed with their triumph over the T.U.C., were more adamant than ever in resisting a compromise; the Prime Minister refused to intervene; and the Cabinet was busy preparing a Trade Disputes Act designed to curtail the powers of the Unions. Meanwhile the miners' strike continued.

Mr. Boothby, a Conservative M.P., and at that time the 'baby' of the House, wrote Mr. Churchill a long and apprehensive letter. 'I told him that the impression was growing every day that the Government had now divested itself of all responsibility for the conduct of our national industries in the interests of the country as a whole, that it had capitulated to the demands of one of the parties engaged in the mining industry, and was now preparing legislative action at their behest in order to compass the destruction of the other ... I asked how ... the Government, having placed the weapon [of longer hours] in the hands of the owners, could stand by and allow the miners to be bludgeoned and battered back district by district. "Bludgeoned and battered they will be," I continued, "in parts of Scotland at any rate. And the instruments? Longer legal hours, cold, and starvation ... If this is to be followed by legislative action calculated to convey the impression that the Conservative Party has utilized the power given to it by the electorate to plunder the funds of the principal Opposition party, and smash the trade unions, then in Scotland at least a fearful retribution awaits it at the polls".'[259]

Winston showed this letter to the Cabinet; and invited Mr. Boothby to become his Parliamentary Private Secretary. Apart from that, he did very little. Although he declared privately that he thought the coal owners were a loathsome lot he was determined that 'not a shilling' of Government money should subsidise the miners' pay packets. He subscribed to the orthodox Tory view that the State must not interfere with the laws of supply and demand. As a result, the coal strike pursued its long, bitter and useless course and ended in the complete defeat of the miners. It cost the country £800,000,000, a sum which,

---

[259] *I Fight to Live*: Robert Boothby.

as Mr. Boothby pointed out, 'could have settled it, at any time, on fair terms. It left a legacy of bitterness which continues to this day.'

*

While the miners were still on strike Mr. Churchill followed the Prime Minister's example and went abroad on holiday. He took a trip to Egypt and Greece (where he painted the Pyramids and the Parthenon) and on the way home stopped in Italy to study Mussolini's new society. Before he departed he gave a statement to the Italian press which shows how far his dislike of Bolshevism had led him. 'I could not help being charmed as so many other people have been by Signor Mussolini's gentle and simple bearing and by his calm detached poise in spite of so many burdens and dangers,' he began. 'If I had been an Italian I am sure that I should have been wholeheartedly with you from start to finish in your triumphant struggle against the bestial appetites and passions of Leninism. But in England we have not had to fight this danger in the same deadly form. We have our way of doing things. But that we shall succeed in grappling with Communism and choking the life out of it — of that I am absolutely sure.

'I will, however, say a word on an international aspect of Fascism. Externally, your movement has rendered a service to the whole world. The great fear which has always beset every democratic leader or working-class leader has been that of being undermined or overbid by someone more extreme than he. It seems that continued progression to the Left, a sort of inevitable landslide into the abyss, was the characteristic of all revolutions. Italy has shown that there is a way of fighting the subversive forces which can rally the mass of the people, properly led, to value and wish to defend the honour and stability of civilized society. She has provided the necessary antidote to the Russian poison. Hereafter, no great nation will be unprovided with an ultimate means of protection against cancerous growths, and every responsible labour leader in the country ought to feel his feet more firmly planted in resisting levelling and reckless doctrines ...'[260]

At first glance this statement strikes the reader as one of the most surprising deflections of Churchill's political career. Yet it is not inconsistent with his classic interpretation of foreign policy. As far as Britain was concerned he was a constitutionalist and a democrat; as far as Europe was concerned he was willing to hold out a hand of friendship to any country, regardless of its system of government,

---

[260] *The Times*: 21 January, 1927.

likely to align itself against Britain's major enemy. At that time he regarded Bolshevism as the greatest threat. Dictators who tried to export their wares were not to his liking. Mussolini, as well as Stalin, was soon to learn the truth of this.

*

Winston seldom spent a week-end away from his country house, Chartwell. His wife was a clever, sympathetic companion who took a keen interest in politics, as well as running the house to Winston's exacting satisfaction and enjoyment.

Chartwell was close enough to London for guests to motor down comfortably for lunch and dinner and almost every Saturday and Sunday there were relays of people coming and going. Winston's favourite relaxation was good political talk which he always got from his close friends, Lord Birkenhead, Lord Beaverbrook and Lloyd George. He liked to sit up late at night, and although he woke early in the morning, often did his work in bed, dictating to his secretary and puffing a cigar.

His bedroom was a high, oak-beamed study equipped with a huge desk which was usually covered with foolscap. On the walls were a picture of his nurse, Mrs. Everest, a contemporary print of the Duke of Marlborough, and a cartoon of Lord Randolph Churchill. When Parliament was not sitting he applied himself to the task of finishing the last two volumes of *The World Crisis*. Often his morning work was interrupted by the shouts and cries of his four children, who ranged in age from eleven to one; and sometimes when the din was too great he put aside his work and joined them in the garden.

They adored his company for Winston was still a good deal of a schoolboy himself. He loved doing things. He put up a tree-top house, built a goldfish pond, and a bathing pool. But best of all he showed them how to dam the lake and make miniature waterfalls. Frequently, like the children themselves, he got so wet he stood dripping outside the house while maids hurried to put newspapers on the floor.

Winston never forgot how he himself longed for his father's confidence, and as a result spent many hours with his own boy talking to him as a grown-up and letting him share his interests. Once when he drove Randolph back to Eton he remarked sadly: 'I have talked to you more this holiday than my father talked to me in his whole life.'

Part of Winston's love of doing things sprang from the interest he took in applying a methodical and systematic technique. Just as he enjoyed writing because he liked to fit the sentences neatly to one another and to build up paragraphs that in turn were carefully linked, so he enjoyed the constructional side of manual labour. Probably this is what attracted him to bricklaying. There was a cottage and a long wall to be built on the estate, so he worked with a professional bricklayer five or six hours a day until he could lay a brick a minute. Then in 1928 he joined the Amalgamated Union of Building Trade Workers, at the invitation of Mr. Hicks, the General Secretary. He paid a fee of five shillings and was rated as an 'adult apprentice'. This drew forth a furious outcry. Winston was the bugbear of the T.U.C. and the Builders' Union immediately passed a public resolution denouncing his act as 'a piece of humiliating and degrading buffoonery', a 'nauseating situation', a 'good joke for Winston Churchill but a painful insult to members of the Union'.

Nevertheless, Winston stuck to his ticket, although his five shillings was never paid into the Union funds; and during the next twelve years constructed with his own hands a large part of two cottages and a swimming pool. Often he urged his guests to come out and talk to him while he worked. Dressed in workman's overalls with a strange and comical hat on his head he liked to discuss the affairs of state. In 1935 when the international situation was darkening and he was growing increasingly alarmed by Baldwin's placid indifference he muttered gloomily to William Deakin, a young Oxford don who was helping him with his *Life of Marlborough* and had been put to work on the cottage: 'I suppose these bricks will be excavated in 500 years as a relic of Stanley Baldwin's England.'

Another of Churchill's interests at Chartwell was his animals. He loved his pet dogs, cats, goldfish, and was even sentimental about his chickens and geese. Once a young man who had been engaged to tutor Churchill's son was staying in the house. He remembers a Sunday lunch when a goose was brought in and placed in front of Mr. Churchill to carve. He plunged the knife in, then paused and said to his wife with deep emotion: 'You carve him, Clemmy. He was a friend of mine.'

*

The public had no opportunity to see this side of Winston. To them he was a pugnacious and formidable figure with an almost machine-like capacity for work, a brilliant mind, an unstable character and a driving ambition. It is understandable that organized labour regarded him as their arch-enemy throughout the five years of his Chancellorship, but although his ideas and sentiments at last fitted the pattern of ultra-Toryism, the Conservatives still found it difficult to accept him. He seemed far more eager to give a dazzling performance than to get at the core of a problem. The four budgets that followed his first were presented with a masterly touch but amounted to little more than ingenious arithmetical exercises designed to prevent the re-imposition of 6d. on the income tax, which he should never have taken off. The only constructive contribution he made was the introduction of the de-rating scheme for agriculture and industry in 1928 with the resounding slogan 'You should not tax the plant and tools of production but only the profits arising from their use.'

As the months passed Winston's following steadily decreased. This was partly due to the fact that a large section of the Tory Party, led by Mr. Amery, bitterly resented the way he clung to his Free Trade principles, refusing to give Protection to British industry which, they felt, was essential if unemployment, then at the million mark, was to be reduced. But probably it was due even more to the fact that his aggressive, overpowering personality and his concern with his own ideas annoyed them just as they had annoyed his Liberal colleagues in the days before the first World War. Lord Beaverbrook points out in his memoirs that Churchill 'up' is quite a different proposition from Churchill 'down'. 'Churchill on top of the wave,' he comments, 'has in him the stuff of which tyrants are made.'[261]

This explains why the press comments about him at this time are harsh and disagreeable. 'If he changes his Party with the facility of partners at a dance, he has always been true to the only Party he really believes in — that which is assembled under the hat of Mr. Winston Churchill,' wrote one newspaper man. 'His life is one long speech. He does not talk. He orates. He will address you at breakfast as though you were an audience at the Free Trade Hall, and at dinner you find the performance still running. If you meet him in the intervals he will give you more fragments of the discourse, walking up and down the room with the absorbed self-engaged Napoleonic portentousness that makes his high seriousness tremble on the verge of the comic. He does not want to hear your views. He does not want to disturb the beautiful clarity of his thought by the tiresome reminders of the other side. What has he to do with the other side when his side is the right side? He is not arguing with you: he is telling you.'[262]

---

[261] *Politicians and the War*: Lord Beaverbrook.

[262] *Certain People of Importance* 1926: A. G. Gardiner.

Even Baldwin found Winston a difficult colleague. He began to tire of his overpowering energy and his dominating manner. He complained that 'a Cabinet meeting when Winston was present did not have the opportunity of considering its proper agenda for the reason that invariably it had to deal with some extremely clever memorandum submitted by him on the work of some department other than his own.'[263]

Baldwin's Government went to the country in 1929. Once again Labour emerged as the largest Party of the three and once again it assumed power with Liberal support. Baldwin confided to a friend that if he ever formed another Government he would not include Winston in it. His inability to fit himself into a team was a disadvantage that outweighed the contribution he had to offer.

Baldwin kept his word, and successive Prime Ministers followed Baldwin's example. Winston was out of office for ten years.

---

[263] *Neville Chamberlain As He Was*: Lord Camrose (*Daily Telegraph*, 15 November, 1940).

Chapter Seventeen — India

THE AGE of the Common Man had very little appeal for Mr. Churchill. He was proud of Britain's great and educated ruling class which had governed the nation for so many centuries and brought it safely through so many perils. This ruling class was no mean, tight, narrow-minded ring. It was the top layer of an intricate class system that automatically embraced men and women with inherited wealth and aristocratic connections, but also accepted newcomers whose energy and talents had lifted them to positions of eminence. In welcoming distinguished strangers the ruling class constantly refurbished itself with vigorous new blood, yet its impact was strong enough to unite its members in a common outlook towards the traditions and splendours of the nation.

This paternal, benevolent and oligarchic Britain was the sort of Britain Winston had been brought up to love and revere. He resented the fact that ever since the Labour Party had become the largest Opposition in the House of Commons a note of 'class warfare' had resounded through the country which, he felt, was aimed at the very foundations of the British system. It was true that Winston himself had once attacked the privileged classes, but that was long ago when he was very young and the privileged class was very safe; his actions could be classified as political wild oats and forgotten.

The class warfare of the post-war period was very different; it appeared to be undermining the common sense of the British working man and making him wonder whether he wished to continue being ruled by his betters. The working man had noticed that millions of pounds had been spent in war; why could not millions of pounds be spent in the peace to give him a better standard of living? He wanted security, higher wages, a better education, and a larger share in the nation's wealth. He also appeared to want a larger influence in the nation's industrial and political life. This last made no sense at all to Winston. Let the working man climb the ladder first; why should he demand the prizes while he still stood at the bottom?

Winston considered the Labour leaders wholly responsible for the agitation that had sprung up and more than once referred to them contemptuously as 'not fit to govern'. He did not blame the working man for being misled by false hopes and promises, nor did he blame him for rebelling against the grave state of unemployment. For the previous four years the unemployment figure had hovered between one and two million men, which, counting the wives and children of the unemployed, directly affected some five million people. Politicians of all parties were bent on finding a cure for unemployment, some on humanitarian grounds, others on political ones. But the truth was that very few politicians were sure of the answer. Professor Keynes put forward a scheme of large borrowings for public works to relieve unemployment which Winston denounced as 'camouflaged inflation'. Lloyd George supported Keynes and drew up proposals of his own along similar lines. But neither the Labour Government nor the Conservative Opposition were impressed by these heretical views. They believed that the cycle of booms and slumps was inevitable, and that the only method of dealing with it was to follow the prescription laid down by orthodox finance: to reduce wages and prices, to balance the budget, and to sit tight.

In March 1930, Winston wrote a series of articles for the *Daily Telegraph* 'On the Abuse of the Dole', in which he pointed out that many people who were switching from one job to another were claiming the compensation merely for a few weeks' unemployment. 'The minor vicissitudes of labouring men such as an occasional month out of work between satisfactory jobs, are borne in almost every other country in the world in silence,' he wrote reproachfully. 'They may cause some embarrassment or even distress to the individual but they do not emerge as a problem of the State.'

*

But none of this was to Winston's liking. He found economics a boring subject which he did not and could not understand. He had nothing new to offer. Yet economics dominated the whole atmosphere of Parliament. He inclined to the view of his Conservative colleagues that the only remedy lay in drastic deflation which would be deeply resented by the working class electorate. He complained to a friend that Parliament had sunk into a morass of figures and statistics and that politics had never before been so dull. There were no great personalities and no great issues that a politician could get his teeth into. Economics cast its particular blight on every subject that was discussed.

But if Winston had no solution to the economic problem itself at least he had a solution for preventing economics from destroying the liveliness of the House of Commons. In June 1930 he delivered the Romanes lecture at Oxford University and made the surprising suggestion that economics should be isolated from politics. 'I see no reason why the political Parliament should not choose in proportion to its Party groupings a subordinate Economic Parliament of say one-fifth of its numbers, and composed of persons of high technical and business qualifications. This idea has received much countenance in Germany. I see no reason why such an assembly should not debate in the open light of day and without caring a halfpenny who won the General Election, or who had the best slogans for curing unemployment, all the grave economic issues by which we are now confronted and afflicted. I see no reason why the Economic Parliament should not for the time being command a greater interest than the political Parliament; nor why the political Parliament should not assist it with its training and experience in methods of debate and procedure. What is required is a new *personnel* adapted to the task which has to be done, and pursuing that task day after day without the distractions of other affairs and without fear, favour or affection.'

No one took much interest in Winston's Economic Parliament, so to relieve himself from the boredom of statistics, he took up his pen. First he wrote *My Early Life*, an amusing and charming autobiography which took him as far as the House of Commons and ended with the words: 'I married and lived happily ever afterwards.' As far as the public was concerned the work was strangely out of character with the Winston they knew. It was wise and tolerant with a gentle humour which he was not afraid of directing towards himself. It seemed much more the reflections of a calm and elderly philosopher than of a pugnacious politician. Next, Winston wrote the fifth volume of *The World Crisis*, *The War on the Eastern Front*, and a series of newspaper articles and essays ranging in subject from one on 'Moses' to 'Shall We All Commit Suicide?' These essays were later reprinted in a book called *Thoughts and Adventures*.

*

But while he was occupied in his literary work a political issue emerged which aroused his emotions and galvanized his fighting spirit to action. Ever since the war India had been agitating for self-government. The urge for independence had been stimulated by Gandhi, the great Hindu religious leader who preached a policy of passive resistance. Millions of Indians regarded this strange man as a saint and were now quietly following his lead and slowly obstructing the wheels of the British administration.

The Viceroy, Lord Halifax (then Lord Irwin), was in favour of granting India the freedom she wanted; first, in drawing up a Federal Constitution; second, in extending self-government in the direction of Dominion status. He communicated his views to the Labour

Government which received them favourably. The Liberals backed the Labour Government and the Tories, surprisingly enough, backed them both. For once there was an all-Party agreement on the policy Britain should follow. Undoubtedly the reason for this accord was the fact that public opinion had been sharply affected by the lesson of Ireland. India was merely asking for the same Dominion status that had been granted to Canada and Australia. There was no reason to believe that she would leave the Empire. If England could retain her good-will by granting concessions in time there was much to gain; if she tried to rule by repression as she had in Ireland there was even more to lose.

Winston, however, did not see the matter in this light. He was horrified at the idea of relaxing control of any kind over India. He was willing to extend Indian self-government within the provinces, but not to grant a Federal Constitution and certainly not to promise them Dominion status. Had not Lord Randolph Churchill once described India as 'that most truly bright and precious gem in the crown of the Queen, the possession of which, more than that of all your Colonial dominions, has raised in power, in resource, wealth and authority, this small island home of ours far above the level of the majority of nations and states'?

Winston was devoid of sympathy for an act of abdication which he not only regarded as foolish but as wholly unnecessary. All this talk of self-government had sprung up because the statesmen in London were pusillanimous and weak. He did not believe force was necessary to hold India; merely a firm resolve and some plain speaking.

Since no one else was going to do the plain speaking Winston took it upon himself. He described the proposed concessions as a 'hideous act of self-mutilation astounding to every nation in the world'. In words similar to those his father had used he tried to rouse public opinion against casting away 'that most truly bright and precious jewel in the crown of the King, which more than all our other Dominions and Dependencies constituted the glory and strength of the British Empire. That great organism would pass at a stroke out of life into history. From such a catastrophe there could be no recovery.'[264]

He became the leading spirit of the Indian Empire Society, a group composed mainly of Conservatives organized to resist self-government. For the first time he found himself working with the Die-

---

[264] Indian Empire Society: 12 December, 1930.

hards of the Tory Party, the same band which had poured contempt upon him for many years.

Throughout his opposition Winston's main attack was against Gandhi, and as the weeks went by his shafts were hurled with increasing violence. On 12 December, 1930, he told a London audience: 'The truth is that Gandhi-ism and all it stands for will, sooner or later, have to be grappled with and finally crushed. It is no use trying to satisfy a tiger by feeding it on cat's meat.' Two months later, on 23 February, 1931, he told the Council of the West Essex Conservative Association that it was 'alarming and also nauseating to see Mr. Gandhi, a seditious Middle Temple lawyer, now posing as a fakir of a type well-known in the East, striding half-naked up the steps of the Viceregal Palace, while he is still organizing and conducting a defiant campaign of civil disobedience, to parley on equal terms with the representative of the King-Emperor.' One month later, on 18 March, he told a huge meeting at the Albert Hall: 'I am against this surrender to Gandhi. I am against these conversations and agreements between Lord Irwin and Mr. Gandhi. Gandhi stands for the expulsion of the British from India. Gandhi stands for the permanent expulsion of British trade from India. Gandhi stands for the substitution of Brahmin domination for British rule in India. You will never be able to come to terms with Gandhi.'

In the course of his campaign Winston accused politicians of all parties who supported Lord Irwin's proposals, of defeatism and a lack of patriotism. This stung Sir Herbert Samuel, the Liberal, to deliver a scathing pronouncement. 'If indeed the truest patriot is a man who breathes hatred, who lays the seeds of war, and stirs up the greatest number of enemies against his country,' he said, 'then Mr. Churchill is a great patriot.'

The Conservative Opposition was furious with Churchill. They told Baldwin that this was the result of putting his trust in a man like Winston, an ambitious schemer, who would never work for any team unless he called the tune. They went on to say that his chief aim was to split the Conservative Party and wrest the leadership from Baldwin. This was not altogether fair for although no one doubts that he would have liked to grasp the prize, and although he may have believed the Indian issue a likely way to do it, his sincerity about India has long since been proved by the consistency of his views. In January 1930 he resigned from the Tory 'Shadow Cabinet' and three months later Baldwin relieved him of his position as Chairman of the Conservative

Finance Group and appointed Neville Chamberlain in his stead. The breach was now complete.

*

Although Winston's main concern was to rally Conservatives against the official Opposition, he still had time to launch an intermittent and powerful torpedo at the Labour Government. One of the most merciless attacks he ever made in the House of Commons was directed at Ramsay MacDonald in connection with the Trade Disputes Act. The Labour Party was determined to repeal the measure which had been introduced by the Tories after the General Strike to clip the wings of the Trade Unionists. Mr. MacDonald himself was believed to be only lukewarm on the subject, giving way half-heartedly to the Left-wing pressure in his own Party. 'What is the Prime Minister going to do about it?' Winston asked in the House of Commons. 'I spoke the other day, after he had been defeated in an important division, about his wonderful skill in falling without hurting himself. He falls, but up he comes again, smiling, a little dishevelled but still smiling. But this is a juncture, a situation which will try to the very fullest the particular arts in which he excels.

'I remember when I was a child being taken to the celebrated Barnum's Circus which contained an exhibition of freaks and monstrosities, but the exhibit on the programme which I most desired to see was the one described as "The Boneless Wonder". My parents judged that the spectacle would be too revolting and demoralizing for my youthful eyes, and I have waited fifty years to see the Boneless Wonder sitting on the Treasury Bench.'

Then Winston proceeded to give an imaginary conversation which had taken place between Ramsay MacDonald and Lloyd George. 'After the usual compliments, the Prime Minister said, "We have never been colleagues, we have never been friends — not what you would call holiday friends, but we have both been Prime Ministers and dog don't eat dog. Just look at the monstrous bill the Trade Unions and our wild fellows have foisted on me. Do me a favour and I will never forget it. Take it upstairs and cut its dirty throat".'[265]

Winston's speech was greeted with howls of appreciative laughter. Even the Labour benches could not suppress their smiles. But Ramsay MacDonald never forgave him.

*

---

[265] *Hansard*: 28 January, 1931.

The Government of India Bill did not pass through its final stage until 1935. It granted India Federal Constitution and gave a solemn pledge that she would be given Dominion status in the near future. Winston fought the Bill to the bitter end. 'I am told that I am alone among men who have held high office in this country in the view I take about Indian policy … If I am alone I am going to receive shortly an ally — a very powerful ally — an ally whom I dread — an ally with a sombre title — his title is The March of Time.'[266]

But Winston was proved wrong. Indian independence, which finally became a reality in 1947, was not a catastrophe. It did not result in the severing of India's ties with the Commonwealth. It did not mark the end of the British Empire. The brightest jewel in the Imperial Crown has become one of the strongest partners in the British family of nations. The March of Time definitely has not turned out to be Winston's ally.

When he made his final attack in the House of Commons and took his seat after a tremendous peroration, Leo Amery, his Harrow school-mate, spoiled the effect by rising and saying in solemn tones: 'Here endeth the last chapter of the Book of the Prophet Jeremiah.' The House roared with laughter. Members had ceased to take Winston seriously on the subject of India.

In 1931 Ramsay MacDonald and Philip Snowden deserted their Labour colleagues and joined forces with the Conservatives in forming a National Government in order to deal with the financial crisis produced by the American crash. The National Government consisted of only a handful of Socialists and Liberals. It was predominantly Conservative, and although Ramsay MacDonald assumed the Premiership, Stanley Baldwin was the real master. Neither man would have Winston in the Government at any price.

---

[266] Constitutional Club: 26 March, 1931.

Part Six
Time for Greatness

Chapter Eighteen — The Life of Marlborough

WINSTON CHURCHILL had always believed in his Destiny. He felt sure that he had been placed on earth to carry out some extraordinary and critical purpose. Part of this belief sprang from his awareness of the famous blood that flowed in his veins, part from his own throbbing energy and supreme confidence. But the belief also stemmed from pure superstition. When, as a young soldier, he narrowly escaped death several times, he dwelt on these experiences with fascination and awe. 'These hazards swoop on me out of a cloudless sky,' he wrote, 'and that I have hitherto come unscathed through them, while it fills my heart with thankfulness to God for His mercies, makes me wonder why I must be so often thrust to the brink and then withdrawn …'

Long after he had written these lines he had other close escapes from destruction; once in the first War when his dugout was blown up by a shell a minute after he had left it; once when his aeroplane crashed; once when he had a collision in a New York taxi.

The recurrent escapes confirmed his faith that his life was being guarded for some great public role, yet in 1931 the role was hard to see. Most politicians regarded his career as finished. His independent and reckless nature had led him into fierce disagreement with his last remaining colleagues. He had quarrelled with all three parties. The Conservatives had reluctantly forgiven him once, and now that their misgivings had been realized they were not likely to forgive him again. The Liberal Party was dead. The Labour Party was beyond the pale. Where was his future?

It is curious that in 1931, at the very moment when his path had apparently ended in a quagmire from which there seemed to be no rescue, his fortunes were, in fact, at last moving on the upward swing which was to carry him to world fame. The change was not discernible to the public for the initial turn of events did not stem from his efforts as a statesman but from his activities as an artist. In 1931 he began writing the life of the first Duke of Marlborough. It was the work, thought and inspiration which he poured into this literary masterpiece, with its story of tyranny and salvation so strangely and strikingly parallel to the unknown story that lay ahead, that prepared him for the leadership of Britain in the second World War.

*

307

Ever since Winston was a child he had read everything he could lay his hands on about his great ancestor, John Churchill. Here was a tale that contained every element of drama; the story of the unknown youth who rose from obscurity to become one of the greatest generals of all time and who saved his country and half Europe from the tyranny of Louis XIV; the handsome youth who fascinated the King's mistress; the penniless youth who became the richest man in Europe; the sought-after youth who loved his wife passionately for fifty years; the ambitious youth who not only won every battle he ever fought but by his brilliant diplomacy virtually became the political master of England. There was nothing missing. Love, danger, intrigue, war, revolution and counter-revolution all threaded their way through his astonishing life.

It is small wonder that Winston was tempted to write the thrilling record. There were masses of papers at Blenheim Palace filed away in cardboard cabinets and carefully docketed, containing valuable information that had never been published. Yet there was something that had always stopped him from writing the story. Marlborough's name had come down through history not only as a hero but as a villain. He had rendered great service to England but his deeds were darkened by accusations of corruption and unforgivable treachery.

Marlborough had risen to power through the favour of James the Second. But when he saw that James was determined to turn England into a Catholic country and make himself an absolute monarch, Churchill deserted him and was instrumental in placing William of Orange on the throne. James fled to France. Six years later, when William organized an attack against the French Fleet at Brest, Marlborough, it is alleged, wrote a letter to James, known as the Camaret Bay Letter, in order that the French might be informed of the impending operation. Some historians attributed this act to Marlborough's desire to re-establish himself with the Jacobites in case James one day was restored to the English throne. Others claim that Marlborough's wish was to see the English commander fail so that he himself might receive promotion. Whatever the motive an act of this nature was vile and unforgivable. Winston refused to write John Churchill's life.

However, one day he visited his father's old friend, Lord Rosebery, who urged him to take up the task, and here is the account he gives of the conversation. "'Surely,' said Rosebery, "you must write *Duke John* [as he always called him]: he was a tremendous fellow." I said that I had from my childhood read everything I came across about him, but that Macaulay's story of the betrayal of the expedition against Brest was an obstacle I could not face. The aged and crippled statesman arose from the luncheon table, and, with great difficulty but sure knowledge, made his way along the passage of the Durdans to the exact nook in his capacious working library where *Paget's Examen* reposed. "There," he said, taking down this unknown, out-of-print masterpiece, "is the answer to Macaulay!"'[267]

Paget's Examen proved conclusively that Marlborough's letter betraying the Brest Expedition was written only after he knew that it had been betrayed already and could do no harm. Winston's strict code of military honour was still not appeased; nevertheless, it gave him the heart to start the book. But as his research proceeded he discovered that the letter Marlborough was accused of having written did not, in fact, exist. Only an alleged copy of the letter had been preserved. Winston was able to prove to the satisfaction of most historians that this copy was a forgery.

*

Soon Winston was more engrossed in his life of Marlborough than in anything he had ever written before. He had always had strong sentimental attachments for Blenheim, the massive Palace that had been built for Marlborough in recognition of his services, for not only had Winston been born there, but he had also proposed to his wife there. Once he remarked to a friend: 'At Blenheim I took two very important decisions: to be born and to marry. I am happily content with the decisions I took on both occasions.' Now he flung himself into the task of clearing his ancestor's name with passionate concern. He singled out Lord Macaulay, the great historian, as the villain of the piece. Macaulay was only one of many historians who had painted John Churchill's character in black lines, but whereas the others were no longer widely read, Macaulay's wonderful sense of drama and lucid, flowing prose still commanded a large public. Besides, Winston felt a sense of personal grievance against Macaulay. As a boy he had been under the spell of the master; he had read and re-read his *History of England*, his essays, and had even learned by heart a great portion of *The Lays of Ancient Rome*. Macaulay had taught him more about style and construction than anyone else and now to come to the conclusion that the historian had deliberately sacrificed the truth, at

---

[267] *Marlborough*: Winston S. Churchill.

the expense of a Churchill, to make his tale more dramatic, roused Winston to real anger.

Throughout the first two volumes of *Marlborough* Winston conducts a duel with Macaulay in the wings. He flings up the historian's remarks and attempts to show that his interpretation was wholly false. 'Unhappily,' Macaulay had written, 'the splendid qualities of John Churchill were mingled with alloy of the most sordid kind. Some propensities which in youth are singularly ungraceful, began very early to show themselves in him. He was thrifty in his very vices, and levied ample contributions on ladies enriched by the spoils of more liberal lovers. He was, during a short time, the object of the violent but fickle fondness of the Duchess of Cleveland. On one occasion he was caught with her by the King, and was forced to leap out of the window. She rewarded this hazardous feat of gallantry with a present of £5,000. With this sum the prudent young hero instantly bought an annuity of £500 a year, well secured on landed property. Already his private drawers contained heaps of broad pieces which, fifty years later, when he was a Duke, a Prince of the Empire, and the richest subject in Europe, remained untouched.'[268]

Macaulay returned to his theme again and again. 'He subsisted upon the infamous wages bestowed upon him by the Duchess of Cleveland.' 'He was insatiable of riches.' He was 'one of the few who have in the bloom of youth loved lucre more than wine or women, and who have, at the height of greatness, loved lucre more than power or fame'. 'All the precious gifts which nature had lavished upon him he valued chiefly for what they would fetch.' 'At twenty he made money of his beauty and his vigour; at sixty he made money of his genius and his glory.'

When Winston tackled these imputations against John Churchill's character he held a strong card in his hand. The fact that Churchill had married a penniless girl. He was handsome and sought after. He could have won a great heiress; indeed, his family had their eye on one and urged him to consider improving his fortunes by doing so; instead he married the hot-tempered, fascinating Sarah Jennings who had neither money nor property; and their marriage became one of the great love stories of the age.

Winston did not only tilt at Macaulay; he delivered a formidable frontal attack: 'His [Macaulay's] literary descendant, Professor

---

[268] *History of England*: Lord Macaulay.

Trevelyan, whose faithful, fair, and deeply informed writings are establishing a new view of these times and the men who made them, has offered the best defence in his power for the historical malversations of his great-uncle. He says (in effect) that Macaulay, with his sense of the dramatic, vilified Marlborough's early life in order by contrast to make the glories of his great period stand out more vividly. He had completed the black background, but died before he could paint upon it "the scarlet coat and flashing eye of the victor of Blenheim". We need not reject this apologia nor the confession which it implies. But what a way to write history! On this showing — the best that can be provided — Lord Macaulay stands convicted of deliberately falsifying facts and making the most revolting accusations upon evidence which he knew, and in other connections even admitted, was worthless, for the purpose of bringing more startling contrasts and colour into his imaginative picture and of making the crowds gape at it. Macaulay's life-work lay in the region of words, and few have been finer word spinners. Marlborough's life is only known by his deeds. The comparison is unequal, because words are easy and many, while great deeds are difficult and rare. But there is no treachery or misconduct of which Macaulay's malice has accused Marlborough in the field of action which is not equalled, were it true, by his own behaviour in this domain of history and letters over which he has sought to reign … It is beyond our hopes to overtake Lord Macaulay. The grandeur and sweep of his story-telling style carries him swiftly along, and with every generation he enters new fields. We can only hope that Truth will follow swiftly enough to fasten the label "Liar" to his genteel coat-tails.'[269]

The attack on Macaulay drew a letter of protest from Professor Trevelyan which was published in *The Times Literary Supplement* on 19 October, 1933. An extract reads as follows: 'I have stated elsewhere that I think Macaulay was wrong in his reading of Marlborough. Indeed, I think it is the worst thing in his History, and I have no wonder that Mr. Churchill's family piety has aroused him to take revenge. All the same, he has no right to call Macaulay a "liar". A "liar" is not a man who misreads another man's character, however badly, or who sometimes accepts inadequate evidence; if that were so, almost all historians would be "liars". A "liar" is a man who makes a statement that he knows to be false. Now, the facts that Macaulay

---

[269] *Marlborough*: Winston S. Churchill.

states, barring the Camaret letter, are not very different from Mr. Churchill's facts. Mr. Churchill admits that he took for patron the man who kept his sister; that he himself took money from his own mistress and invested it well; that he deserted James while high in his military service; that he afterwards corresponded with the Jacobites. I agree with Mr. Churchill that his desertion of James was in the circumstances commendable, and the other three actions by the standards of the times not unpardonable. But there is a surface case against Marlborough, and many people in his own day thought ill of him. An historian who, before the days of our modern research, was deceived by these phenomena into thinking Marlborough a bad man was not necessarily dishonest.'

*

Winston's attack on Macaulay was only one small aspect of his biography. It constituted the stepping stones by which he led Marlborough to the summit from which, he believed, posterity should view him. But the importance of the work lies not only in his central figure but in the skill with which he brings alive all the leading characters of the time. Sarah Jennings, Godolphin, Prince Eugene, Queen Anne, Bolingbroke, and many others walk confidently through his pages and their complicated relations with one another, developed with a true touch of genius, reveal a century of tumultuous history which slowly unrolls before the reader's fascinated gaze. As a history it is as dramatic as Lord Macaulay's own, written in the same grandly flowing prose. As a literary work it is on the same colossal scale as Tolstoy's *War and Peace* and handled with such technical brilliance that one can admire it as an artistic achievement even though the characters are limited to a frame-work of fact.

Yet what makes the *Life of Marlborough* truly distinctive is the feeling that no professional historian could have written it. The story of Marlborough is the story of a struggle for power. Sometimes the struggle was in ruling circles in England, sometimes on the battlefields, sometimes at a foreign court, but throughout the book it is a strong and constant clash. This subject, the essence of history, had always interested Winston more than any other. He had spent many months of his life studying its causes and effects and he had witnessed it at first-hand in the years preceding the Great War and in the war itself. Besides, his long experience in Parliament had given him special knowledge of the rivalries and emotions, of the jostling for position behind the scenes, and he drew upon his rich knowledge in interpreting the characters and the actions of a bygone day. His chapter on the Camaret Bay Letter is a masterpiece of evidence and argument that could only have been written by a man who understood every current of political life.

Altogether, the biography was deeply satisfying. It gave Winston the opportunity to vindicate his ancestor and also the opportunity to study the art of war, an art which had always thrilled and fascinated him. He could write proudly of Marlborough that 'he never fought a battle that he did not win, nor besieged a fortress that he did not take'. But even more important than the battles was the glorious cause for which they were fought: the freedom of England and the independence of Europe. Here was a theme to which he responded with all the fire of his innermost being. 'Europe drew swords in a quarrel which, with one uneasy interlude,' he wrote, 'was to last for a quarter of a century. Since the duel between Rome and Carthage there had been no such world war. It involved all the civilized peoples; it extended to every part of the accessible globe; it settled for some time or permanently the real relative wealth and power, and the frontiers of every important European state.'

He wrote these words in the preface to his first volume which was published in 1933, the year that Hitler came to power in Germany.

*

During the early thirties Marlborough became Winston's chief preoccupation. Although a National Government which was overwhelmingly Conservative in composition had replaced the Labour Government in 1931, he was not disappointed in being excluded from its counsels. He had not expected office. Indeed, he had announced publicly that he would not accept a position in a government that pursued a policy over India of which he disapproved, when the controversy was at its height. He took a lively interest in the parliamentary debates, but free of the responsibility of a Ministry he spent long week-ends and most of his parliamentary recesses at Chartwell, where he did his work.

Writing was not the painstaking labour to Winston that it is to most people. When he was a young man of thirty he once addressed the Authors' Club in London and told his audience that 'no one could set himself to the writing of a page of English composition without feeling a real pleasure in the medium in which he worked, the flexibility and the profoundness of his noble mother tongue. The man who could not say what he had to say in good English could not have very much to say that was worth listening to at all.'[270]

Winston had the ability to marshal his thoughts rapidly and words came easily. He liked being involved in a major work. 'Writing a long and substantial book,' he explained recently, 'is like having a friend and companion at your side, to whom you can always turn for comfort and amusement, and whose society becomes more attractive as a new and widening field of interest is lighted in the mind.'[271]

He set about the task of collecting material with characteristic precision. He employed several scholars to comb the archives and sort through documents at Blenheim, in London and Paris. He also engaged the services of naval and military experts to help him reconstruct the famous campaigns. In the meantime he did an enormous amount of research himself, for he was never prepared to accept the findings of any of his assistants without subjecting them to a searching examination which often developed into a heated, if somewhat one-sided, argument. Besides that, he visited every battlefield on which Marlborough fought, and spent hours studying the composition of the armies until he knew the strategy and tactics as well as Marlborough himself.

He made one of these expeditions abroad in the summer of 1932, accompanied by his family and Professor Lindemann. They travelled slowly along the line of Marlborough's celebrated march in 1705 from the Netherlands to the Danube. They spent a day on the battlefield of Blenheim, then drove to Munich where they stayed a week.

Winston soon discovered that the Germans were concerned with only one topic and that was the Hitler Movement which was gaining thousands of new recruits every day. He asked many questions about it, and was interested when a lively, talkative young man, who spoke perfect English, came up to him in the Regina Hotel introducing himself as Herr Hanfstaengl, and talked enthusiastically about the Führer. Winston invited him to dine and the young man amused the company that evening by playing the piano and urging everyone to sing the old familiar songs. Winston learned that Hanfstaengl was on intimate terms with Hitler and often entertained him in a similar manner. During the course of the evening the German suggested that

---

[270] *Memories and Reflections*: The Earl of Oxford and Asquith.

[271] *The Gathering Storm*: Winston S. Churchill.

Winston should meet the Führer who, he said, came to the hotel every day at five. 'I had no national prejudices against Hitler at this time,' wrote Winston. 'I knew little of his doctrine or record and nothing of his character. I admire men who stand up for their country in defeat, even though I am on the other side. He had a perfect right to be a patriotic German if he chose. I had always wanted England, Germany and France to be friends. However, in the course of conversation with Hanfstaengl, I happened to say, "Why is your chief so violent about the Jews? I can quite understand being angry with Jews who have done wrong or are against the country, and I understand resisting them if they try to monopolize power in any walk of life; but what is the sense of being against a man simply because of his birth? How can any man help how he is born?" He must have repeated this to Hitler, because about noon the next day he came round with rather a serious air and said that the appointment he had made for me to meet Hitler could not take place, as the Führer would not be coming to the hotel that afternoon. This was the last I saw of "Putzi" — for such was his pet name — although we stayed several more days at the hotel. Thus Hitler lost his only chance of meeting me. Later on, when he was all-powerful, I was to receive several invitations from him. But by that time a lot had happened, and I excused myself.'[272]

*

It was at this point that the struggle for Europe in Marlborough's time began to identify itself in Winston's mind with the new struggle that seemed to be emerging in his own day. He returned to Britain with deep apprehensions. The resurgence of a martial spirit which he had witnessed in Germany offered a sharp and disturbing contrast to the pacifist mood that gripped England.

In 1932 Britain was still in the throes of an economic depression largely caused by the American crash of 1929. The unemployment figures touched the three million mark and were the worst in the nation's history. This, people said, was the price of the war. First came the slaughter and the suffering, then came the dislocation, the strikes, the poverty and the hardship. Whatever happened, there must never be another war. And since the pacifists seemed to have the only solution for making war impossible, the English public became overwhelmingly in favour of disarmament. This fitted in nicely with the Government's financial predicament; the Exchequer was strained

---

[272] *The Gathering Storm*: Winston S. Churchill.

to its utmost limits, and Baldwin was only too glad to back a policy which had almost become a necessity.

Disarmament as a deterrent to war was a sound proposition if all nations agreed to play the same game, but disarmament by some and rearmament by others was bound to fail. Winston's intensive study of the struggle for power had not convinced him that human nature had altered much. He could understand the feeling of revulsion of the victors against war that had caused so much dislocation to their agreeable way of life. He could also understand the feelings of the vanquished, smarting under the humiliation of defeat, and determined to redress their grievances.

Churchill believed that Germany's grievances should be removed, but he did not think it wise to make concessions through weakness. In Germany he had heard whispers of 'British decadence' and had not failed to notice how much bolder the German demands were becoming as German strength increased. Shortly after Winston returned from Munich in the summer of 1932 she flatly demanded the right to rearm. *The Times* regarded the proposition favourably and spoke of 'the timely redress of inequality', but Winston warned members of the House of Commons not to 'delude themselves'. 'Do not let His Majesty's Government believe,' he continued, 'that all that Germany is asking for is equal status ... That is not what Germany is seeking. All these bands of sturdy Teutonic youths, marching through the streets and roads of Germany, with the light of desire in their eyes to suffer for the Fatherland, are not looking for status. They are looking for weapons, and, when they have the weapons, believe me they will then ask for the return of their lost territories and lost colonies, and when the demand is made it cannot fail to shake and possibly shatter to their foundations every one of the countries I have mentioned ... The removal of the just grievances of the vanquished ought to precede the disarmament of the victors. To bring about any tiling like equality of armaments (between the vanquished and the victor nations) if it were in our power to do so, which it happily is not, while those grievances remain unredressed, would be almost to appoint the day for another European war — to fix it as though it were a prize fight. It would be far safer to re-open questions like those of the Danzig Corridor and Transylvania, with all their delicacy and difficulty, in cold blood and in a calm atmosphere and while the victor nations still have ample superiority, than to wait and drift on, inch by inch and stage by stage, until once again vast combinations, equally matched, confront each other face to face.'[273]

Two months after Winston's speech, in January 1933, Hitler came to power. But the British Government took notice neither of Churchill nor Hitler. In March 'The MacDonald Plan' was put forward urging further disarmament upon the French. Winston attacked it with all his force. 'Thank God for the French Army,' he declared to the disgust of a large section of the House. 'When we read about Germany, when we watch with surprise and distress the tumultuous insurgence of ferocity and war spirit, the pitiless ill-treatment of minorities, the denial of the normal protections of a civilized society to large numbers of individuals solely on the ground of race — when we see that occurring in one of the most gifted, learned, scientific and formidable nations in the world, one cannot help feeling glad that the fierce passions that are raging in Germany have not found, as yet, any other outlet but upon Germans. At a moment like this, to ask France to halve her army while Germany doubles hers, to ask France to halve her air force while the German air force remains whatever it is, is a proposal likely to be considered by the French Government, at present at any rate, as somewhat unseasonable.'[274]

The French Government agreed with Winston Churchill and refused to reduce the size of their army. Instead they offered to destroy a large part of their heavy artillery. Hitler's answer to this concession, which he regarded as insufficient, was not only to quit the Disarmament Conference but to leave the League of Nations as well. This, said the pacifists, was the logical consequence of France's refusal to co-operate. The strength of this view was revealed a fortnight later when a by-election was fought at East Fulham. A safe Conservative seat was lost to a pacifist by a ten thousand majority.

Winston watched these manifestations uneasily. He had no faith in disarmament. He believed that the only way to prevent war was through strength. He recognized the new Germany of Hitler as a potential aggressor and he knew that Britain's duty must be to oppose the unlawful expansion of her power. He had a firm belief in the simple, old-fashioned formula which Britain had always followed, based on the maintenance of the Balance of Power. In writing his life

---

[273] *Hansard*: 23 November, 1932.

[274] *Hansard*: 23 March, 1933.

of Marlborough he had reflected deeply on this principle, and reaffirmed his faith in it. In a speech to the Conservative Members Committee on Foreign Affairs in March 1936 he outlined his conception clearly and simply; and since this conception has always determined his attitude, and still determines it to-day, it is perhaps worth while to print in part what he said:

'For four hundred years the foreign policy of England has been to oppose the strongest, most aggressive, most dominating Power on the Continent, and particularly to prevent the Low Countries falling into the hands of such a Power. Viewed in the light of history, these four centuries of consistent purpose amid so many changes of names and facts, of circumstances and conditions, must rank as one of the most remarkable episodes which the records of any race, nation, state, or people can show. Moreover, on all occasions England took the more difficult course. Faced by Philip II of Spain, against Louis XIV under William III and Marlborough, against Napoleon, against William II of Germany, it would have been easy and must have been very tempting to join with the stronger and share the fruits of his conquest. However, we always took the harder course, joined with the less strong Powers, made a combination among them, and thus defeated and frustrated the Continental military tyrant whoever he was, whatever nation he led. Thus we preserved the liberties of Europe, protected the growth of its vivacious and varied society, and emerged after four terrible centuries with an ever-growing fame and widening Empire, and with the Low Countries safely protected in their independence. Here is the wonderful unconscious tradition of British foreign policy. All our thoughts rest in that tradition to-day. I know of nothing which has occurred to alter or weaken the justice, wisdom, valour, and prudence upon which our ancestors acted.'

*

Winston was convinced that the next war would be largely decided in the air, and uppermost in his mind was the thought of the swiftly growing German air force. The chief disadvantage of being out of office at this time was the fact that he had no official information to support his contentions. However, he was determined not to allow tills difficulty to clip his wings, and at once set about creating an intelligence service of his own. He began to build up contacts both abroad and at home. He had close friends at the War Office and the Foreign Office who now became frequent visitors to Chartwell. He renewed acquaintanceships in Ministerial circles in France, and began to establish new lines in Berlin. He gladly received any newspaper correspondent who he thought could tell him anything and opened the doors of his house to Germans who disliked the Hitler regime as much as he did. Chartwell became a little Foreign Office of its own with its stream of visitors supplying information, working out statistics, doing research, and analysing events through searching arguments and careful discussions. Refugees from Nazi Germany and, as time went on, from Austria and Czechoslovakia made their way to Winston's home. But probably the most important member of his 'inner circle' was Frederick Lindemann, the Professor of Experimental Philosophy at Oxford, who had accompanied him abroad on his summer trip to Munich. Lindemann spent countless week-ends at Chartwell compiling statistics and advising Churchill on the latest technical and scientific developments which covered many fields, including radar and projected missiles. The two men often sat up discussing these subjects until two or three in the morning.

Winston's intelligence service was soon supplying him with valuable information which made his speeches to the House of Commons important events. Although Germany had been forbidden a military air force under the Versailles Treaty he learned that her large civil aviation force and her national glider clubs had been organized and designed so that they could be expanded instantaneously for war. He warned the House that Britain was only the fifth air power in Europe while the Germans, 'those very gifted people, with their science and with their factories, with what they call their "Air Sport", are capable of developing with great rapidity a most powerful air force for all purposes, offensive and defensive, within a very short period of time.'[275]

Eight months later Winston had precise information on which to base his arguments. 'I assert first,' he told the House of Commons, 'that Germany already, at this moment, has a military air force — that is to say, military squadrons, with the necessary ground services, and the necessary reserves of trained personnel and material — which only awaits an order to assemble in full open combination; and that this illegal air force is rapidly approaching equality with our own. Secondly, by this time next year, if Germany executes her existing programme without acceleration, and if we execute our existing programme on the basis which now lies before us without slowing down, and carry out the increases announced to Parliament in July last,

---

[275] *Hansard*: 8 March, 1934.

the German military air force will this time next year be in fact at least as strong as our own, and it may be even stronger. Thirdly, on the same basis — that is to say, both sides continuing with their existing programmes as at present arranged — by the end of 1936? that is, one year farther on, and two years from now — the German military air force will be nearly fifty per cent stronger, and in 1937 nearly double. All this is on the assumption, as I say, that there is no acceleration on the part of Germany, and no slowing-down on our part.'[276]

The House was startled by this information but Mr. Baldwin allayed its fears by categorically denying Winston's figures. 'It is not the case that Germany is rapidly approaching equality with us ... Her real strength is not fifty per cent of our strength in Europe ... As for the position this time next year ... we estimate that we shall have a margin in Europe alone of nearly fifty per cent.'[277]

However, it soon became apparent that Mr. Churchill's private intelligence was far better than the official channels on which the Government relied. In March 1935 the German Chancellor stated openly that the German Air Force had achieved parity with the British. And in May of the same year Stanley Baldwin was forced to make an astonishing retraction to the House. 'Where I was wrong was in my estimate of the future. There I was completely wrong. We were completely misled on that subject ...

'I will repeat here that there is no occasion, in my view, in what we are doing, for panic. But I will say this deliberately, with all the knowledge I have of the situation, that I would not remain for one moment in any Government which took less determined steps than we are taking to-day. I think it is only due to say that there has been a great deal of criticism, both in the press and verbally, about the Air Ministry as though they were responsible for possibly an inadequate programme, for not having gone ahead faster, and for many other things. I only want to repeat that whatever responsibility there may be — and we are perfectly ready to meet criticisms — that responsibility is not that of any single Minister; it is the responsibility of the

---

[276] *Hansard*: 28 November, 1934.

[277] Ibid.

Government as a whole, and we are all responsible, and we are all to blame.'[278]

Strangely enough, 'Mr. Baldwin's Confession', as Winston soon dubbed it, did not have an adverse effect on his popularity. If anything, his popularity slightly increased, for the British public was deeply impressed by his honesty. They liked a man who could admit he was wrong. Winston had the dazzle and the eloquence but Stanley Baldwin was the man you could rely upon. At the General Election a few months later they showed their confidence by returning him with a handsome majority.

---

[278] *Hansard*: 22 May, 1935.

Chapter Nineteen — The Balance of Power

WINSTON WAS angry and disappointed not to be included in Stanley Baldwin's new Government. The India issue was closed; his warnings about Germany were being fulfilled; and the Government had received a mandate to re-arm. It was widely forecast in the press that he would be asked to take over the Admiralty and he confidently expected the offer to be made. 'The growing German menace made me anxious to lay my hands upon our military machine,' he wrote. 'I could now feel very keenly what was coming. Distracted France and timid peace-loving Britain would soon be confronted with the challenge of the European Dictators. I was in sympathy with the changing temper of the Labour Party. Here was the chance of a true National Government. It was understood that the Admiralty would be vacant, and I wished very much to go there should the Conservatives be returned to power.'[279]

However, as soon as the election results were known Baldwin announced through the Conservative Central Office that Churchill would not be asked to join the Government. Winston believes that his exclusion was a sop to the pacifist element in the House, but remembering that Baldwin had complained in the late twenties that Churchill flooded the Government with memoranda and advice and that 'a Cabinet meeting when Winston was present did not have the opportunity of considering its proper agenda,' it seems more likely that he was merely adhering to his resolve never again to have him as a colleague.

However, the Prime Minister was one of the shrewdest Party managers in the history of Conservatism and it stands to reason that he would have put his reservations aside if Winston had commanded any following in the country. But in 1935 Churchill had practically no support either in Parliament or among the people. It was a curious situation. The public freely acknowledged his great gifts; they admired his courage; they read his books; they were impressed by his superb oratory. Yet they would not follow him. They believed him to be emotionally unsound. They had watched his career and listened to his wonderful eloquence for thirty-five years and formed the impression that his thirst for adventure always led him in search of heroic parts.

---

[279] *The Gathering Storm*: Winston S. Churchill.

He dramatized himself and the stage on which he performed. In his hands incidents swelled into large events. They remembered the young Minister who had sent field guns to Sidney Street; the Home Secretary who had dispatched troops all over Britain in the railway strike of 1911 without waiting for the local authorities to ask for them; the First Lord of the Admiralty who had asked to take command of the army defending Antwerp; the Minister for War who had secured Allied intervention in the Russian revolution; the Minister for Colonial Affairs who drafted the Chanak communique. They remembered his warnings that the Labour Party would destroy the constitution of the country, and that self-rule for India would mark the downfall of the British Empire. He had exaggerated situations before. How could they know he was right this time?

But personal misgiving was not the only reason for Winston's failure to command a following. The public felt that he was offering them little hope of a better world. They had no faith in power politics. The idea of a Grand Alliance, based on the balance of power, had been tried often before and had often failed. On looking back it is clear that the only hope of arousing the people of Britain and France lay in the League of Nations. Here was a great new concept; here was a concert of nations joined together in a common desire to establish for the first time a reign of international law; to substitute the principle of negotiation for the act of war.

The detractors of the League argued that it had been hopelessly crippled, soon after birth, by the withdrawal of the United States. Nevertheless, the fact remains that throughout the twenties and most of the thirties Britain and France together, if they had had the will, could have enforced the League's authority. But could they have commanded public support? During the twenties the vast number of people who supported the League regarded it merely as a 'moral force'. The Disarmament Conferences were held under its aegis and helped to swell the impression that it was an instrument of pacifism rather than an authority for the maintenance of order.

In the early thirties this conception gradually began to change. Europe was growing increasingly frightened of Germany and by the middle of 1934 disarmament was abandoned. Many people said this spelt the death of the League. It had failed to deal either with the Chaco clashes in 1928, or with the Manchurian incident in 1931. Now that rearmament was beginning again, the last vestige of its peaceful purpose seemed to have been stripped from it. Churchill fought against this feeling of despair and told the House as early as 1932 that he deprecated 'the kind of thought that, unless the League can force a general disarmament, unless it can compel powerful nations in remote regions to comply with its decisions, it is dead — away with it.'

*

Nevertheless it is a curious fact that even Winston Churchill did not understand the potential power of the League as a weapon for rallying public opinion. In the summer of 1935 it became apparent that Mussolini had designs on Abyssinia. The situation could scarcely have been more awkward. Italy was an ally of Britain and France and the three nations had pledged themselves to stand together against further aggression. On the other hand Abyssinia was a member of the League of Nations. If she was attacked what was the duty of Britain and France?

Winston's attitude on this question was understandable. Almost alone among the leading British statesmen he realized the full gravity of the German menace. In his desperate and lonely efforts to build up a strong balance of power he had no wish to see Italy estranged from France and Britain. On 11 July, 1935, he expressed his uneasiness to Parliament and cautioned the Government to move slowly. 'We seemed to have allowed the impression to be created that we were ourselves coming forward as a sort of bell-wether or fugleman to lead opinion in Europe against Italy's Abyssinian designs. It was even suggested that we would act individually and independently. I am glad to hear from the Foreign Secretary that there is no foundation for that. We must do our duty, but we must do it with other nations only in accordance with the obligations which others recognize as well. We are not strong enough to be the lawgiver and the spokesman of the world. We will do our part, but we cannot be asked to do more than our part in these matters ...

'As we stand to-day there is no doubt that a cloud has come over the old friendship between Great Britain and Italy, a cloud which, it seems to me, may very easily not pass away, although undoubtedly it is everyone's desire that it should. It is an old friendship, and we must not forget, what is a little-known fact, that at the time Italy entered into the Triple Alliance in the last century she stipulated particularly that in no circumstances would the obligations under the Alliance bring her into armed conflict with Great Britain.'

A month later he was invited to the Foreign Office and asked how far he was prepared to go against Italian aggression in Abyssinia. He replied that he thought the Foreign Secretary was 'justified in going as far with the League of Nations against Italy as he could carry

France,' but that he ought not 'to put any pressure upon France because of her military convention with Italy and her German preoccupations.' This, of course, was tantamount to doing nothing for as Churchill himself admitted: 'In the circumstances I did not expect France would go very far.'[280]

Winston's point of view was understandable, nevertheless it was a serious mistake. Here was the man who had been asking his countrymen to take the lead against the treaty-breaking of Germany, now advising them to hang back over the flagrant aggression of Italy, knowing full well that unless Britain took the lead the act would be condoned. His attitude opened him to a charge of cynicism and expediency and revealed a complete misunderstanding of the drastic change that was taking place in British public opinion. There had been some indication of this evolution earlier in the year when the League of Nations Union sent out a questionnaire under the heading of The Peace Ballot. The two most important questions were these: 'Do you consider that if a nation insists on attacking another, the other nations should combine to compel it to stop by: (a) economic and non-military measures? (b) if necessary military measures?' Eleven million people answered (a) in the affirmative and nearly eight million answered (b) in the affirmative.

Stanley Baldwin was conscious of which way the wind was blowing and he fought the election of October 1935 on a promise to uphold the League of Nations. This same month another significant event occurred. The Labour Party dismissed its pacifist leader George Lansbury (mainly due to the influence of Ernest Bevin who told a large audience that he was 'tired of having George Lansbury's conscience carted about from conference to conference'), and put in his stead Major Clement Attlee, a Socialist who had been an infantry officer in the late war.

The British Government went ahead and rallied the support of fifty nations in the laying down of economic sanctions against Italy. Once the step had been taken, once Italy had been estranged, Winston gave the League his unqualified support. In a strong and eloquent speech in the House he professed his hope that sanctions would prove a decisive stumbling block to Mussolini's conquest, and declared with emotion that the League of Nations had 'passed from shadow into substance, from theory into practice, from rhetoric into reality'. He announced

---

[280] *The Gathering Storm*: Winston S. Churchill.

courageously that if he were asked how far he would go in support of the League Covenant he would go 'the whole way with the whole lot'.[281]

But disillusion was soon to set in: for Winston Churchill, for the British people, for the whole world. Baldwin's sanctions were only sham sanctions. He was determined to prevent war at all costs — although we know to-day that if the Royal Navy had taken action the matter would have been settled in a very few weeks. The Prime Minister was not prepared to impose the only sanction that really mattered — oil sanctions. Furthermore, once the gesture had been made against Italy he did not rule out the idea of a settlement. In January the British and French Foreign Secretaries met by accident at Geneva and concocted a plan, known as the Hoare-Laval proposals, which gave Italy a fifth of Abyssinia in return for calling off the war.

This cynical compromise profoundly shocked the British people and rocked the Government to its foundations. Stanley Baldwin was forced to withdraw the proposals and apologize to the House. Sir Samuel Hoare was forced to resign and Anthony Eden took his place. Sham sanctions continued and Italy went ahead and completed the conquest of Abyssinia. It was a dismal story.

*

Winston was in Spain and North Africa during the Hoare-Laval crisis. If he had been in England he might have been able to exert enough pressure to force Baldwin to take him into the Cabinet, for the latter's prestige had sunk to its lowest level. However, he profited from the lesson. He perceived that a new force had come into being in England. He understood the deep urge of the people for a righteous stand and he saw that it was only by championing the League of Nations that he could rally the masses to his cause: the cause of maintaining a balance of power on the side of Britain. Two months later, in March 1936, he told the Conservative Members Committee on Foreign Affairs: 'You must not underrate the force which these ideals [the League of Nations] exert upon the modern democracy. One does not know how these seeds are planted by the winds of the centuries in the hearts of the working people. They are there, and just as strong as their love of liberty. We should not neglect them, because they are the essence of the genius of this island. Therefore, we believe that in the fostering and fortifying of the League of Nations will be found the best means

---

[281] *Hansard*: 24 October, 1935.

of defending our island security, as well as maintaining grand universal causes with which we have very often found our own interests in natural accord.' He then outlined his three, simple contentions: 'First, that we must oppose the would-be dominator or potential aggressor. Secondly, that Germany under its present Nazi regime and its prodigious armaments, so swiftly developing, fills unmistakably that part. Thirdly, that the League of Nations rallies many countries, and unites our people here at home in the most effective way to control the would-be aggressor.'

The old cry 'Disarmament and the League' was dead and in its place Winston tried to substitute the slogan 'Arms and the Covenant'. Throughout 1936 he commanded a growing following. Labour and Liberal leaders who, only a few years before, had regarded him as an arch-enemy, were now marching behind his banner. Sir Walter Citrine, the great Trade Union figure and one of the leaders of the General Strike, occasionally sat on his platform. But although Churchill had the moral backing of the Labour Party he failed to win the practical support that was so vital to his cause. The Socialists voted repeatedly in favour of the League of Nations but at the same time they refused to back any increase in armaments. This fantastically muddled policy was put forward on the grounds that Labour did not trust the Tories to use weapons in defence of the League.

Winston was also supported by a number of Conservative M.P.s but they were only a small splinter group, for the bulk of the Parliamentary Conservative Party was staunchly behind their leader, Stanley Baldwin. And Baldwin was still determined not to take any risk, no matter how minute, which might lead to war. In March 1936 Hitler electrified Europe by marching into the Rhineland, in direct contravention of all the treaties. France was paralysed with fear, and refused to move unless Britain moved with her. But Baldwin still would not commit himself and urged the French to take the matter to the League. As we know to-day, if the French Army had advanced they would have forced Germany to move back with scarcely a shot fired. Hitler had occupied the Rhineland against the advice of his military experts with only a handful of troops. It was a gigantic bluff. He was gambling on the inertia of the democracies and if his gamble had not succeeded it is more than likely his whole regime would have crumbled. Thus one more chance to avert war was lost.

While France stood back trembling and undecided Winston tried to galvanize the world through collective action. 'If the League of Nations were able to enforce its decree upon one of the most powerful countries in the world found to be an aggressor,' he told the House of Commons on 13 March, 'then the authority of the League would be set upon so majestic a pedestal that it must henceforth be the accepted sovereign authority by which all the quarrels of the people can be determined and controlled. Thus we might upon this occasion reach by one single bound the realization of our most cherished dreams.'

The people of Great Britain were ready to make a stand but they were not given the chance to do so. The country's rulers were not prepared to risk anything, no matter how large the gain. Prominent men and leading newspapers began to play the crisis down. After all, at the same time that Hitler had invaded the Rhineland he had offered the democracies a nonaggression pact. *The Times* and the *Daily Herald* both expressed their faith in his offer. Such leading statesmen as Lloyd George and Lord Lothian said, respectively, that they 'hoped we should keep our heads' and that 'after all, they are only going into their own back garden.' Winston pointed out that if Germany fortified the Rhineland, which she was bound to do, it would 'enable German troops to be economized on that line, and will enable the main forces to swing round through Belgium and Holland'. But those in responsible positions were not prepared to listen.

Winston continued to hammer home his theme throughout the years and his following continued to grow. He castigated Baldwin for not fulfilling his promise that British air power would not be 'inferior to any country within striking distance of our shores', and turned the full force of his vehement and polished rhetoric upon him. 'The Government simply cannot make up their minds, or they cannot get the Prime Minister to make up his mind. So they go on in strange paradox, decided only to be undecided, resolved to be irresolute, adamant for drift, solid for fluidity, all-powerful to be impotent. So we go on preparing more months and years — precious, perhaps vital, to the greatness of Britain — for the locusts to eat.'[282]

Stanley Baldwin's stock once again was declining; Winston's stock once again rising. Once again he might have regained high office, but for the strange intervention of fate. An event occurred which tipped the scales heavily the other way — the Abdication Crisis.

*

Everyone knows the deftness and skill with which Stanley Baldwin handled the Abdication Crisis. As Philip Guedalla put it, 'the King

---

[282] *Hansard*: 12 November, 1936.

was handled with a firmer touch than the King's enemies'. He gave the Sovereign two clear choices: he could either renounce Mrs. Simpson and keep the throne, or wed Mrs. Simpson and abdicate. There was to be no morganatic marriage. The Prime Minister was treading on firm ground for public opinion was strongly behind him. He knew the British people would never accept a thrice married woman as their Queen.

It was characteristic of Winston to take the King's side and plead the King's cause. He could not possibly have hoped to gain from it: indeed he had everything to lose. But he had a romantic nature and a sympathy with the monarch's wish to marry for love. More than this, he had a deep sense of loyalty. He had known Edward VIII since his childhood, and as Home Secretary had read out the proclamation creating him Prince of Wales. The King sent for him on his own initiative to ask for advice and help. As Lord Birkenhead had once pointed out Winston 'never failed a friend no matter how embarrassing the obligation appeared at the time'. He felt it his duty to serve the King until the end.

He drew his sword and attacked Baldwin for trying to rush the issue, and pleaded with the House of Commons for delay. Public sentiment was so strong, however, that a storm of wrath broke on his head. He was accused of lacking all principle and trying to make political capital of the matter. He was accused of trying to form a King's party and wreck the constitution. He was accused of his usual bad judgment. The tragedy was that the following he had gathered, so important for the life of Europe, began to melt away, while Stanley Baldwin, a discredited Prime Minister, was once again installed high in public favour. 'There were several moments when I seemed to be entirely alone against a wrathful House of Commons. I am not, when in action, unduly affected by hostile currents of feeling; but it was on more than one occasion almost physically impossible to make myself heard. All the forces I had gathered together on "Arms and the Covenant", of which I conceived myself to be the mainspring, were estranged or dissolved, and I was myself so smitten in public opinion that it was the almost universal view that my political life was at last ended.'[283]

The history of the thirties makes tragic reading. If even a small part of Winston Churchill's advice had been heeded the second great world catastrophe would never have taken place. He will be remembered in

---

[283] *The Gathering Storm*: Winston S. Churchill.

history as a man of war, but no statesman has ever tried more valiantly to save the peace. 'My mind was obsessed by the impression of the terrific Germany I had seen and felt in action during the years of 1914 to 1918 suddenly becoming again possessed of all her martial power,' he wrote, 'while the Allies, who had so narrowly survived, gaped idle and bewildered.'[284] Under Stanley Baldwin the Allies continued to gape; under Neville Chamberlain they moved forward — but on the wrong road.

The vacillation of the French and British and the blindness of the Americans during the late thirties almost passes comprehension. Nearly every foreign correspondent in Europe was aware of the derision in which the dictators held the democracies, and the determination of the dictators to strike while the going was good. There is a mass of journalistic warnings on the subject. In 1937 Winston had a long conversation with the German Ambassador in London, Herr von Ribbentrop. The latter told him that Germany must have a free hand in Eastern Europe, and Winston replied that he was sure that the British Government would not agree to it. 'In that case,' said von Ribbentrop, 'war is inevitable. There is no way out. The Führer is resolved. Nothing will stop him and nothing will stop us.' This conversation was not unique. In Germany similar sentiments were expressed freely to anyone who would listen. Indeed it would be difficult to find another period in history where the aggressive designs of a nation were so unconcealed.

It is therefore even more remarkable that of all the statesmen in the Western world Winston Churchill alone perceived the danger from the start and consistently pointed out the only course to follow. He never, for one moment, took his eyes off the balance of power, and every action he urged was to strengthen the balance in favour of Britain and France. During the first half of the thirties he begged the democracies to build up their strength. 'If you wish to bring about a war, you bring about such an equipoise that both sides think they have a chance of winning. If you want to stop a war, you gather such an aggregation of force on the side of peace that the aggressor, whoever he may be, will not dare to challenge.'[285] This advice was not followed. During the second half of the thirties he begged the democracies to combine to

---

[284] Ibid.

[285] *Hansard*: 13 July, 1934.

uphold law and order. 'Why not make a stand while there is still a good company of united, very powerful countries that share our dangers and our aspirations? Why should we delay until we are confronted with a general landslide of those small countries passing over, because they have no other choice, to the overwhelming power of the Nazi regime?'[286]

But even more remarkable than his prescience was his unflagging courage. His boldness illuminates the darkness of the thirties and saves it from the scathing judgment of posterity. When in 1937, despite all his warnings and prophecies, he was shunned by his Party and ignored by Parliament, a lesser man might have turned from the House of Commons in despair and occupied himself with his own affairs. But Winston never faltered. Whether the tide was with him or not he sailed on. He was derided by his enemies, patronized by his friends, and mocked by the press, yet he continued to work feverishly to stave off the approaching calamity.

Although Stanley Baldwin excluded Churchill from office, he offered him a sop. In 1935 he invited him to sit on the newly constituted Committee of Air Defence Research. A man of smaller stature might have refused the offer, arguing that if his Party did not think highly enough of him to employ him in a Ministerial capacity they would have to do without his services in minor spheres. But Winston was determined to serve, no matter how humble the capacity. He asked that Professor Lindemann should be placed on the Technical Sub-Committee so that they might work together. For the next five years he mastered every aspect of scientific air defence. He heard Professor Tizard make his report on radio-location, which resulted in the setting up of an experimental organization. In 1939 when the Air Committee held its final meeting twenty radar stations were in operation between Portsmouth and Scapa Flow and it was possible to detect aircraft from fifty to one hundred and twenty miles away flying above ten thousand feet. Winston was also given free access to the Admiralty and made it his business to acquaint himself with every detail of the new building programme, and the latest developments in guns, armour and explosives. Thus when he became Prime Minister he had more knowledge of the technicalities of sea and air defence than any other statesman called to lead a nation in war.

---

[286] *Hansard*: 14 March, 1938.

Winston's persistent and lonely efforts to save his country from war for nearly ten years, unsupported by any single political party in the House of Commons, are without parallel in English history. Many politicians have opposed the Government but they have usually had the backing of a Party. Winston stood alone. In 1920 an anonymous writer in the *Daily News* had written prophetically: 'Politics for Mr. Churchill, if they are to fulfil his promise, must be a religion. They must have nothing to do with Mr. Churchill. They must have everything to do with the salvation of mankind.' Winston had found his cause; and no one would argue to-day that it was not concerned with the salvation of mankind.

*

The year 1937 was one of the most painful of Churchill's life. His influence had fallen to zero, partly because of his attitude over the Abdication Crisis, partly because Hitler and Mussolini remained quiet and people began to feel that perhaps there would not be a war after all. Churchill's stock remained at low ebb throughout the early months of 1938, and it was at this period that I first met him. His son, Randolph, took me to Chartwell one day for lunch. Mr. Churchill was down by the pond, in a torn coat and a battered hat, prodding the water with a stick, looking for his pet goldfish which seemed to have disappeared. He was in an expansive mood and at lunch the conversation centred, as it usually did, on politics. He expressed his fear that England would refuse to show her hand until it was not only too late to avoid war, but too late to win a war.

As he talked one could not help being struck by the restless energy and frustration of the man. In spite of his writing, his weekly contributions to the press, his long and masterly speeches in the Commons, one was aware that only a quarter of his resources were being used, and you felt that he was like a mighty torrent trying to burst its dams.

The sense of frustration was not difficult to understand. Shortly after this luncheon, I heard him speak in the House of Commons. The date was 24 March, 1938, two weeks after the German invasion of Austria. As I looked down from the gallery on the sea of black coats and white faces, he seemed only one man of many; but when he spoke his words rang through the House with terrible finality. He stood addressing the Speaker, his shoulders hunched, his head thrust forward, his hands in his waistcoat pockets. 'For five years I have talked to this House on these matters — not with very great success. I have watched this famous island descending incontinently, fecklessly, the stairway which leads to a dark gulf. It is a fine broad stairway at the beginning, but after a bit the carpet ends. A little farther on there are only flagstones, and a little farther on still these break beneath your feet. Look back over the last five years. It is true that great mistakes were made in the years immediately after the war. But at Locarno we laid the foundations from which a great forward movement could have been made. Look back upon the last five years — since, that is to say, Germany began to rearm in earnest and openly to seek revenge. If we study the history of Rome and Carthage we can understand what happened and why. It is not difficult to form an intelligent view about the three Punic Wars; but if mortal catastrophe should overtake the British Nation and the British Empire, historians a thousand years hence will still be baffled by the mystery of our affairs. They will never understand how it was that a victorious nation, with everything in hand, suffered themselves to be brought low, and to cast away all that they had gained by measureless sacrifice and absolute victory — gone with the wind!

'Now the victors are vanquished, and those who threw down their arms in the field and sued for an armistice are striding on to world mastery. That is the position — that is the terrible transformation that has taken place bit by bit. I rejoice to hear from the Prime Minister that a further supreme effort is to be made to place us in a position of security. Now is the time at last to rouse the nation. Perhaps it is the last time it can be roused with a chance of preventing war, or with a chance of coming through to victory should our efforts to prevent war fail. We should lay aside every hindrance and endeavour by uniting the whole force and spirit of our people to raise again a great British nation standing up before all the world; for such a nation, rising in its ancient vigour, can even at this hour save civilization.'

When Mr. Churchill sat down there was a deep silence for a moment: then the show was over. The House broke into a hubbub of noise; Members rattled their papers and shuffled their way to the lobby. A prominent Conservative came up to the gallery to take me to tea. I was talking to a friend, and when we asked him what he thought of the speech he replied lightly: 'Oh, the usual Churchillian filibuster; he likes to rattle the sabre and he does it jolly well, but you always have to take it with a grain of salt.' This was the general attitude of the House of Commons in those days. Many years later Churchill wrote: 'I had to be very careful not to lose my poise in the great discussions and debates which crowded upon us … I had to control my feelings and appear serene, indifferent, detached.'[287] In view of the circumstances, this was no small feat in itself.

*

Unlike Stanley Baldwin, Neville Chamberlain had a positive policy. This policy was completely contrary to Winston's belief in the balance of power, and to the age-old formula which Britain had always followed in refusing to allow any single Power to dominate the Continent of Europe. Chamberlain believed that Britain and Germany could come to a peaceful understanding about spheres of interest. Let Germany extend her influence on the Continent, let Britain look to her Navy and her Empire.

Chamberlain had not been in office long before he set about putting these ill-fated theories into practice. He forgave the Nazi invasion of Austria and journeyed to Italy to try and establish friendly relations with Mussolini. This brought about the resignation of Anthony Eden, whose heart was in the right place, but who had never had the moral strength to dissociate himself from Baldwin's vacillating policies.

Then came Munich. Chamberlain flew to Germany three times, and returned home with the famous agreement which gave Czechoslovakia's Sudetenland to the Germans. Winston cried out, 'One pound was demanded at the pistol point. When it was given, two pounds were demanded at the pistol point. Finally the Dictator consented to take £1 17s. 6d. and the rest in promise of goodwill for the future.'[288] But Chamberlain enunciated his belief that it was 'peace with honour' and what is more 'peace in our time' and the whole world acclaimed him as a saviour. Never had he been so popular. But this dream was not to last for long. Only six months after Munich, after a solemn declaration from Hitler that he had no 'evil intentions towards Czechoslovakia', the German army moved into Prague. At last the scales fell from the blind eyes of the British leader; at last he saw that Germany meant business. From that moment the policy of appeasement was over, and England and France slapped a guarantee on Poland. But the Germans had every form of military superiority. The British could never catch up.

At this point Winston Churchill regarded war as inevitable. There was only one faint hope left, and that was an alliance with Russia.

---

[287] *The Gathering Storm*: Winston S. Churchill.

[288] *Hansard*: 5 October, 1938.

Although Winston had been the Soviet Union's most hostile critic during the twenties, he welcomed Russia's entry into the League of Nations in 1934, for he saw it as an added reinforcement to the balance of power. A few months before the Munich Agreement he spoke out plainly, describing her as 'a country whose form of government I detest ... but how improvidently foolish we should be when dangers are so great, to put needless barriers in the way of the general associations of the great Russian mass with resistance to an act of Nazi aggression.'[289] After Munich he spoke again, begging Chamberlain to accept the Soviet offer of a Triple Alliance which would bind Great Britain, France and Russia in a guarantee for the safety of the states in Central and Eastern Europe. But Poland feared Russia as much as Germany; Mr. Chamberlain hesitated: the alliance was never established. Instead, in the summer of 1939 Stalin did a deal with Hitler which burst upon the world as the Soviet-German Pact. Germany's hands were now free for other business. In September the second World War began.

---

[289] Free Trade Hall, Manchester, 9 May, 1939.

Chapter Twenty — Prime Minister in War

WHEN THE Admiralty Board learned that Mr. Chamberlain had asked Churchill to take over the Navy, they signalled to the Fleet: 'Winston is back.' It was a dramatic return. Just twenty-five years previously Churchill had guided the Royal Navy through the opening months of the first World War. Then, as now, he was the most dominating figure in the Government; then, as now, he was spoken of as a probable war Prime Minister. But then he had stumbled; this time his step was firm and sure.

From the first day he was the true leader of Britain. When Chamberlain broadcast to the nation on the morning of 3 September, 1939, he spoke as a broken-hearted man. 'Everything that I have worked for, everything that I have hoped for, everything that I have believed in during my public life has crashed into ruins!' This was true enough, but it was scarcely the way to rouse the nation. Chamberlain could not rid himself of the past, and as a result he was unable to regard the war as anything but a calamity. Winston on the other hand accepted it as a challenge, and not only dismissed the past but buried all recrimination with it.

I saw an amusing example of this for myself, for a few months after war began a member of the Churchill family invited me to lunch at Admiralty House. Conversation in the Churchill household was always political, and previously one could have been certain of a number of witty sallies at Mr. Chamberlain's expense. On this occasion, however, one of Mr. Churchill's children attempted a mild joke and I was astonished to see a scowl appear on the father's face. With enormous solemnity he said: 'If you are going to make offensive remarks about my chief you will have to leave the table. We are united in a great and common cause and I am not prepared to tolerate such language about the Prime Minister.' I honoured Mr. Churchill's sentiments, but having heard the same joke from his own lips a few months before, I found it difficult to suppress a smile.

*

The first seven months of the war provided a strange hiatus. It was the long uneasy lull before the curtain lifted on the grand climax. The British people had been warned of the strength and ferocity of the German Air Force and had braced themselves for a rain of bombs on their towns and cities. Instead there was silence in the West while Hitler concentrated his attack on Poland and divided the spoils with

Stalin according to a prearranged plan. Next, Stalin devoured the Baltic States, and invaded Finland; after an inauspicious start the Russian Bear finally smashed the small Finnish army and in March 1940 an armistice was signed.

All this time Britain and France looked on helplessly. To-day the world knows how badly prepared they were for the conflict. The German Air Force was twice the strength of Britain's and the German Army was soon to demonstrate its might against the soldiers of France. The two democracies were eager to help Finland, and the British hurriedly began to train divisions for an ice-bound war. The troops were not ready in time; but even if they had been, there was not an earthly chance of persuading Norway and Sweden, who were desperately clinging to their neutrality, to allow a passage through to Finland.

As a result British soldiers began to sing about 'hanging out the washing on the Siegfried line' and Americans began to refer to 'the phoney war'. This last jibe was a miscalculation of the determination of England; nevertheless it touched a chord that was real. In the early days of the war both Britain and France were wholly concentrated on defensive warfare. France had poured out her strength and money on the Maginot Line, and Britain had concentrated on fast fighters. When you asked military people how the war would be won they answered confidently that Germany would smash herself against the French fortifications and dissipate her air force against the English defences.

The democracies had no plan for assuming the offensive; besides this there were strong subversive elements in the population, particularly in France. The extreme Left had taken its signal from Moscow and denounced the war as a capitalist-imperialist project. The extreme Right, on the other hand, still hankered for an understanding with Germany. Poland was gone. How could Britain and France revive her, they argued? Wasn't it better to have a strong Germany in Central Europe as a bulwark against Bolshevism than to smash the only barrier and open the way for the barbaric Slavs? Even in England one could hear this argument. In the winter of 1939 I remember talking to an Englishman who later became one of Churchill's most energetic and loyal colleagues. 'I would give everything I possess,' he said, 'if I could put an end to this senseless war. I would sign a peace with Germany now and stop the conflict before the whole of Europe is brought to ruin.'

These were some of the sentiments of the phoney war. They were not widespread, but they existed. Winston lost no time in combating them no matter from what quarter they came. He referred to the 'thoughtless dilettanti or purblind worldlings who sometimes ask us: "What is it that Britain and France are fighting for?" To this I answer: "If we left off fighting you would soon find out."'[290] He referred to Hitler as 'a haunted, morbid being, who, to their eternal shame, the German people in their bewilderment have worshipped as a god.' And he referred to the frightened neutral countries who were sitting on the fence, warning them that their plight was lamentable, 'and it will become worse. They bow humbly and in fear to German threats of violence, comforting themselves meanwhile with the thought that the Allies will win … Each one of them hopes that if he feeds the crocodile enough, the crocodile will eat him last …'[291]

At the same time that Winston was attacking the enemy, combating the defeatist elements on his own side, and trying to galvanize the neutrals into action, he was giving the people of Britain the firm clear lead they wanted. 'Now we have begun; now we are going on; now with the help of God, and with the conviction that we are the defenders of Civilization and Freedom, we are going on, and we are going on to the end.'

Hitler at once recognized his true enemy, and lost no time in singling out Winston as the villain of the piece. Early in October the German leader broadcast to the world employing the tactics that up until now had been so successful. There was no need, he said, for a war with the West. Poland was dead, it would never rise again. Why fight about it? 'I make this declaration only because I very naturally desire to spare my people suffering. But should the views of Churchill and his following prevail, then this declaration will be my last. We should then fight … Let those repulse my hand who regard war as the better solution!'

Winston gave him a plain answer in a broadcast on 12 November, 1939. 'You may take it absolutely for certain that either all that Britain and France stand for in the modern world will go down, or that Hitler, the Nazi regime, and the recurring German and Prussian menace to Europe will be broken and destroyed. This is the way the matter lies, and everybody had better make up their minds to that solid, sombre fact.'

---

[290] Broadcast, 30 March, 1940.

[291] Broadcast, 20 January, 1940.

*

Meanwhile Winston was not idle as First Lord of the Admiralty. The Royal Navy was the only strong force the British possessed and from the first day of the war the senior service was on the offensive. Winston worked an eighteen-hour day. Plans were drawn up for a blockade of Germany; convoy arrangements were made; mine-sweeping was organized; ships were requisitioned; new building began; and, above all, enemy raiders and submarines were hunted down. By the end of 1939 Winston announced that the British had sunk half Germany's submarines. But he was wise enough to know that many great battles were coming. Germany's production in all fields was enormous; the war was only in its infancy.

Chamberlain on the other hand did not appear to grasp the situation. On 5 April, 1940, he made an astonishing statement to the Conservative and Unionist Associations: 'After seven months of war I feel ten times as confident of victory as I did at the beginning … I feel that during the seven months our relative position towards the enemy has become a great deal stronger than it was.' He went on to elaborate the theme that the breathing space Hitler had afforded the Allies had made the whole difference to the war; he could not seem to understand that during this period Germany, too, had been building up. 'Whatever may be the reason,' he said, 'whether it was that Hitler thought he might get away with what he had got without fighting for it, or whether it was that all the preparations were not sufficiently complete — however, one thing is certain; he missed the bus.' Three days later Hitler invaded Norway and Denmark.

*

The story of the Quisling 'Fifth Column' inside Norway, the landing of the British troops and their dismal withdrawal ending in a complete German victory is well known. The House of Commons was angered by the defeat and met on 7 and 8 May to debate the events. Admiral of the Fleet Sir Roger Keyes declared that if his countrymen had been bold enough to seize Trondheim, the key to central Norway, the German invasion could have been frustrated. He charged that the Navy had been let down by Whitehall.

It is ironic that this accusation played a large part in the fall of the Government, as for once Chamberlain was not to blame. Churchill himself, the First Lord of the Admiralty, had not welcomed the idea of a frontal attack on Trondheim. The assault was to have been a combined naval, military and air operation, and Winston felt that the risks which the Home Fleet would have run were far too great. But when the plan was pressed forward strongly by all the Chiefs of Staff and the Secretary of State for War, he acquiesced. Arrangements went ahead but at the last moment the Chiefs of Staff developed cold feet and said that on reconsidering the situation they believed that the frontal attack was too perilous. Instead, they recommended a pincer movement on Trondheim from North and South. Although Winston had never been enthusiastic about the first operation and people even whispered that 'the iron of the Dardanelles had entered his soul' and he had no longer the courage to strike boldly, he was indignant at such a late change of plan. Nevertheless, he again acquiesced. Chamberlain was also disappointed but in face of the opposition of both the Chiefs of Staff and the Vice-Chiefs of Staff he felt he could not interfere.

These were the facts and yet the blame for not attacking Trondheim settled on Chamberlain. So Hitler had missed the bus? Speaker after speaker flung the Prime Minister's unhappy remark in his face.[292] Winston tried to defend him, as he was bound to do, but told the House of Commons plainly that the defeat was not merely due to mistaken strategy, but to the failure of the Government to maintain air parity with the Germans.

The House, however, was not in a mood for excuses. Although Members of Parliament had no one to blame but themselves for the state of British arms and equipment, they insisted on action and successful action at that. It may strike the onlooker as unreasonable, but democracies function that way. All their wrath turned on Chamberlain for his bad advice and guidance. Mr. Leo Amery, a staunch Conservative, attacked the Prime Minister and his colleagues in an impassioned speech ending with Oliver Cromwell's stinging words to the Rump of the Long Parliament: 'You have sat here too long for any good you have been doing. Depart, I say, and let us have done with you! In the name of God, GO!'

A vote of censure was put down against the Government and when Winston defended Chamberlain Lloyd George rose and advised him not to allow himself to be converted into an air raid shelter to keep the splinters from hitting his colleagues. Mr. Chamberlain called on his

---

[292] When Winston first heard the news of the German invasion of Norway he, too, made a statement just as wide of the mark as Chamberlain's. He spoke joyously of 'the strategic blunder into which our mortal enemy has been provoked.' Fortunately this observation was overlooked.

friends to save him from defeat and Lloyd George pointed out with deadly effect that it was not a question of who were the Prime Minister's friends. 'It is a far bigger issue. The Prime Minister must remember that he has met this formidable foe of ours in peace and war. He has always been worsted. He is not in a position to put it on the ground of friendship. He has appealed for sacrifice. The nation is prepared for every sacrifice so long as it has leadership. I say solemnly that the Prime Minister should give an example of sacrifice, because there is nothing which can contribute more to victory in this war than that he should sacrifice the seals of office.'

The Members went through the lobby and although there was normally a Conservative majority of nearly two hundred and fifty, Chamberlain won by only eighty-one votes. He realized that his Government no longer commanded the confidence of the House, and when he put out feelers to the Liberal and Labour followers for a coalition he was told that neither party would serve under him. He then offered the King his resignation.

10 May was a momentous day. In the morning news came that the attack on the West had begun and that German troops were streaming across Holland; that night the King sent for Winston Churchill and asked him to form a Government. 'As I went to bed at about 3 a.m.,' he has recorded, 'I was conscious of a profound sense of relief. At last I had the authority to give directions over the whole scene.'[293] Even though the situation was grave Winston Churchill's spirits were far from low.

*

Many books have been written about the second World War, chief of which are the six detailed volumes that Mr. Churchill himself has contributed. The story of the British war effort falls into two distinct parts: first, the struggle to survive, and second, the alliance with Russia and the United States in securing the victory and designing the peace.

The struggle to survive covers the twelve months that Britain fought alone, from the fall of France in June 1940 to the German attack on Russia in June 1941. The high-lights of this grim year are still fresh in the minds of most people; the partition of France; the formation of the Vichy Government; the air attack on Britain; the blitz on London; the

---

[293] *The Gathering Storm*: Winston S. Churchill.

Desert War; the defeat of Greece; the Commando raids along the Norwegian and French coasts.

During this desperate period Winston Churchill became the most inspiring figure in the Western world. He symbolized the fierce spirit of liberty, and clothed Britain's determination to fight in words that no other Englishman could have summoned. In his account of the war he declares modestly that he was merely interpreting the strong mood that gripped the country. He cites as an example the fact that when Hitler made his final peace offer in the summer of 1940 the British Cabinet regarded it as so supremely foolish that not a single member even raised it for discussion. Nevertheless Winston's knowledge of military matters and his close concern with all operational undertakings animated the British effort with a vigour and a boldness it had been lacking until then. And his interpretation of the Mother Country's cause not only thrilled millions of people all over the globe but raised British prestige to the highest level in history.

The truth was that Winston had at last found his destiny. The world looked to him for a lead and all the pent-up energy of the immense machine that throbbed in his heart and mind was brought into play. He no longer knew the frustration of ideas that could not be brought alive, vitality that could not be spent, ingenuity that could not be tested. The tremendous task that had fallen upon him equalled his stature as a man, and he grasped the supreme power of the State with eager hands.

The whole of 10 Downing Street throbbed with an energy it had not seen since the days of Lloyd George, and perhaps hoped not to see again. The routine of Government was turned topsy-turvy. Churchill stayed in bed half the morning dictating and stayed up half the night talking. Every afternoon, after lunch, he had a nap. Chiefs of Staff, Ministers, civil servants, had to adapt themselves to this routine as best they could. Most of them had to be at work at nine or ten in the morning; even so, woe betide them if they were not men enough to come when he sent for them after dinner to stay up until the early hours of the morning.

I do not mean to suggest that Churchill's leadership was not of the most precise, orderly kind. On the contrary, he was a master organizer and at once set about shaping a small, efficient machine that could take decisions swiftly and work with the maximum effect. First he organized a War Cabinet comprised of only four members besides himself: two were Labour leaders, Clement Attlee and Arthur Greenwood, and two were Conservatives, Mr. Chamberlain and Lord

Halifax.[294] This War Cabinet met almost daily and took all the supreme decisions of the war. Besides this tiny, all-powerful, directing force there were sixty or seventy other Ministers of all Parties who formed the membership of the Coalition Government, but the latter were responsible only for their own departments; as Winston pointed out it was only the members of the War Cabinet 'who had the right to have their heads cut off on Tower Hill if we did not win.'

Needless to say Churchill was the over-riding figure in the War Cabinet. Never before in history has a Prime Minister exerted such wide powers; never before has a Prime Minister exercised so much control over the operational side of a conflict. He was not only the King's First Minister but Leader of the House of Commons and, even more important, Minister of Defence as well. In this last capacity he initiated a new system which centred authority in his own hands. The Chiefs of Staff instead of reporting to their own Ministers, the men in charge of the War, Air and Admiralty departments, reported directly to him. He then asked the War Cabinet for permission to have the Joint Planning Committee, a body of professional staff officers of all three services, work under him as Minister of Defence rather than under the Chiefs of Staff. Thus, by permission of the War Cabinet, he became virtually a dictator.

He revelled in both the immense power and responsibility of his task, and arranged his day with careful thought. He woke up at eight, summoned his secretaries, read all the telegrams and reports that had come through the night, then from his bed dictated a flow of minutes and memoranda, a large part of which was taken to the Chiefs of Staff at their morning meeting. Every afternoon he went to bed for an hour or longer, like a child, and slept soundly. This gave him the extra strength to remain at work until the early hours of the morning.

The two links between himself and the military machine, and himself and the political authority, were General Ismay and Sir Edward Bridges. These men interpreted his wishes, carried out his orders, and smoothed his path in every direction. The huge mass of instructions from the Prime Minister which flowed through their hands were always in writing for Churchill was a firm believer in the written word. He had had enough experience of Government to know how often verbal orders led to misunderstandings; besides, he had no wish to have his name used loosely. Soon after he became Prime

---

[294] Membership of the War Cabinet grew to seven later in the war.

Minister he issued the following directive to Ismay and Bridges: 'Let it be very clearly understood that all directives emanating from me are made in writing, ... and that I do not accept any responsibility for matters relating to national defence on which I am alleged to have given decisions unless they are recorded in writing.'[295] Altogether, Churchill's directives, memoranda, telegrams and minutes amounted throughout the war to nearly 1,000,000 words, enough to fill half a dozen good sized volumes, even though most of them were models of brevity and precision. A one-line minute which he penned to a high civil servant read as follows: 'Pray remember that the British people is no longer able to tolerate such lush disorganization.'

*

No one can study Churchill's part in the war without being staggered by the scope of his interests and his colossal output. His contribution falls into distinct parts: first, his directives on military operations and second, his public leadership. In the first capacity one has only to study the minutes that are reproduced in his history to gather an idea of the enormous range he covered, and the powerful influence he had upon the course of the war. When Britain was alone, waiting for the full fury of the German attack to descend upon her, Churchill insisted that the nation should not merely sit back with brave endurance but should immediately take the initiative. 'The passive resistance war,' he wrote in a directive to General Ismay, 'in which we have acquitted ourselves so well, must come to an end. I look to the Joint Chiefs of the Staff to propose me measures for a vigorous, enterprising and ceaseless offensive against the whole German-occupied coastline. Tanks and A.F.V.s [Armoured Fighting Vehicles] must be made in flat-bottomed boats, out of which they can crawl ashore, do a deep raid inland, cutting a vital communication, and then back, leaving a trail of German corpses behind them.'[296]

Amphibious warfare had always fascinated Churchill, no doubt as a result of the ill-starred Dardanelles venture which had been his particular brain child, and which, if it had been truly amphibious, probably would have resulted in the defeat of Germany in 1915. In July 1940 he set up Combined Operations under Admiral Sir Roger Keyes, which initiated the daring commando raids that put Britain on

---

[295] *Their Finest Hour*: Winston S. Churchill.

[296] *Their Finest Hour*: Winston S. Churchill.

the offensive. Time and again one finds him urging amphibious tactics. He repeatedly urged the commanders of the desert war to mount a surprise landing from the sea but this advice was never heeded. And later on, when the attack on Italy was in preparation one finds him anxious to employ the sea-borne landings boldly. 'Why crawl up the leg like a harvest bug from the ankle upwards? Let us rather strike at the knee!'

Churchill's flat-bottomed boats were invented and not only played a major part in the commando raids, but became absolutely essential equipment for the final cross-Channel invasion of France. But undoubtedly his most important contribution was the idea of the great artificial harbours around which the D-day operation was built. He had conceived this idea as far back as 1917 when he prepared a scheme for the capture of the two Frisian islands, Borkum and Sylt, which he submitted to Lloyd George. In this paper he suggested making an artificial island in the shallow waters of Horn Reef. '*A number of flat-bottomed barges or caissons, made not of steel, but of concrete*, should be prepared ... These structures would be adapted to the depths in which they were to be sunk, according to a general plan. They would float when empty of water, and thus could be towed across to the site of the artificial island. On arrival at the buoys marking the island sea-cocks would be opened, and they would settle down on the bottom. They could subsequently be gradually filled with sand, as opportunity served, by suction dredgers ... *By this means a torpedo- and weather-proof harbour, like an atoll, would be created in the open sea, with regular pens for the destroyers and submarines, and alighting-platforms for aeroplanes.*'[297]

Churchill fortunately did not publish this document when he came to write *The World Crisis* and now he began toying with this particular brain child again. Frances Perkins quotes President Roosevelt as saying: 'You know, that was Churchill's idea. Just one of those brilliant ideas that he has. He has a hundred a day and about four of them are good.' But Roosevelt apparently was unaware that Winston had been mulling over the project for many years, for he continued: 'When he was up visiting me in Hyde Park he saw all those boats from the last war tied up in the Hudson River and in one of his bursts of imagination he said, "By George, we could take those ships and others like them that are good for nothing and sink them off shore to protect

---

[297] Ibid.

the landings." I thought well of it myself and we talked about it all afternoon. The military and naval authorities were startled out of a year's growth. But Winnie is right. Great fellow, that Churchill, if you can keep up with him.'[298]

But it was not only in the field of amphibious war that Churchill made his contribution. He gave advice over the entire operational field. Scarcely an undertaking was formed that he did not submit to the Chiefs of Staff detailed and technical papers advising on how the plan should be executed. This was almost without parallel; no British political leader, with the possible exception of Pitt the Elder, had ever exerted such a powerful influence on strategy and tactics; not even Roosevelt, who by rights was Commander-in-Chief of the American Army, attempted to assume any like responsibility. 'During the war,' testified General Eisenhower, 'Churchill maintained such close contact with all operations as to make him a virtual member of the British Chiefs of Staff; I cannot remember any major discussion with them in which he did not participate.'[299]

Even Lloyd George's ascendancy in the first World War never reached the same scale. Lloyd George had been the inventor of the small, all-powerful War Cabinet which Winston copied. This Cabinet, like Churchill's, had supreme control as long as it had the support of Parliament. It had the authority to dictate strategy and insist that generals carried out its policies. But in the first War this right was never exercised, for public opinion was strongly averse to political interference in military matters. The professional soldier was king. The design of a battle was regarded as a matter for generals, and generals alone.

This had disastrous results. To-day very few experts would care to defend the strategy of the first War, with its terrible and unnecessary slaughter. Lloyd George tells how strongly he opposed the futile holocaust of Passchendaele. He protested repeatedly both orally and in writing, but he was not strong enough to carry the Cabinet in reversing the commanders on the spot. In his memoirs he gives a vivid discourse on this subject. He denounces the generals who sent their armies time and again to needless doom in scathing tones: 'Such highly gifted men as the British Army possessed were consigned to

---

[298] *The Roosevelt I Knew*: Frances Perkins.

[299] *Crusade in Europe*: Dwight D. Eisenhower.

the mud by orders of men superior in rank but inferior in capacity, who themselves kept at a safe distance from the slime which they had chosen as the terrain where their plans were to operate.' Lloyd George makes the final summary: 'Looking back on this devastating war and surveying the part played in it by statesmen and soldiers respectively in its direction, I have come definitely to the conclusion that the former showed too much caution in exerting their authority over the military leaders. They might have done so either by a direct and imperative order from the Government or by making representations followed, if those were not effective in answering that purpose, by a change in the military leadership.'[300]

Churchill took these lessons to heart. He was determined to dominate the military machine from the start. As with Lloyd George, his power was dependent on the War Cabinet, and the War Cabinet on the House of Commons. But in 1940 he was the leader of a completely united nation. The War Cabinet were inspired by him, and were content to take the burden of home affairs off his shoulders and let him direct the military effort. But it must be remembered that his authority depended on this body. If, for example, the Chiefs of Staff had resented his advice or interference, and had secured the backing of the War Cabinet, he would have been forced to give way. But the issue never arose. The War Cabinet gave him firm support throughout the struggle, and the only man who sat in it continuously from beginning to end, Clement Attlee, the leader of the Labour Party, never faltered in his loyalty. During the difficulties of January 1942 Churchill records that Attlee 'sustained the Government case with vigour and even fierceness.'[301] It is also worth emphasizing that no crisis ever took place between Churchill and his Chiefs of Staff; not one of them ever threatened to resign during the whole six years of conflict. This is some proof that the Prime Minister with his wide knowledge of military history, and his detailed study of tactics, was enough of a professional soldier to give advice that was useful and often brilliant. 'Discussion with him,' writes Eisenhower, 'even on purely professional grounds, was never profitless.'

Winston's suggestions for the conduct of the war covered a vast sphere. Sometimes he advised on the movement of ships; on coastal

---

[300] *War Memoirs of David Lloyd George.*

[301] *The Hinge of Fate*: Winston S. Churchill.

fortifications; on the strength and position of Air Force squadrons; the deployment of troops; equipment of all kinds; the relative merit of different weapons; new inventions; scientific experiments; and hundreds of other subjects. On several occasions he pressed the Chiefs of Staff to over-rule commanders on the spot who did not agree with directives sent them from London. Churchill directly influenced the decision not to evacuate Calais, and refused to accept General Wavell's advice to make terms with the Iraq Government over the Habbania incident. General Eisenhower was fascinated at the control he exerted. When he spent a week-end at Ditch-ley he saw for himself the extent of Churchill's influence. 'Operational messages arrived every few hours from London headquarters,' he wrote, 'and Mr. Churchill always participated with the British Chiefs in the formation and despatch of instructions, even those that were strictly military, sometimes only tactical, in character.'[302]

Churchill's authority was very remarkable since, as he himself pointed out to Roosevelt and Stalin, he was the only one of the three who could be dismissed instantly at any time. Stalin was not an elected representative; and Roosevelt was secure for his four-year term. Harry Hopkins delivered a speech at Teheran in which he said that he had made 'a very long and thorough study of the British Constitution which is unwritten, and of the War Cabinet, whose authority and composition are not specifically defined.' As a result, he said: 'I have learned that the provisions of the British Constitution and the powers of the War Cabinet are just whatever Winston Churchill wants them to be.'[303] This was a tribute to Churchill's persuasiveness for the hard truth was that, unlike the other two leaders, Winston exercised his authority only by permission of the War Cabinet; and the War Cabinet was willing and able to grant this authority only so long as he commanded the confidence of Parliament.

Once or twice this confidence was in doubt. In the early months of 1942 Churchill's position was seriously undermined. The previous six months had been grim and anxious. Greece and Crete had been over-run; Yugoslavia was invaded; the British Army had suffered set-backs in North Africa; the British Navy had lost two battleships the *Prince*

---

[302] *Crusade in Europe*: Dwight D. Eisenhower.

[303] *The White House Papers of Harry L. Hopkins*: Robert E. Sherwood.

of Wales and the *Repulse* which were sunk by the Japanese at Singapore. The press was openly hostile and for the first time since he had taken office the Prime Minister was under fire. In some quarters there was even talk of his resignation, and the extreme Left exerted pressure to put Stafford Cripps in his place. Winston faced the storm and on 29 January, 1942, demanded a Vote of Confidence from the Commons. The result was surprising. Only the Independent Labour Party, numbering three members, refused to support him, and since two were tellers, only one vote was recorded against him. Less than six months later his leadership was again challenged. This time criticism was precipitated by the fall of Tobruk. A Conservative put down a Motion of Censure against him, but once more he had a sweeping victory. The vote was 475 to 25. Despite Hopkins' compliment, Churchill was always acutely conscious of the fact that his leadership was dependent on Parliament.

However, it is not impossible to draw a parallel between Winston's leadership and that of his ancestor the soldier Duke of Marlborough. Professor Trevelyan writes that Marlborough 'acted as head of the State in war-time for all military and diplomatic affairs, but he left to his colleagues the management of Parliament.' Winston left to his colleagues the management of home affairs. They both concentrated on war, diplomacy and foreign relations. Marlborough was a commander who assumed the role of statesman, while Churchill was a statesman who assumed the role of commander.

*

All this was behind the scenes. The public saw the Prime Minister as a fighting man who expressed in stirring language the emotions they felt but could not put into words. He lifted millions of men and women out of their humdrum lives and inspired them with a sense of mission; he emblazoned the British cause across the world as the defence of freedom and justice. He represented in his own person the spirit of indomitable England. When he accepted office in 1940 he told the House of Commons, 'I have nothing to offer but blood, toil, tears and sweat.' Whereupon, in a characteristic manner, the nation drew a deep breath of relief and took new heart.

His fierce and moving speeches, sometimes filled with passion, sometimes with humanity, made him the spokesman of all the democratic world. No one who was in the House of Commons on 4 June, 1940, when France was being over-run, will forget the thrill of emotion that went through the assembly when he said in his strange rough voice: 'We shall go on to the end, we shall fight in France, we shall fight on the seas and the oceans, we shall fight with growing confidence and growing strength in the air, we shall defend our island, whatever the cost may be, we shall fight on the beaches, we shall fight on the landing grounds, we shall fight in the fields and in the streets, we shall fight in the hills; we shall never surrender, and even if, which I do not for a moment believe, this island or a large part of it were subjugated and starving, then our Empire beyond the seas, armed and guarded by the British Fleet, would carry on the struggle until, in God's good time, the new world, with all its power and might, steps forth to the rescue and the liberation of the old.'

*

No single man had worked harder to prevent the second World War than Winston, yet once the conflict had begun no leader enjoyed the excitement of the clash more than he. From youth his imagination had been stirred by the great battles that had decided the history of Europe, by the relentless struggle for power between men of different nations and different creeds. Churchill was a fighter and the stakes were high: for the first time in his life he had the opportunity of employing all his genius and energy in a cause in which he passionately believed. 'In my long political experience I had held most of the great offices of State,' he wrote, 'but I readily admit that the post which had now fallen to me [the Premiership] was the one I liked best. Power, for the sake of lording it over fellow-creatures or adding to personal pomp, is rightly judged base. But power in a national crisis, when a man believes he knows what orders should be given, is a blessing.'[304]

He had always been a fearless man and derived excitement from physical danger. During the London blitz it was with the greatest difficulty that he was persuaded not to sleep at 10 Downing Street, which was a natural target for German bombers, but to move to the shelter in a Government building by Storey's Gate, which came to be known as the 'Annexe'. Often when there was the drone of enemy planes overhead, when the guns were thundering and flashing and there was the steady crash of bombs exploding, he insisted on going up on the roof to see the sights. On one of these occasions an air raid warden approached him timidly and said: 'If — if you'll kindly excuse me, sir, would you mind moving?' 'Why?' growled Winston. 'Well, sir, you are sitting on the smoke vent, sir, and the building's full of smoke.'

---

[304] *Their Finest Hour*: Winston S. Churchill.

Throughout his life it had always been Winston's nature to dramatize whatever part he was called upon to play and the war gave him a natural and an extensive scope. From childhood he believed he had been put on earth to perform a special service, and when the Premiership was offered to him at the very moment that German troops were streaming across France he was certain his mission was being realized. 'I felt as if I were walking with Destiny, and that all my past life had been but a preparation for this hour and for this trial.'[305]

Conscious of his great position, Churchill was every inch a Prime Minister. Occasionally I had the honour of being invited to 10 Downing Street for lunch. A low-ceilinged room below the ground floor which, I believe, was once the servants' hall, had been turned into a dining-room, and there were seldom more than seven or eight guests. Winston usually came into the room in a blue siren suit looking remarkably like a teddy bear with an air as autocratic as a monarch. I used to watch the guests struggling between surprise at his comic appearance and awe at his dignity. The success of the lunch depended entirely on what sort of mood he was in; sometimes he ate in such sullen silence your heart sank as you imagined that the war had taken some grave turn for the worse; at other times he was buoyantly talkative and held the table with a brilliant monologue. But whatever the atmosphere, Mr. Churchill was always unquestionably the master. No one dared pursue a topic of conversation that did not meet with his approval; no one dared to ask any questions or take any liberties. Many guests would have found royalty easier to deal with.

Winston was aware of the fact that he was making history and as a result he wrote his minutes and directives with care so that they would bear the scrutiny of posterity. He saw the great battle Britain was fighting in its true historical perspective and it is not at all surprising that on more than one occasion he compared his position with that of Marlborough. For example, in *Their Finest Hour* he comments on the close relationship he maintained with the King and Queen. 'I valued as a signal honour the gracious intimacy with which I, as First Minister, was treated, for which I suppose there has been no precedent since the days of Queen Anne and Marlborough during his years of power.'

---

[305] *The Gathering Storm*: Winston S. Churchill.

But the fact that Winston executed his task with pride, and even relish, does not mean that he had a cold heart. On the contrary he was always deeply moved by suffering he saw with his own eyes. During the London blitz he often toured the Metropolis to inspect the damage, and on more than one occasion people saw him in tears. When he saw a small shop in ruins he was so upset, imagining the owner's distress at losing not only a home but a livelihood, and perhaps his savings as well, that he resolved then and there that compensation for all damaged property must be paid by the State. Thus the policy of war damage came into being.

On another occasion General Eisenhower witnessed an example of Winston's emotionalism. 'One day a British major-general happened to refer to soldiers, in the technical language of the British staff officer, as "bodies",' writes the General. 'The Prime Minister interrupted with an impassioned speech of condemnation — he said it was inhuman to talk of soldiers in such cold-blooded fashion, and that it sounded as if they were merely freight — or, worse, corpses! I must confess I always felt the same way about the expression, but on that occasion my sympathies were with the staff officer who, to his own obvious embarrassment, had innocently drawn on himself the displeasure of the Prime Minister.'[306]

Although Churchill carried the great burden of the war with zest, anyone who imagines that he never suffered from its weight is mistaken. More than once it seemed almost crushing. In his war memoirs he tells how in June 1941 he went to his home at Chartwell, alone, to await the news of General Wavell's final attempt to destroy Rommel's army; and how when he learned that the attack had failed he wandered about the valley disconsolately for some hours. On one or two occasions I also saw him deeply depressed. In the autumn of 1940 I motored to Chequers for lunch. Mrs. Churchill was away and only his daughter Mary and daughter-in-law Pamela were there. Just before lunch was announced one of Churchill's private secretaries came into the room and handed him a message from the Foreign Office. He read it standing before the mantelpiece in the drawing-room. Then, unexpectedly, he handed it to me. The message was a report picked up from the Berlin wireless stating that Pétain had agreed to turn over to the Germans all aerodromes and ports in unoccupied France.

---

[306] *Crusade in Europe*: Dwight D. Eisenhower.

Churchill was plunged into a state of gloom. He came into the dining-room but ate very little and sat half way through the meal with his elbows on the table holding his head in his hands. The secretary who had brought the news reminded him that it was only a report from Berlin and likely to be untrue, but the Prime Minister would not be consoled. 'If it is true, it is a bitter blow,' he said.

At last lunch mercifully ended and Churchill went out for a walk. I left about four o'clock and before I went he came back into the drawing-room as vigorous and as lion-hearted as ever. He had received a message that the report was false.

A few months later I went again to Chequers, this time to be the godmother of Randolph Churchill's son, Winston junior. The christening took place in a small chapel about a mile from the house. Due to a breakdown in my car I did not arrive until the ceremony had begun, and found a place reserved for me between Mr. Churchill and his son. I had always heard that the Prime Minister's emotions were easily stirred and at times he could be as sentimental as a woman, and on this occasion I had proof of it, for he sat throughout the ceremony with tears streaming down his cheeks. 'Poor infant,' he murmured, 'to be born into such a world as this.'

After the christening we returned to Chequers for lunch. Only the family, Lord Rothermere, and the three godfathers, Lord Beaverbrook, Lord Brownlow and Brendan Bracken, were present. Beaverbrook rose and proposed a toast to the baby, then turned to Churchill whose birthday it had been the day before, and proposed a toast to him. Beaverbrook was eloquent and reminded us that we had the honour to be in the presence of a man who would be remembered as long as the civilized world existed. Once again I looked up to see Churchill weeping. When he was called upon to reply he rose, and in a voice unsteady with emotion, said: 'In these days I often think of Our Lord.' Then he sat down. I have never forgotten those simple words and if he enjoyed waging the war let it be remembered that he understood the anguish of it as well.

*

But Churchill was enormously resilient. He never remained downcast for long. Indeed his moods could change so rapidly that frequently those who worked with him were uncertain how to handle him. He often punctured his own indignation by a flashing witticism that completely altered the whole atmosphere. Once when he was fuming about his difficulties with General de Gaulle he said suddenly: 'Of all the crosses I have to bear, the cross of Lorraine is the heaviest.' On another occasion his cousin Clare Sheridan tells how she was working on a sculpture of him. She had been given permission to sit in his bedroom in the morning, and while he sat up in bed reading his reports and telegrams, to get on as best she could. She had finished the high forehead and determined mouth, and was moulding the jutting chin. Churchill who had been concentrating fiercely on his papers suddenly jumped out of bed to take a look at what she had done. His forbidding expression melted into a warm smile. 'Forget Mussolini,' he said, 'and remember that I am the servant of the House of Commons.'

Chapter Twenty-One — The Big Three

WHEN THE war ended the Russian Bear glowered over half of Europe. Stalin had emerged with all the spoils. He had enlarged the Soviet boundaries by hundreds of miles; he had substituted Communism for political freedom in seven sovereign European states; he had extended his influence throughout the Far East. It was not surprising that William Bullitt, a former American Ambassador to Moscow, wrote an article entitled: *How We Won the War and Lost the Peace*, for no one could pretend that the post-war world was what the democratic leaders had envisaged.

When Churchill and Roosevelt met at Newfoundland in 1941, four months before the Japanese attack drew the United States into the conflict, they had drawn up a remarkable document, the Atlantic Charter, setting forth the peace aims on which they both agreed. They wished to see the independence of small nations firmly established; the rights of man upheld; the free and democratic system of government spread as far and wide as possible. What happened to the vision? Did the democratic leaders blunder? What responsibility does Churchill bear?

*

It was a peculiar twist of fate that ordained Churchill to be the first, and so far the only, British Prime Minister to visit Joseph Stalin. No Englishman had fought against Bolshevism with greater passion. In 1919 he was largely responsible for the Allied military intervention against the Red Army; in the nineteen-twenties he preached the evils and dangers of the Marxist creed on a hundred platforms; in 1937 he declared: 'I will not pretend that, if I had to choose between Communism and Nazism, I would choose Communism.' The dictatorship of the proletariat with its repressive and terrible regimentation, its slaughter of the bourgeoisie, its atheism, its elimination of all the refinements of life, outraged and repelled Churchill's sensibilities. Yet when Nazi Germany attacked the Soviet Union he did not hesitate to hold out his hand.

On the evening of 21 June, 1941, he was walking on the croquet lawn at Chequers with his secretary Mr. Colville. He knew from intelligence reports that a German attack on Russia was only a matter of hours. He told Colville that if Hitler believed he would rally the Right-wing forces in Britain he was mistaken, for England would fight on the side of the Soviet Union. Colville asked Churchill whether, in view of his position as an arch anti-Communist, this was not bowing down in the House of Rimmon. 'Not at all,' replied Winston. 'I have only one purpose, the destruction of Hitler, and my life is much simplified thereby. If Hitler invaded Hell I would make at least a favourable reference to the Devil in the House of Commons.'[307]

The next morning the news broke that Germany had opened her attack on Russia and that same evening Winston publicly cast his lot with the Soviets. 'No one has been a more consistent opponent of Communism than I have been for the last twenty-five years,' he told the British people in a broadcast. 'I will unsay no word that I have spoken about it. But all this fades away before the spectacle which is now unfolding. The past with its crimes, its follies, and its tragedies, flashes away. I see the Russian soldiers standing on the threshold of their native land, guarding the fields which their fathers have tilled from time immemorial … Can you doubt what our policy will be? We have but one aim and one single irrevocable purpose. We are resolved to destroy Hitler and every vestige of the Nazi regime. From this nothing will turn us — nothing. We will never parley, we will never negotiate with Hitler or any of his gang. We shall fight him by land, we shall fight him by sea, we shall fight him in the air, until, with God's help, we have rid the earth of his shadow and liberated its peoples from his yoke. Any man or state who fights on against Nazidom will have our aid. Any man or state who marches with Hitler is our foe … That is our policy and that is our declaration. It follows therefore that we shall give whatever help we can to Russia and the Russian people.'

This statement raised the curtain on the uneasy and temperamental partnership with the Soviet Union that dissolved so swiftly after the close of the war. Churchill wrote Stalin a letter and the Dictator replied thanking the Prime Minister for his support. The relationship between the two men was bound to be dramatic, for each had long recognized the other as a formidable and implacable opponent. For years they had studied each other's moves with careful attention; they despised and feared each other's system of government; they upheld philosophies diametrically opposed. They could clasp hands on only one issue: survival against Germany. Yet their personalities were not altogether unlike. Both were dominating, blunt and practical, and neither left the other in any doubt as to his views. They enjoyed good food, good

---

[307] *The Grand Alliance*: Winston S. Churchill.

drink, and they both liked to sit up late talking. From the point of view of conviviality they had something in common.

Churchill's first meeting with Stalin took place in Moscow in August 1942, just fourteen months after the Soviet Union had been drawn into the war. Winston was received with appropriate ceremony, and driven to a luxurious country house on the outskirts of the city, which was known as State Villa No. 7. In one of his first interviews with Stalin an amusing exchange took place which perhaps illustrates the difference of approach between the Eastern and Western mind. Winston was charmed to find, in the grounds of State Villa No. 7, a fountain and a tank full of goldfish. He assumed that Stalin had heard that goldfish were one of his hobbies and had ordered the tank to be especially installed. At one of his first interviews with the Russian dictator he told him how delighted he was with the fish, and thanked him for being so thoughtful. Stalin looked slightly taken aback, for he probably did not even know the tank existed. But he instructed the interpreter to tell the Prime Minister that he was gratified he liked the fish and would he care to take them back to London with him? This time it was Churchill's turn to be taken aback for he had no desire to carry a bowl of ordinary goldfish to England. He thanked the dictator but said he would have to refuse his offer as the fish would not travel well in a bomber. Stalin nodded and spoke to the interpreter who said: 'Since the Prime Minister is unable to take the fish with him, would he care to have them for breakfast?'

*

Churchill's dealings with Stalin were always difficult, and often unpleasant. From the moment the German attack began, the British arranged to send the Russians millions of pounds' worth of supplies, including rubber, oil, aluminium, cloth, tanks, guns and planes. Some of the materials came from British factories, others from American firms earmarked for England under Lend-Lease. Shipping these supplies to Russia entailed a great sacrifice for Churchill, as they were desperately needed by the British themselves to equip their armies in the Middle East and build up air supremacy over the Germans. Besides this, Britain had the difficult task of delivering the goods. The Royal Navy had to organize and operate convoys to Murmansk and Archangel through the dangerous Arctic passage, a performance which continued throughout the war. Yet Britain received very little thanks for her effort, for the Russian dictator wanted only one thing: a second front.

Stalin's demand for a second front came the month after the Germans launched their attack on him. It was not only an impossible request but, considering the circumstances, one of the most brazen ever made. After all, it was Stalin, by his pact of friendship with the Nazis in 1939, who had given Hitler the signal to begin the war. He had helped the Germans to tear Poland to pieces, invaded Finland and occupied the Baltic States. Then he had sent Germany a flow of materials in order to expedite the attack on France. When the air assault on England began, Molotov had even gone so far as to meet von Ribbentrop in Berlin to discuss 'dividing up' the British Empire. Now, in 1941, having been caught unawares by his treacherous ally, Stalin imperiously and unashamedly demanded that the British should re-open the second front which he himself had helped to destroy only twelve months previously.

Churchill explained to the Russian dictator that his demand was out of the question. An amphibious operation against strongly fortified positions demanded hundreds of landing craft and thousands of pounds of equipment which would take many months to accumulate. Nevertheless Stalin kept hammering this theme, and continued to hammer it, until the invasion plans were completed two years later. At times the relations between Britain and Russia seemed near a breaking-point, for Stalin refused to see the operational difficulties involved. In September 1941 Mr. Maisky, the Soviet Ambassador, called on Churchill emphasizing the extreme gravity of the situation, and when Winston explained as he had done so often before the impossibility of a second front at that time, he began to threaten him. 'When I sensed an underlying air of menace in his appeal,' writes Churchill, 'I was angered. I said to the Ambassador, whom I had known for many years, "Remember that only four months ago we in this island did not know whether you were not coming in against us on the German side. Indeed, we thought it quite likely that you would. Even then we felt sure we should win in the end. We never thought our survival was dependent on your action either way. Whatever happens, and whatever you do, you of all people have no right to make reproaches to us." As I warmed to the topic the Ambassador exclaimed, "More calm, please, my dear Mr. Churchill," but thereafter his tone perceptibly changed.'[308]

---

[308] *The Grand Alliance*: Winston S. Churchill.

Stalin's demands were not only confined to military matters. From the very beginning he kept his political objectives well in view. Seven months after his country was invaded he formally asked Britain and the United States to recognize Russia's 1940 frontiers; these, of course, included the great territorial gains he had seized, as Germany's ally, in Poland, Finland and the Baltic States. It was remarkable that he could remain calculating enough to make these requests at a time when his armies were being hurled back, and the very existence of his country was at stake. His timing was shrewd for it must not be forgotten that for two years the Allies laboured under the spasmodic fear that Russia might sign a separate peace.

Churchill at first reacted strongly against Stalin's demand then, two months later, surprisingly enough, he acceded to it and tried to persuade Roosevelt to accept it. His argument was that the Russians had already liquidated so many people in the Baltic States that there was very little left to protect. The President, however, was adamant, insisting that the demands were not in keeping with the Atlantic Charter. The reason Churchill gives in *The Hinge of Fate* for his sudden deviation is lame and unconvincing. He says he did not feel 'the moral position could be physically maintained' and that 'in a deadly struggle it is not right to assume more burdens than those who are fighting a great cause can maintain.' This attitude is not at all in keeping with Winston's character and one can only regard his explanation as a poor excuse for one of the very few lapses of this type in his career. However, before the war was over it was Roosevelt, and not Churchill, who was paving the way for the fulfilment of Russia's political aims.

*

The attitude of the Soviet Union in its dealings with Britain was haughty and often insulting. Churchill writes that they 'had the impression that they were conferring a great favour on us by fighting in their own country for their own lives. The more they fought the heavier our debt became.'[309] British personnel stationed in Russia were invariably treated with cold hostility. Permits were withheld and information denied them, as though they were enemy aliens. Even the British sailors who ran the convoys to Murmansk and Archangel were so badly used that Churchill was forced to issue a series of vehement protests.

---

[309] *The Grand Alliance*: Winston S. Churchill.

Stalin sometimes ignored Winston's telegrams altogether, at other times delayed his replies for weeks at a time. Occasionally the tone of his message was friendly but more often it was laden with reproaches. Churchill declares that he bore them with a patient shrug for 'sufferance is the badge of all who have to deal with the Kremlin.'

However, when the two leaders met face to face they did not get on badly. Although they disagreed on the issues involved they were fascinated by each other's reactions. At their first meeting Stalin teased Churchill for having taken a leading part in the Allied military intervention in Russia at the end of the first war. He declared that when Lady Astor visited the Soviet Union she had told him that Churchill had misled Lloyd George and was therefore entirely to blame. Then she went on to assure him that Churchill was finished. 'I am not so sure,' Stalin had replied. 'If a great crisis comes the English people might turn to the old war-horse.' Winston laughed at this recital. 'Have you forgiven me?' he asked. Stalin replied with a smile: 'All that is in the past and the past belongs to God.'[310]

The next night Churchill got a little of his own back on Stalin. The dictator invited him to dinner at his flat in the Kremlin. Only Molotov and an interpreter were present. Stalin's daughter waited on the table but she did not sit down. The Marshal uncorked rows of bottles and the three men sat talking from 8.30 until 2.30 in the morning. They carried on a light-hearted conversation but every now and then the vein became more serious. This time it was Churchill's turn to probe into the past, and he gives a fascinating account of it in his Second World War. '"Tell me," I asked, "have the stresses of this war been as bad to you personally as carrying through the policy of the Collective Farms?" ... "Oh no," said Stalin, "the Collective Farm policy was a terrible struggle." "I thought you would have found it bad," said I, "because you were not dealing with a few score thousands of aristocrats or big landowners, but with millions of small men." "Ten millions," he said, holding up his hands. "It was fearful. Four years it lasted. It was absolutely necessary for Russia, if we were to avoid periodic famines, to plough the land with tractors. We must mechanize our agriculture. When we gave tractors to the peasants they were all spoiled in a few months. Only Collective Farms with workshops could handle tractors. We took the greatest trouble to explain it to the peasants. It was no use arguing with them. After you have said all you

---

[310] *The Hinge of Fate*: Winston S. Churchill.

can to a peasant he says he must go home and consult his wife, and he must consult his herder … After he has talked it over with them he always answers that he does not want the Collective Farm and he would rather do without the tractors." "These were what you call Kulaks?" I asked. "Yes," said Stalin … "It was all very bad and difficult — but necessary."[311] This appears to have been the most intimate conversation Churchill ever had with Stalin.

*

Although the two men got on well personally, Churchill could never rid his mind of the terror that lay behind Stalin's rule. When he discussed the Collective Farm policy he could not escape the vision of the three million Kulaks who had been cruelly exterminated in the enforcement of the system. He found it difficult to put out of his mind the killing and the suffering, the concentration camps and the slave labour on which Stalin's absolute power rested.

These feelings were sharpened in the spring of 1943 when the Polish Government accused the Russians of the massacre of fourteen thousand officers who had been taken prisoner by the Soviets when the latter invaded Poland. Sikorski claimed that he had proof that their bodies lay in mass graves in the Katyn Woods. The Soviets did not deny that they were dead but claimed that the slaughter was done by the Germans when they overran the region. Churchill was sickened by the crime and after probing the evidence found it difficult to believe that the deed had been perpetrated by anyone but the Russians. When the war ended this evidence was strengthened still further by the fact that although many German war criminals were tried at Nuremberg, the Soviet Government did not attempt to clear its own name by proving them guilty of the atrocity. Instead, they avoided all mention of the Katyn murders.

Churchill's abhorrence of the totalitarian disregard for human life evinced itself in a personal incident at Teheran. Stalin gave a dinner for Churchill, Roosevelt and four or five of their closest advisers. In the course of the evening the dictator declared that when the war was over the German General Staff must be liquidated. The whole force of Hitler's armies, he claimed, depended on fifty thousand officers and technicians, and all these must be rounded up and shot. Churchill was repelled by the idea of such coldblooded murder and said: 'The British Parliament and public will never tolerate mass executions. Even if in

---

[311] Ibid.

war passion they allowed them to begin, they would turn violently against those responsible after the first butchery had taken place. The Soviets must be under no delusion on this point.'[312]

Stalin insisted on pursuing the subject, and repeated that fifty thousand must be shot. Churchill reddened with anger and declared that he would 'rather be taken out in the garden here and now and be shot myself than sully my own and my country's honour by such infamy'.[313] The other members at the table were obviously embarrassed at the turn the conversation had taken and signalled to Winston that it was all a joke. Whereupon Elliott Roosevelt, the President's son, who had joined the party uninvited, rose from the end of the table and made a speech saying how whole-heartedly he agreed with Stalin, and how sure he was that the United States Army would support it. This impertinent and fatuous intervention was more than Churchill could bear. He left the table and walked off into the other room. A few minutes later Stalin himself, grinning broadly, clapped a hand on his back and explained it was all in fun. Churchill was not convinced then, nor is he now, that the Marshal was joking. The incident is important, for Winston's refusal to lend himself even to a jest involving moral principles is some indication of how wide was the chasm between him and the Russian master.

*

Churchill was always conscious of this division. He knew that when the war ended Russia would be the dominant power on the Continent. Why did he think that the Soviet Union with its system of absolute rule, the complete antithesis of political freedom, would be willing to sit back and watch Roosevelt and himself furthering the spread of Western democracy under the terms of the Atlantic Charter?

The answer is that Churchill did not believe that Stalin would watch the process with favour, but he hoped that if the British and American partnership was close and strong enough, he would be forced to acquiesce to it. This was the whole basis of his post-war conception. In a letter to Field Marshal Smuts on 5 September, 1943, he said: 'I think it inevitable that Russia will be the greatest land Power in the world after this war, which will have rid her of the two military Powers, Japan and Germany, who in our lifetime have inflicted upon

---

[312] *Closing the Ring*: Winston S. Churchill.

[313] Ibid.

her such heavy defeats. I hope however that the "fraternal association" of the British Commonwealth and the United States, together with sea and air power, may put us on good terms and in a friendly balance with Russia at least for the period of rebuilding. Further than that I cannot see with mortal eye, and I am not as yet fully informed about the celestial telescopes.'[314]

Since Churchill's plans for the post-war world were based on the keystone of a strong Anglo-American alliance, it is not surprising that he should have bent all his energies towards establishing a firm and intimate relationship with President Roosevelt. But it would be wrong to give the impression that Winston was motivated chiefly by self-interest. Logically the partnership seemed right; before the war Winston had developed this same theme in his *History of the English-Speaking Peoples*. But leaving logic aside, he had a profound, almost romantic, admiration for the United States which he liked to refer to as 'the great Republic'. Emotionally he was deeply stirred by the vision of Britain, with her age and wisdom, and America, with her youth and power, endowing the world with safety and peace.

Churchill never failed to dramatize himself and since he was half-English and half-American by birth he felt he had been appointed by Destiny to bring the partnership about. He was especially conscious of this when he made his historic address to the Congress of the United States in December 1941. 'The occasion was important,' he writes, 'for what I was sure was the all-conquering alliance of the English-speaking peoples. I had never addressed a foreign Parliament before. Yet to me, who could trace unbroken male descent on my mother's side through five generations from a lieutenant who served in George Washington's army, it was possible to feel a blood-right to speak to the representatives of the great Republic in our common cause. It certainly was odd that it should all work out this way; and once again I had the feeling, for mentioning which I may be pardoned, of being used, however unworthy, in some appointed plan.'[315]

Churchill's friendship and affection for Roosevelt were certainly not manufactured. He had a deep, even fierce, loyalty to the President which sprang from Roosevelt's courageous help to Britain in her most desperate hour. Churchill never forgot how in January 1941 Harry

---

[314] *Closing the Ring*: Winston S. Churchill.

[315] *The Grand Alliance*: Winston S. Churchill.

Hopkins had appeared in London with a message from his chief. 'The President is determined that we shall win the war together. Make no mistake about it. He has sent me here to tell you that at all costs and by all means he will carry you through, no matter what happens to him — there is nothing that he will not do so far as he has human power.'[316]

This won Churchill's everlasting gratitude; even now when he relates the incident his eyes fill with tears. 'He is the greatest friend Britain has ever had,' he declared with emotion. And from then on, he allowed no Englishman to forget it. No one, not even a member of Winston's most intimate circle, has ever been permitted to make a disparaging remark about the President; and this rule still holds good to-day.

But apart from Winston's indebtedness, he was charmed by Roosevelt's easy, friendly manner; he was also impressed by his ingenuity in moulding public opinion and his adroitness at winning elections — talents which had never come easily to Churchill. Both men enjoyed the rough excitement of political life and both were always considerate of the domestic problems the other had to take into account. Their friendship began in 1939 when Churchill was First Lord of the Admiralty and Roosevelt wrote him a sympathetic letter. This started a long and intimate correspondence, unprecedented between the heads of two great Powers, which continued until Roosevelt's death. Since both men were capable of making up their minds and taking decisions on the spot they soon fell into the habit of by-passing their ambassadors and communicating directly on almost all important matters. Sometimes when affairs were pressing they rang each other up on the telephone.

They met on ten separate occasions during the war. These discussions took place on an average at six-monthly intervals. The first meeting was in Newfoundland in 1941. After that Churchill made four trips to Washington; two to Quebec; one to Casablanca, one to Cairo and Teheran, and one, finally, to Yalta.

But it was in Washington that the Churchill-Roosevelt friendship flowered best. The President welcomed Churchill at the White House as a member of the family. He was given a room across from Harry Hopkins' and the three invaded each other's bedrooms as unselfconsciously as schoolmates. Roosevelt liked to go to bed early but when Churchill was there he was so fascinated by the conversation

---

[316] Ibid.

that he stayed up far later than usual. Even so, Hopkins and Winston usually out-sat him and carried their talk into the early hours of the morning. The three men always lunched together, and although dinner was usually a more social affair, including members of the family, or of the President's inner circle, it still remained a small friendly group. Roosevelt liked to mix the cocktails and when he left the drawing-room Churchill always insisted on wheeling him to the lift.

Some idea of the informality of the White House is revealed in Harry Hopkins' favourite story. He claims that one morning when the President was wheeled into Churchill's bedroom, the Prime Minister emerged from the bath stark naked. The President apologized and turned to go but Churchill bade him remain. 'The Prime Minister of Great Britain,' he said, 'has nothing to hide from the President of the United States.' Robert Sherwood asked Winston if this story was true and says the latter replied that it was nonsense, 'that he never received the President without at least a bath towel wrapped around him. And he said, "I could not possibly have made such a statement as that. The President himself would have been aware that it was not strictly true".'[317]

As far as Churchill was concerned, no trace of jealousy ever marred his relationship with the President. It is one of Winston's characteristics that once he has formed a deep personal friendship he is completely faithful, never allowing selfish motives to influence him. He was loyal to Lloyd George when both were spoken of as potential Prime Ministers; now he was loyal to Roosevelt when both were world leaders. An interesting feature of his relationship with the President lay in the fact that whereas Winston was the head of a Government Roosevelt was the head of a State. Churchill never lost sight of this fact, and instead of resenting it, took great pleasure in showing Roosevelt a marked deference; this undoubtedly did much to keep relations between the two men running smoothly.

Up until the end of 1943 Churchill was certainly the dominant figure in the partnership. He not only had a far greater knowledge of military matters than Roosevelt, but until 1944 the British had more divisions in contact with the enemy in both the European and Japanese theatres of war than the Americans. The only areas where the Americans could speak with a commanding voice were in the Pacific and Australasia.

---

[317] *The White House Papers of Harry L. Hopkins*: Robert E. Sherwood.

In these circumstances Churchill had the right to speak in a commanding voice, which he did not hesitate to do.

But all the time that the two men were concentrated on the military side of the war, Churchill never lost sight of his main objective: the bringing of Great Britain and the United States together in what he had termed to General Smuts, was 'a fraternal association'. His ideas on this subject were far from orthodox, and when he visited Washington in 1943 he explained them to Roosevelt and Vice-President Wallace. He told the latter that he would like the citizens of Great Britain and the United States, without losing their present nationality, 'to be able to come and settle and trade with freedom and equal rights in the territories of the other. There might be a common passport, or a special form of passport or visa. There might even be some common form of citizenship, under which the citizens of the United States and of the British Commonwealth might enjoy voting privileges after residential qualification and be eligible for public office in the territories of the other, subject of course to the laws and institutions there prevailing.'[318]

Winston developed this same theme in a speech to Harvard University on 6 September, when he said: 'This gift of a common tongue is a priceless inheritance, and it may well some day become the foundation of a common citizenship. I like to think of British and Americans moving freely over each other's wide estates with hardly a sense of being foreigners to one another.'

*

President Roosevelt, however, did not share Churchill's conviction that the hope of the world lay in a fraternal association between the English-speaking peoples. He respected British institutions, but like many other Americans he was suspicious of British Imperialism. These suspicions grew deeper as the war developed until they became almost an obsession with him. He saw the challenge to the Atlantic Charter coming not from totalitarian Russia but from the colonial possessions of his Allies. 'The colonial system means war,' he told his son, Elliott. 'Exploit the resources of an India, a Burma, a Java; take all the wealth out of those countries, but never put anything back into them, things like education, decent standards of living, minimum

---

[318] *Closing the Ring*: Winston S. Churchill.

health requirements — all you're doing is storing up the kind of trouble that leads to war.'[319]

This observation was not only a ridiculous travesty of the British colonial system, but even its conclusions were false. The two world wars of this century and the present threat to peace have not sprung from discontented colonies but from the armed might of dictators anxious to spread their totalitarian rule. It seems astonishing that Roosevelt could be more concerned with British colonial rule than the extension of Soviet authority which carried with it, as a matter of course, severe and brutal 'liquidations'. Yet apparently this was the case, for at every major discussion with Churchill it was not the problem of Russia but of Britain's overseas possessions that came up for discussion. More than once he urged England to give up Hong Kong as a gesture, and in the spring of 1942 he pressed Churchill to grant India her independence at once, suggesting in a paper which must rank as one of the most naive documents ever drafted by a head of state, that she model her provisional government along the lines of America's original thirteen states.

Churchill stood his ground firmly. Glory in the British Empire was as much a part of him as his life's blood. Far from excusing England's over-lordship, he saw her rule as a great benefaction; was she not spreading the English tongue and with it all her light and learning and civilized institutions to the farthest corners of the earth? Besides, he argued with Roosevelt, if Britain withdrew she would leave a gap which undoubtedly would tempt some less civilized Power to assume her place.

Churchill could not convince Roosevelt, and both men stubbornly held their ground. What Winston failed to grasp until the Teheran Conference, however, was the fact that ingrained American anti-colonialism was having a marked effect on Roosevelt's attitude towards Russia. 'Of one thing I am certain, Stalin is not an Imperialist,' the President remarked to the Polish leader, Mikolajczyk. This belief, based on instinct rather than logic, drew him away from Britain and towards the Russian camp. He apparently viewed Stalin in almost exactly the same light that Chamberlain had viewed Hitler; if he could implant a feeling of trust in the dictator everything would turn out all right. 'I have a hunch,' he told William Bullitt, who had been the American Ambassador in Moscow, 'that Stalin doesn't want

---

[319] *As He Saw It*: Elliott Roosevelt.

anything but security for his country, and I think that if I give him everything I possibly can and ask nothing in return, noblesse oblige, he won't try to annex anything and will work for a world of democracy and peace.'[320]

One can only comment that a hunch was a strange basis for a nation's foreign policy. Although it can be argued that up until 1939 Russia had shown no imperialistic tendencies as far as her armies were concerned, her rule was being spread by Communist Parties all over the world which were often financed and controlled from Moscow. Far from being a static faith, Communism was a militant crusade, openly in conflict with the institutions of Western democracy.

Roosevelt, however, was not the only American who had trust in Russia. Many leading officials, including Harry Hopkins and General Eisenhower, shared his beliefs. Eisenhower wrote that 'judging from the past relations of America and Russia there was no cause to regard the future with pessimism'; and Harry Hopkins, six months after the Yalta Conference, wrote glowingly: 'We know or believe that Russia's interests, so far as we can anticipate them, do not afford an opportunity for a major difference with us in foreign affairs. We believe we are mutually dependent upon each other for economic reasons. We find the Russians as individuals easy to deal with. The Russians undoubtedly like the American people. They like the United States. They trust the United States more than they trust any other power in the world … above all, they want to maintain friendly relations with us … They are a tenacious, determined people who think and act just like we do.'[321]

The American attitude towards Russia can only be described as appallingly ingenuous. The tragedy lay in the fact that although Churchill and Roosevelt were in accord about a world of free, independent nations, the President's failure to understand the nature of Soviet totalitarianism allowed Stalin to drive a wedge between the two democracies and walk off with the spoils.

*

The turning point in the relations between Roosevelt and Churchill took place at Cairo and Teheran in December 1943.

---

[320] *How We Won the War and Lost the Peace*: William C. Bullitt.

[321] *The White House Papers of Harry L. Hopkins*: Robert E. Sherwood.

The Teheran Conference was the first meeting of 'The Big Three', and it was almost exclusively a military conference. The leaders decided on the programme which was to prove the grand climax of the war. Britain and America would launch a cross-Channel invasion in May; about the same time they would use the Allied force in Italy to strike at Southern France; and Russia would co-ordinate a large-scale offensive on the Eastern front.

The Big Three were in full accord on this strategy. Much nonsense has been written about Churchill's reluctance to strike across the Channel. He believed that an invasion of France was right and inevitable, but his experience of the huge and useless blood-letting on the Western front in the first War cautioned him not to undertake it until the enemy had been sufficiently weakened by attacks in other theatres to ensure its success. At Teheran, however, Churchill was in agreement with Roosevelt and Stalin that the time to invade was in the spring. He also was in favour of the joint operation in Southern France, although as an alternative he would have preferred President Roosevelt's proposal that the Allied Army in Italy advance through the Ljubljana Gap to Vienna. However, he had no fixed thoughts on this subject and when Stalin raised objections and plumped in favour of Marseilles Churchill backed the project.

There was only one point on which he did not see eye to eye with his two colleagues. Churchill believed that one-tenth of the Allied strength should be used in a third operation in the Eastern Mediterranean. He argued that there was an air force massed for the defence of Egypt standing idle; also that there were two or three divisions in the Middle East which could not be used elsewhere because there was no available shipping to move them to the main theatre. Why not employ them? If, by a small effort, Rhodes could be captured, the whole Aegean would be dominated by the Allied Air Force and direct sea contact established with Turkey. This might bring Turkey into the war, which would open up the Black Sea, and with it, unlimited possibilities. Surely, he argued, such a huge prize was worth a minor effort which would not detract in any way from the other major undertakings.

Roosevelt, however, was not only uninterested in the project but the fact that Winston pressed it so hard aroused his suspicions. Was Churchill seeking some selfish gain for Britain in the Balkans? At the end of the first day in Teheran he remarked to his son, Elliott, 'I see no reason for putting the lives of American soldiers in jeopardy in order to protect real or fancied British interests on the European continent. We are at war and our job is to win as far as possible, and without adventures.'[322]

Other American leaders shared Roosevelt's suspicions. Even General Eisenhower believed Winston had hidden motives for after the war he wrote: 'I could not escape a feeling that Mr. Churchill's views were unconsciously coloured by two considerations that lay outside the scope of the immediate military problem ... The first of them was his concern as a political leader for the future of the Balkans ... The other was an inner compulsion to vindicate his strategical concepts of World War I, in which he had been the principal exponent of the Gallipoli campaign.'[323]

Churchill has never been a devious, or for that matter, even a subtle man. He rarely leaves anyone in doubt as to what he thinks or what he wants. Yet the inclination to attribute concealed motives to his arguments on military strategy has become so widespread that many writers to-day state them as facts. For example, Chester Wilmot in his brilliant and authoritative book *The Struggle for Europe* asserts, 'During 1943 ... Churchill became increasingly concerned about the necessity of restraining Stalin's ambitions ... The Prime Minister sought to devise a plan of campaign which would not only be a military success, but would ensure that victory did not leave the democratic cause politically weaker in any sphere.'

There was no foundation for this statement. The truth is that it was not until 1944, when the great invasion was only a matter of a few months, that Churchill seriously concerned himself with the design of the post-war world. Up until Teheran he had given surprisingly little thought to the blue-print. He had decided in his own mind that the only hope for a secure world lay in an Anglo-American alliance, far closer than anything that had evolved so far; and that this combination would deal with the problem of Russia when the time came. He had then turned all his thoughts and energies on securing the victory.

Churchill himself makes it plain, in his fifth volume of memoirs, that at Teheran he was thinking in terms of military strategy only when he advanced his arguments about Turkey. He emphasizes that he was in complete agreement with the cross-Channel invasion and the attack on the South of France; and that he merely wanted a third, and a very

---

[322] *As He Saw It*: Elliott Roosevelt.

[323] *Crusade in Europe*: Dwight D. Eisenhower.

minor, operation in the Eastern Mediterranean at the same time in order to employ all available forces. 'This was the triple theme which I pressed upon the President and Stalin on every occasion,' he writes, 'not hesitating to repeat the arguments remorselessly. I could have gained Stalin, but the President was oppressed by the prejudices of his military advisers, and drifted to and fro in the argument, with the result that the whole of these subsidiary but gleaming opportunities were cast away. Our American friends were comforted in their obstinacy by the reflection that "at any rate we have stopped Churchill entangling us in the Balkans". No such idea had crossed my mind. I regard the failure to use otherwise unemployable forces to bring Turkey into the war and dominate the Aegean as an error of war direction which cannot be excused by the fact that in spite of it victory was won.'[324]

*

However, it was not the military aspects of the Teheran Conference that upset Churchill. It was Roosevelt's aloof, almost hostile attitude. At Cairo, before the two leaders proceeded to Teheran, Roosevelt lectured Winston sharply about his outlook towards colonialism. The Prime Minister remarked that he thought Chiang Kai-Shek had designs on Indo-China. 'Winston ... you have four hundred years of acquisitive instinct in your blood and you just don't understand how a country might not want to acquire land somewhere if they can get it. A new period has opened in the world and you will have to adjust yourself to it.'[325]

Churchill arrived in Cairo hoping to hold preliminary and private talks with Roosevelt about the forthcoming invasion. But the President insisted on Chiang Kai-Shek being present, and he also invited Russian observers (who declined the invitation) despite Winston's protests. This gesture was undoubtedly made to show Churchill that Britain had no right to regard her relationship with the United States as either favoured or exclusive.

At Teheran the President continued the same tactics. He refused bluntly to meet Churchill alone on the grounds that 'the Russians wouldn't like it'. Yet at the same time he had several meetings with Stalin from which Winston was excluded. The latter was astonished and hurt by this behaviour which was contrary to his own code of

---

[324] *Closing the Ring*: Winston S. Churchill.

[325] *Roosevelt and the Russians*: Edward Stettinius.

friendship and loyalty. But Roosevelt went even further. When, after three days at Teheran, he felt he had not made as much progress with Stalin as he would have liked, he tried to ingratiate himself with the Russian dictator by making fun of Churchill. 'I began almost as soon as we got into the conference room,' he told Frances Perkins. 'I said, lifting my hand to cover a whisper (which of course had to be interpreted), "Winston is cranky this morning, he got up on the wrong side of the bed". A vague smile passed over Stalin's eyes, and I decided I was on the right track ... I began to tease Churchill about his Britishness, about John Bull, about his cigars, about his habits. It began to register with Stalin. Winston got red and scowled, and the more he did so, the more Stalin smiled. Finally Stalin broke out in a deep, hearty guffaw, and for the first time in three days I saw light. I kept it up until Stalin was laughing with me, and it was then that I called him "Uncle Joe". He would have thought me fresh the day before, but that day he laughed and came over and shook my hand.'[326] John Gunther, the American journalist, asked someone who was there if the incident had really taken place. 'Yes,' replied the official, 'and it wasn't funny either.' It was certainly not Churchill's idea of humour, nor, for that matter, of statesmanship. It turned The Big Three into The Eternal Triangle, with Roosevelt the female, almost feline, character, and Stalin and Churchill, both aggressively male, the respective villain and hero of the piece.

*

Churchill pondered the lessons of Teheran deeply. Roosevelt's actions made it plain that he was not only unwilling to regard Britain as a favoured partner, but that he was prepared to put as much trust and faith, and perhaps even more, in totalitarian Russia than in democratic Britain. This came as a profound shock to Winston. His whole foreign policy was based on the concept of an English-speaking authority. If the foundations were faulty there was only one alternative: to act on his own and try to safeguard Britain against the consequences of a Soviet domination of Europe.

Five months later, in the spring of 1944, these new and pressing worries began to manifest themselves. On 4 May, he sent a minute to the Foreign Office: 'A paper should be drafted for the Cabinet, and possibly for the Imperial Conference, setting forth shortly ... the brute issues which are developing in Italy, in Roumania, in Bulgaria, in

---

[326] *The Roosevelt I Knew*: Frances Perkins.

Yugoslavia, and above all in Greece … Broadly speaking, the issue is, Are we going to acquiesce in the Communization of the Balkans and perhaps of Italy …? I am of the opinion on the whole that we ought to come to a definite conclusion about it, and that if our conclusion is that we resist the Communist infusion and invasion, we should put it to them pretty plainly at the best moment that military events permit. We should of course have to consult the United States first.'[327]

A month later, in June, I was invited to 10 Downing Street for lunch. It was the day after the great invasion had begun and the papers were filled with little else. Mr. Churchill appeared in a blue siren suit and he seemed worried and preoccupied. He scarcely referred to the invasion, but in the middle of lunch launched forth into an angry discourse on foreign affairs. 'When this war is over,' he growled, 'England will need every ally she can get to protect herself against Russia. I'm sick of these parlour pinks, always criticizing the internal regimes of countries. I don't care a whit what people do inside their own countries so long as they don't try to export their ideas, and as long as their relations with Britain are friendly. Spain is ready to make her peace with Britain and I am ready to accept it; the Italian Monarchy is friendly to Britain and I would like to see it preserved. The idea of running foreign affairs on personal prejudices is criminal folly.'

*

The Red Army had not, at this date, made any serious inroads into the Balkans, but Churchill knew that time was short. If any part of Eastern Europe was to be saved from domination, someone must act and act quickly. Without consulting Roosevelt he wrote Stalin suggesting that Russia grant Britain a free hand in Greece and Yugoslavia in return for the controlling interest in Bulgaria and Roumania. When the American Secretary of State, Cordell Hull, learned of this proposal he angrily denounced it as an attempt to 'carve up the Balkans'. Churchill, however, was undeterred and during his visit to Moscow in October 1944 worked out in actual percentages both nations' respective spheres of interest. The State Department branded the agreement as 'Churchiavellian' but Winston insisted that it was his only hope of preventing Stalin from gaining control of the whole area.

Meanwhile Churchill had not been idle nearer home. For the first time he began to think of military strategy in terms of political aims.

---

[327] *Closing the Ring*: Winston S. Churchill.

It was apparent in July, a month after cross-Channel invasion had begun, that the Southern France operation was no longer strictly necessary. Originally the Allies had considered the port of Marseilles vitally important to handle the flood of troops and supplies scheduled for the main assault. But now the invaders possessed ports in Brittany which, Winston argued, would do just as well. If instead of sending the Anglo-American Army from Italy to Marseilles he could persuade the Americans to advance towards Vienna, much of Central Europe might be saved from the Soviet influence. Since Eisenhower wielded supreme authority it was on him that Churchill turned all his persuasive powers, resulting in what the General has described as 'the longest-sustained argument I had with Prime Minister Churchill during the war'. But Eisenhower was still suspicious. 'I felt that the Prime Minister's real concern,' he wrote, 'was possibly of a political rather than a military nature. He may have thought that a post-war situation which would see the Western Allies posted in great strength in the Balkans would be more effective in producing a stable post-hostilities world than if the Russian armies should be the ones to occupy that region. I told him that if this were his reason for advocating the campaign into the Balkans he should go instantly to the President and lay the facts on the table ... But I did insist that as long as he argued the matter on military grounds alone I could not concede validity to his arguments.'[328]

This time Eisenhower's surmise was right, but his advice to Winston to approach the President was gratuitous. Winston had already argued out the matter with Roosevelt but the latter had insisted that in view of the Teheran agreement he could not 'agree without Stalin's approval to any use of force or equipment elsewhere.'

This setback did not diminish Winston's resolve. He was more determined than ever to play every card in his hand to protect British interests regardless of American opinion; and he did not have long to wait. Before the end of the year grave situations arose in Italy and Greece. Both these countries were battlefields; both had an Allied army which was predominantly British; and both recognized the necessity of preserving law and order. The Italian crisis was provoked by the resignation of the Bonomi Coalition Government. Carlo Sforza, an anti-Fascist who had lived many years in the United States, flew to Rome and tried to establish himself as the leading Republican

---

[328] *Crusade in Europe*: Dwight D. Eisenhower.

spokesman. He was violently opposed to the monarchy and it became apparent to Churchill that if post-war politics were allowed to flare up while the country was in a state of upheaval the large Communist Party already in existence might manage to install itself. Winston did not like or trust Sforza; he felt he was being foisted on Italy by an unthinking American public opinion, and he was determined not to allow the country to slip into extremism by mismanagement. He therefore made it clear that Britain would not look with any favour upon an Italian Government which included Sforza as Prime Minister or Foreign Secretary. This caused a storm of protest in the United States. In a public statement on 5 December Stettinius, the American Secretary of State, rapped Churchill over the knuckles for his suspected interference in Italian affairs. Churchill sent a furious cable to Roosevelt and in the House of Commons on 8 December, 1944, said bitterly: 'Poor old England! (Perhaps I ought to say, "Poor old Britain!") We have to assume the burden of the most thankless tasks, and in undertaking them to be scoffed at, criticized and opposed from every quarter; but at least we know where we are making for, know the end of the road, know what is our objective ... We have not attempted to put our veto on the appointment of Count Sforza. If to-morrow the Italians were to make him Prime Minister or Foreign Secretary, we have no power to stop it, except with the agreement of the Allies. All that we should have to say about it is that we do not trust the man, we do not think he is a true and trustworthy man, nor do we put the slightest confidence in any Government of which he is a dominating member. I think we should have to put a great deal of responsibility for what might happen on those who called him to power.'

Churchill won the battle, for Sforza failed to establish himself as a leader, but the relations between London and Washington were distinctly cool. Then came the Greek trouble. For some time three elements in Greece had been struggling for power; the royalist faction which centred around George II; the anti-Communist faction, centred around Colonel Zirvas; and the Communist-led resistance force known as E.L.A.S. and E.A.M. This last group had been active in the fight against Germany, but now they were busy trying to grasp the power of Government by terrorist methods. British troops were called in to maintain order and blood was shed. The American public did not know much about the partisans except that they were violently anti-Nazi, and once again opinion flared up against the British. It rose so high that Admiral King, the United States Naval Chief of Staff, ordered Admiral Hewitt, the American Commander in the Mediterranean, not to allow any American L.S.T.s to carry supplies into Greece. Hopkins intervened and the order was countermanded, but not before Churchill had sent angry protests. The Prime Minister then took unexpected action by flying to Athens on Christmas Day. He succeeded in bringing hostilities to an end by establishing a temporary regency under Archbishop Damaskinos and obtaining from King George of Greece the assurance that he would not attempt to return to Greece 'unless summoned by a free and fair expression of the national will.' Temporarily, at least, the crisis subsided; nevertheless the atmosphere of the Yalta Conference, which was held a few weeks later and which proved to be the last meeting between Roosevelt, Churchill and Stalin, was not as happy as it might have been.

*

Most of the troubles of the post-war world have been blamed on Yalta. But the truth is that this conference took very few new decisions, for the pattern of Europe had been moulded over the previous two years. Only one Yalta decision can be severely criticized and that is the large concession which Roosevelt made to Stalin throughout the Far East in return for the dictator's promise to enter the war against Japan. This concession made Stalin the virtual master of Manchuria and, in effect, the master of North China. Many members of the British delegation were strongly opposed to the plan, and Eden begged Churchill not to put his signature to it. The Prime Minister replied 'that the whole position of the British Empire in the Far East was at stake' and if he refused to sign he might find himself excluded from any further say in these affairs.

As far as Europe was concerned, however, the Russians made no new gains on paper. The frontiers of Poland were thrashed out; German reparations were discussed; the design of the United Nations was sketched; the three-power occupation of Germany, which had been agreed upon in principle by the Foreign Ministers in October 1943, was extended to include France. The most important and hopeful event in the eyes of Britain and America was the fact that the Soviet Union reiterated its promise to uphold the Atlantic Charter which was firmly pledged to the freedom and independence of the small states of Europe. If Russia meant what she said, peace was assured.

Should the democratic leaders have placed an implicit faith in Russia, or should they have attempted to safeguard their interests wherever they had a right to do so? Roosevelt believed the first and Churchill the second, which led to severe altercations between the two Governments in the months to follow.

Since the Russians had promised to allow free elections in Central and Eastern Europe, Roosevelt was confident that democracy would establish itself as soon as the Nazi grip was broken. But he felt strongly that the only way to keep Russia to her bargain was to accept her word as her bond. Any outward suspicion or ill-will on the part of the democracies, he believed, would bring down the structure in ruins. Consequently American policy recognized only one objective: to destroy the German Army. Once that was accomplished it was believed that Europe would right itself of its own accord.

Churchill was highly sceptical of this thinking. Although he agreed with the President that post-war policy must be based on the assumption that Russia would honour her pledges, he saw no reason why, at the same time, the Allies should not grasp the initiative when they could, and guard their interests against any possible contingency. After all, Stalin was still insisting that the Lublin Committee, which was a Moscow-controlled body, should become the rulers of Poland. And only a few weeks after Yalta he had summoned the King of Roumania and ordered him to install a Communist Prime Minister. Was this the furtherance of democracy? What did the Russians mean by the word anyway?

Churchill felt strongly that the Allies should fashion their military strategy in accordance with certain obvious political aims. The Western Powers should liberate key cities and territories whenever the opportunity presented itself. This was important not only from the point of view of psychology and prestige but for hard-headed, practical reasons as well. Their advance would not be in contravention of any agreements they had made with the Russians; yet it would place them in a position to see that the pledges Stalin had given on free elections were really upheld.

Czechoslovakia became one of the major points of issue. In April, as the Allied Army moved towards its frontiers, the British Chiefs of Staff made it clear that they felt great advantage would be derived from liberating Prague. General Marshall passed this information on to Eisenhower with the comment: 'Personally, and aside from all logistic, tactical, or strategic implications, I would be loath to hazard American lives for purely political purposes.'[329]

Eisenhower agreed with Marshall; and since he did not feel that an advance into Czechoslovakia would have any bearing on his sole aim, the destruction of the enemy's armed forces, he halted his troops on the frontier. Although he received frantic appeals for help from Prague which was being subjected to a severe German attack he remained stationary; and when, on 4 May, the Russians asked him formally not to move forward any further, he agreed. Three days later he received a wire from Churchill begging him to proceed to Prague, but, instead, he instructed the Czechs to refer their requests for aid to Moscow. The following week Czechoslovakia was liberated by the Russians.

Berlin raised an even more heated issue. General Montgomery became convinced in September 1944 that if the Allies made a 'powerful and full-blooded thrust' into Germany, they could capture the Ruhr and liberate the German capital. But although Berlin had been listed by SHAEF in a pre-D-Day plan as the Allies' ultimate goal, in the months that followed Eisenhower had come to regard it as increasingly unimportant. From a military point of view he decided it was better to move forward more slowly on a broad front rather than concentrate his forces in a single thrust.

Churchill felt passionately on the subject of the German capital. Berlin was not only a great prize but he believed it would give the Allies an invaluable bargaining point. Although they would be obliged to move back into the zones of occupation that had been agreed upon by the Russians, it would provide them with an opportunity, and their only opportunity, to see that Stalin carried out his treaties as well. On 3 April, five weeks before the war ended, he took up the matter with Roosevelt: 'If they [the Russians] also take Berlin will not their impression that they have been the overwhelming contributor to the common victory be unduly printed in their minds, and may this not lead them into a mood which will raise grave and formidable difficulties in the future'? But Roosevelt's reply was curt. He said that he 'regretted at the moment of a great victory we should become

---

[329] *Why Eisenhower's Forces Stopped at the Elbe*: Forrest Pogue. This article was printed in *World Politics*, April 1952, published by the Princeton University Press. The extract is from an official paper, *W.-*74256 28 April, 1945, *Shaef Cable Log*.

involved in such unfortunate reactions.'[330] A few days later, on 7 April, Eisenhower informed the Combined Chiefs of Staff: 'I regard it as militarily unsound at this stage of the proceedings to make Berlin a major objective, particularly in view of the fact that it is only thirty-five miles from the Russian lines.'[331]

Churchill continued to urge his point of view with desperate insistence. When Truman succeeded Roosevelt a week later, he turned his fire on him. But the new President merely replied that 'the tactical deployment of American troops is a military one.' And the American Army was adamant. General Omar Bradley sums up the situation in his book *A Soldier's Story*. 'I could see no advantage accruing from the capture of Berlin that would offset the need for quick destruction of the German army on our front. As soldiers we looked naively on this British inclination [the desire to go to Berlin] to complicate the war with political foresight and non-military objectives.' Consequently, Churchill lost his battle, and the Russians liberated Berlin as well as Prague.

*

To-day the results are apparent for all to see. Within three years Czechoslovakia was a Communist country; the Russian sector of Germany was decapitated from the rest, despite Soviet assurances at Potsdam that trade would flow freely between the Eastern and Western zones; and the whole of Eastern and Central Europe was paralysed into subservience to Moscow. In many cases the Russians not only broke their treaties but they did not even try to honour them.

What differences would it have made if Churchill had gained his way and Eisenhower had secured control of Germany? Remembering the rise of Left-wing opinion all over the world at the end of the war, could the Allies have dealt with Russia with a firm hand or would public pressure have been too strong against them? No one can answer these questions, and it may be argued that it was necessary for the democracies to learn by bitter experience; otherwise the close *entente* which exists between the English-speaking world might not have come into being.

---

[330] Ibid.

[331] *Why Eisenhower's Forces Stopped at the Elbe*: Forrest Pogue. The above quotation is from an official document, *Eisenhower to Marshall F. W. D.*, 18710, 7 April, 1945.

But whatever conclusions one draws it is difficult to see how the costly innocence of the American leaders, with their failure to understand that all wars have political objectives and carry with them political responsibilities, can escape severe condemnation. When all is said and done, Communism and not Democracy has been the victor over a large part of the world.

**Part Seven
The World of To-Day**

Chapter Twenty-Two — Leader of the Opposition

MR. CHURCHILL'S overwhelming defeat at the General Election of 1945, held only a few weeks after the surrender of Germany, was regarded as astonishing news, even by his own countrymen. For Winston it was a stunning and ironic reverse, first because he was at the very summit of his power and fame, and second, because no statesman emphasized the superior qualities of the British people more forcibly than he. During the war, when someone congratulated him on a broadcast, saying: 'You are giving the people the courage they need,' he replied quickly: 'You are mistaken. They already have the courage. I only focus it.' To have been rejected by a people towards whom he felt such pride and possessiveness was a bitter blow.

During the first years of his Premiership Churchill had declared privately that he would not commit the same mistake Lloyd George had made in seeking to retain power once hostilities had ended. He remembered how, in the difficult months that followed the war, L.G.'s prestige had gradually dwindled until in 1922 he was dismissed from office never to return again. However, when Churchill took over the leadership of the Conservative Party in 1940 many people were sceptical about his sticking to his resolve. His action was criticized at the time by those who considered that as head of a great coalition government he should remain above Party politics; and even his friends warned him that it might be a mistake to commit himself so far in advance.

But it was not Winston's nature to play the role of a detached Elder Statesman; and it would have taken a man of far less sanguine disposition to refuse to offer himself to the electorate when all the world was acclaiming him. Leading Conservatives were aware that a new wind of social consciousness was blowing through England, but they believed that Churchill's fame could keep them in power; and Churchill believed this too. Although from time to time he had been pressed to make some positive statement on peace-time domestic policy, he was so absorbed by the problems of the war that except for one or two occasions he refused to put his mind on internal affairs. Besides, he was confident that when the time came the British people, who had followed him so loyally throughout the conflict, would heed what he had to say about the days to come.

This was a severe miscalculation for the British people has never pledged itself to a single man except in times of extreme emergency.

Nowhere in the world is the Party system so highly developed as in England. The electorate was not looking for a personality, but for a programme; and the only programme that was forthcoming was that put forward by the Labour Party with its emphasis on social reform and a long over-due redistribution of the national income. The working classes remembered the hard times they had had between the wars; first the soaring prices and the bad housing, then the long years of unemployment. And they also remembered that except for two short spells the Conservative Party had dominated the parliamentary scene for most of the twenty-one years. Besides, had not Mr. Churchill fought the Tories throughout the thirties and accused them of allowing the country to drift into war? Why had he attached himself to them anyway?

*

Churchill himself did not add to his own chances. If the public needed a reminder that he had always been rejected as a peace-time leader on the grounds of bad judgment and instability, they had it, to use a figure of speech, straight from the horse's mouth. Overnight the statesman vanished and in his place appeared an irresponsible politician hurling invective at his opponents and offering few proposals of his own. He sounded the first gun in a radio broadcast telling the country that Socialism would result in 'a Gestapo'. It was a childish blunder to attack Labour leaders like Attlee, Morrison, Bevin and Cripps, who had won the respect and admiration of the public for their loyal service in Winston's Coalition Government. I heard the broadcast at Lord Rothermere's house and I remember the silence when he had finished. 'If he continues like that,' said our host, 'the election is as good as lost.'

But Winston did not change his tactics. Next, he turned his fire on the Chairman of the Labour Party Executive, Professor Laski, insisting that the latter would be the 'boss' of any Labour Government that got into power. Since the Party Chairman is only an annual appointment this was patently nonsense. *The Times* tried to play down Winston's attacks but Churchill, buoyantly confident, and with an old-fashioned tendency to regard an election as something of a lark, insisted on reviving his charges at every opportunity.

There is no doubt that the electorate was greatly shaken by his campaign. People were in a serious mood and wanted facts, not political stunts. Although the Conservatives put forward a Five Year Plan under the guidance of Lord Woolton, it contained few constructive ideas. The result was that the Conservatives fought the battle equipped with little more than Churchill's photograph while the Socialists went into action with a carefully planned programme. This seemed to confirm the suspicions of the working class that the Prime Minister took little interest in domestic matters. In one speech Winston referred to milk for babies, and the comments of the people in the village where I was staying were: 'What's 'e know or care about babies' milk? Guns is 'is speciality and any time there's a war we're glad to let 'im run it but when 'e talks about babies' milk we know someone's put 'im up to it and it's not 'im speaking at all.'

Although it was obvious that opinion was hardening against him even the pessimists believed he would win a majority of thirty seats. The result of the Gallup Poll published in the *News-Chronicle* showed a landslide which proved to be accurate within one per cent, but Britain was not 'poll-conscious' and few people paid any attention to the figures. Two days before polling day I heard Churchill address an enormous gathering at Walthamstow Stadium on the outskirts of London and was amazed at the amount of opposition and heckling he received. He was interrupted so often he could scarcely get through his speech. When he had finished, his daughter Sarah invited me to a private room to have beer and sandwiches with them before he went on to his next engagement. As a war correspondent for the previous eight years I had seen a number of countries invaded and overrun by the enemy and when Churchill saw me he exclaimed: 'What a bad omen! For the first time I have my doubt about this election. You only appear when the established regime is crashing to the ground!'

Neither he nor I had any idea how prophetic his words were to prove. Up until the last he was confident of victory. He even arranged a small dinner party in advance to celebrate the results. One of the guests told me afterwards that she had never sat through a more depressing meal. Churchill's daughters were in tears and the old man himself sat immobile as though too stunned to speak.

*

Defeat burned deep into Churchill's soul. He felt he had been badly treated by an ungrateful population, and when he wrote his first volume on the second World War he allowed himself the bitter comment: 'Thus, then, on the night of the tenth of May, at the outset of this mighty battle, I acquired the chief power in the State, which henceforth I wielded in ever-growing measure for five years and three months of world war, at the end of which time, all our enemies having surrendered unconditionally or being about to do so, I was immediately dismissed by the British electorate from all further conduct of their affairs.'

This resentment was unlike Winston, for throughout his long political life no man had taken greater care to hide his disappointments from public view. He had always made a point of treating an election as a good healthy English game with winners and losers shaking hands amiably in the traditional sporting fashion. But in this case the shock and humiliation were too great and it took him many months to overcome a feeling of deep resentment.

However, as far as Parliament was concerned his manners were distinguished. He refused to allow vindictiveness to creep into his speeches and faced the House with a courage and aplomb which aroused general admiration. His peculiarly disarming quality of forgive and forget was expressed when he had bronze plaques made, adorned with the oak and the acorn, which he sent to all those who had served in his war-time Government. Socialists whom he had branded as future Gestapo leaders were surprised to receive these souvenirs with their names inscribed bearing the words: 'Salute the Great Coalition, 1940-1945'.

Churchill also managed to retain his sense of humour. When an acquaintance suggested that he should tour England so that the thousands of his own countrymen who had never seen him could have a chance to honour him he growled: 'I refuse to be exhibited like a prize bull whose chief attraction is its past prowess.'

Many of Churchill's friends urged him to leave Parliament and devote himself to writing a history of the war. The Labour Government had a huge majority and was bound to run its full course; and it was always possible that it would be re-elected for another five years after that. Considering the heavy responsibility that Churchill had carried, and in view of his unique position as the greatest living statesman in the world, they felt it was undignified for him to occupy himself in day to day altercations in the House; he should reserve himself for the big occasions — 'the Test Matches', as one of them put it, 'not village cricket'. But Winston insisted that he 'liked' village cricket, and as for leaving Parliament, that was unthinkable. 'I am a child of the House of Commons,' he announced solemnly. His friends then argued that even if he remained in Parliament he at least should give up the Leadership of the Opposition. It was an exacting job, and undignified for one who could command world attention whenever he chose.

But Winston had no intention of retiring from this position either. He knew that the leadership of the Conservative Party was the only course that might take him back to No. 10 Downing Street again, and the truth was that a few months after his defeat he resolved to become Prime Minister again. He had had enough experience of the back benches to know that real political power only lies in high office. Although he realized that another election probably would not come before he was seventy-five he still felt full of vigour; more important still, the conviction that he could manage things much better than anyone else, which he had carried with him all his life, still burned strongly within him. 'It would be easy for me to retire gracefully in an odour of civic freedoms,' he told a Conservative Party Conference on 5 October, 1945, 'and the plan crossed my mind frequently some months ago. I feel now, however, that the situation is so serious and what may have to come so grave, that I am resolved to go forward carrying the flag so long as I have the necessary strength and energy and so long as I have your confidence.'

So to those friends who urged his resignation from the Party leadership he replied firmly: 'My horse may not be a very good one, but at least it's better than being in the infantry.'

*

As Leader of the Opposition it was Mr. Churchill's duty to oppose, and he plunged into the attack against the Labour Government with obvious relish. On 28 November, 1945, he told a large Conservative Party audience that the verdict of the country at the polls was 'a hideous lapse and error in domestic affairs'. 'I hope you will believe,' he said, 'that it is with no personal bias, soreness or conceit that I declare that the vote of the nation at the General Election was one of the greatest disasters that has smitten us in our long and chequered history.' These were strong words, and annoying words too, for the electorate does not like being told it is a fool. However, Winston went on to develop the two main themes which were to be his battle-cries for the next five years; first, that the Labour Government by its misguided and spiteful economic policies would lead the country to industrial ruin, and second, because of their doctrinaire and unpatriotic theories they would carry the country towards totalitarianism.

Neither of these prophecies was fulfilled; in fact, the direct opposite proved true. Although the Labour Government took over a nation which had exhausted her wealth and resources in a gigantic war effort and was literally facing bankruptcy, five years later, almost to the month, it was in a position to announce that Britain was the first country in Europe able to stand on her own feet and pay her own way. And far from flirting with totalitarianism, under the leadership of Ernest Bevin the Labour Government not only established itself as a formidable foe of Communism but was playing a leading role in spreading the democratic faith throughout the world. 'Ours is a philosophy in its own right,' explained Prime Minister Attlee in a broadcast in January 1948. 'Our task is to work out a system of a new and challenging kind which combines individual freedom with a planned economy; democracy with social justice. The task which faces not only ourselves but all the Western democracies required a Government inspired by a new conception of society with a dynamic policy in accord with the needs of a new situation. It could not be accomplished by any of the old Parties, nor by a totalitarian Party, whether Fascist or Communist.'

The Labour majority of 1945 undoubtedly will take its place alongside the Liberal sweep of 1906 as one of the great reforming Parliaments of British history. But the programme that it carried through, like that of its forerunner, has been so largely accepted by the country as a whole that even from the short perspective of to-day it is difficult to see what all the fuss was about. A large amount of social legislation was passed which now has the support of most Conservatives; a number of basic industries were nationalized, almost all of which were in need of vast sums of capital equipment, and which to-day only a few of the most rabid Tories would like to see back in private hands.

Why, then, the reader may ask, was Churchill's opposition so violent? Did he really believe in the disaster he predicted, or was it merely part of his fight to regain power? There is little doubt that in the first years of the Parliament Winston viewed the future with dire apprehension. But it should not be forgotten that home affairs opened up a field of thought for him which had been closed for nearly a generation. During the ten years before the war he had been wholly absorbed by foreign relations; and during the five years of his Premiership he had been so occupied with military matters that he had delegated the country's domestic problems to his Labour colleagues. Aside from this, his long political life had not been distinguished for his judgment or understanding of internal issues. Probably the least satisfactory period of his career was the five years between 1924 and 1929 in which he had served as Chancellor of the Exchequer.

The cold science of economics had never held the slightest attraction for him. He had a few simple, fundamental views on finance which had been instilled in him as a youth and from which he had never deviated. 'I was brought up to believe that taxation was a bad thing,' he told the House of Commons on 27 October, 1949, 'but the consuming power of the people was a good thing … I was brought up to believe that trade should be regulated mainly by the laws of supply and demand and that, apart from basic necessaries in great emergencies, the price mechanism should adjust and correct undue spending at home, as it does, apart from gifts and subsidies, control spending abroad … I still hold to these general principles.'

What Winston failed to understand in those grim days after the war was that Britain was actually facing starvation. It would have been impossible for any Government, whether Conservative or Socialist, to let the laws of supply and demand work freely. The country was desperately in need of cars, textiles, china, kitchen utensils, in fact everything one could mention; yet unless Britain starved her home markets she could not export enough goods to feed herself, for she had to buy the raw materials with which to manufacture, and many of these raw materials were in short supply. This meant that the strictest control on industry was absolutely necessary in order to ensure that the key industries received necessary materials.

Winston did not understand these theories. They were contrary to all he had been taught, and he refused to open his eyes to the fact that the situation itself was quite unlike any other that the country had faced. 'Whoever thought of starving the home trade as a peacetime measure of stimulating exports?' he told a Conservative Party meeting in November 1945. 'Sir Stafford Cripps is under the profound delusion that he can build up an immense, profitable export trade while keeping everything at the minimum here at home. Look what he is doing to the motor car industry … He is a great advocate of "Strength through Misery".'

Winston decided that all the controls and restrictions imposed by the Socialists were merely part of a spiteful ideology. The Government's decision to continue high taxation on the largest incomes, in order to be able to ask the wage earners not to press for larger wages, was construed by him as pure malice; and the principle of maintaining a rationing system while goods were in short supply was interpreted as bureaucracy gone mad. 'The Socialist belief,' he told a Conservative Rally at Blenheim Palace on 4 August, 1947, 'is that nothing matters so long as miseries are equally shared and certainly they have acted in accordance with their faith.' In October of the same year he told the House of Commons: 'The reason why we are not able to earn our living and make our way in the world as a vast, complex, civilized country is because we are not allowed to do so. The whole enterprise, initiative, contrivance, and genius, of the British nation is being increasingly paralysed by the restrictions which are imposed upon it in the name of a mistaken political philosophy and a largely obsolete mode of thought ... I am sure that this policy of equalizing misery and organizing scarcity, instead of allowing diligence, self-interest and ingenuity, to produce abundance, has only to be prolonged to kill this British Island stone dead.'

During the next five years Churchill painted a horrific picture of what was happening in Britain. He claimed that the Labour Government was a disaster almost as great as the second World War; he declared that the country was 'hag-ridden by Socialist doctrines', that it was 'torn by feud and faction, and strangled by incompetence and folly'. He accused the Labour leaders of 'squalid Party motives', of 'cheap and bitter abuse', of 'crazy theories and personal incompetence', and of a 'dismal and evil reign'.

These polemics were characteristic of Churchill when he was fighting a battle. He always saw an issue as a stirring and vital challenge. Fierce partisanship was the very essence of his nature, and this time, with a glittering prize awaiting the victor, he threw himself into the fray with increased ardour. A large section of Conservative support, however, was embarrassed by his invective, and felt that perhaps he was conjuring up a savage dragon in order to continue in the role of Britain's saviour. Even in the Conservative Parliamentary Party there began to be discontent. Winston was so unpredictable, they complained. He only made sporadic appearances in the House, and instead of trying to organize the Opposition as a team, he often made speeches without even consulting his shadow Cabinet. The Conservatives had not won a single by-election; it was obvious, said their back-benchers, that they must produce a policy, yet Winston refused stubbornly to commit himself to any programme. It was rumoured that he had never even bothered to read the Tory Industrial Charter which R. A. Butler had produced so painstakingly. Perhaps things would be better, they whispered, if Winston resigned and Eden took his place. At this point, in 1949, *Picture Post* ran an article entitled: 'Is Churchill a Liability to the Tories?' and Lord Beaverbrook's *Sunday Express* stoutly replied: 'When Mr. Churchill is in his seat, the Opposition breathes fire. When he is not, the Tory front bench has the venom of a bunch of daffodils.'

Although the discontent of the Tory back bench continued, the Members found that it was not easy to remove a leader, and far less easy to remove a leader of Churchill's determination. Although the latter was well aware of the agitation in favour of Eden he clung firmly to his saddle and remained unperturbed. 'When I want to tease Anthony,' he remarked slyly to a friend, 'I remind him that Gladstone formed his last administration at the age of eighty-four.'

Winston was right to remain unruffled for when the results of the 1950 General Election were known Conservative criticism abruptly ceased. The Tories had cut down Labour's majority to only six; this made another election in the very near future inevitable, and if the swing continued against the Government, which it was likely to do as long as Britain was undergoing hardships, Churchill was certain to become Prime Minister again.

He now began to change his tactics. It was wise to do so for in June 1950, five months after the election had taken place, his prophecies of industrial disaster had been proved completely false; Britain was able to forgo Marshall Aid, two years earlier than even the Americans had expected, and to pay her own way. However, a month later the war in Korea broke out and before the year was over Attlee had pledged the country to a large defence programme. Rearmament and stockpiling began to send up prices of raw materials all over the world, and England, which had hoped for easier days, found herself confronted with new economic worries. The cost of living was rising and the terms of trade were moving against her; these were the issues on which Churchill concentrated.

*

When one looks through the press cuttings between the years 1945-51 one is staggered that even a man of Churchill's capacity could have poured out such an avalanche of passion, energy, and work. He wrote five volumes of the history of the second World War; he exhibited new paintings at the Royal Academy; he made important speeches in America and half the capitals of Europe; he was the most celebrated figure at all the great functions of the day; he received honorary degrees from the Universities and civic freedoms from countless cities; he awarded medals, signed souvenirs, addressed rallies and was accorded tumultuous ovations whenever he went abroad.

At home, he acquired five hundred acres of land near Chartwell and plunged into farming; he loved animals, and was as pleased as a child with the marmalade kitten his wife gave him and the French poodle sent to him by a friend; he delighted in his goldfish, hung a drawing of his pet cat in an honoured position and watched after his beautiful black Australian swans with tender solicitude. When a fox killed the mother swan leaving behind an enraged father and six three-week-old cygnets he telephoned the superintendent of the Zoo for advice, and a man was sent out to remove the young ones to safety. But Winston's interest in animals did not stop here. In 1949 he took out the chocolate and pink racing colours that both his father and grandfather had used, and bought a colt which soon became famous on the turf as Colonist II. In 1950 he entered this horse in the Winston Churchill Stakes at Hurst Park in the hope of breaking the run of successes of French owners, who had triumphed every year since the race started in 1946. As a tribute to Churchill the clerk of the course printed on the programme the memorable words starting with, 'Let us, therefore, brace ourselves to our duties ...' Colonist II did not win, but he came in second.

Churchill's work on his history of the second World War was a major operation. But he still held to his theory that it was foolish to indulge in detailed work that others could do for him. His first step, therefore, was to assemble a large and competent staff to check facts, sort material, produce memoranda, collect information, and give advice. He gathered around him naval, military and air experts, scientists, historians and classical scholars, not to mention a competent team of secretaries who worked day and night on eight hour shifts. Winston did all his writing by dictation, sometimes turning out eight or nine thousand words a day. As the work progressed he began to receive offers for the serial rights from editors all over the world. 'I'm not writing a book,' Winston commented to a friend, 'I'm developing a property.' *Life* magazine bought the serial rights for a sum that was said to be near two million dollars.

Five volumes of the book have now been published and literary critics, soldiers and historians have hailed it as one of the classics of all time. It stands in a category of its own, for no other great statesman has ever had the ability to write as a great historian; and no great historian has ever been provided with more dramatic material. 'When before, through all the centuries of this island's history, has such a theme matched such a pen?' commented the *Spectator*.

*

For recreation, while he was writing his book, Churchill turned back to his old love, painting. During the war he had been forced to abandon this pastime, but now he re-embraced it with enthusiasm, and according to the art critics, painted better pictures than he had ever done before. In 1947, for the first time, he exhibited pictures at the Royal Academy; and when, a few years later, he was asked to contribute a painting to a society of amateur artists he announced that he was 'a professional'.

An amusing account of Winston, as an artist, was given by Sir John Rothenstein, an eminent critic and Director of the Tate Gallery. In February 1949 Churchill invited Rothenstein to lunch at Chartwell and told him that he would be grateful for any criticisms of his paintings he would care to make. 'Speak, I pray, with absolute frankness,' he said, as he led his guest into lunch. 'As soon as we sat down,' wrote Rothenstein, 'he began to talk about Sickert. "He came to stay here," said Mr. Churchill, "and in a fortnight he imparted to me all his considered wisdom about painting. He had a room specially darkened to work in, but I wasn't an apt pupil, for I rejoice in the highest lights and the brightest colours."' Mr. Churchill spoke with appreciation of Sickert's knowledge of music-halls, and he sang a nineteenth-century ballad Sickert had taught him — not just a line or two but to the end.

'"I think," he went on, "the person who taught me most about painting was William Nicholson. I noticed you looking, I thought with admiration, at those drawings he made of my beloved cat."

'Back in the studio,' continued Rothenstein, 'fortified by a bottle of champagne, I found his invitation to give my opinion of his work without reserve much less alarming. Mr. Churchill was so exhilarating and so genial a companion that, before I had been with him a few hours, the notion of speaking with absolute frankness seemed as natural as it had earlier seemed temerarious.

'My first detailed criticism of one of his paintings had an unexpected, indeed a startling, result. I offered the opinion, with regard to a landscape — a wood on the margin of a lake — that the shore was too shallow, too lightly modelled and too pale in tone to support the weight of the heavy trees with their dense, dark foliage, so that, instead of growing up out of the earth, they weighted it down. "Oh," Mr. Churchill said, "but I can put that right at once; it would take less than a quarter of an hour," and he began to look out the brushes and colours. "But surely this painting," I said, "must be among your earliest." "I did it about twenty years ago." "Well then," I objected, "surely it is impossible for you to recapture the mood in which you painted it or indeed your whole outlook of those days."

"You are really persuaded of that?" he grumbled, abandoning with evident reluctance the notion of repainting.'[332]

Sir John Rothenstein's verdict on Mr. Churchill's work was that 'he is able to paint pictures of real merit which bear a direct and intimate relation to his outlook on life. In these pictures there comes bubbling irrepressibly up his sheer enjoyment of the simple beauties of nature …' The highest peaks of his achievement, in Rothenstein's opinion, are 'The Goldfish Pool at Chartwell' (1948), 'The Loup River, Alpes Maritimes' (1947), 'Chartwell under Snow' (1947), and 'Cannes Harbour, Evening' (1923). These and twenty other paintings have been exhibited at the Royal Academy.

*

Although Mr. Churchill's work as a Party leader paved the way for his return to No. 10 Downing Street, it was the least important and least distinguished of his activities during his six years in opposition. From a political point of view, his most valuable contribution came in the old, familiar field of foreign affairs. On home subjects he was the party politician, but on world problems he never failed to fulfil his part as the great world statesman.

As far as foreign policy was concerned there was no break or defection in the course Churchill had pursued for the last forty years. He still believed it vitally necessary to build up a strong balance of power against any nation which threatened to dominate the European continent; but now no balance could be decisive without commitments from the United States. Winston's foreign policy was clear-cut and simple; first, the fraternal association with America which he had preached to Roosevelt without success; and second, a Western Europe united against aggression to which America and Britain would pledge their mutual aid. This was exactly the same policy that Churchill had advocated against the German threat in the thirties, but in those days most of the countries of Europe preferred to act independently, and the United States insisted on remaining aloof.

In view of the consistency of Churchill's thought, it seems surprising that his speech, delivered in Fulton, Missouri, on 5 March, 1946, should have caused such a sensation. But the war had ended only eight months previously and many Americans still clung to Roosevelt's belief that there was a special affinity between the

---

[332] *Mr. Churchill: The Artist*: Sir John Rothenstein (*Sunday Times*, 7 January, 1951).

Russian and American people; and that good will and co-operation were bound to blossom with mutual trust. Churchill made it clear to his audience that he considered this a sentimental daydream and pointed harshly to the facts. 'From Stettin in the Baltic to Trieste in the Adriatic an iron curtain has descended across the Continent. Behind that line lie all the capitals of the ancient states of Central and Eastern Europe ... The Communist Parties, which were very small in all these Eastern States of Europe, have been raised to pre-eminence and power far beyond their numbers and are seeking everywhere to obtain totalitarian control. Police government is prevailing in nearly every case, and so far, except in Czechoslovakia, there is no true democracy.'

This speech was of historic importance. It marked the end of Roosevelt's policy of blind trust towards the Soviet Union, and marked the beginning of Churchill's policy of peace through strength, based on the 'fraternal association of the English-speaking peoples'. 'I will venture to be precise,' he told his listeners. 'Fraternal association requires not only the growing friendship and mutual understanding between our two vast but kindred systems of society, but the continuance of the intimate relationship between our military advisers, leading to common study of potential dangers, the similarity of weapons and manuals of instruction, and to the interchange of officers and cadets at technical colleges.' To-day, this close association is no longer a dream but the chief factor in maintaining the peace in Europe.

*

Churchill's second goal, a united Europe, was far less clearly defined in his mind than his relationship with America. What part was Britain to play? Was she to encourage continental Europe to form a federal bloc, but to stand aloof herself retaining a position as the third point of the triangle between United Europe and the United States? Or was she to consider herself not only part of Europe, but the leader and organizer of Europe, and, as such, to head a powerful union which could talk to the United States on equal terms with equal power behind it?

At first it is clear that Winston favoured this second course. The vision of Europe as a single entity had been the dream of conquerors for centuries past; now with a leader of Winston's stature its realization seemed to move into the realms of possibility by good will and mutual desire alone. There was such an upsurge of feeling for the idea that Churchill had no difficulty in forming an all-party European

Movement to promote the aim of ultimate unification. In a speech at the Albert Hall in London on 14 May, 1947, he started the ball rolling but he was careful not to commit himself to any definite action. 'It is not for us at this stage to attempt to define or prescribe the structure of constitutions. We ourselves are content, in the first instance, to present the idea of United Europe, in which our country will play a decisive part, as a moral, cultural and spiritual conception to which we can all rally without being disturbed by divergences about structure. It is for the responsible statesmen, who have the conduct of affairs in their hands and the power of executive action, to shape and fashion the structure. It is for us to lay the foundation, to create the atmosphere and give the driving impulsion.'

The European Movement began to gather followers all over the Continent and almost exactly a year later, in May 1948, a momentous 'Congress of Europe' representing a dozen nations assembled at The Hague. Churchill made a stirring speech calling on the Governments of Western Europe to authorize a European Assembly which would enable its voice 'to make itself continuously heard and we trust with every growing acceptance through all the free countries of the Continent'. And this time he went further toward the federal idea. 'The Movement for European Unity must be a positive force, deriving its strength from our sense of common spiritual values ... It is impossible to separate economics and defence from the general political structure. Mutual aid in the economic field and joint military defence must inevitably be accompanied step by step with a parallel policy of closer political unity. It is said with truth that this involves some sacrifice or merger of national sovereignty.'

As a result of the Hague Conference twelve Governments including the Labour Government of Britain authorized the setting up of a Council of Europe. The first meeting of the historic assembly took place in Strasbourg in the summer of 1949. I attended this meeting and arrived to find the whole city in an atmosphere of celebration. The green and white flags of United Europe fluttered from all the buildings, the restaurants were garlanded and festooned, and cameramen and reporters from all over the world arrived to record the proceedings. Winston Churchill was given a luxurious villa and provided with one of the best cooks in France. United Europe would be born with all the refinements that civilization could offer.

But Churchill's speech, which was regarded as the highlight of the conference, came as a startling douche of cold water. Once so warm and enthusiastic about United Europe, he shocked and chilled the assembly by his sudden indifference. He made it clear that he was not in favour of an overall authority and talked in terms that were so vague as to be almost meaningless. 'I am not myself committed to a federal or any other particular solution at this stage. We must thoroughly explore all the various possibilities, and a committee, working coolly and without haste, should, in a few months, be able to show the practical steps which would be most helpful to us ... To take a homely and familiar test, we may just as well see what the girl looks like before we marry her.'

What happened to Churchill in the twelve months since the Hague Conference? Why had he changed his mind about the part Britain should play? The most obvious answer was the fact that in Britain itself there was practically no support for the federal idea. Although Winston had collected a handful of English intellectuals and politicians, most of the enthusiasm for United Europe came from the Continent and not from England. Both the Labour Party and the Conservative Party were dead against any commitment which might impair British sovereignty. And since politics is the art of what is possible and a General Election was only a few months off, it is clear that Winston felt impelled to heed public opinion.

Apart from this, however, Churchill himself was cooling off on the idea of a supreme political authority. The more he studied the implications of a United Europe with Britain as a member state the less he liked it. After all, Britain was the most heavily developed industrial power in Europe with a standard of living far higher than her neighbours. Federation eventually must mean a common currency and a common financial budget. Foreigners did not pay their taxes, and some of their civil services were notoriously corrupt. Did this mean the British public would find itself financing its neighbours? And because of the lower standard of living on the Continent would foreign goods swamp the British markets and cause unemployment? And would it be wise to allow foreign legislatures, some of them riddled with Communism, to control British coal and steel on which the very survival of the nation depended?

The more Churchill examined the economic consequences of Union the less he liked it; and the more he studied British reactions the less he was convinced that his proud and insular countrymen would ever give their sanction to such a course. One needs only to recall the national reaction in 1940, when the Continent was overrun and England stood alone, to realize how difficult such a step would have been. In those days English people received the news of the fall of

France and the return of the British Army with open relief. 'Now we're together again,' they sighed. 'Now everything will be all right.'

The Federalists on the Continent were bitterly disappointed by Churchill's change of heart. During the war he had offered France common citizenship, and had talked the same language to the United States. A great vision glowed in his mind which still burned brightly in the first years of the post-war era. He talked of a 'transformation of the Western world' and referred to a 'Federal Constitution for Europe', saying, 'I hope this maybe eventually achieved.'[333]

Now he had come round to the view of Mr. Ernest Bevin, the Foreign Secretary, that the only possibility as far as Great Britain was concerned was 'inter-governmental' co-operation. This was a crushing blow to the Continental Unionists, for it meant the end of any hope of a Parliament of all Europe. As M. Schuman, the French Foreign Minister, announced in November 1949, 'Without Britain there can be no Europe.' He might also have added, 'Without Churchill there can be no complete European Union,' for it is clear that no other man save Winston could have aroused the enthusiasm or commanded the world-wide following that would have made the transformation possible.

Without Churchill's support the grand design of United Europe perished; but in its stead have come the beginnings of a smaller federation between six of the Continental countries and a closer understanding between all nations of the West, economically, militarily and spiritually, than ever before. Another age may see the whole dream fulfilled.

---

[333] Albert Hall, London, 14 May, 1947.

Chapter Twenty-Three — Prime Minister Again

CHURCHILL COMPLAINED that the 1950 General Election was 'positively demure'. He had no such criticism of the contest that followed twenty-one months later. The General Election of October 1951 was fought by the Conservatives on the high cost of living at home, and the deterioration of British prestige abroad. The Persians had announced their intention of nationalizing the Anglo-Iranian Oil Company, and trouble was brewing in Egypt. This, said the Tories, was the fault of weakness and indecision on the part of the Socialists. The Labour Party retaliated by reminding the public of Mr. Churchill's impulsiveness, and warning voters that precipitous acts were capable of landing Britain in another war. Churchill angrily denounced these attacks and on the day of the poll itself issued a writ against the *Daily Mirror* which printed a front-page picture of a revolver with the headline: 'Whose Finger on the Trigger?' and ran a story that Winston intended to deliver an ultimatum to the Russians if he were returned to power.[334] Nevertheless his resentment subsided that night when the final results were nearly complete and he learned that once again he was Prime Minister, this time by a small majority of twenty-two.

A month later he attended the Lord Mayor's banquet at the Guildhall and told his audience: 'Though I have very often in the last forty years or so been present at your famous Guildhall banquets to salute the new Lord Mayor, this is the first occasion when I have addressed this assembly here as Prime Minister. The explanation is convincing.' He smiled. 'When I should have come as Prime Minister Guildhall was blown up, and before it was repaired I was blown out. I thought at the time they were both disasters.'[335]

At last the 'affront', as he termed it, that he had received from the British people in 1945 had lost its sting. At last he was Prime Minister not through extraordinary circumstances but by an elected majority in

---

[334] Mr. Churchill's action against the *Daily Mirror* was settled out of court. He accepted a profuse apology from the *Daily Mirror* which was published in all newspapers on 24 May, 1952. The *Daily Mirror* agreed to pay Mr. Churchill's costs and to make a contribution to a charity named by him.

[335] *The Times*: 10 November, 1951.

the House of Commons. And this represented the final ambition of fifty-two years of political life.

At seventy-seven he seemed strong and vigorous, still towering over his parliamentary colleagues like a Colossus. The country held its breath waiting to see how and where the master of the sensational and unexpected would direct the Ship of State. But once again Churchill surprised his audience. There was to be nothing dramatic in his approach to the serious problems facing the British economy, or for that matter in his handling of world affairs. Britain was to continue the same course which she had pursued ever since the war with very few deviations: austerity at home, and a strict adherence to the Atlantic Treaty abroad.

All those who would have raised their voices loudest if Churchill had ventured into uncharted waters now cried out against his orthodoxy. On 20 December, 1951, the *Observer* printed a profile of the Prime Minister in which it said: 'Any consideration of Mr. Churchill's career as a whole brings one up against the extraordinary fact that, for all its majestic scope, it remains to this day tragically unfulfilled and fragmentary. His political role certainly has not been meteoric and disastrous, like Napoleon's or Hitler's. But neither has it been linked to a definite achievement, like Richelieu's or Chatham's, Washington's or Lincoln's, Bismarck's or Lenin's. So far, he leaves no completed work, for even the war he won has not been ended. He leaves glory, tragedy and unfinished business.'

This is a superficial and unjust judgment. Leaving aside the fact that the writer has compared Churchill to statesmen who, with the exception of Chatham, created unity out of civil war and disorder within their own countries, the suggestion that Churchill's life presents no theme or no definite achievement is absurd. Now that his political work is nearly ended, the pattern stands out boldly: a fierce belief that the freedom of man, and of Christendom itself, must be guarded, and can only be preserved, by the combined efforts of the English-speaking people. It was the vision of this alliance that prompted Mr. Churchill in the early thirties to begin writing an Anglo-American history; it was faith in this alliance that gave him heart for his prodigious task in 1940. Throughout the war he hammered his conviction to Roosevelt, and although the American leaders were not ready to accept his premises in 1944, the events of the last eight years have drawn the two countries together in an association which almost marks the fulfilment of Mr. Churchill's heart's desire. Never before in peace time have the affairs of two free nations been so tightly interwoven. Although some people regret the fact that Winston has not used his influence to draw the countries of Europe close to the British orbit so that the Anglo-American partnership could develop on terms of equal power, it was Churchill's inspiration that gave birth to the Council of Europe, and the Council may yet illuminate the minds of the statesmen who follow him. But if the English-speaking alliance continues to be a foundation stone for the United Nations, and the United Nations continue to stand up against aggression and to insist upon negotiations as the only civilized method of settling difficulties between nations, Mr. Churchill's immortality is assured. He led the free world in its darkest hour, and when the battle was won he used his counsel and influence to bring millions of people together on a path of common endeavour.

Yet it is not only as a statesman that he must be judged. No one can meet this extraordinary man without a feeling of awe. He not only stands head and shoulders above a century of powerful statesmen but his vitality, his mastery of the English language, his contribution to literature, his scientific inventiveness, his painting, his far flung interests from house building to racehorses, and even his astonishing constitution, place him in a category far removed from mere mortals. The range of his talents forces one to compare him with Leonardo da Vinci, and no doubt the world will have to wait as long again to see his like reborn.

Yet although his accomplishments place him apart as a giant, students of the future may find his character the most unusual subject of all. For over fifty years Churchill has attracted world-wide interest. At various times he has provoked his countrymen to anger, admiration, indignation, laughter, gratitude, fury and veneration. But whatever the feeling, he has never failed to fascinate, for the swift, changing facets of his personality embody the frailties of human nature with the highest capacity for service and leadership. With Churchill it is possible to see selfishness flash into generosity; mischievousness retreat before a strict code of Victorian morality; impulsiveness melt into wisdom; dejection surge into wit; flouts and jeers dissolve into a warm and loyal friendship. And shining through all the contradictions of his mercurial temperament is a burning courage, and a deep faith in the power for good within the human race. He will be remembered as a statesman, but he will be cherished as a man.

Made in the USA
Middletown, DE
23 January 2020